THE
FLOWER
AND THE
LEAF

THE
FLOWER
AND THE
LEAF

A Contemporary Record of American Writing Since 1941

by

MALCOLM COWLEY

Edited and with an
Introduction by
DONALD W. FAULKNER

VIKING

VIKING
Viking Penguin Inc., 40 West 23rd Street,
New York, New York 10010, U.S.A.
Penguin Books Ltd, Harmondsworth,
Middlesex, England
Penguin Books Australia Ltd, Ringwood,
Victoria, Australia
Penguin Books Canada Limited, 2801 John Street,
Markham, Ontario, Canada L3R 1B4
Penguin Books (N.Z.) Ltd, 182–190 Wairau Road,
Auckland 10, New Zealand

First published in 1985 by Viking Penguin Inc.
Published simultaneously in Canada

LIBRARY OF CONGRESS CATALOGING IN PUBLICATION DATA
Cowley, Malcolm, 1898–
The flower and the leaf.
1. American literature—20th century—History and
criticism—Collected works. I. Faulkner, Donald W.
II. Title.
PS225.C68   1985   810'.9'0052   83-40645
ISBN-0-670-32009-9

Pages 391-92 constitute an extension of this copyright page.

Printed in the United States of America
by R. R. Donnelley and Sons Company, Harrisonburg, Virginia
Set in Garamond

I think of the tangled reasons why
this man should flourish, this one die
obscurely of some minor hurt;
why this one sought his death by sea
and this one drank himself to death
and this one, not of our company,
but born on the same day as Hart,
should harvest all the world can give,
then put a gun between his teeth;
or why, among friends who live,
this one, misled by his good heart,
and this, forsaken by a wench,
should each crawl off to nurse his grief.
I saw the flower and the leaf,
the fruit, or none, and the bare branch.

From "The Flower and the Leaf"
                    Malcolm Cowley

Contents

Part Three
ASSESSMENTS AND RETROSPECTIONS

Contents / ix

Introduction

Malcolm Cowley has considered it a privilege to be born before the turn of the century, as one among others in a literary generation that Gertrude Stein called "lost," but Cowley himself called "lucky." To succeeding generations the adventures of those belonging to this group have become part of literary lore. Their rites of passage included a college experience or a similar departure from native ground, important to them not so much for encounters with literary tradition as for meetings with kindred spirits; military service of some sort (and in most cases) during the First World War; a sojourn in Paris that sometimes lasted for years; then a period of intellectual wandering through either the politics of commitment or the self-testings of interiority; and meanwhile a time of flowering and of bearing fruit, or none.

There are few periods in American literature when a generation has been so tightly knit or has felt such a strong sense of identity. Though individuals grew apart and, buffeted by critics or events, modified their picture of the world or otherwise suffered the vicissitudes of their careers, a bond of age and common experience held them together. Cowley defined the strengths and weaknesses of that bond and helped to forge it. He added to it dimensions of understanding that went beyond common immediacies. As critic, poet, editor, and literary historian, he endeavored to place his generation within the emerging tradition of a national literature. In the process he helped to broaden our perceptions of that literature itself.

He wrote books when he had time for them, but much of his contribution to our self-knowledge took the form of short essays or book reviews. During the forty years of literary activity that this collection partly covers (there are also the books), Cowley wrote more than five hundred articles, ranging from his weekly contributions to *The New Republic* during the early 1940s to his retrospective pieces of the early 1980s. Few other writers of his time have made such a searching and continuous contribution to American letters. Few other writers have had the imagination and the energy to engage in such an effort.

Many of the articles in this collection occupied only a few magazine pages. There are several longer essays, too, but the shorter ones testify to what can be accomplished both critically and stylistically within a limited space. As Cowley has noted in an Epilogue to his *Think Back on Us . . .* (1967):

> The relatively short book review was my art form for many years; it became my blank-verse meditation, my sonnet sequence, my letter to distant friends, my private journal. I did not fall into the illusion that it was a major form; no, it was dependent for its subject matter on the existence of novels or plays or poems worth writing about. Nevertheless it was *my* form; and for years I neglected obligations to family and friends in order to get the review written. As writers tend to do with any form imposed upon them by accident, I poured into it as much as possible of my adventures among events and opinions.

Cowley had become a weekly reviewer by accident, taking up the position at *The New Republic*, where he was literary editor during the 1930s, at a time when the need for more in-house writing became apparent. But the accident was fortunate since, if taken together, the reviews, articles, assessments, meditations, and retrospections he wrote at the time and later encompass the history of a significant period in American letters. They also reveal the insight and the interpretive imagination of one who both witnessed that history and, with many collaborators, helped to shape it.

2

The Japanese attack on Pearl Harbor in December 1941 was the beginning of a new era. The two preceding years had been a time of bitter arguments between isolationists, or America Firsters, and supporters of the Western Allies. Once America was plunged into the war, those arguments were in some measure forgotten. The country at large resigned itself to necessity; "We're in this business now," Cowley remembers people saying, "and we'll have to come out on top." There was little of the frenzied patriotism that had been whipped up in 1917, but there was, people also said, no less determination.

In the intellectual world, the reality of war created a kind of unity that had been only talked about in years past. But the unity had come after staggering disillusionments and bitter dissensions. In the years 1936–38 the Spanish republic had become a symbol to American intellectuals; it was the star to which their reformist hopes were hitched. The republic fell, largely as a result of international duplicity; there had been no hope for it after the British and the French prime ministers flew to Munich in September 1938 and bowed to Hitler's demands in the effort to appease him. Eleven months later Stalin signed his non-aggression pact with Hitler and thereby turned his back on the Western intellectuals who had, until then, widely supported his foreign policy even though they had more and more misgivings about what was happening inside Russia. Tidings of incredible purges, state-engendered mass starvation, and the persecution of artists and politicians alike were seeping out of a country that many had regarded as the hope of the world.

There seemed to be no end to catastrophes. The worst of all, for many writers who had spent years in Paris, was the fall of France in June 1940. Having returned to America after mastering their profession, these self-styled exiles of an earlier decade were now reminded by France's abject defeat that the freedoms they cherished as ideals might easily be destroyed along with the liberties they enjoyed in fact. "The fall of France was my trauma," Cowley said in a letter to this editor. He continued:

The Nazi-Soviet pact had affected me, but somewhat less deeply. After the British and the French surrendered at Munich, I was expecting a drastic change in Russian policy, though nothing quite so drastic as that drinking of toasts to Hitler. The pact was a bill of divorcement between Russia and the Men of Good Will in the West, of whom I was one. Russia had ceased to be an admired country, having adopted a new policy that promised to be fatal to our hopes. The invasion of Poland, then of Finland, were ominous signs, but still I had vestiges of faith in the radical movement, which had once been a force for progress, and I did not break with it publicly. Then came the invasion of France, the country I loved best after my own, and I was shaken to the depths. I wrote an open letter of resignation from the League of American Writers, which had been following the Communist Party line of strict neutrality, and I wrote several articles about France in the effort to understand why and how she had surrendered.

In the great debate between America Firsters (cheered on by the Communists until the invasion of Russia in June 1941) and supporters of the Western Allies, Cowley had taken the side of the Allies. He continued to support them after the alliance had been reduced to only Britain fighting on doggedly. In foreign affairs he had moved close to the Roosevelt administration. That brought him under fire from the Communist press. He was excoriated in *The Daily Worker* and cartooned in *The New Masses* as a lackey of J. P. Morgan. He had broken cleanly with the radicals because—as it becomes clear in retrospect— he saw that the freedoms of his own country were threatened and saw, too, that many of his former associates were capitulating to an abstract faith instead of maintaining the canons of reason.

Cowley's embrace of an individualism in pursuit of community was part of an ethic that runs deep in his Western Pennsylvania roots. It allowed him to feel at home with individuals as diverse in their literary and political opinions as William Faulkner, Louis Aragon, Allen Tate (author of *Reactionary Essays*), and Nelson Algren, to mention only a few. Always he valued a man's character above his opinions; that was another facet of what he called his "personalism." His upbringing between a rural and an urban environment, with half the year spent in each, had broadened his sympathies. Combined with his equanimity and rationality, it had given him an openness toward American writers and cultural movements that few have been able to match.

During the early Depression years, that very openness had helped to get him involved in the radical movement. Cowley never joined the Communist Party, but he became a so-called fellow traveler and, he says, a fervent one for a time. One finds it hard to connect his generally benign spirit with fervor, and in any case the feeling had largely ebbed away before the Russo-German Pact. Shortly before Pearl Harbor and the publication of his second book of poems, *The Dry Season*, Cowley went to work for the government's Office of Facts and Figures (OFF), an organization that was the forerunner of the Office of War Information and the USIS. Archibald MacLeish was the head of OFF and Cowley's post was that of Chief Information Analyst. OFF came under attack for painting a rosy picture of America's war effort. Cowley himself was violently abused by several journalists in a chorus led by Westbrook Pegler, whose syndicated column charged him with being a subversive. The bombardment was intensified by the Dies Committee on Un-American Activities and there were speeches against Cowley on the floor of Congress.

A crushing blow was *Time*'s review of *The Dry Season*, belatedly published in the issue of February 16, 1942. The review was unsigned, like everything else in *Time*, but the files of the magazine record that it was written by Whittaker Chambers, who was also responsible for giving it a prominent place. Instead of being printed with other reviews, it appeared in the front pages of the magazine as part of a section called "U.S. at War." Some of it reads:

> Most inopportune book of the month is *The Dry Season*, a slim, sage green volume of 17 poems by Malcolm Cowley, sometime literary editor of the *New Republic*, now chief information analyst of the Office of Facts and Figures. Congressman Martin Dies recently charged Cowley with having had "seventy-two connections . . . with the Communist Party and its front organizations." Two of the poems in *The Dry Season* seem designed to make Dies lift his calculations to 74.
>
> "Tomorrow Morning" is an appeal to the "Mechanics of the morning, you of the blunt hands, the sensitive fingers," to remember in the society of the future the anonymous intellectuals who were "swept by the same flood of passion toward the morning that is yours.". . .
>
> "The Last International" is Chief Analyst Cowley's prescient vision of the dead march of his comrades "against the Capitol.". . .
>
> "Comrades," pleaded Poet Cowley, "not weaponless, not to crumple under fire. No farther, comrades." But the comrades marched right on, even in the face of "an enormous thundercrack.". . .

The article was calculated to bring down an avalanche on a minor government official. Quoting out of context from a book of poems, finding and featuring lines that expressed a revolutionary spirit, it pictured Cowley as a disloyal American who probably carried bombs in his briefcase together with copies of *The Communist Manifesto*. Of course he answered the review, if with a feeling of "What's the use?" The last lines of his answer were:

> It is only by desperate juggling that the poems can be torn from their context in a book, that half a dozen lines can be torn from their context in the two poems and given a political meaning they do not possess, and that the whole discussion can be moved forward seventy-five pages in the magazine, from the book section, where it belongs, to the Washington section—where, presumably, it proves that the country all of us love is in grave danger of being overthrown by a determined rabble of poets and literary editors. The country has graver dangers, this year.

The rejoinder was printed, but with this ambiguous comment: "TIME cheerfully concedes that ex-Literary Editor Malcolm Cowley is no danger to the country.—ED."

Before his letter appeared in the issue of March 16, Cowley had resigned from OFF. Although he might have stayed on to fight the accusations and might have won his case, he recognized that, given the mood of Congress, such an effort would have caused some damage to the war effort. The Washington affair had ended in a debacle. Cowley retired to his home in Connecticut, where he literally cultivated his own garden and vowed never again to engage in politics or enter government service. Though he remained a keen observer of political and social life—and wrote during wartime with devotion to the American cause—he no longer took confrontational positions.

The change was a blessing for him, if one that was pretty well disguised. Always interested in the social context of American literature, Cowley turned his attention to the field in earnest. He was writing from what was still, in the war years, a rather isolated country village, far from the literary world, and that perspective simplified his task. He was able to see events and tendencies in their broad outlines.

The first section of this book, "The War Years and After," contains some of his observations on the changing trade of writing. Before making them, however, he had a necessary task to perform, namely, to pass judgment on the faults of Communism as a religion that had attracted many thousands of proselytes during the Depression years. His sober conclusions went into an essay, "Communism and Christianism," that is the earliest by date (1941) of those reprinted in this volume. After publishing the essay—in Klaus Mann's little magazine *Decision*, which went almost unread—he launched into projects that attracted wider attention. One of them was his classic profile of Maxwell Perkins, who, at Scribner's, had brought Fitzgerald, Hemingway, and Thomas Wolfe to the public eye while himself remaining in the background, a sort of Gray Eminence. Cowley's profile also described a revolution in American letters, with its effect on the publishing trade. Other subjects treated at the time were the war as reported by correspondents, the death and rebirth of French patriotism, and the tragedy of Central European exiles, a whole generation of brilliant writers dispersed and destroyed by Hitler. There is a lively account of the battle that raged after the Bollingen Award was given to Ezra Pound. The section ends with "Some Dangers to American Writing" (1954), a perspective on the literary situation during the McCarthy era. Taken together the pieces record the tragedies (and some comedies) of the war and its aftermath as observed from the home front.

Reserved for a second section, "The Usable Past," are essays connected with another important development of the 1940s and 1950s. This was a new spirit of nationalism, carried to an extreme by Henry Luce in his magazines, all of which prophesied that the next hundred years would be an American Century. Cowley, ever temperate, had misgivings about that spirit in some of its manifestations, as when writers who had once been dissenting voices began to celebrate conformity. Still, he had always been a firm supporter of American writing, which he thought had earned its place among the great literatures of the world. His search for American traditions is reflected in an affectionate memoir of Hawthorne and in a pathbreaking essay on the first edition of *Leaves of Grass*. Some of his essays on contemporary writers are also included here because of the effort he makes in them to attach those writers—most notably Hemingway—to modes of thinking and feeling that are as old as the Republic.

Cowley's explorations of the American past were unexpectedly aided by Mary Mellon and what was then the precursor of the Bollingen Foundation. In 1944 Mrs. Mellon established what she called her Five Year Plan, a system of granting stipends for five years to various writers of promise. Cowley was chosen as one of the first four-person group at a stipend of $5,500 a year (there was never to be a second group). By far the most productive of the four, Cowley used the monies not only to finance his scholarly work but also to pay off the mortgage on the remodeled barn that was to be his home for the rest of his life. He wrote about standard American authors as if he were the first to have read their works and studied their lives. His interest in them was as much for what they had contributed to American literature as for how they had developed as individual talents; their individuality was not eclipsed for his readers by being placed in its historical context. His various findings appeared as essays, though less regularly in *The New Republic* and more often now in other magazines, since he was gaining a wider audience.

In 1949 Mary Mellon's Five Year Plan came to its end. Cowley then became associated with The Viking Press as a part-time literary consultant. He helped to establish the Viking Portable Library as an esteemed series of one-volume anthologies widely used in colleges. It was a time when American literature, formerly a neglected subject, was being almost universally taught in American and foreign universities. Cowley accepted a few appointments as visiting professor, but never for more than an academic quarter or at most a semester, since writing, not teaching, was his central task.

His first teaching assignment, as Walker-Ames Lecturer at the University of Washington in 1950, brought to the fore that old specter of his radicalism during the Depression years. The inanities of the attack on his appointment are recounted in the essay "Gammon for Dinner" (reprinted in the first section of this book). It is unlike anything written in Cowley's generally even-tempered style. The attack collapsed of its own weight and Cowley, who had proved to be an inspiring teacher, was offered many other assignments, most of which he refused.

The third section of this book "Assessments and Retrospections," is chiefly devoted to his writing of those later years. For Cowley there had been a change in the literary landscape. Most of his old colleagues, those of whom he had written over the years, had published their last works, had become the subject of biographies or critical studies, or had simply passed from life. Their work now demanded a different treatment. Instead of examining the shape of American writing as a "usable past"—and as a portent of the future—he turned his attention to individual writers and what each of them had contributed to our common heritage. He offered sharp but usually sympathetic generalizations. Dreiser, for example, "is the clearest example in American literature, and perhaps in American life, of a man who possessed genius in its raw state, genius almost completely unfortified and unrefined by talent. He is our great primitive." Willa Cather, who abhorred social purposes in fiction, nevertheless performed services to American society:

> For one example, she humanized the land itself, the wide, gently rolling, but savage land of her girlhood, endowing it with folk memories and warm associations. She celebrated the pioneers, not so much the Anglos among them as the Central Europeans and especially the Czechs, giving them a place they deserved in her American gallery of heroes and wonders. Not a Catholic herself, she rendered the poetry of the Church, giving that too a place in her gallery. She made her readers feel that culture is all of a piece, depending almost as much on gardens and kitchens as on classrooms and concert halls. All these are social lessons, not painted on the text but woven into the fabric. Let us not forget that Miss Cather's integrity as an artist was also, in its way, a social lesson.

Besides such overviews of important writers, this section also contains tributes in which Cowley brings his dead friends back to life. In all it might serve as a chronicle and partial summation of American writing in our century.

3

Malcolm Cowley's efforts and concerns have long been taken out of context. As the experience of American writers in Paris during the

1920s acquired the patina of myth, his writing—especially *Exile's Return*—was taken as comfortably reinforcing a certain nostalgia. The sharp insights he developed over a long career in the writer's trade have gone generally unheralded. An example from the early 1960s might serve as an emblem for the way in which Americans have come to regard that "lucky generation" less as pillars of a national literature than as a mythical baseball team that broke records long ago.

In the July 1963 issue of *Esquire* there is a two-page photo spread of a rather odd assemblage of artists: Marcel Duchamp, Virgil Thomson, Kay Boyle, and Malcolm Cowley among others. All are over sixty. All display a calm disdain toward the photographer. The accompanying text, written by Cowley, bears an editorial title, "The Last of the Lost Generation." The group, unfortunately, looks more like the survivors of a Wild West gang. Cowley offers a précis of each pictured character. Enjoyable as his account may still be, it is also a painful moment captured. Here are men and women who helped to shape a modern aesthetic rolled out for inspection like museum pieces. In describing his own somewhat distracted image, Cowley says that his thoughts are wandering to how he might assemble a half-million words of essays and reviews into books that made sense as books.

Since that group photograph appeared in *Esquire*, Cowley has published nine of those books, including essays, histories, memoirs, and a collection of old and new poems—"Not bad for an old codger," I could hear him say before he went back to his desk. Much of his recent work—as is the case with essays produced throughout his life—remains uncollected. It is rare that an author of such note—whose work, produced with infinite care, belongs with American literature, not merely with criticism—should find so much of it dispersed in the back numbers of magazines.

It is my hope that the present assemblage will help to remedy that neglect of his work in its broader aspects. The task of putting the book together has been a pleasant one, since Cowley is always easy and rewarding to read. "A writer is a man or woman who has readers," he used to tell his students. One of his aims is to make the reader of any first sentence go on to the second, then to the third, and so to the end of the piece, which he tries to make a definite rounding off. He strongly believes in narrative as a central element not only in fiction and drama but also in nonfiction and even in poetry. Many of his essays are essentially stories, though with close reasoning and accurate observation fitted into the narrative framework. There are passages that come close to poetry and others that open windows on a busy landscape. He is fanatical about the English language, including the form it has assumed in this country. Jargon in all its manifestations, including the academic variety, is what he detests. He likes to brood over a judgment until it can be expressed in simple words that will be remembered. Thus, he says of James Gould Cozzens and John O'Hara, two realistic novelists for whom I have only a lukewarm admiration, "Cozzens is an architect in fiction; O'Hara is a sort of hydraulic engineer, with a primary interest in flow, not form." He says of Louis Aragon's wartime poems (not widely read in this country, though one enjoys hearing about them) that they give the effect "of a complex situation reduced, after years, to a statement as simple as that of the old Scotch ballads. He was the Border minstrel of this war." At times Cowley comes close to being a Border minstrel of the republic of letters.

I would hope that the pieces gathered here will help to reveal his stature as an author to a new generation of writers and readers. A new generation of critics might profit from examining both his judgments and his writing style. At a time when many critics are neglecting the communicative function of writing, specifically the critic's role as mediator between reader and writer, Cowley's work is as helpful, fresh, and vital as when it first appeared. As for readers in general, they may find, to their surprise, that these observations on literature and the world surrounding it are more to be trusted than those later proclaimed by a bureaucracy of critics, and less likely to be thrust aside. Cowley's opinions are nothing if not honest, thoughtful, and above all deeply aware of the situations to which they were a response. They have a central theme: the defense of literature and the writing profession.

It was a rewarding effort to bring these pieces together, for they provide a view of an American century—not the one that Henry Luce dreamed about, but an actual century—as well as offering a perspective on this country's rise to a high position in world letters, and much besides. Cowley has written of those times with the confidence of one who is laying ground for things to come. His awareness is not that of someone who nostalgically looks back; it is the awareness of an establisher. We younger writers must assume responsibility for what is still to appear. We can acknowledge, with gratitude, the integrity with which Cowley has approached the recent past.

Acknowledgments

I thank the following individuals for their contributions, both direct and indirect, to the preparation of this volume:

First and foremost I thank Malcolm and Muriel Cowley, whose patience, guidance, openness, and friendship have been most deeply appreciated. I thank John A. Harrison, Robert Bailey, and the staff members of the newspaper and periodical rooms of the Yale University Libraries for their assistance in tracking down much of this material. I also thank Diane U. Eisenberg for her *Malcolm Cowley, A Checklist of His Writings*, 1916–1973 (Carbondale: Southern Illinois University Press, 1975), without the aid of which my collecting this material would have been much more difficult; and Clinton Kraus of Montpelier, Vermont, who provided numerous issues of *The New Republic* that aided in the preparation of this volume.

I also acknowledge the helpful suggestions of R. W. B. Lewis, Cleanth Brooks, John E. Smith, and Charles Feidelson, all currently or formerly of Yale University. The suggestions of James M. Kempf and Hans Bak, whose studies of Malcolm Cowley have been as astute as they are pioneering, have been of great assistance. Arvin Brown, artistic director of the Long Wharf Theater, provided helpful information on Cowley's Stanford class, of which Brown was a member.

I note as well the important compilations and studies undertaken by Henry Dan Piper, Lewis P. Simpson, and George Core, whose work helped set the stage for the present volume. Beyond these, I thank those people at Viking, Alan D. Williams, Walter Bode, and Lucine T. Bellocchio, who aided my work in a spirit of kindness, affability, and professionalism. And last, I thank those many friends who offered support during the stages of this book's development, among them John W. Spalding and Leslie Horan, and Dennis Danaher, longtime follower of good writing, for speaking out his mind on my selections.

Donald W. Faulkner

PART ONE

THE WAR YEARS AND AFTER

AMERICAN LITERATURE
IN WARTIME

L iterature as a business is prospering as never before, with book
after book selling more than a quarter of a million copies in hard
covers, but literature as an art is in a dead season. Looking at the bookshelves from week to week, the critic sees little to encourage him. He
sees correspondents' stories cabled home from North Africa or New
Guinea, although they might as well have been mailed by slow boat
and sunk in mid-ocean, the supply of manuscripts being inexhaustible
and the chapters interchangeable. He sees inspirational books ghost-
written for heroes who found God in a foxhole and a contract waiting
in Hollywood. He sees discussions of the peace based on the notion
that the world hasn't really changed since 1914. He sees memoirs by
feature writers and news photographers who met such interesting people. He sees women's-magazine serials dealing with the great problem
of divorce and how to prevent it—why, the war is the answer, with
trumpet calls, Old Glory, and so to bed. He sees family sagas by ladies
who don't want us to forget that they came from very distinguished
families. He sees historical novels that might have been written in collaboration by Miss Ginger Rogers and Parson Weems. He sees book
after book manufactured on the assembly line—the 1943 models, re-
conditioned and stripped of chromium, but with the old dependable
motors inside.

It is not their presence that depresses him so much as the absence of
other books he had hoped to find. Where are the novels about America
in emotional confusion and Europe under the terror? Where are the
true pictures of refugees in Marseilles waiting for the ship sirens that
never sound, or of harassed officials in Washington, or of airplane
plants in Southern California (the Joads are working there now), or of
corporations everywhere waving the flag while they scramble for still
higher profits and lower taxes? Where are the correspondents' books

on a level with the best of those written during the 1930s? Where are the political treatises by authors who recognize that we are entering a new age? Where shall we turn for a discussion of our real problems at home? And, to ask an older question, where are the war poets?—not the battle poets or the patriotic rhymesters, but soldiers writing honest verse about what they see and feel. The need and the public appetite for books are present as never before in our lives, but the authors seem to be stricken with inertia in the face of changes too swift and events too sudden, vast, and complicated for them to handle.

Of course we know that many people find it impossible to write books in wartime. Most of the younger authors are living in a G.I. world where they have little time for literature. Many of the middle-aged authors are in uniform too, perhaps serving as war correspondents or as intelligence officers with air squadrons, while others have government jobs that leave them too tired to write. American authors in general are more deeply involved in the war than they were in 1918; this time the radicals are even more patriotic than the conservatives. There are, however, enough able writers still in civilian life—women, 4F's, and over-thirty-eights—to produce better books than most of those we have been reading since 1941. Seeking other reasons for the low level of American literature in wartime, we may find that some of them are connected with defeats that were suffered long before Pearl Harbor.

I don't propose to review the literary history of the last twenty-five years. Time and again the critics have discussed some of its chief features, including the reaction against social literature after the First World War and the reaction against personal and formalistic writing that occurred during the 1930s. Sometimes it seems that the record of the interwar period was that of a swinging pendulum or an alternation between two poles: between the public and the private, the objective and the subjective, the naturalistic or photographic and the fantastic or abstract. Sometimes the same individuals moved in both directions at different times: for example, Archibald MacLeish's first book was a collection of poems called *The Tower of Ivory*, a title that might have been applied to almost all his work during the first decade after Versailles. Even future writers on international politics were concerned at the time with a realm of fantasies: John Gunther published an artificial romance called *The Red Pavilion* and Vincent Sheean contributed to the little magazines. In the 1930s, on the other hand, both Sherwood Anderson and Waldo Frank wrote strike novels, using the same technique they had developed for treating subjective themes. By that time subjectivity was out of fashion. The private world was almost deserted for the world of factories, breadlines, and international revolutions.

When we look at the period in retrospect, it seems that the social movement among writers reached its highest point in 1937. That was the year of the Federal Theatre and the sit-down strikes; it was also the crucial year of the war in Spain. American writers had been devoting more and more attention to what happened in Europe, and now there was no question of where their sympathies lay. Hundreds of them joined the League of American Writers, which was actively campaigning for the Loyalists. The League published a pamphlet called *Writers Take Sides*, of which I have lost my copy; nevertheless I can remember the contents. Out of something like 418 writers who had answered a questionnaire, there was only one who favored Franco (it was Gertrude Atherton). Perhaps a score of the others were cautious or undecided, but all the rest enthusiastically supported the Spanish Republic. Many young American writers served in the Abraham Lincoln Battalion, while older ones visited Spain as correspondents and came home to do propaganda work. There were hundreds of writers who organized Loyalist meetings, signed petitions to the President, and raised funds for medical relief. They wrote poems, too, in surprising numbers and with greater eloquence than most American or English poets have shown when treating the war against Germany and Japan. In a sense, the conflict in Spain was *their* war, and the defeat of the Spanish Republic was their defeat.

Spain was also the subject of the novel that Ernest Hemingway published at the end of 1940. *For Whom the Bell Tolls*, besides being the best and almost the only good war novel of the last ten years, has so far been the last major work produced by any member of his generation. This remark is not intended as a prophecy, since I feel that some of these writers have still to do their best work, but for three years most of them have fallen into a curious half-silence. There are a few exceptions: Faulkner and Wilson have done some of their best writing, but in shorter pieces. Dos Passos has been working on a biography of Jefferson and has meanwhile published two short novels, the first of which was so bitterly disillusioned that it must have been painful to write; at any rate it was painful for me to read. Among those a few years younger than the postwar generation, Farrell has taken a long step down from Studs Lonigan to Danny O'Neill, and Steinbeck a still longer step from *The Grapes of Wrath* to *The Moon Is Down*. It may be that I am neglecting still younger writers, and yet I feel that literary history will not have much to say about the last three years.

This does not mean that I am trying to establish a causal relationship between the Spanish civil war and the present state of American letters; what happened was much more complicated. The fall of the Spanish Republic came midway in a whole series of disasters, a litany we have learned by heart: the Moscow trials, the invasion of Austria, the surrender at Munich, the seizure of Prague, and the Russo-German Pact. This last, among other things, was Stalin's declaration to the world that he had lost faith in the power of the Western liberals to influence their governments and that he no longer cared whether they were his friends. External defeats lead to internal dissensions, and the literary world in New York was no exception to this rule; it was divided by as many quarrels as a colony of exiles. Then came the fall of France, which was the deepest of all the emotional shocks to those Americans who had lived there in the postwar decade and had learned to regard France as a second fatherland. I can remember a friend of mine, an aviator in the other war, standing at attention with the tears streaming down his cheeks when somebody put a new record on the phonograph and it turned out to be the "Marseillaise."

Then, too, there were professional reasons for discouragement. The social realism of the 1930s had proved to be a less fertile movement than many writers had hoped. It had produced one novel that grows in stature with the years—I mean Dos Passos' *U.S.A.*—and another novel, *The Grapes of Wrath*, that has faults and falsities but still retains the power of a popular myth. It had produced a quantity of good reporting and a few effective dramas, chiefly the early plays of Clifford Odets, but it had also produced many plays and novels that followed the same threadbare pattern of conversion. Considering that it claimed to speak for the popular heart, the movement was strangely argumentative and prosaic. There was the verse of the Social Symbolists, who wrote about the Scottsboro trial in such strained metaphors that they might as well have been using medieval Latin, but there were almost no folk poets. People had begun to feel the need of books with more warmth, inwardness, and freedom.

The point I am trying to make depends on a whole series of events, literary and political, but the Spanish war might stand as a symbol for them all. One effect it had on writers was to separate them from the public at large, which had been less interested in Spain and was now less disturbed by the victory of the fascists there. During the 1930s American writers had been drawing closer to their audience and had gained strength from this relationship, but now they were farther apart than ever. A more serious effect of the war on those whose sympathies had been deeply engaged was that it produced a postwar mood of disillusionment or even despair, and this in the midst of a prewar situation. Like the public itself, if for different reasons, American writers were emotionally confused and unprepared for the events that would soon follow.

The younger writers, those now in the army, were in some ways even more unprepared than were those already established in their profession. Two years ago I talked with several of them at length, when I taught for a week in a writers' school on a hilltop in the Berkshires. The students in my class were between nineteen and twenty-five years old, all of them likable in their different ways and some quite talented. They may have learned something from me; there is no doubt whatever that I learned a great deal from them.

The first thing that surprised me was what appeared to be their total lack of interest in the European war. It was August 1941, another black month for the Allies. Hitler had failed to win the Battle of Britain, but elsewhere everything was going brilliantly for his designs. Erwin Rommel, the Desert Fox, was threatening to conquer Egypt and close the Suez Canal. The Japanese were advancing into Indochina. In Russia some of Hitler's armies had been temporarily halted at the Smolensk Gate, but others were sweeping through the rich Ukraine. Our own fate was being decided along with that of the world. If Russia collapsed, as seemed likely at the time, it was hard to see how the

English-speaking countries could hold out alone. But the battles were raging far from that magic mountain, where, so far as I could see or hear, there was not even a radio to report the news. About two o'clock the mailman came with letters and a single copy of *The New York Times*. It was seized and carried away by one of the students who had formerly been a Young Communist and who, after losing his political faith, had retained the habit of reading the papers. Nobody seemed to mind.

On Monday I suggested an experiment in automatic writing. A dozen students carried their portable typewriters into the classroom, sat at a long table, and wrote at top speed for two hours. The rules of the game were that nobody should pause or erase and that everybody should say whatever came into his head. It is good training for writers, young or old, so long as it is regarded purely as an exercise. It teaches them to write fast—a lesson I was never able to learn—and to think at the typewriter. Sometimes it also reveals ideas or episodes or images that have been hidden away beneath their conscious minds and that will make good stories or poems if developed later, consciously and at their leisure.

Nobody was asked to read aloud what he had written, but several of the students insisted on doing so. Their automatic writing was, in general, fanciful, grotesque, humorous, with more than a little sexual symbolism; sometimes a student would blush and skip a page. Sometimes he would speak with a firmer voice as he came to an episode obviously suggested by his reading of Franz Kafka; here was something recognizable by his audience as literature. I was impressed by the fact that there was not a single direct reference to the war. There were several deeply felt harangues against the monotony of American middle-class life and one girl was obsessed by the fear of becoming a housewife in Bronxville. Nobody showed any realization that, if Hitler won—as he then seemed to be on the point of doing—middle-class life in Bronxville would become an impossible Utopia.

During the week I held a two-hour conference with each student, reading his poems or stories and listening to his problems. One girl, a gifted poet of nineteen, told me that she had outgrown her excitement about society at large. The former Young Communist was writing Symbolist verse; he worshiped Mallarmé in the same fanatical spirit that he had once worshiped Marx. One evening the students gathered at their own suggestion for a reading from Rainer Maria Rilke's Paris notebooks. These I enjoyed less than the students did, for they lacked the unself-protective candor of good diaries; I may have been unjust to Rilke, but it seemed to me that he was too much concerned with his prose effects. Afterward the class discussed the years when he had lived alone in Munich (after serving briefly in the army) and had scrupulously refrained from writing anything about the war. They thought he had followed the proper course.

Listening to them talk, I began to feel that Rilke and Kafka, as literary symbols, were the equivalents of Eliot and Joyce after the other war, representing the same reaction against political interests and any compromise with the public taste. I began to feel that my calendar was shaped like a clock; the hands had made a complete revolution, and now I was back in Cambridge at a meeting of the Harvard Poetry Society. Would Cummings read one of his early poems about a saintly harlot? Or had the calendar made a double turn, and was I listening to the Rhymers' Club in London before my birth? Was that the young poet Lionel Johnson in the corner, explaining why he did not mind being separated from men and women: "In my library," he said, "I have all the knowledge of the world that I need." Remembering Johnson's tragedy, and that of almost all his friends except Yeats, I wondered whether writers learned anything but tricks of style from their predecessors.

At the last meeting of the class I gave a lecture which, as I remember it, was pretty severe. I said in effect that by not making an effort toward intellectual and emotional understanding of what was happening in the world, the students were neglecting one of their chief duties as writers. Afterward I received several interesting letters from them. One poet said, "I remember feeling there was plenty of evidence that I wasn't unaware of what was happening, in spite of the phony statement that I had outgrown excitement about society. In my stream-of-consciousness writing, didn't you notice the part about hands snagged on the wire and the vision of Hitler meeting his beak over the Andes? And didn't I read the part about the refugee climbing a tree?" She was right to scold me for lack of attention. Although none of the students had mentioned the war directly, there were several of these vague allusions that betrayed their worries. There was also a general mood of apprehension at the school that summer, leading to little quarrels and rebellions; but there was no conscious interest in political events. The subject was suppressed in writing and conversation, as sexual subjects used to be. It reappeared like sex in the form of indirect symbols and irrational actions.

These students on the magic mountain had special abilities and training, but in other respects they were not much different from the rest of their college generation. You could picture a whole age group of young writers prepared to spend years in study and partial solitude while perfecting their ability to express a personal vision—in other words, you could picture them as ready for a world that at worst would leave them alone and at best might permit them to serve a long apprenticeship in the art of letters, something like the years that Flaubert spent alone in his mother's house. The one thing for which they were not prepared, intellectually or emotionally, was to be seized and transported into a world without solitude, where their time would be measured by the top sergeant's whistle. All this helps to explain why very few young writers have come forward during the last three years: even those in civilian life are not yet adjusted to a new situation. Another wartime generation faced somewhat the same problems in 1918, not to mention its troubles afterward. Fortunately the mistakes and delays of writers in their twenties are seldom fatal.

For the last ten or a dozen years, American literature has been dominated by the writers who came of age during or shortly after the First World War—that is, by Hemingway, Dos Passos, Fitzgerald, Faulkner, and Wolfe among the novelists, by Cummings and Crane among the poets, by Wilson and his contemporaries among the critics, not to mention a dozen other names in all fields. They had talent to start out with, but they also had special opportunities. Besides giving them an emotional shock, the war opened new perspectives and new countries. Money was plentiful in the postwar years, travel was cheap, leisure was possible, and it was easier for new men to get a hearing. All these facts help to explain why so many of the writers admired today were born in the seven years between 1894 and 1900.

It may be that the generation coming of age during the Second World War will have an even greater opportunity. Partly it will depend on political events that are impossible to predict, but there is not much doubt that the public will be eager for new writers. I have no clear notion what those writers will say, and I should question whether their ideas before the war are a good indication of what they will think in the future. A better guide would be what they are thinking today, but civilians can't be sure of that, and I wonder whether the soldiers themselves have had time to make up their minds about it. If there is a postwar disillusionment, it can hardly take the same form as in the 1920s, considering that most young Americans went into this war with comparatively few illusions. I should expect that literature will be more personal, imaginative, and lyrical than it was in the 1930s, and it may also be more affirmative (though personally I distrust the word). For the rest, all one can say about it is that it will be interesting, and different.

COMMUNISM AND CHRISTIANISM

In spite of its appeal to deeply religious emotions, Communism is not a religion in the usual sense of the word. Good Communists do not believe in God, or in a future life, or in any mysteries beyond the ultimate scope of human logic. Calling themselves humanists, not superhumanists or deists, they are hostile by tradition to every form of worship from aboriginal totemism to the most enlightened Christian sects. The hostility goes back to Marx himself, and they often quote his opinions as the last word in any religious argument. Marx was opposed to Christianity for two reasons (outside of its falsity, which he took for granted). In the first place, he did not like to see meekness and self-humiliation exalted as high virtues. Proud of himself, proud of the human race, he demanded "the overthrow of all the social relations in which man is regarded as a degraded, enslaved, abandoned and contemptible creature." In the second place, he was angry because Christianity held forth the promise of rewards in heaven, and thus kept people from struggling against earthly injustice. He said very early in his career, "The destruction of religion as the illusory happiness of the people"—in the preceding sentence he had called it their "opium"—"is the necessary condition for the real happiness of the people." Through all the changes in the Communist Party line, this sentence from *The Holy Family* has remained an official doctrine.

But it is a doctrine that has led from the beginning to inconsistencies of conduct. Marx himself, while fighting against Christian morality, was inspired with moral fervor and wrote in a style that often suggests the prophets of the Old Testament; like them he called for justice on the oppressor and promised a return of the golden age. After his death, still other religious traits began to appear in the behavior of the Marxist parties; and this was only to be expected, considering that most of their members had received a Christian or Jewish training and found it natural to seek equivalents for the lost faith of their child-hood. The process was at first almost wholly unconscious; but after-ward, in Russia, it was deliberately encouraged by the party leaders in order to strengthen the Communist hold on the peasantry. They seem to have felt the need of providing devotional practices and symbols: for example, slogans like prayers chanted by thousands of marchers, and ikons of Stalin, which by 1933 had almost universally replaced the ikons of the saints. In spite of Communist doctrine, Holy Russia had become holier still.

And there is a question whether even the doctrine is as completely secular as Communists believe. There have been other religions with-out mysteries, as note the official faith of the Roman republic; even Christianity in the age of Descartes was usually presented as a logical creed that could be proved by the laws of scientific evidence. There have been other religions that did not promise a life beyond the grave; even Judaism was for a long time ambiguous on this point, and the Sadducees explicitly denied that men were immortal. Finally, there have been other religions that worshiped no god, and this is certainly the case with Buddhism, which consists primarily in the doctrine of salvation by the Four Noble Truths and which, in its orthodox form, does not recognize the divinity of Buddha. Granting that Commu-nism is the only great faith that is lacking in all three of these ele-ments, we can still question whether their absence makes it completely nonreligious. Psychologists would say that it leads to def-inite and even extreme types of religious behavior. Anthropologists would say that it performs the functions of a religion, since it embod-ies rites and institutions that help to give a whole society the feeling of unity, purpose, and confidence in the future. Theologians might say—if they approached the subject with open minds—that some of its doctrines provide a rough functional equivalent for God, heaven, and the sacred mysteries.

It is true that the same remarks would partly apply to other political parties and to many movements of reform. The single tax, women's suffrage, birth control, consumers' coöperatives, and nonviolent re-sistance have all been described as semireligious crusades. As Emile Durkheim said in his *Elementary Forms of Religious Life*, "There can be no society"—and he might almost have added, no group—"that does not feel the need of upholding and reaffirming at regular intervals the collective sentiments and collective ideas which make its unity and its personality. This moral remaking cannot be achieved except by the means of reunions, assemblies and meetings where the individuals, being closely united to one another, reaffirm in common their common sentiments; and this leads to ceremonies that do not differ from regular religious ceremonies either in their purpose and the results they produce or in the processes utilized to attain those results."

In this broader sense, the presence of religious characteristics in Communism is surprising only to the Communists themselves, who as a class are not much interested in anthropology. But there is also a narrower sense in which Communism can be described as a religion. It was founded like Christianity as a movement to redeem the oppressed of all the world, and for nearly a century it has been struggling with Christianity for the loyalty of the masses. The natural result is that it has come to embody more and more Christian elements or equivalents, just as Christianity in the course of its long struggle with Paganism made a practice of borrowing from the enemy in order to defeat him. By now the results of this process should be more widely recognized. In point of creed or doctrine, in point of cult or observance, and in point of churchly organization, there are at present dozens of parallels between Communism and the various Christian sects.*

*Some of the same parallels would apply in the case of Fascism, the other great political religion. This is partly because most of the Fascist leaders received their early training in Catholic schools, and partly because they copied much of their political organization from the Communists with whom they were struggling. Both Fascism and Communism are theocratic, in the sense that they place temporal and spiritual authority in the same hands. But whereas Communism aspires to be a universal religion like Christianity, and welcomes disciples of all races, the German Fascists have reverted to a tribal faith strangely resembling that of the early Semites. Hitler's German god is like Jahve, the volcano-god whom the Hebrews are said to have followed after the death of Moses (cf. Freud's *Moses and Monotheism*). The German conquest of Europe is conducted in the same spirit as the Hebrew conquest of Canaan, the Promised Land, this being an earlier synonym of *Lebensraum*.

Here, for example, are a few of the doctrinal parallels:

Instead of God, the Communists believe in history as a final principle and omnipotent judge. They regard "the great task of making history" as the highest activity open to mankind; it is their equivalent for doing God's will on earth. To be cast "into the dustbin of history" is like being cast into hell.

Instead of Divine Providence, the Communists believe in the Marxian dialectic as the principle that shapes our lives in society. Since the dialectic consists of three parts—thesis, antithesis, synthesis—it also bears some relation to the Christian Trinity; and it is the subject of quite as many learned disputations.

Instead of Divine Grace, they believe in a spirit emanating from the working class; almost by magic it transforms one's doubts and weariness into renewed hope. But if a man rejects this spirit, says Michael Gold in *The Hollow Men*, he suffers "a disintegration of personality and . . . loses much of his humanity, and can no longer distinguish good from evil."

Instead of Christ, they believe in Lenin the Redeemer, whose body is as carefully preserved in a shrine of pilgrimage as are the pieces of the True Cross. Trotsky for the orthodox takes the place of Judas.

Instead of Holy Writ, they believe in the writings of the Communist fathers, Marx and Engels together having composed their Old Testament and Lenin their New Testament. Stalin may or may not be fitted into the canon; Trotsky is accepted only by heretical sects corresponding to the Gnostics and Manicheans. The proceedings of the Comintern—Stalin once called it "the Holy of Holies of the working class"—resemble the Acts of the Apostles.

Instead of the doctrinal disputes among the Christian churches, they have still fiercer disputes over questions that are sometimes amazingly similar. Thus, the quarrel between Stalinists and Trotskyists was in one of its aspects concerned with the difference between salvation by faith and salvation by works, the Stalinists laying their emphasis on works and the Trotskyists on rightness of doctrine.

Instead of the picture that the Bible presents of the world's progress—from creation to last judgment to resurrection—they offer another pattern that is not wholly different. The golden age or Garden of Eden, which they situate in the past, is the communism of primitive tribes. The spirit of evil, the old Serpent, is the impulse toward amassing wealth at the expense of one's neighbors. The yielding to this impulse is Original Sin, still present in the hearts of all except the workers, who are the Elect. The world revolution will be Judgment Day, and the heaven to which they look forward is the classless society of the future. That heaven has so often been promised as a consolation for earthly misfortunes and the all too frequent mistakes of party leaders that Communism, too, might be called the opium of the people.

But besides these parallels between Communism and Christianity as creeds, there are others to be noted in churchly organization. The Catholic hierarchy has its counterpart in Russia, and indeed in every country with an organized Communist Party. Instead of a Pope, the Communists revere Stalin, whose rare speeches have no less force than papal encyclicals. Instead of bishops, they obey the members of the Central Committee. The Political Bureau of that committee is like a college of cardinals, with authority to choose a new Pope. The district and section organizers correspond to the lower ranks of the clergy.

The Communist Party itself has no exact equivalent in Christian organization. As a matter of fact, it has varied in size and function, sometimes resembling a religious order and sometimes including almost the whole congregation of the faithful; its nature depends on the tasks of the moment and the policies of its leaders. Thus, in 1930 the American party was small and devoted, having been freshly purged; whereas in 1938, toward the end of the People's Front period, it was large and full of doubtful elements. But the party in all countries, and during most periods, includes militant and usually secret sub-organizations that resemble the seventeenth-century Jesuits.

Economically the party is supported like the Christian sects, by tithes levied on its members and by voluntary contributions. In Russia it is the established church and forms part of the governmental structure. In countries where it is forbidden by the government, or is struggling to make a place for itself, it receives help from the Comintern—just as Christian churches in China are supported by the Board of Foreign Missions. As for domestic missions, they are carried out among the Chosen People (not the Jews but the workers) as well as among the

Gentiles (who are the middle classes) and the Laodiceans (who are the untrustworthy intellectuals). But the Trotskyists and Bukharinists, being heretics beyond redemption, deserve to fall into the hands of the Gaypayoo (which has often been compared to the Inquisition, and not without reason).

Russia is regarded by the Communists as their Holy Land, and Mecca has often been used in cablegrams as their code word for Moscow. But actually the parallels are more with the position of Italy and Rome in Catholicism. The old debate over the temporal power of the Pope has been mirrored and magnified in the disputes over Russian interests as opposed to or identified with the interests of the world revolution.

There are dozens of parallels between the two religions as cults, as patterns of conduct to be followed by their members. Almost all the intellectuals who join the Communist Party think of themselves as being completely detached from religious habits of thinking, completely logical, realistic, affranchised; and yet without making objections and usually without understanding the symbolic value of what they are doing, they undergo the same rites of indoctrination as if they were joining one of the more militant Christian sects. They listen to sermons on the new faith, they study its doctrines, they learn its sacred legends, they sing its hymns—some of which are deeply moving—and they begin to speak its special dialect, which in the course of years has acquired the effect of a sacerdotal language. Having been sponsored by a member in good standing, they are received into the congregation (unless the party is being persecuted, in which case they may have to serve a sort of novitiate in order to demonstrate their reliability). Their sign of membership is the red party-card, which many of them carry in the same spirit that a Catholic carries the crucifix. Some of them receive party-names, the ostensible purpose of which is to protect them from exposure, but which also have the religious function of denoting the new personality they have acquired by entering a new world.

Their Sunday now becomes Tuesday evening, when the American party holds its unit meetings. If these are as dull as Granville Hicks says they are, they have an even closer resemblance to church services than I had suspected; and those who attend them can leave with a comforting sense of having mortified themselves in the cause of duty. Then there are the holy festivals of Communism: May Day with its parades and November 7 with its great meetings to commemorate the Russian revolution. There are other meetings that are like public prayers for deliverance or public curses on the infidel; there is the daily round of party chores; there are the entertainments, benefits, costume balls; and in all these activities the new Communists are so deeply involved that they are likely to change their whole pattern of behavior. If they deviate from the party line, they are forced to confess their sins and do penance, on pain of being expelled not only from the party but from most of their social relationships; they would not suffer more if they lived in a Catholic country and were excommunicated. If they follow the party line faithfully through all its curves, they are rewarded with party honors and the admiration of their friends. Meanwhile they feel a deep sense of unity with the struggling masses of all the world—the Russian shock brigaders, the Chinese fighting native and foreign Fascists, the tortured German leaders—and in present tribulations they are upheld by the conviction that the future is theirs. As Ruth McKenney wrote in an article for *The New Masses*:

> Communists today are in the great stream of humanity, brothers to the forgotten men who invented speech, comrades to the Greek architects who discovered form—they sail beside Columbus, and sit in Galileo's studio, they hold the basin for Harvey as he discovers the circulation of the blood, and march with the *sansculottes* to the attack on the Bastille. . . . They have discovered the direction in which production is changing, from the anarchy of capitalism to the logic of socialism. And so Communists can act upon their knowledge, midwives to the future. Communists can make history, and so transcend their lives by knowing the only immortality open to human beings—putting a mark on tomorrow.

I know that Ruth McKenney is not a party leader, let alone being an authority on Marxism, but she speaks with more candor than the leaders and pundits; she reveals the deep religious feelings of the best party members. With this clue, we can understand why thousands in this country became so strongly attached to Communism that they have refused even to consider evidence by which their faith might be shaken (some of them in 1941 had stopped reading the newspapers, which they said printed nothing but lies). We can understand why others retained the Communist frame of mind when they wandered off into heretical sects, all of which continued to be spiritually centered on Moscow; and why still others, while becoming reconciled with bourgeois democracy, insisted on defending it with a fanaticism and unwillingness to compromise that were totally foreign to the democratic spirit; and why still others, who had become alienated not only from Communism but from the whole progressive movement, at last joined other churches, usually of an authoritarian cast (there were even converts to Fascism); and why still others actually suffered from that disintegration of personality mentioned by Michael Gold. They had all formed habits of action and feeling which they could not easily break; there was a void in their lives that had to be filled. In the immediate future, the world must reckon with that pressing need.

2

I can claim no originality in drawing these religious parallels. Most of them have already been pointed out by others, though not usually in any systematic fashion. A few writers, among them Edward Dahlberg, have gone much farther than I should like to follow. In the last chapter of *Can These Bones Live*, Dahlberg compares the Russian proletariat to "the body of sacrifice which gives dionysiacal rebirth to the fatherland, just as the mithraic bull, identified with the people, was burned and eaten by them so that a total resurrection and oneness could be symbolized." This, it seems to me, is only a picturesque way of saying that the Soviet masses have paid a heavy price for trying to build a happier future; in so far as their sacrifice was voluntary, they were not victims like the mithraic bull, though many of them acted like early-Christian martyrs. But my real objection to most of the writers who have made these comparisons is that they are imbued with the spirit of nineteenth-century scientific skepticism, based on the physical sciences and naïvely ignorant of human society. When they say that Communism has religious elements, they are implying that it is unscientific, out-of-date, and a little ridiculous.

Thus, Edmund Wilson, in a chapter called "The Myth of the Dialectic,"* says that Marx always believed "in the triad of Hegel: the *These*, the *Antithese* and the *Synthese*; and this triad was simply the old Trinity, taken over from the Christian theology, as the Christians had taken it over from Plato. It was the mythical and magical triangle which from the time of Pythagoras and before had stood as a symbol for certainty and power and which probably derived its significance from its correspondence to the male sexual organs." Wilson might easily have added examples of trinitarian thinking from Egypt, Babylon, and India, or from the political or the academic world of our own day; or he might have mentioned the triangular situations that are the subject of so many three-act plays and fictional trilogies; the triad is inescapable. To me the astonishing feature of his argument is the unspoken assumption behind it: that anything ancient and almost universal in human thought is by the same token false, the truth being a creation of modern times and scientific enlightenment. It would seem to me more fruitful to examine whether a conception as widely employed as the triad is the symbol of any psychological or social or historical reality (outside of the male sexual organs, which have already been used to explain everything from the Empire State Building to the two thieves crucified on either side of Christ). Likewise Edward Dahlberg, after presenting in a grotesquely magnified form the religious myths of Soviet Russia, pours forth his pity on poor humanity for accepting them. He asks when man will throw away "his manikin baby gods, the toy buddha dictator, his plaything ikons: the little magical Christmas states, the toy tanks, war games and flags, the infant cubical fatherlands with the doll-house knockers and emblems on the door: the Nazi scarab, the hammer and sickle, the red, white and blue. . . . O, let man laugh the *gods* out of this world, so that the heart can live in it!" Here the unspoken assumption is that the ideal society is composed of independent individuals believing in nothing they cannot see or touch and acting on the principles of enlightened self-interest: in other words, the heavenly city of the Utilitarian phi-

---

To the Finland Station. This happens to be the weakest chapter in a valuable book.

losophers. In Dahlberg's judgment, Russia failed to attain that ideal because it kept a place for gods, symbols, and myths.

But the truth, I believe, is quite opposite to what these critics suggest. Instead of being an element of weakness, the religious side of Communism helps to explain its strength and continued life. Although its cosmology, its history, its economics, its sociology, its politics, and its picture of the future have at one point after another been brought into question by the experiments and the experience of our own century, its religious force simply cannot be denied. It was precisely because Marx believed in the dialectic as a demiurge and in history as a god working for justice to the working class; it was because thousands sacrificed their happiness and their lives to spread his beliefs; it was because those beliefs were adopted by the Russian masses as a new pentecostal faith and became surrounded with the myths, the poetry, the symbols of a church—it was for all these reasons that Communism has been able to gain millions of converts, many of whom have maintained their faith in the midst of trials ranging from ordinary social disapproval and economic penalties up to imprisonment, torture, death. No other religion of our times has had so many martyrs; and thinking of the thousands who have died for it in Central Europe, the hundreds of thousands in Spain, the millions in Russia and China (many of them executed for the mere suspicion of having Communist leanings), one doubts that any religion of the past has ever had so many martyrs in so short a space of years. Communism is now showing, moreover, an ability to maintain bitter resistance in the face of the strongest army the world has known—and this summer of 1941, reading fragmentary accounts of the battles waged by the Red Army, the guerillas dying behind the lines, the towns completely destroyed to keep them from falling into the hands of the invaders; reading and comparing these stories with the rather shameful record of the conquered Western nations, one finds it hard to criticize the Communists; there are always others to pursue that task.

Yet we cannot judge a religion merely by the number of its martyrs; there are always the survivors to be reckoned with. We cannot judge it merely by its ability to create armed forces, to manufacture planes and tanks, lest we be tempted to believe that if Fascism conquers Communism in battle it will be a still higher faith. A religion must be judged by its capacity to produce admirable lives, not only in times of war and revolution, but also in the daily relations of society; not only in heroic failure but also in rather humdrum success. And although our data are incomplete, Russia having so far existed in a state of continual crisis, still it would seem that by this standard of judgment Communism is in many respects inferior even to the decayed and diluted Christianity of the Western world.

Most writers condemning the ethics of Communism have for years made one charge against it. They accuse it of having adopted the principle that the end justifies the means, whereas the truth, in their estimation, is that ends and means are really identical and good never comes of evil. But doesn't it? Those ethical philosophers would speak with more authority if we could be sure that they never—and "never" is a big word—punished their children or told harmless fibs to their wives. When someone shows them a mediocre painting or poem, do they *never* say, "Yes, that's very nice," or even, "I do like that," in the desire to please the painter or the poet?—though certainly they realize that the good end of sustaining his ego is being used to justify the bad means of falsehood. And—granting that many of them are high-principled pacifists and nonresisters—can we be sure that they never eat meat or wear furs or set out poison for mice (or phone the exterminator to come and get rid of them) and never accept money derived from the exploitation of the working classes? *Never* to do or condone or profit by evil while hoping that good may come of it would condemn one to the life of a Hindu mystic (who in turn is doing evil to his own body). Obviously means and ends cannot be wholly separated, any more than cause and effect; obviously the character of a spy or jailer or policeman, even if he is serving an enlightened government, is going to be influenced by his calling. But for practical purposes, and in spite of everything the philosophers have written, we are left with the daily problem of deciding what means are justified by what ends.

The real charge against the ethics of Communism is that the means or instruments used in attaining its ends are too often living men and women. By habitually treating people as instruments—and on the face of the record, "habitually" is not too strong a word—it violates a principle which was not given its definitive statement until Kant wrote his

Critique of Pure Reason, but which nevertheless has always been close to the heart of Christian thought. Christianity sets an absolute value on the individual; Communism has in practice recognized no absolute value except society as a whole, or rather the future of society.

Some results of that practice are written in the history of Russia during the last twenty years, and in the history of the Communist parties elsewhere; even after rejecting the many slanders and questioning all statistics, we are left with a few well-attested facts. Thus, we know that individuals in great numbers have been sacrificed to the future of society (and too often without their consent or prior knowledge); they have been lied to and about, used as scapegoats, sent on fatal missions, worked to death in labor camps, and starved to death in a famine that was kept secret and therefore went unrelieved for the good of the state. We know that individuals have been punished for crimes of which they were merely suspected, and even for crimes known to have been committed by others—all the subordinates losing their jobs or their freedom or their lives when the factory manager or government commissar was convicted of treason; and we know that they have been punished for what they thought was doing their duty as good Communists—on the principle, abhorrent to Christians, that the objective effect of an action is to be judged rather than the good or bad intentions of the man who performed it. We also know that all those sacrifices were ordered, and all these punishments inflicted, by leaders acting on what they possibly thought was the highest principle of morality, and that their conscious aim was almost always to insure the survival of the workers' state. But the workers' state has become such an abstract principle that at times it seems hardly intended for real workers to live in—pity, kindness, gratitude, friendliness to individuals have not much part in it. One is reminded of a colony of bees, where the sick or wounded members are driven out of the hive to die, lest they spread contagion; there is no law except the survival of the swarm.

And the fact is that a movement like Communism, which lays so much stress on society as a whole, is tempted to paint a somewhat bare and simplified picture of the individual. He needs food, clothing, shelter, and sex; he acts in the light of logic and according to what he thinks are his best interests; for the rest, he is either naturally good or else he can be kneaded and shaped into goodness by an all-knowing state that controls the schools, the press, and the instruments of production. That is roughly the conception of the human unit on which Communist policy seems to depend; it is one that was widely held in the nineteenth century. But the Economic Man and the Reasoning Man of the nineteenth-century philosophers have been largely destroyed by later researches into the nature of men's thinking and men in society: by Freud and Pavlov, by Frazer and Durkheim, to mention only four of the pioneers. There is not much place for their discoveries in Communist ideology—except for a simplified form of Pavlov's conditioned reflexes, which seem to be accepted partly because Pavlov was a Soviet citizen. One can read a great deal of Communist literature without finding anything but angry sneers at concepts like the unconscious, associational thought, symbolic and vicarious actions, semantics, cultural patterns, the Oedipus complex, or the cult of the dying god—many of which will have to be modified or abandoned, but all of which have been a basis for new studies of human behavior.

And an interesting feature of those studies is that they are leading to a richer and more complicated picture of what Franz Boas calls "the specific characteristics of the human species." It seems to be a species with an infinite capacity for changing itself, but also with an infinite capacity for retaining the same fundamental patterns of action and belief. The same rites appear in Malaya and Mexico and, under new disguises, in Soviet Russia. The same antisocial vices are repeated in new forms—or if finally stamped out, they disappear at the same moment as virtues with which they were somehow connected. Apparently the progress of the race is not toward the eventual solution of class conflicts or any other conflicts, but rather toward their transformation and reappearance in new fields. And this chain of thought leads one to question whether the classless society for which Communists are working is either possible to the human species or would, if forcibly achieved, satisfy the specific human needs. Perhaps they have been sacrificing men and women to an unattainable ideal. Perhaps the Christian picture of human nature, which recognizes, if it does not solve, the problem of evil, is not only more emotionally satisfying but also, in the end, more realistic.

TOWN REPORT:
1942

This isn't a piece about Middletown or Anyburg or Sauk Center. The country towns here in New England all bear a family resemblance to one another, but they also have individual characters that can be learned only by living in them. They are more or less united as communities, more or less friendly to newcomers, more or less dominated by cliques that are more or less conservative and sometimes corrupt. But all of them are different from small towns in other parts of the country, and I suspect that all of them have been rapidly changing since the war, in fashions that are not always apparent to their own inhabitants.

I suspect, but I can't be certain. One effect of this war has been to broaden our political interests while narrowing our social horizons. Friends who live within thirty miles of us used to be regarded as neighbors; now we can see them only by saving gasoline for weeks to have a little surplus. Our cousins in Pennsylvania might as well be living in Omaha, or the moon. And so, in setting down the wartime record of one little town, I wonder whether it is at all unusual or whether it is typical of the country as a whole.

Sherman is a town only in the New England sense; in New York it would be an unincorporated village, in Pennsylvania a township, and farther west nothing more than a school district. It consists of about twenty-five square miles of land shaped like a narrow slice of pie—a valley ten miles long with a lake in the south, farmland in the north, and a range of wooded hills on either side. The back roads are full of abandoned farms like those described in Slater Brown's novel, *The Burning Wheel*. North of the village, locally called the Center, there are twenty fairly prosperous dairy farms. Summer cottages are clustered along the shores of the lake and scattered through the hills. The winter population is about 450.

Small as it is, the town has its own probate judge and its own representative in the Connecticut General Assembly. As for local officials, it has so many of them that I have never been able to make an accurate count, although thirty-five are listed by name in the annual report, which doesn't bother to mention three or four constables. Most of these officials are elected for terms of one or two years, but a few are appointed, including the dog warden, who happens to be a Democrat. The first selectman, who acts as a mayor or burgess, more than earns his salary of $500 a year. With a few exceptions, the other officials either serve without pay or else receive fees for the work they actually perform. One of them makes a living by holding three town offices and driving the school bus.

Except for Republican politics, Sherman has no native industries, and there are only three products of any importance: milk, scenery, and good roads. About one-third of the inhabitants are supported by dairy farming, and most of the others either work on the roads, which are maintained or subsidized by the state, or else they supply various goods and services to the summer people who come to enjoy the scenery. At least that is what they used to do before the war.

Sherman today has twenty-nine men and two women in the armed forces—about seven percent of its people and substantially more than the average for the nation. About one-third of them enlisted voluntarily, including an aviation cadet and two army nurses, besides half a dozen men in the navy. I heard that one boy thought seriously of becoming a conscientious objector, but he changed his mind at the last moment, and it now seems that he has become an uncommonly good soldier. Most of the men neither try very hard to get into the army nor take any steps to keep out of it. There is a somewhat passive attitude, as if they said—and in fact I have heard more than one man saying—"When Uncle Sam wants me, he'll come and get me and I'll be ready to go."

Uncle Sam doesn't want the farmers, most of whom are now in their fifties, but they complain of not being able to find help, and this at a time when they are being asked to keep bigger herds. The summer people had to mow their own lawns or let them grow into hay. To keep a maid is a dream that most of the housewives have forgotten. Building has stopped completely, and many of the carpenters and plumbers are finding jobs in airplane factories; at any rate they are moving to Bridgeport and Hartford. Sherman has only two war workers now living here, a grandfather more than seventy years old and one of his younger sons. They work twelve hours on the night shift at Bridgeport, besides driving fifty miles each way.

It is surprising how little talk one hears about the war. Maybe it's because I don't get around as much as I should, or don't catch everything that is said. I note, however, that the radio at the grocery store was turned on for the World's Series but not for news reports of the fighting in the Solomons. Ten years ago when farmers on the back roads talked about "the war," they meant the American Revolution, during which this countryside was infested with marauding Tories. The Civil War and the First World War left no such lasting impressions, for the fighting was far away—and New Guinea is even farther. What is near at hand is food and fuel rationing, high prices, and the shortage of unrationed articles like prunes and alarm clocks and bacon. About all these matters there is grumbling, but rather less than I expected to hear. Sometimes a man will say, "Those people in Washington . . ." as if he blamed them for everything that was going wrong; but the same man will volunteer as an airplane spotter or a fire warden. Nobody thinks that we will lose the war, but there are signs of deep uncertainty about the future. People say, "It's no use making plans any more," and that is a bitter remark for New Englanders, who like to know what they will be doing in twenty years.

So far the most obvious change in Sherman life has been produced by the rationing of gasoline and tires. Eight miles from a railroad station, the town had learned to live on rubber. There is a state highway two hundred yards from my house, and I used to hear the hum of tires as cars shot past at seventy miles an hour. Now the highway is empty half the morning, and then a car passes as slowly and silently as if it were driving behind a hearse. Nobody can take long trips. Hardly anybody thinks of driving to New Milford or Danbury—the nearest large towns—without inviting his neighbors to come too.

At first the church suffered from gasoline rationing, but I understand that with people learning to share rides, attendance is almost back to normal. Sunday school has been resumed, after being abandoned during the summer; the children are now taken there in the school bus. There is absolutely no sign, however, of the religious revival that is supposed to be felt in wartime. Activities that used to be connected with the church are now centered in the town hall.

Indeed, that little white Gothic chickencoop has become more important than any other building in Sherman. It used to stand empty from week to week, being opened only for town meetings and an occasional square dance or chicken supper. The town clerk kept his books and papers at home. Now the hall is open every day, with the clerk at his desk, the selectmen or the assessors meeting, and the rationing board receiving applications (which, incidentally, it handles with great fairness). In the evenings the hall is lighted for meetings connected with war or politics—for lectures on gas masks, fire protection, or first aid; for Republican caucuses and rallies of the fire company. One feels that the community has been drawn together by the new tasks it is called upon to perform.

Some of its former activities have been discontinued; for example, there are not many purely social gatherings. Sherman used to be known as the eatingest town in Connecticut. Two years ago its women compiled and published a *Sherman Cookbook*, with local recipes that are widely followed—and they are good ones, too. It used to be that every event was celebrated and every organization was financed by a covered-dish luncheon, a clambake, a turkey dinner, or a cake and jelly sale. But public meals are difficult to arrange in wartime, and many of the organizations that depended on them for support have become inactive.

Meanwhile the war has created new organizations—too many of them by far, and with functions that in some cases are vague or conflicting. The rationing board, however, has a definite job and is doing it well; it will end by exercising a tremendous power over civilian lives. The observation post has been in continuous operation since the day after Pearl Harbor. It has the services of 150 airplane spotters in summer and 90 in winter, each of them standing guard for three hours a week. A service committee has been forwarding letters and packages to the Sherman boys in the armed forces.

The local defense council is charged with supervising a host of activities, those listed in its report as Air Raid Wardens, Agriculture, Auxiliary Police, Emergency Housing and Evacuation, Finance, Fire

Wardens, Courses, Medical, Women's Division, and Salvage—in other words, the whole complicated pattern created in Washington by the Office of Civilian Defense, on the model of what had been done in England. The trouble is that events here aren't following the English model. Serious air raids are becoming more unlikely and it is the countryside instead of the cities that is being evacuated. I should guess that the muddle in civilian defense cost the administration more votes than the loss of the Philippines.

And yet new organizations continue to proliferate. An hour ago I was interrupted by a visitor who urged my wife to become the coordinator of something or other; I didn't catch all of the high-sounding title. The actual work involved was organizing a course in forest-fire prevention to compete with courses already being given in first aid, home nursing, and nutrition, not to mention others. In spite of having a coordinator, the new course would apparently not be coordinated with earlier activities, even those of the local fire wardens. The visitor, who was very nice and rather apologetic, had to carry out his instructions from Washington, where the course had been carefully and no doubt soundly planned, but without any notion of what is actually being done in towns like this.

A great deal is being done, and done willingly, in spite of all the confusion. Although some of the defense activities are being performed in a perfunctory fashion, as perhaps they deserve to be, others are taking root in local life. To mention one example, the naming of fire wardens led naturally to the organization of a local fire company, a step that had been hopefully discussed for several years. Until the war we had been forced to depend on the fire company from New Milford, which does excellent work in its own town, but which is so far from Sherman that often a house burned down before it arrived—and even then it charged $50 for making the trip. After the chief fire warden suggested that we could do the work ourselves, the selectmen appropriated $1,500 to buy a second-hand fire truck, and the firemen collected money to buy hose. A firehouse is being built by volunteer labor, with materials furnished by the town. It is an achievement like those we used to admire in travelers' stories from Russia.

When the time came for the national scrap collection, it was the fire company that undertook to do the job. We gathered at nine o'clock one Sunday morning—twenty-five or thirty men and seven or eight trucks, each with a route assigned to it. The driver of the truck on which I rode was the Republican candidate for the General Assembly. I was running against him and we joked about it sometimes during the morning, when we weren't too busy carrying old iron, but nobody was much concerned about our political rivalry, considering that no Democrat has carried the town since Cleveland's second term. At almost every house a pile of scrap was waiting. People said, "I had three old cars, too, but I guess they were shipped to Japan." Or else, "The Japs got in ahead of you, Howard. You'll have to go out to the Solomon Islands if you want to find my tractor." For people here, the scrap iron sold to Japan has come to stand for all the errors in our foreign policy.

From one house we hauled away a weatherbeaten Ford that was rooted in weeds and looked like an enormous vegetable; from another we drove off in a caravan, with a hayrake hitched to the back of the truck and a buggy hitched to the hayrake. The big pile in a corner of the schoolyard had been growing all morning and afternoon; it was now about as large as a brownstone house lying on its side. Digging into it, one could reconstruct almost everything the town had ever been. There were saws and axes, ox chains, farming implements (some used for crops no longer grown in western Connecticut), dozens of heavy milk cans, old trucks and tires, kiddie cars, a box of tennis balls—in all, the record of a town that had passed from lumbering to herding to general farming, and then to a mixed economy of dairying and providing vacations for city people; that had traveled in a century and a quarter from pioneering to week-ending—and now was moving in what direction? If it had not been for the war, Sherman might have become an outer suburb, with gentlemen's estates in the midst of desolate fields. So far, the war has preserved its farms and has carried Sherman backward in time through the automobile age toward the period when it was an isolated community furnishing most of its own food and its own amusements. It is in most ways a better and friendlier town in wartime than it was in peace.

That Sunday we collected twenty-five tons of its relics, or about 110 pounds for each inhabitant. It was more than the state or the national average, but less than we might have collected if we had planned our work more carefully or continued it longer. And that might stand as a general comment on our effort in wartime: it is better than the average, and in spite of some confusion it is probably better organized, like the community itself, but it is not half the effort we are capable of making or will have to make before the end of the war. As for what is being done in towns bigger and smaller than Sherman, I haven't heard and I would like to know.

THE RED AND
THE BLACK

M any of the best books of the last twenty years were not written
for the public at large. Being textbooks instead of trade books,
they were not reviewed or advertised except in professional journals,
and were not placed on sale except in college bookstores. Even when
they were later published in trade editions, as sometimes happened,
they still had a pedagogical look that frightened the reviewers away;
and yet some of these books were superior in all respects, including
simple readability, to almost everything that appeared on the best-
seller lists.

French Literature and Thought Since the Revolution belongs to this category of textbooks that the public should hear about. Edited by two
Dartmouth professors, Ramon Guthrie and George E. Diller, it is intended for college students with three years of high-school French. It
looks forbidding, with its ponderous title, its separate introductions
to each of seven sections, its small-type biographies of every author
represented and its footnotes that take nothing for granted—not even
that the reader will know who Chopin was. It will probably never be
seen by the literary critics, let alone the mass of readers with three
years of high-school French, and yet it gives a better picture of literature under the French Republic than any other book I know.

The earlier sections include most of the passages that, by dint of
being learned by heart, have acquired an indefeasible right to be reprinted in anthologies; but they also include other material that is not
widely known even in France. The editors don't bother to pretend, as
many professors do, that the great French authors had no social background and no political convictions. In the last section of 150 pages,
they are dealing with Symbolism and all the schools that followed it.
Here, besides a taste for modern writing that is rare in the colleges,
they reveal the born teacher's conviction that even the most obscure

poems can be clarified for his students by explaining the poet's ideas and the symbols he used to express them. Their notes perform the remarkable feat of making Rimbaud and Mallarmé intelligible to the common reader.

One's first impression after watching this review of French authors in their ordered ranks—the Classicists followed by the Romantics, who were followed in turn by the Naturalists and the Symbolists, while all the wild rebels scouted on the flanks without ever disturbing the tramp of disciplined feet—one's first impression is that the 125 years after Waterloo were one of the great periods in world literature. Poetry, fiction, history, criticism, self-analysis, pure fantasy: all these forms were broadened, intensified, or in any case transformed. Never before were so many fields so thoroughly cultivated at the same moment by men who were also amateurs of painting, music, food, love, and conversation, all the arts of enjoying the world. And these activities in every field were closely tied together: that is one's second impression. Reading this anthology published two years after the fall of the French Republic, one feels that every aspect of its life was part of a unified whole.

That is by no means the impression we used to have. Those of us who had lived in France felt that the whole country was divided, not into the three parts that Caesar listed, but merely into two, the Red and the Black—the France of the revolution and the France of pensions and property. Even in a village fifty miles from Paris, the division was clear. On one side were most of the men who worked with their hands, the women washing clothes in the sunlight, the children bathing in the river, the doctor's two sons home from school, the penniless artist down the road and the girl who took care of him—in short, everybody who laughed aloud, who was reckless and generous, who lived in the open air. The black France was represented by the retired colonel and his wife, the priest's housekeeper, the notary playing whist with his friends—every family that had a parlor with drawn blinds, that dressed correctly, that was afraid of drafts and complained about the servants. And this division in one village seemed to be repeated everywhere in France, from the Chamber of Deputies down to the dram shop at the corner. Sometimes it seemed to be a division between rich and poor, or between radical and conservative, or between pagan and pious, or even between young and old; but these were not infallible tests. There were rich old men, Catholics and even Royalists, who belonged to the red France; there were radical politicians and labor leaders who belonged in spirit to the Blacks (and who would prove it later by their support of Vichy). Sometimes the essential difference seemed to be one of temperament, between those who took risks and those who avoided them; between those who had nothing to lose and those who thought they had nothing to gain—perhaps between those who loved and those who were afraid of life.

What one feels after reading this new anthology is not that the division was imaginary—it was so real that it caused the defeat of France—but rather that it expressed two interrelated aspects of the same culture. The red France depended on the black, which in turn depended on the red; they were the two poles of a magnet, the two sides of a coin. Artists revolted against the bourgeoisie, Romantics against Classicism, Impressionists against the Salon; yet they never carried their revolt so far as to break the frame that united them all— all, Baudelaire and his hated stepfather, Flaubert and Madame Bovary (and even Homais the pharmacist), Rimbaud and his mother, Alphonse Daudet and his reactionary son, Barrès in his rebellious youth and Barrès in his age, Dreyfus and the anti-Dreyfusards, yes, even the men of the Commune and their executioners. Here was something different from Marx's picture of thesis and antithesis struggling together and giving birth to a new social order. This conflict seemed almost static, year after year, as if it were only the marble frieze of a battle.

Yet the nature of the struggle was changing imperceptibly. At first both the red France and the black had been strengthened by combat. Later, as more and more people became involved, the whole country was weakened; with its forces consumed internally, it was reduced to inertia. No projects could be completed, not even those on which almost everyone was agreed, like building a railway across the Sahara, or a ship canal from Bordeaux to the Mediterranean, or even the modernization of French industry. Everybody complained of the stationary population, and everybody should have known that it was not caused by the birth rate, which was higher than in Germany or England, but chiefly by the mortality among children. No public measures were taken to reduce that mortality. The country was deadlocked; and when it appeared that the deadlock might be broken by the triumph of red France, the other France failed to resist the invader. That was the end: the apparent triumph of the Blacks, ruling behind a wall of German tanks, but their actual confession of defeat.

Today it is certain that France after this war will be a different country. Much that we loved in the old France will have been destroyed along with much that we hated; dependent on each other they are dying together like stags with their antlers locked. A new generation will have other conflicts and will create a new literature to express them.

THE DISPOSSESSED

Besides being a somewhat bombastic title for an unassuming book of memoirs, *Today We Are Brothers* is a statement partly false in its implications, since brothers in adversity are not always brothers in arms or even friends in need. But the subtitle, *The Biography of a Generation*, is strictly accurate. If Leo Lania's publishers had told him, "Forget about your autobiography, it wouldn't sell in these times, and instead write the case history of any Central European intellectual during the period between two wars"—if the author had followed this advice, inventing an archetypical hero and getting him involved in adventures designed to reveal the spirit of the age, he need have added only a few incidents to his own story. He need have changed nothing at all.

Like many other writers of his generation, Lania began with a sense of divided nationality, for he was born in Kharkov—where his father died during the 1905 revolution—and educated in Vienna. He wrote his first stories there while he was still a student at the Academic Gymnasium. Soon he learned to regard himself, not as a Russian or an Austrian, but as a member of the new intelligentsia. This, he says, "was a caste apart, more aristocratic than the aristocracy, more exclusive than a religious order." For the honor of being known as intellectuals, young people starved themselves and ran away from home. For the crime of being intellectuals, they would later go into exile.

Lania was eighteen when the war broke out, and soon he volunteered for service at the front. Almost surrounded by Russians in a disputed trench, he directed the artillery fire of a whole Austrian division; he was recommended for a gold medal. But besides being a brave soldier, Lania had also been writing for a Socialist paper, and so he received a silver medal instead; Socialists could never be more than second-class heroes. Back in Vienna he had his first real love affair, with a girl of good family who was desperately resolved to live her own life. As he describes Helly drinking, Helly dancing wildly, Helly spiteful or in tears, it seems to me that in those days I knew a dozen like her, each convinced that she was unique and alone.

All through the book, Lania practices an unobtrusive talent for presenting figures from life as if they were types chosen to illustrate the history of our times. He was such a type himself for the first two years of the revolution; he was the conspirator traveling across international frontiers with money and documents sewed into the lining of his coat. Later, after leaving the Communist Party, he became another type: the disillusioned radical trying to get ahead in the world. He nearly starved in Berlin during the inflation; but one night a famous dancer took him with her to a gambling hell. Going through his clothes in the morning, he found a five-dollar bill that he had put aside from his temporary winnings; it paid his rent for a month and left him with enough change in German marks to start a new career as a free-lance journalist. As for the dancer, Anita Berber, she was admired in those days for her utter depravity. When she died in 1926, there was a mob at her funeral—film directors, prostitutes, financiers, bartenders, and half-men dressed in women's clothes. Her husband came late, still wearing a dinner jacket from the night before; in his mouth was a red geranium, which he coquettishly laid on her coffin. He was another type; they all were types.

By this time, Lania himself was beginning to be the type of successful writer; his novels sold and his plays were produced by Piscator and Reinhardt. He was often to be seen at Schwanneke's bar, which, he says, "was a literary institution. . . . In other capitals, 'society' was the nobility or the upper middle class; in Berlin at this period it was the leading artists and writers. Schwanneke's was our salon and our home." But the Nazis were winning their street brawls outside the door, and by 1932 even Schwanneke's was beginning to be unsafe. Lania left the country just in time, losing his furniture, his books, and his manuscripts.

He gives only one brief chapter to his seven years as an exile in Paris. They were difficult years, spent moving from one furnished room to another, but Lania was luckier than most; his wife believed in him, his wits had been sharpened by his early adventures in Berlin, and he wasn't too proud to do any honest work that came his way. Some of his companions relapsed into idleness and self-pity. "I am like a dead man on leave," said the film director Alex Granovsky a short time before his death. "Like our whole generation. We are lost."

Lost they were, and Lania never explains exactly why, but in terms of concrete experiences he tells almost the whole story. There are of course a few episodes that he omits, usually because they formed no part of his own career—for example, he was never sent to a concentration camp, and he seems to have taken no part in the Spanish adventure. The Russo-German Pact of 1939 is another crisis in the life of the intellectuals that he fails to mention; its effects are eloquently described in *Scum of the Earth*, by Arthur Koestler. The escape of the luckier refugees from France is described not only by Koestler and Lion Feuchtwanger but also by Lania himself in an earlier book, *The Darkest Hour*. For the rest, almost everything is here—the revolutionary fervor, the disillusionment, the crazy days in Berlin when all values were inflated and meaningless, the brief days of glory at Schwanneke's bar, the flight across the German border, the discovery that exile was only the prelude to greater disasters—in short, all the incidents, all the human types, all the background material for understanding one of the great collective tragedies of modern times.

It is indeed a greater tragedy than Lania allows himself to realize, in his determination not to yield to self-pity. A whole generation of writers—not to mention artists, musicians, film directors, and political theorists—were subjected to a lifelong process of deprivation. First they were deprived of their childhood country, the *petit pays* dear to every European—the grape-grown hillside in the Rhineland, the *Bezirk* in Vienna, or the village on the wide Galician plain. Then, by a conflict in ideals, they were deprived of their families. Then they lost their fatherland, if they had not lost it already; for those who had been subjects of Francis Joseph, the fatherland was simply abolished. They even lost the revolutionary ideals that for many intellectuals had taken the place of nation, family, and home.

In Berlin, where most of them spent the postwar years, they married, had children, earned a little fame; but in 1932 the process of deprivation was renewed—and very quickly they lost their hold on the public, their material possessions and even the privilege of being published in the German language. When France fell in 1940, they lost Europe as a whole; middle-aged and empty-handed they had to seek their fortune overseas. Nor is this by any means the full story of what they suffered. Old friendships and happy marriages ended in quarrels, for it is a false view of human nature to believe that adversity holds people together. Old beliefs held with religious fervor were destroyed by Munich and the Russo-German Pact. Even their faith in themselves was weakened, since it is true that punishment, no matter how little deserved, creates a sense of guilt in the victims. Worst of all their losses, perhaps, was that of an aim and an illusion. They had believed firmly that they were working for and possessing the future, but now, exiled from their own countries, the intellectuals were also exiled into the past.

There is no use calling the roll of the talented German and Austrian writers who died in concentration camps or who committed suicide either in France, when they learned that the Gestapo was about to catch up with them, or else in America when they found that they were too exhausted to start a new life. Walter Hasenclever, Irmgard Keun, Otto Pohl, Walter Benjamin, Ernst Toller, Stefan Zweig—the list would have to be much longer to include the names of all those who, in Koestler's words, "killed themselves hurriedly, secretly; stole out of life as they had stolen over barbed wire and frontier posts, after even this last exit permit had been refused to them." A whole generation has been outlawed, and much of it has been physically destroyed. To find a parallel, one would have to go back many hundreds of years— to the Emperor Shih Hwang, who beheaded a host of scholars because he thought they were partisans of the old order, and ordered his soldiers to burn every book they found. But most of the books had already been memorized, and many of the scholars were saved by their neighbors.

To me the most terrifying feature of Lania's story is not the attack on the Central European intellectuals; it is the fact that almost nobody came to their defense. We know of course that the German nation was stunned and terrified; we know that any critic tolerated by the Nazis who dared to make a gesture toward helping a proscribed author would certainly be proscribed in turn. But even under the worst tyrannies, people find ways of showing their sympathy for victims whose sufferings really move them. Public support for churchmen opposed to Hitler was so strong that most of them were never sent to concentration camps; a few, like Bishop von Galen, are still speaking out from the pulpit. This happened in spite of the fact that the Germans were not an especially religious nation; before 1933, they seemed to be more interested in literature; no other people in western Europe bought so many books or crowded so many theatres. And yet when their contemporary writing was abolished overnight, the Germans protested not at all. There is nothing in recent history that has illustrated so forcefully the divorce of contemporary literature from contemporary life. The intellectuals paid with all their possessions for their pride in being a separate caste.

And what about our own country?—since the implications of Mr. Lania's story are not confined to Europe. If we ever had fascism here under whatever name—and its name might well be the Patriotic All-American Party—would the intellectuals fare any better? Would they find themselves any closer to the public at large than their German colleagues after the fall of the Weimar Republic? I hope for many reasons these questions will never have to be answered.

KOESTLER:
THE DISENCHANTED

When Malaga was lost in the early spring of 1937, Arthur Koestler fell into the hands of the Rebels. He had once met Queipo de Llano, the Rebel general; he had even published an interview telling the truth about him, and that was crime enough to condemn a journalist. Without being tried, he was sentenced to death.

That spring, Koestler was thirty-one years old. He was a Hungarian subject, an exile from Germany, and a roving correspondent for *The News Chronicle*, the bravest paper in London. For the last six years he had been a Communist Party member; he had spent some time in Moscow and had traveled through Central Asia as a guest of the Soviet government. He had also finished his first novel, which was a curious book for any Communist to have written.

The Gladiators, which would not be published in this country until 1939, was a novel purporting to deal with Spartacus and the Servile War. Its main outlines were indeed historical, but it was full of anachronisms that seemed to be deliberate—as if Koestler was saying that he didn't care when Lucullus returned from the East or what the Roman slaves were given to eat; one year or another, horse beans or maize, it was all the same to him, because he wasn't really writing about the Romans. His real subject was not one particular revolt against Roman landlords beginning in 73 B.C., but all the revolts in recorded history. He was, moreover, telling a fable for our own times, in which one could recognize familiar people and topics—Anarchists, Trotskyists, party liners, deviations, the end justifying the means. Spartacus himself was presented, not as a Thracian gladiator, but rather as a combination of Lenin in Smolny Institute and Christ on the cross. It was of course permissible for any Communist to discuss the reasons why his revolt was a failure, but Koestler went far beyond political issues or historical events. Painfully, awkwardly, shifting his attention from one character to another as if afraid of coming to the point, he managed to imply—as if against his will—that every revolution must be abortive or betrayed and that any revolutionary leader, after becoming a dictator by the logic of his position, must end by destroying those he is fighting to save.

Thus, Koestler in Malaga had been sentenced to die for a cause that he had already begun to question. During the hundred days when he was waiting to face a firing squad—first in Malaga and then in Seville—he felt no sense of solidarity with his fellow prisoners as a group; in more senses than one, he was kept in solitary confinement.

The story of his Spanish adventures appeared in England the following year; it was called *Spanish Testament*. A shorter version, omitting all the chapters that dealt with the war in general and including only his personal experiences, has just been published here under the new title of *Dialogue with Death*. It is not the greatest prison narrative even of our own times, but it is among the easiest to read. Whereas *The Gladiators* was technically an apprentice work, *Dialogue with Death* has the characteristics of Koestler's mature writing: the gift for straightforward narrative, the taste for introspection, the observations on human nature—often full of wisdom—the interest in moral issues, which leads him to pass severe judgments on himself, and finally the air of complete candor with which he tells his own story. "The main difficulty," he says in a foreword, "was the temptation to cut a good figure"; and this is an especially great temptation to men playing even a minor part in politics, since they assume that any reflection on themselves would also be a reflection on the party to which they belong. Koestler, by avoiding it—by presenting himself as a quite unheroic but living figure—managed to write a book that is no less moving today than it was when we still hoped for victory in Spain.

After his release from prison—which he owed partly to his friends in England and partly to a series of accidents involving the Hearst newspapers and a collection of filthy postcards—Koestler had a moral crisis. He resigned from the Communist Party and began writing a novel about the Moscow trials; it would not be finished until a few weeks before the fall of France. Meanwhile he had been having a series of adventures that would be the subject of another autobiographical work. He had been arrested by the French police and had spent the winter in the concentration camp at Le Vernet, which in most respects was worse than the German camp at Dachau. Released by the intervention of his English friends, he had returned to Paris, where he lived under constant threat of being sent back to prison and yet was never told the nature of the charges against him. Then, after the German invasion, he had escaped to the south, enlisted in the Foreign Legion, and finally made his way to England. All these adventures are described in *Scum of the Earth*, which is the most personal, the most eloquent, and apparently the most exact of all the narratives dealing with the fall of France.

As for the novel that he finished and sent to the printer at almost the last possible moment—a few days later and it would have been seized with his other manuscripts by the French police—it was later published here as *Darkness at Noon*. Though it deals with the Russian trials, it obviously contains elements borrowed from Koestler's own story. Thus, most of the Russian characters are composite portraits of Communists he knew. The prison he describes so graphically is like no building that ever stood in Moscow; it actually resembles the Model Prison in Seville. The men who pass his hero's cell on the way to execution were condemned to death by Franco, not by Stalin. And Koestler was able to write his convincing account of a prisoner examined by the Gaypayoo because, at the moment of writing, he was himself being persecuted by the French political police. Throughout the book he is blaming Russia not only for her own sins but for those of her opponents; though he would answer this statement—and not without good reasons on his side—by saying that all dictatorships are forced to use the same methods, whatever their ultimate goals may be.

But although *Darkness at Noon* is not a safe guide to contemporary politics, and although much of its force as a pamphlet was destroyed when Hitler crossed the Russian border, it has other values that make it worth rereading. Its real theme is not the wickedness of the Russian dictatorship, but rather the everlasting conflict between the political universe and the moral universe. In developing this theme, the author leads us to deeper and deeper psychological levels, as if we were being guided downwards through a series of caves. At first we believe—and Rubashov the hero believes—that he is an innocent man about to be executed for crimes of which he was absolutely incapable. Then, going deeper into his own case, he is forced by the examining magistrates to admit that he is guilty by the Communist standards he has always proclaimed. Groping still deeper into his mind, he decides to reject Communist standards, but that is no solution; judged by the older principles of Christian ethics, his conduct has been even more deserving of punishment. Rubashov's explorations of his own personality are cut short by a pistol shot, but the reader gets a hint of further depths, especially if he is familiar with Koestler's two autobiographical works. It seems clear enough that the hero represents the author; that in this book Koestler is symbolically standing trial before his own conscience, is confessing the errors of his past life as a Communist, and is himself being led to execution in the cellars of the Lubyanka Prison. *Darkness at Noon* is a powerful work of fiction partly because it is, for its author, a ritual of sacrifice and atonement.

But it is also important because it stands for the literature of a new period. During the six or eight years before the Spanish civil war, the mood of the younger writers had been Utopian and even apocalyptic. They thought that bourgeois society would soon be destroyed, but they hoped—and many of them believed with a deep religious feeling—that a happier world would be erected on its ruins by a process somewhat resembling the Russian five-year plans. André Malraux was the great new figure of this period, finding new symbols to express its faith in the future. The hero of *Man's Fate*, waiting to be burned alive with two hundred other Communists after the suppression of the revolt in Shanghai, has no fear whatever of dying. "He had fought for what in his time was charged with the deepest meaning and the greatest hope; he was dying among those with whom he would have wanted to live; he was dying, like each of these men, because he had given a meaning to his life. What would have been the value of a life for which he would not have been willing to die? It is easy to die when one does not die alone." Malraux's novel about the Spanish war was even more confident, although this time the mood seemed a little forced. Its title in English was *Man's Hope* and in French simply *l'Espoir*.

By the time it was published, however, most of the hopefulness had vanished. In the new period that was beginning in literature as in politics, the prevailing mood would be one of defeat and disenchantment. It is not a mood or a time that makes writing easy, and the new period has not yet produced any novelists of Malraux's stature. Koestler is a lesser figure, but so far he has been its most effective spokesman. And the death of Rubashov, in *Darkness at Noon*, forms a curious contrast with the death of Malraux's hero, as if a century had intervened. Rubashov is dying for a faith in which he no longer believes. What he discovers while waiting for the end is not a sense of comradeship, but rather the feeling of individuality that he had lost during his political career. As the guard leads him into the cellars of the Lubyanka, he reflects that "it was easy to die with the visible certainty of one's goal before one's eyes. He, Nicholas Salmonovich Rubashov, had not been taken to the top of a mountain; and wherever his eye looked, he saw nothing but desert and the darkness of night."

MR. CHOLERTON'S
BEARD

American and British correspondents in Russia since the war seem to have led a life as perfectly communalized as that of boys in boarding school. They had the same sort of rooms in the same hotels: the Grand in Kuibyshev and the Metropole in Moscow. They ate three times a day at the same table, until—though they were fond of one another—they grew desperately tired of looking at familiar faces. After breakfast they listened while their secretaries translated the same items from the same Russian newspapers; then they wrote practically the same stories and submitted them to the same censor. In the evenings they drank vodka from the same bottle while playing chess or poker; or else they went to the ballet, where their favorite production was *Swan Lake*. Those who had seen it thirty-five times were awarded the imaginary order of the Golden Swan. Occasionally the monotony was broken by a visit to some quiet sector of the front, conducted almost in the spirit of a high-school picnic. Several of the correspondents were permitted to make individual tours of factories or collective farms, and in fact they often tried to break through the invisible wall that surrounds foreigners in Russia; but most of them ended with the same feeling of frustration. After a year they went home by way of Teheran and Cairo, sat down at their typewriters, and hastily wrote the same book.

I have been reading that book all spring, under several different titles. Walter Graebner of *Time* and *Life* called it *Round Trip to Russia* and Henry C. Cassidy of the Associated Press called it *Moscow Dateline*. More recently, James E. Brown of International News Service called it *Russia Fights*. Larry Lesueur of Columbia Broadcasting System adapted his title from John Reed: it is *Twelve Months That Changed the World*. All these authors describe the same events: the cold winter in Kuibyshev, the return to Moscow, the German summer offensive, Winston Churchill's visit (and the curious rumors to which it gave rise), the epic fight among the correspondents over the question whether their secretaries should be permitted to eat at the same table, the coming of Wendell Willkie, and the defense of Stalingrad. All of them end by expressing the hope that Russia and America will continue to be friends after the war, but chiefly they write about their own misadventures. Reading their texts one after the other, you get a curious impression. It is as if some mock-heroic poem had survived from ancient times, not in its original version, but in more or less imperfect manuscripts that differ because they were copied by careless scribes.

The carelessness was what impressed me when I came to compare these four volumes. You expect American correspondents to differ in matters of interpretation, but at least they get their facts straight—or so it is always said. They are trained to spell names correctly, to remember dates and statistics. But these four authors fail to agree on the simplest and most neutral facts, even when they had every chance for accurate observation. To mention a trivial example, there is the question of Cholerton's beard. A. T. Cholerton of *The London Telegraph* was dean of the correspondents; the others saw him every day and were deeply impressed by him. Graebner says that he wore "a long brown beard." Cassidy says that it was "a stubby black beard" and Brown calls it "a goatee." Lesueur avoids difficulties by simply calling Cholerton "full-bearded." I wonder what he looked like with his long, stubby, brown, black, full goatee; and I wonder how much he knew about Russia. Brown calls him "the best-informed" of all the Moscow correspondents. Cassidy says that during his sixteen years in Moscow, Cholerton had "accumulated a vast store of information and misinformation, all of which became hopelessly muddled."

Often two correspondents get involved in a quarrel over dates. For example, Lesueur says that he reached Kuibyshev on November 22, 1941. Cassidy says that he heard about Lesueur's arrival on Thanksgiving Day, November 20. Lesueur says that they left for Moscow by plane on December 14. Cassidy says that they left on December 13, and adds that there were thirteen passengers. In this case I would follow Cassidy, because Lesueur's narrative, which is published as a diary, shows some internal evidence of having been composed long after the events which it describes. Some time I should like to read a war diary which was actually written at the time and was not revised for publication.

But these are simple inconsistencies compared with those which occur in their separate accounts of a visit to a ruined village which seems to have been called Pogoreloye-Gorodische, though every correspondent has a different spelling. Here is the story, so far as I can put it together:

The correspondents were instructed by the Soviet Press Department to meet in front of the Metropole at 4:55 or 5:00 on the morning of August 30, 31, or September 1, depending on which account you follow. Promptly, or after a delay of half an hour, they piled into four (Brown), five (Graebner), or six (Lesueur) Soviet limousines and drove off to the front.

They stopped at a village which Graebner calls Lotoshino and Brown calls Istra, where they talked with a group of children. One of them, says Lesueur, had lost his arm when he exploded a German ammunition dump. Brown says that he had lost his fingers playing with an unexploded hand grenade in his own front yard.

As they drew closer to the front, the Russian chauffeurs of the four, five, or six ZIS or Ziss limousines were instructed to drive at a distance of 1,600 yards (Lesueur) or 150 feet (Graebner) from one another. Brown, more cautious, says "far apart." Finally all the cars were parked in a forest near the lines, and the correspondents were conducted through the ruins of Pogoreloye, if that is how you spell it. A Soviet major (or regimental commander, according to Brown, though of course he might have been both) explained to them how the Russians had taken the village, where the Germans had been firmly entrenched, had a force almost equal to the Russians, and had known for days that the attack was coming. Graebner, Brown, and Lesueur were standing side by side while the major talked—in very good English, Brown says—and yet if we compare their accounts, we seem to be reading about three different battles. Graebner's story is the most businesslike:

At 3:30 A.M. on the morning of August 4, the Russians feinted with a scout battalion north and east of the town. This roused the whole of the 161st German infantry division, which was immediately strengthened by all available reserves. Its job done, the Russian scouting battalion retreated before dawn, leaving the field clear to the Red artillery, much of which was concentrated in the fields where we were then standing. At this point in the narrative, the major announced that it was time for lunch.

Brown quotes the major's words directly, as if he had taken them down in shorthand:

> "We started a barrage at 10 o'clock at night, and, shortly after midnight, we made our first attack. The Germans thought it was the main attack, but we used only shock troops, keeping our regular infantry in reserve. We were beaten off, and, for about two hours, the front was quiet. Then, at three o'clock, we attacked in full strength, taking the enemy by surprise. They never recovered; we had every position before dawn."
>
> This account of the engagement appeared so simple that one of the correspondents expressed amazement that the Russian strategy was successful, that the Germans were caught off guard.
>
> "It was simple only as I explain it," said the commander.

In any case, it wasn't so simple that any two correspondents heard the same words. Here is Lesueur's account, also enclosed in quotation marks:

> "We immediately launched fighting patrols against the enemy lines to scare them into bringing up their nearest reserves. Two hours later, when we were sure the Germans were waiting in the front lines, we let loose with one of the heaviest artillery barrages of the war, advancing nine miles over German dead in the first day alone."

A legal expert, after comparing these stories, might conclude that the Russians attacked and captured a town; he could be sure of almost nothing else. And the contradictions don't end with that single battle. Graebner says that the Russian authorities insisted on sending the correspondents back to Moscow that night, although many of them wanted to sleep in the cars till dawn. Brown says that the correspondents insisted on driving back to Moscow that night, but the authorities refused and made them sleep in their cars till dawn. Incidentally Graebner, Lesueur, and Brown were all in the same car. "Where did you sleep on the night of August 30?" a prosecuting attorney might ask them. "It was the night of September 1," Lesueur would answer, "and anyway I didn't sleep very well."

Like most Americans, I am intensely curious about Russia. Like most Americans, I have to get all my information about it at second hand. I used to think that most books about the Russians were untrustworthy because the authors were trying to prove a political point and because, consciously or unconsciously, they were concealing part of the evidence. These four authors have no particular thesis; they are foreign correspondents whose business is to present all the essential facts; and yet they can't agree on such simple matters as the strategy of a single battle or the shape of A. T. Cholerton's beard. How can we trust them when they make generalities about the vast Soviet Union or the future of modern civilization?

I don't mean to say that their books, or their one book, is or are completely valueless. *Moscow Dateline* seems to contain fewer inaccuracies than the others and its author had the advantage of being on good terms with the Russian authorities. *Mother Russia*, by Maurice Hindus, is full of important observations about the changes in Soviet life since 1936, but its author is a student and something of a Russian patriot instead of a foreign correspondent. Although Hindus was a member of the famous expedition to the front, and even had an adventure that is described by Graebner and Brown, he wrote nothing about it at the time. Instead he went back to Pogoreloye ten weeks later, talked to the inhabitants, and wrote a scholarly essay on what happened during the German occupation.

James E. Brown's *Russia Fights* adds very little to the story. Brown had an exciting trip with a convoy to Murmansk, but afterwards in Moscow he suffered from a serious illness, and he writes like a tired man; perhaps he was also a little hard of hearing. In any case he seems to have had no Russian friends and not much curiosity about how the Russians lived. Ambassador Davies, in a brief introduction, calls him a typical American correspondent.

Larry Lesueur, on the other hand, came to Moscow with an immense appetite for experience and a pretty large capacity for getting into scrapes. During a visit to the front, a Cossack orderly invited him to take a ride on the general's white horse. The horse fell into a mudhole, and the orderly insisted on cleaning him completely before they rode back again. By that time a whole troop of cavalry was scouring the woods for Lesueur, thinking that he might have been picked off by snipers. Back in Moscow he gave a pint of blood to the Red Army and jumped from the parachute tower in the Park of Culture and Rest. He had a passion for meeting pretty Russian girls, and one of them finally consented to have supper in his room at the Metropole, although he says that it took a good deal of coaxing. Her name was Katya; she had disturbing black eyes and carried a red Komsomol card. It was Katya and her family who showed Lesueur a side of Russian life that he couldn't have learned from any number of conducted tours. Once he asked her what she thought Russia's post-war plans would be. "Why ask me?" she answered tartly. "There won't be any Russians or Germans alive after the war. What do England and America plan?" In general, *Twelve Months That Changed the World* seems pretty inaccurate about facts and figures, but not about people, and it is easy to read. It is the only book about the Hotel Metropole boys that has any heart interest. When Lesueur said goodbye, just before his return to the States, Katya quoted a line from Pushkin: "If you find one better than me, you'll forget me; if you find one worse, you'll remember." Lesueur thought he would remember.

THE STREETS OF
PALERMO

On May 15, 1796, a French republican army came marching into
the streets of Milan. It was led by General Bonaparte, who was
very young at the time and still devoted to the Revolution. As for the
Milanese, they had been governed for 250 years by Spanish and Austrian tyrants, with the support of the Church. What happened during
the next few days is described by Stendhal in the first chapter of *The
Charterhouse of Parma*. "A whole people," he says, "discovered that
everything which until then it had respected was supremely ridiculous, if not actually hateful. The departure of the last Austrian regiment marked the collapse of the old ideas: to risk one's life became the
fashion. . . . People had been plunged in the darkest night by the
continuation of the jealous despotism of Charles V and Philip II; they
overturned these monarchs' statues and immediately found themselves
flooded with daylight." And Stendhal continues (I am quoting from
the Scott Moncrieff translation):

> The French soldiers laughed and sang all day long; they were all
> under twenty-five years of age, and their commander-in-chief,
> who had reached twenty-seven, was reckoned the oldest man in his
> army. This gayety, this youthfulness, this irresponsibility fur-
> nished a jocular reply to the furious preachings of the monks, who
> for six months had been announcing from every pulpit that the
> French were monsters obliged, upon pain of death, to burn down
> everything and to cut off everybody's head. In the country districts
> one saw the French soldier at the cottage door, engaged in dan-
> dling the housewife's baby in his arms.

The Italian Church today has a different attitude toward the invaders.
But I thought of those French soldiers dandling babies (and organizing

country dances, as Stendhal goes on to say) when I read how the Americans in Sicily were helping the children to milk their goats and when, in a newsreel, I saw them passing their canteens full of wine to a laughing crowd of Sicilian women. I thought of Milan in 1796 when I read how the Seventh Army marched into the streets of Palermo, where it was received with exactly the same feeling of liberation.

That feeling took a little time to develop. The first Allied soldiers in Sicily had a mixed reception: smiles and hostile looks; gifts from the villagers and snipers' bullets from the hills. John Gunther told about three sentries whose throats were cut in the darkness; there must have been others. By the second week, however, it became clear that no civilians were resisting the invasion except a few die-hard fascists, perhaps aided by parachute troopers. The mass of the population had decided that anything, even a city bombed into rubble, was a cheap price to pay for getting rid of despotism.

When the Americans entered Palermo, on July 23 and 24, innkeepers broached their hidden casks of wine. People lined the streets and pelted our men with flowers, lemons, cantaloupes and even watermelons—"But it should be emphasized," General Patton said, "that all the fruit was tossed in a spirit of friendliness." There were hundreds of uniformed Italian soldiers in the crowd. Some of them cheered and others ran out to kiss the hands of the Americans riding past in half-tracks. It was as if America was being thanked for rescuing the shipwrecked from a desert island. It was as if the whole city was shaking itself free from a nightmare that had lasted for twenty years.

Like the French in Milan, the Americans in Palermo are the soldiers of an idea and the soldiers of a revolution. The idea is not one that clearly exists in their own minds. Talk to them and they will say, as likely as not, that they are fighting "to get it over with as soon as possible and then go home." Even to the Italians, the idea is nothing so generalized as the Four Freedoms. It is simply the picture of a society where people have enough to eat, and aren't pushed around by men in uniform, and have a chance to get rich if they save their money. The revolution is that of Thomas Jefferson rather than that of Karl Marx, and in Europe today it has more explosive force than all our four-ton blockbusters.

But although it is our strongest weapon, it is ineffective when used alone. Not many Europeans will sacrifice themselves, their families, and their whole communities to defend an ideal that seems to have no chance of military success. That is one of the reasons why our propaganda was almost totally wasted for a year after Pearl Harbor, when the British and American armies were taking no forward step. But when the moral weapon is supported by an aggressive military policy and by a sufficient weight of guns, it is capable of performing the only miracles known to modern warfare. General Bonaparte's campaign in northern Italy was one of these, and there are others today, though as yet they have been on a smaller scale. A cockney pilot runs out of gas and lands on the Italian island of Lampedusa. There he receives the surrender of the entire garrison. An American pilot falls into the sea off the west coast of Sicily and is rescued by four Italian fishermen. Shortly afterwards he returns to our lines with thirty-seven prisoners, including a lieutenant-colonel. Except on the Russian front, there have been few such individual exploits against the Germans, who have been protected by a political weapon of their own. But the German collapse in Tunisia was almost a major miracle, and everybody knows that its causes were moral as well as military.

In Palermo, an American soldier battled his way through a crowd of people who were pressing his hands and kissing his cheeks. He exclaimed, "Who's nuts in this crowd? I'm beginning to think it's me." It was somebody else; in fact it was a whole group of men who were thousands of miles from the fighting lines. It was the American and British leaders who think we are fighting merely to restore the old order in Europe. It was the men who imagine that our armies are those of the Holy Alliance, not those of the American and French and Russian revolutions.

MAX PERKINS
IN 1944

M any book publishers share the opinion that their colleague Maxwell Evarts Perkins, vice-president of Charles Scribner's Sons, is
the best editor in the trade. At the same time, they regard his methods
as old-fashioned almost to the point of being other-worldly. He never
attends their professional gatherings and he refuses to go to booksellers' conventions. He never accepts invitations to other publishers'
cocktail parties or gives parties of his own to celebrate the publication
of Scribner books. He doesn't send notes to book reviewers telling
them that something on his spring list is the greatest event since *Gone
with the Wind*. He doesn't invent plots for best-selling novels and call
in his authors to write them. He doesn't ask literary agents for hot tips
or look through the magazines for new names. His authors say that he
never talks to them about potential sales or movie rights. Despite his
refusal to do all of these things, which are routine among the higher-
powered editors at other publishing houses, he is known for making
more literary discoveries and semi-discoveries than anybody else in the
field (F. Scott Fitzgerald, Ernest Hemingway, Thomas Boyd, Ring
Lardner, Thomas Wolfe, John P. Marquand, Erskine Caldwell, and
Marjorie Rawlings are a few of the authors he helped to launch on their
careers); there is usually a Perkins book near the top of the best-seller
lists (in 1943 six Scribner publications were book-club choices, with
aggregate printings of 1,677,000 copies in the first nine months of the
year); and it is believed that more books have been dedicated to him
than to any other man alive. Among the authors who have dedicated
books to Perkins are Hamilton Basso, Thomas Boyd, Van Wyck
Brooks, Roger Burlingame, Struthers Burt, Taylor Caldwell, Ann
Chidester, Charles Townsend Copeland (who addressed him as "Great
Publisher and Steadfast Friend"), August Derleth, F. Scott Fitzgerald,
Caroline Gordon, Nancy Hale, Josephine Herbst, Francis Lynde,

Dawn Powell, Chard Powers Smith, Arthur Train, and Thomas Wolfe, who hoped that *Of Time and the River* would be "in some way worthy of the loyal devotion and the patient care which a dauntless and unshaken friend has given to each part of it." Besides the dedications, there have been dozens of authors' acknowledgments, or "without-expressing-my-gratitudes," as publishers sometimes call them. "But I cannot take my leave," says Charles Breasted, for example, in the preface to his recent biography of his father, "without expressing my gratitude . . . to my friend, Maxwell Perkins, for his inexhaustible patience and helpfulness and his consummate editorial judgment in enabling me to reduce a two-volume manuscript to one."

Perkins is a New Englander, even though he was born in New York and, except for three months in a Boston settlement house, has never worked anywhere else. The Manhattan Yankees, among whom the Perkins and Evarts families belong, are a small but recognizable tribe. They are the sort of people who are ridden by scruples and who, before going to bed, like to pass judgment on everything they have done during the day. They also like to follow their own peculiar rules of conduct. Perkins' maternal grandfather, William Maxwell Evarts, who was Secretary of State under Rutherford B. Hayes, once told his young friend Henry Adams, "I pride myself on my success in doing *not* the things I like to do but the things I don't like to do." Perkins has that same Puritan bent. Yet this bookish, professorial, modest, upright man has chosen a profession in which he has to deal constantly with writers, who as a class have distinguished themselves as barroom brawlers, drawing-room wolves, breakers of engagements, defaulters of debts, crying drunks, and suicidal maniacs.

The juxtaposition of Perkins with some rather dashing men of letters, including Hemingway and Wolfe, has led him into many predicaments. One came up when Perkins was reading the manuscript of Hemingway's third book for Scribner's. Old Charles Scribner II, a rather churchly gentleman who ruled his staff like a benevolent despot, had been disturbed by some of the language Hemingway had used in his second book, *The Sun Also Rises*. Perkins told him that there wouldn't be any trouble this time, except for three words. "What are they?" Mr. Scribner asked. Perkins, who never uses a stronger phrase than "My God," and that only in moments of great emotion, found that he simply couldn't say them. "Write them, then," said Mr. Scribner. In his chicken-track hand, Perkins scrawled two of them on a memo pad and handed it to him. "What's the third word?" Mr. Scribner asked. Perkins hesitated. "What's the third word?" said Mr. Scribner again, giving the pad back to him. Finally Perkins wrote it. Mr. Scribner glanced at the pad. "Max," he said, shaking his white head, "what would Hemingway think of you if he heard that you couldn't even write that word?"

Perkins has been working at Charles Scribner's Sons for thirty-four years. During that time, American literature has undergone a couple of noisy revolutions. Perkins himself, in his quiet and self-effacing way, had a lot to do with one of them. What he did was to introduce the bad boys of letters into one of the citadels of Victorian publishing.

Scribner's, founded in 1846, is not the oldest publishing house in this country. Harper & Brothers go back to 1817, D. Appleton & Co. (now D. Appleton-Century) to 1825, J. B. Lippincott to 1836, and Putnam's to 1838. Little, Brown, founded in 1847, grew out of a Boston bookstore that had been in existence since the eighteenth century. But Scribner's has the distinction, which it shares with Lippincott, of having always been under the management of one family. Ninety per cent of the voting stock is still held by the Scribners. The present Charles Scribner is not only the third man to bear that name but also the fifth president of the firm and the grandson of the first president. The three other presidents, all sons of the founder, were John I. Blair Scribner, Charles II, and Arthur. Charles Scribner IV, son of the fifth president, is an ensign in the Navy and plans to enter the family business after the war.

Until the nineteen-twenties, Scribner's had another distinction, too. It was the most genteel and the most tradition-encrusted of all the publishing houses that had survived from Victorian days. No word unfit for a young girl's ear could appear in a book that Scribner's published. Because ladies were employed in the office, gentlemen could not smoke there. The furniture looked—and some of it still does—as if it had been purchased from the estate of a very old country doctor.

Most of the employees were even more elderly than their desks, and in publishing circles people said that nobody left Scribner's until he was carried out.

The second Charles Scribner, born in 1854, was not only president of the firm but also a sort of grandfather image; his wrath was feared like Jehovah's. His first assistant and the firm's chief editor, for a long period beginning in 1887, was William Crary Brownell, born in 1851. One of Scribner's young men, who went to work for the company in the nineteen-twenties, still remembers the first time he saw him. "Mr. Brownell was stretched out on a leather couch in his office, just beyond the room where we were having a sales conference," the young man recalls, "taking his afternoon nap, his white beard slowly rising and falling and one fly slowly circling about it. The scene made quite an impression on me." Another member of the staff, almost as old as Brownell, used to lunch by himself at the University Club, where he sometimes shouted and pounded on the table while arguing with an imaginary companion. The incumbent sales manager was reputed never to have read a book. When a new Scribner novel came out, he would take a copy home to his wife. She would read it over the weekend and the office force would gather on Monday morning to hear her verdict. "My wife cried over that book," he would sometimes say, and everybody knew it would be a best-seller.

There wasn't much chance for a book that even mildly disturbed the conventions. Scribner's had a distinguished list of British authors, including Meredith, Stevenson, Barrie, and G. A. Henty, who wrote eighty books for boys, an achievement surpassed only by Horatio Alger's record of a hundred and thirty (not all of them written by himself). Among the famous, and distinctly respectable, Americans Scribner's published were John Fox, Jr., Thomas Nelson Page, Dr. Henry van Dyke, Richard Harding Davis, F. Hopkinson Smith, Henry James (his last half-dozen books, at least), and Edith Wharton (up to *The Age of Innocence*). Theodore Roosevelt was a valuable publishing property, but most of the staff believed that as a politician he was too radical. Galsworthy represented the younger generation and was thought to be a little subversive, although sound at heart. Scribner's did not publish the realists who emerged during the so-called

American Renaissance—Dreiser, Anderson, Sandburg, and so on. Instead, the firm took a sudden leap from the age of innocence into the
middle of the lost generation. That leap was the result, for the most
part, of Perkins' urging, but he made his suggestions so quietly that
hardly anybody noticed what was happening.

The revolution began, in 1917, with the threat of a libel suit
against Scribner's and one of its authors, an Irish novelist and critic
named Shane Leslie, who was then teaching at the Newman School,
in Lakewood, New Jersey. Leslie was contrite about the expense that
Scribner's had been put to in avoiding the suit. In an attempt to make
amends, he came into the office with the manuscript of a novel written
by a former student of his, F. Scott Fitzgerald. Perkins liked the novel,
then called *The Romantic Egotist*, but he thought it needed some revision before it would be ready for publication. He said so in a letter to
the author, who had meanwhile entered the Army. Fitzgerald asked
him, as a favor, to submit it as it stood to two other publishers. Both
of them rejected it with form letters. Just before going overseas, Fitzgerald came to New York, had a long talk with Perkins, and decided
to revise the manuscript. As a matter of fact, he completely rewrote it
twice and it wasn't published until 1920. *This Side of Paradise* seems
innocent enough today, but then it was the terrifying voice of a new
age and it made some of the older employees of Scribner's cringe. On
the Monday after the first bound copies came into the office, everybody
gathered to hear whether the sales manager's wife had cried. "That
book? I wouldn't think of showing it to my wife," the sales manager
said. "I picked it up with the fire tongs and dropped it in the fire."

This Side of Paradise sold fifty-two thousand copies, which was almost unprecedented, in those days, for a first novel. Fitzgerald then
wrote *The Beautiful and Damned*, which sold forty-four thousand copies
and, incidentally, was dedicated to Perkins. Full of enthusiasm for his
editor, Fitzgerald told all his literary friends about him and told Perkins about the friends. One of them was Ernest Hemingway, who was
a young newspaperman living in Paris. Perkins sent to Paris for a copy
of his first volume of stories, *in our time*, which had just been brought
out there by the Three Mountain Press. Then he wrote Hemingway
and offered to publish his next book in America. But Horace Liveright

had already sent a cable to Hemingway and signed him up for *in our time*, with options on his next two books.

The matter might have ended there, with an exchange of courtesies—Hemingway writing Perkins that he didn't even have a copy of his own book, Perkins sending him the copy he had ordered from Paris, Hemingway returning it to Perkins with an inscription—if it had not been for the fact that the public showed very little interest in the Liveright edition of *in our time*, which sold less than five hundred copies the first year. Liveright was dubious about making an advance payment for Hemingway's second book, and when he saw a reader's report on the manuscript, he was sure that he shouldn't make it. It was *The Torrents of Spring*, which not only looked unsalable to Liveright but also did a good deal of kidding of Sherwood Anderson, one of Liveright's most profitable authors. The manuscript was rejected and the contract between Hemingway and Liveright was thereby nullified. Hemingway came back to New York in 1925 and called on Perkins, who gave him an advance on the book of $1,500, which looked bigger to him, he has said, than the $150,000 he received from Paramount for the movie rights of *For Whom the Bell Tolls*.

By 1925 Ring Lardner, another member of the new literary generation, had been a Scribner author for about a year. Fitzgerald, who, like Lardner, lived in Great Neck, had persuaded him to collect some of his magazine pieces and give them to Perkins. It was quite an achievement, for Lardner didn't keep copies of his stories and had a hard time remembering where they had been published. "Maybe it was the *Saturday Evening Post*," he would say hopefully of some story. The manuscript which Lardner turned in to Scribner's consisted largely of photostats made from back issues of magazines in the Public Library. The book was published under the title of *How to Write Short Stories*. It was Lardner's seventh book, but it was the first to be seriously reviewed; the others hadn't been read except by the hammock trade. At Scribner's there had been an editorial meeting lasting all afternoon before the book had been accepted. The older Scribner employees felt that Lardner was merely a sportswriter and just one more of Perkins' roughneck authors. Perkins claimed that Lardner was literature. What eventually won the argument for Perkins' side was a letter from Sir James M. Barrie, who said that Lardner was the most exciting American story writer he had read, although it was a pity, he added, that Lardner hadn't written about cricket instead of baseball.

The older men at Scribner's continued to be outraged not only by Lardner but by all the indecorous authors whom Perkins had been introducing one after the other. One ex-Scribner man recently wrote to a friend, "I remember the old fellow in charge of the stockroom opening a book and with quivering fingers pointing to a word. He said, 'To think that Scribner's would publish a book with that word in it!' The book was *The Great Gatsby*, the word was 'son of a bitch.' " The letter continued, "There was a moment of crisis when the question was: would Scribner's publish Hemingway's *The Sun Also Rises?* Old Charles Scribner, Sr., ran the place then with a very firm hand and no two ways about it. We knew that Perkins had to go to bat for Hemingway, and it was reported with hushed voices one evening that Charles, Sr., had turned down the book and Perkins was going to resign. I don't believe that now, but I did then. Anyway, that was the lineup: van Dyke and Galsworthy or Hemingway and Fitzgerald, with Perkins representing the latter."

For his part, Perkins insists that Mr. Scribner was quick to recognize the talent of Perkins' new author, but it is known that the old man was worried about the moral standards of Hemingway's heroines. He used to say fretfully, "I always felt that a woman at least ought to have some affection for a man." He wrote his friend Judge Robert Grant of Boston, asking for his comment on *The Sun Also Rises*. The judge, himself still a novelist at seventy-four, replied, "You *have* to publish the book, Charles, but I hope the young man will live to regret it."

In 1929, Scribner's published Thomas Wolfe's first novel, *Look Homeward, Angel*, which was a moderate financial success; it sold seventeen thousand copies in the trade edition before coming out in reprints. That year, too, Scribner's issued a biography, with nearly disastrous results: *Mrs. Eddy*, by Edwin Franden Dakin. The Christian Science Church made formal protests, but old Mr. Scribner refused to withdraw the book. One self-appointed champion of Mrs. Eddy appeared in the office and threatened to use malicious animal magnetism against the publishers. Charles Scribner, Sr., died in 1930, and his brother Arthur, who succeeded him as president, died in 1932. A number of impressionable people at Scribner's thought that malicious animal magnetism had something to do with it.

Old Brownell had died in 1928. His office was inherited by the poet John Hall Wheelock, who had been moved upstairs into an editorial post after fifteen years in the Scribner bookstore. Wheelock also inherited Brownell's leather couch. Young Charles Scribner, the new president, lived in Far Hills and belonged to the New Jersey foxhunting set. Like most Princeton men of his generation—he was class of '13—he had admired Fitzgerald and Hemingway from the beginning; also, he liked to smoke in the office. All these changes, combined with the changing character of the list of authors, meant that Scribner's was losing its mid-Victorian atmosphere. It became progressively less Victorian, reaching its low in the 1930s, when the office force, arriving in the morning, would find Thomas Wolfe, after a night on the town, asleep on the directors' table in the library.

The friendship between Wolfe and Perkins has been best described by Wolfe in his last novel, *You Can't Go Home Again*, in which Perkins is the editor called Foxhall Edwards and Wolfe is, of course, the hero, George Webber. "The older man," the novelist wrote, "was not merely friend but father to the younger. Webber, the hot-blooded Southerner . . . had lost his own father many years before and now had found a substitute in Edwards. And Edwards, the reserved New Englander, with his deep sense of family and inheritance, had always wanted a son but had had five daughters, and as time went on he made of George a kind of foster son."

For a whole year—1933—Wolfe worked ten to fourteen hours a day on *Of Time and the River*, and he began to acquire the disposition of a morose elephant. "People seem to expect a great deal of me in my next book," he wrote to his mother in Asheville, "and I am very nervous about it." He was also nervous about money, even though Scribner's had been taking good care of him. In the past three years, Wolfe had received more than $15,000, including an advance of $5,000 on his new book, paid in monthly installments of $250; a short-story prize of $2,500 from *Scribner's Magazine*; a Guggenheim fellowship, also of $2,500; and royalties from the American, English, Swedish, and German editions of *Look Homeward, Angel*. He was unmarried and hated to spend money on clothes or furniture, but he ate and drank on a scale commensurate with his six feet seven inches and his two hundred and fifty pounds. In February, 1933, he complained to his mother, "I have my back right up against the wall at the present time and have almost no money."

In his letters to his mother, he sounded as if he thought that everybody except Perkins—"the best friend I ever had"—was leagued in a conspiracy against him. These letters were full of phrases like "I have been hounded and driven crazy . . . beset and pressed on all sides . . . badgered, tormented, and almost driven mad at times by fool questions, fool letters from fool people, the tantrums of crazy women . . . cheap, slanderous, cheating, and canting swine—I see no reason why I should not tell them plainly what they are." Wolfe was not a man to keep his opinions to himself. Sometimes, at parties, he would begin to scowl and his face would go white; his friends would attempt to get him out of the room before he lowered his head and charged. Perkins told him, after one such scene, "You don't really hate those people. You hate yourself because your work is going badly." Wolfe promised he wouldn't act up again.

About half past eleven on the night of December 14, 1933, he came, late, to an appointment with Perkins in the editor's office and dropped a heavy bundle on his desk. It was two feet high, wrapped in brown paper, and tied with strong twine. When Perkins opened it, he found the manuscript of *Of Time and the River*, on several kinds of white and yellow paper. It totaled more than three thousand typewritten pages—nobody knows how many more, because the pages weren't numbered—but in any event it was too long to publish in one volume. "It was all disproportioned," Perkins has said. Wolfe wrote his mother, "God knows a lot of it is still fragmentary and broken up, but at any rate he can now look at it and give me an opinion on it." Perkins went through the manuscript carefully and told one of his associates, "This book has to be done."

It took Wolfe and Perkins, working together, more than a year to do it. The first step was for Perkins, in his own phrase, to "mark up" the manuscript. This meant pencilling brief notes in the margin, in his high, angular script—"Ought to be cut out," or "Repetition," or "Needs to be explained." At that time, Perkins was living in town, and the two men began meeting at eight o'clock five or six evenings a week in Perkins' office.

Perkins would glance at one of his marginal notes and say, "I think this section should be omitted."

Wolfe would answer, after a long, sulky pause, "I think it's good."

"I think it's good too," Perkins would say, and mean it, "but you have expressed the thing already."

The two men would argue for hours, while cigarette butts and sheets of paper piled up on the floor. Sometimes, in the midst of an argument, Wolfe would glance at a rattlesnake skin with seven rattles—a gift from Marjorie Rawlings—which hung from a coathook above Perkins' overcoat and under his hat. Wolfe, whose touch was rarely light, liked to call this collection of objects "The Portrait of an Editor," a joke that had an undertone of resentment. Usually he ended by doing as Perkins suggested, but passages cut out of the novel were never thrown away. Wolfe carried them home to Brooklyn Heights and put them in a big wooden packing case—eventually there were three such cases, the two largest being three feet high, three feet wide, and four feet long—in the centre of his parlor. In them he also kept cooking pots, old shoes, an electric flatiron, and bundles of receipted bills. He saved his discarded scenes as plumbers save lengths of pipe, and eventually fitted them into other novels. Thus the longest of the passages omitted from *Of Time and the River* became the second half of *The Web and the Rock*.

By February of 1934, work on *Of Time and the River* was going well. Sometimes, when the marginal note said "Needs transition," Wolfe pushed aside other manuscripts on a corner of Perkins' old-fashioned desk and wrote the necessary pages in his huge, sprawling, but legible hand, the words so widely spaced that five of them made a line and ninety filled a page. Wolfe had to have all his work copied; he never learned to type, because, he said, his hands were too big for the keyboard, just as his feet were too big for the pedals of an automobile. In April, the two men still hoped that the novel would be ready for fall publication, but Wolfe had developed a habit of writing new chapters, which he submitted at the evening sessions with a look of both penitence and pride. The book became like Penelope's web; whatever the two men unravelled by night, Wolfe rewove by day. One week he added a passage of some thirty thousand words, describing the death of the hero's father. Perkins thought that most of it was unnecessary, but he recently told an associate, "It was too good to let go."

In the middle of October, Perkins felt that the book was finished. "I don't think you should do anything more to it, Tom," he said, but Wolfe had been working on it so long that he couldn't stop. It wasn't until January 14, 1935, that the novel was in page proofs. Then Wolfe was forbidden to make any more changes. Suddenly he felt as if he had been released from bondage. He celebrated by eating an eight-pound porterhouse steak. Perkins took his first vacation in three years. He paid a visit to Hemingway in Key West and, with his help, he landed the first fish he had caught since he was a boy. Two weeks before anybody at Scribner's expected him, Perkins was back at his desk. When *Of Time and the River* was finally published, in March, 1935, it bore this dedication: "To Maxwell Evarts Perkins, a great editor and a brave and honest man, who stuck to the writer of this book through times of bitter hopelessness and doubt and would not let him give in to his own despair, a work to be known as 'Of Time and the River' is dedicated with the hope that all of it may be in some way worthy of the loyal devotion and the patient care which a dauntless and unshaken friend has given to each part of it, and without which none of it could have been written."

In the autumn of 1937, Wolfe transferred himself and his three packing cases of unpublished manuscript to another publisher. People often wonder how such a close relationship came to be broken. Perkins said nothing at the time it happened and has said very little since. In his last novel, Wolfe explained at great length that there was a fundamental difference in temperament. Foxhall Edwards (Perkins), he said, was as much a fatalist as the author of Ecclesiastes, whereas Wolfe believed that the world could be changed for the better. In simpler terms, Perkins had been an independent Democrat for fifty years but had turned against the New Deal at the moment when Wolfe, after a German friend had been persecuted by the Nazis, was beginning for the first time to think of himself as a radical. Both men, however, were much more interested in people than in politics. The principal reason for the separation—it was never a quarrel—seems to be that Wolfe's pride was touched. He had told everybody how much he owed to Perkins' editing, and everybody believed his story, which grew in the telling, until Wolfe began to feel that his own contribution was being slighted. Once, after this attitude had crystallized, he said to another Perkins author, "I'll show them that I can write my own books. I'll show them that I'm not a robot." One of his friends said that he was like a son who had risen rapidly in his father's factory and then resigned, just to prove that he could be as successful on his own. Wolfe chose Harper, in preference to two other publishers who were bidding for his work, after he found that Edward C. Aswell, Harper's editor, had been born in the same week of the same month of the same year as himself. This time there wouldn't be any question of foster parentage.

The separation weighed on Wolfe's conscience. The last, long section of *You Can't Go Home Again* takes the form of a letter to Foxhall Edwards. "Dear Fox, old friend," he concludes, "thus we have come to the end of the road that we were to go together. My tale is finished—and so farewell." A somewhat different version of the letter was actually mailed to Perkins; it was a leavetaking note of a hundred and thirty-two handwritten pages. On the day that his last illness took a fatal turn, Wolfe scrawled another letter to Perkins in pencil. Perkins hurried to visit him at the Johns Hopkins Hospital in Baltimore, but by the time he reached the hospital, Wolfe was too near death to see him. Wolfe's will made Perkins executor of his involved estate. In this capacity, Perkins had to read the proofs of Wolfe's last three books, which were edited by Aswell. It was in these proofs that he saw for the first time Wolfe's portrait of Foxhall Edwards. The portrait was largely a caricature, but after publication people began to confuse it with Perkins' real personality. For example, Wolfe said that Edwards went to Groton, and now many people take for granted that Perkins went to Groton instead of St. Paul's. Perkins' first comment, made to Aswell, was simply, "That man he calls the Fox—I don't think Tom got him quite right." Then, a few days later, he added, "That man Tom calls the Fox—I took the passage home to show my wife and daughters, and they think he did get him right."

THE ASSASSINATED
POET

The Silence of the Sea is a little book, hardly more than a short story, that gains much of its interest from the circumstances surrounding its writing and publication. The author, who signs himself Vercors, is still in France; if his real name were known, he would be sentenced to death, along with the other Frenchmen who printed the book or helped in its distribution. The original edition carried a brief notice on the title page: "Editions de Minuit. This volume, published at the personal expense of a patriot, came from the press on February 20, 1942, under the Nazi occupation." It was dedicated to the memory of Saint-Pol-Roux, *poète assassiné*. Later the story was reprinted in London, and thousands of copies were scattered over France by the Royal Air Corps. The present translation, an extremely good one, was made by Cyril Connolly.

After all these preliminaries, the story itself seems a little unflavored and wholesome, like a cup of cocoa when you had been expecting wine. A German officer has been billeted in a French country house, where he shows himself eager to be liked by the owner (who tells the story) and falls in love with the owner's niece. He was a composer in civilian life and a student of French literature; he wants to think that the two countries can now live at peace. Every day he pays a visit to his unwilling French hosts; every day he tells them about his boyhood or delivers a friendly lecture on the future; but the owner and his niece remain obdurately silent. Then, during a visit to his colleagues in Paris, he learns that the France he loves is to be destroyed, economically and morally. "There is no hope," he tells his hosts, before leaving for the eastern front. And the niece speaks to him for the first time: "Adieu," she whispers, as if saying farewell to the old Germany of music and scholarship; henceforth there will be nothing but hatred between the two nations.

The story seems to have had an overwhelming effect on its French readers. This was partly because it appeared during a prolonged moral crisis, the nature of which is still misunderstood in this country; particularly we fail to realize that the crisis has now ended. But in 1940, when France was overrun by the Germans, even her best citizens were plunged into a state of lethargic despair. They suffered much less from the sense of military defeat than from the feeling that their nation had deserved nothing better, being so divided by internal conflicts—as Gide wrote in his *Journal*—and so given over to private selfishness and political corruption that it was scarcely fit for self-government; they asked themselves whether the Nazi invasion might not be a deserved retribution and even a promise for the future. At this period, the Nazis succeeded in making a number of converts among the artists and writers. One of these was Drieu la Rochelle, who had German support when he took over the *NRF*, formerly the best of the literary journals. There were distinguished names in the first issues that appeared under his editorship. A year later, however, he was forced to confess that "Almost all the intellect, almost all the poetic spirit of France, are against us."

Something had happened in the meantime: a rebirth of patriotism, a *redressement*, a stiffening of the backbone. In some of the books that have reached us from France, we can note the exact moment of change: with Aragon, for example, it happened one morning in August 1940, when he heard an old French ballad "troubling," as he said, "the green pool where silence lay nightlong." With André Gide, always refractory and counter-suggestive, it was reading a book by a collaborationist author, Chardonne, that made him realize the depths of self-delusion (and bad writing) into which some of his colleagues were sinking. With Vercors, whoever he may be, it was the moment when the German officer pointed to his bookshelves and said that the Nazis proposed to extirpate French culture—"Not only your modern writers! Not only your Péguy, your Proust, your Bergson. . . . But all the others! All those up there! The whole lot!"

For still other Frenchmen, the critical incident was the death of the poet to whom this little book is dedicated. It is a story worth telling at some length.

Before the First World War, visitors to the seacoast village of Camaret, in Brittany, were sure to notice a strange building with two round towers that gave it the look of a Spanish castle reproduced in cardboard on the stage. If they lingered in front of it, the owner himself might emerge and bow deeply. "I am Saint-Pol-Roux the poet. This," he would say with a wave of his hand, "this is my manor house. Might I ask you in for a glass of vermouth?" Some of his casual visitors stayed for dinner, stayed for charades or a pantomime, and emerged late at night, aching with laughter and perhaps a little in love with the poet's wife; she had been the leading lady of *Louise*, after spending her youth in the streets of Montmartre. Saint-Pol-Roux had written the book of *Louise*, but under a pseudonym, having too great respect for the profession of poet to let his name appear on the playbill of a light opera. Nevertheless he lived for years on the money it earned; and when funds ran short he wrote begging letters to the crowned heads of Europe, telling them that it was their duty as monarchs to keep a gifted poet from starving. Some of the letters were answered with gifts.

The story begins to sound like something written by Leonard Merrick, all Latin laughter and bohemian recklessness (and a little cheap in the bargain); but it had a beginning and a sequel that were in a different key. Saint-Pol-Roux, born in 1861 and married in middle life, had once been known in Paris as the Magnificent; that was because of his splendid costumes and his torrential speeches. He was a leader among the Symbolist poets of the 1890s, a disciple of Mallarmé, a friend of Gauguin, and a leader admired by dozens of the younger writers. His poems appeared in all the little reviews, all the anthologies, and they had been honored with a chapter in Remy de Gourmont's *Book of Masks*. About this time, he wrote his masterpiece, *La Dame à la Faulx*, an extravagantly poetic drama of real distinction which, for a wonder, was all but accepted by the Comédie Française. Later the great director Antoine wanted to have it read at one of his Saturday mornings at the Odéon, but the offer was refused. "I will not come in by the servants' entrance," said Saint-Pol-the-Magnificent.

He retired to the coast of Brittany, where he built his manor house and where, after a time, he was almost forgotten. He could find not even a publisher, let alone a producer, for his new poetic dramas. He ceased to appear in anthologies or be mentioned by the critics. It seemed that he had entered the realm of the *poètes manqués*, the vast cemetery where failures are buried alive. And he had private as well as professional sorrows: his wife died young; his favorite son, Cécilian, was killed in Belgium during the war; his savings were wiped out in the postwar inflation. For years this poet who loved good company was left alone in his cardboard manor, with only his youngest child, a daughter named Divine, and a usually unpaid but faithful servant. Then, in the 1930s, Saint-Pol-Roux was discovered by the Surrealists, who began reprinting his work, after saluting him as their ancestor and a genius unsurpassed in modern French poetry. He became the center of a cult that he was now too old to enjoy.

And his life was destined to take one more strange turn, as a result of the invasion. On the night of June 23–24, 1940, a little band of German soldiers broke into the manor, looking for wine or loot. It wasn't an episode typical of the German occupation, which began by being "very correct," as the French said among themselves; but every invading army has its drunken soldiers. The poet, who expected everybody to obey him, brandished his cane and ordered them out of the house. Rose, the servant woman, flung herself in front of him and the shot killed her. The poet was untouched, but fragile with age, and he fell to the floor with an apoplectic stroke. What followed was a scene of grotesque horror that Goya might have drawn. One of the soldiers attacked Divine. There were more drunken pistol shots and a bullet shattered her knee. When the Germans went out, she crawled into the garden to scream for help, but nobody came because of the curfew and she lay there all night in the rain. Next morning Divine and her father were taken to the hospital, where the poet died.

Her story spread through the Occupied Zone by word of mouth, although it was also mentioned guardedly in several French and Swiss magazines. *Fontaine*, published in Algiers, said in November 1940, that the poet's death was the result "of recent events which, we hope at least, can some day be revealed." It revealed them in April, 1943, after the American occupation. By that time, however, they were known all over France. And the result was that Saint-Pol-Roux, who believed in the divine right of kings and poets, who was completely indifferent to politics and had even withdrawn from literary life, retiring to the last promontory in the Atlantic, became a political symbol and, by his death, helped to create a new spirit in the French nation.

GERTRUDE STEIN'S WAR

N obody else, among all the writers who have told us about life in occupied France, has made the story so intimate, homely, immediate, as if a squad of Germans were quartered in your own kitchen and the Maquis were prowling the roads outside your door. *Wars I Have Seen* is directed to the plain reader, and it is by all means the best book that Gertrude Stein has published in more than a generation. For the first time since *Three Lives*, in 1908, she has an intelligible and important subject outside of Gertrude Stein.

There is a mystery about her career in the intervening years, or rather there are several mysteries. For example, there is the mystery how this woman who has spent more than forty years abroad, with only one visit home, has remained such a thoroughgoing American, so that she might have just stepped off the boat with a cow-college diploma and the latest copy of *The Saturday Evening Post*. There is the mystery how she understood so much of modern art, when it was a question of meeting the right artists or buying their pictures, and yet in writing about modern art revealed a sturdy innocence concerning the ideas on which it is based. But the great mystery about Gertrude Stein is how this woman with a real influence on American prose, so that her first book marks an era in our literature; this woman famous for her conversation, able to change the ideas of other writers, able to hold and dominate big audiences when she lectures, should at the same time have written books so monumental in their dullness, so many pyramids and Parthenons consecrated to the reader's apathy.

I am not speaking of her exoteric works like *The Autobiography of Alice B. Toklas* and the present volume, but rather of her experimental essay-poem-novels like *Tender Buttons* and *The Making of Americans* and *Lucy Church Amiably*. And the trouble isn't at all that these books have no meaning. If we felt they were pure nonsense, we could find some pleasure in the word patterns, the puns, the rhymes, the mere sound of it all; everything would be dada, would be good fun. The trouble is that they do have a meaning, somewhere in the author's mind: a definite subject that eludes and irritates us and sets us off on a vain search as if through a pile of dusty newspapers for an item which we are sure must be there, but which we are equally sure we can never find.

When at last Miss Stein published a book that anybody could understand at a first reading—*The Autobiography of Alice B. Toklas*, in 1933—there was a general murmur of relief and admiration. Everybody was so delighted to find a meaning in her prose that almost nobody bothered to ask whether the meaning was worth all those years of sleepy suspense and dull mystification. On second reading the *Autobiography* is a disappointing book. You are impressed not so much by its childlike directness and its wealth of amusing or malicious gossip as by the lack of anything else.

So far as the *Autobiography* has any subject outside of Gertrude Stein, it deals with the order of precedence among writers and artists. This bears a curious resemblance to the pecking order among barnyard fowls, a favorite study of the ethologists. Outside my window this morning three bluejays are giving a demonstration of their pecking order. Mr. X, the biggest jay, is stuffing his beak with broken crusts of bread from a pile in the snow, while Mr. Y and Mr. Z are perched above him in the lilac bushes. Mr. Y gets tired of waiting and hops down for his share of the crusts, but Mr. X frightens him away with a great ruffling of feathers. Mr. Z sits there meekly under his shabby topknot; he looks like an author overwhelmed by unfavorable reviews.

The pecking order among birds is established, so far as I can observe, by a mixture of strength and boasting. The pecking order among artists is established in almost as simple a fashion: sometimes by the mere statement that Mr. Z or his ideas or his misadventures "did not interest" Miss Stein. In *The Autobiography of Alice B. Toklas* we find the formula applied to dozens of her acquaintances. Thus: "Robert Jones was very impressed by Gertrude Stein's looks. He said he would like to array her in cloth of gold and he wanted to design it then and there. It did not interest her."—"Mrs. Van Vechten told the story of the tragedy of her married life but Gertrude Stein was not particularly interested."—"There was always Glenway Wescott but Glenway Wescott at no time interested Gertrude Stein. He has a certain syrup but it does not pour." Miss Stein in the *Autobiography* has a certain pepper, but it clogs in the shaker. There is no reason why the reader should be particularly interested.

Wars I Have Seen starts out to give us more in the same self-centered vein: more about the early life of the very great author, more about her becoming a legend, more about how it felt to be the spoiled youngest child in a family of five boys and girls. "There you are you are privileged," she says. "Nobody can do anything but take care of you, that is the way I was and that is the way I still am, and anyone who is like that necessarily liked it. I did and do." In the midst of a cataclysm, this privileged character sets down her memories of the little wars she heard or read about in girlhood; some of them, she says, were the nicest sort of wars. But her attention keeps being distracted by present events, much as a rheumatic twinge or the ticking of an alarm clock will intrude into a pleasant dream about the past. Soon the sleeper wakens to feel that there are intruders in the house.

The intruders, of course, are the Germans; and here in an occupied village the effects of their presence are felt in a thousand indirect ways. Thus, "you lose a stocking and it was the best one, it was lost in the stream when they were washing, there is no soap, this is 1943, and so they wash in running water and the stocking went down the stream and it was the very best woolen stocking, only one but of what use is only one stocking, and we neither of us slept very much that night." Or again, the twinge that brings the sleeper back to the present may be some neighbor's misfortune, say that of two young men who are being deported to Germany and come to Miss Stein for advice; or that of the restaurant-keeper's wife, who thinks it a shame to see her husband going off between two policemen just as if he were a criminal. Everybody, so it seems, is being arrested, and a professional thief condemned to two months' imprisonment for stealing turkeys has to wait three months before there is room for him in jail.

More and more absorbed in her neighbors' troubles, Miss Stein forgets her glamorous childhood and even the business of being a great author. She goes plodding along the roads with her cane and her white poodle, six miles to one village, eight miles to another, in search of cakes and cabbages and conversation. She talks to everybody, in the voluble French that she is proud of, still speaking with an American accent after forty years away from home. "Everything is dangerous," she says, "and everybody casually meeting anybody talks to anybody and everybody tells everybody the history of their lives, they are always telling me and I am always telling them." These lives and casual meetings and homely dangers form the substance of her book, which in turn becomes an utterly convincing picture of a people and a time.

At the beginning of *Wars I Have Seen* you are bothered by Miss Stein's American but excessively personal style, with its flatness of statement, its repetitions, its deliberate errors in grammar, and its absence of commas, except where the sense calls for a period or a semicolon. Later you become reconciled to your reading; or perhaps the style itself becomes a little simplified and humanized through the author's preoccupation with her subject. For the first time she forgets herself in her subject, and her readers forget themselves too, and forget Miss Stein, as they follow the life of a French village from day to day.

Everything in her story is reduced to a village scale. Thus, the first echo of the resistance movement is the dull sound of a train exploding as it emerges from the nearest tunnel. German tyranny is the town drunkard shot in the street for not being home before curfew. The last battle for freedom is a local battle fought in the marshes just across the Rhone: the baker's nephew killed five Germans and the town butcher's boy killed four. The sense of liberation is a man whistling in the street at midnight, where nobody had whistled for five years, and the children crying "Pomm, pomm, pomm" as they killed imaginary invaders with wooden tommy guns.

All these are trivial details, but they add together, they gain strength through numbers; and the result is a sharp, immediate, overwhelming story of France in defeat and resurrection. It is such a story as Miss Stein has never told before, in all her abstract and self-centered works of art. And it leads to a real climax, when the first American soldiers drift into Culoz on a wave of popular delirium. For the author, it was as if they had snatched her from Babylonian captivity. For the villagers, it was like the second enactment of a miracle remembered from their youths.

A little French girl was praying to see an American soldier and, a few days later, her mother asked Miss Stein if she couldn't manage it somehow, because otherwise the little girl might lose her faith in prayer. Miss Stein took her to visit five M.P.'s who were living in a box car. They gave her chewing gum and chocolate and holy medals from Rome, and the little girl sang old French songs for them. Miss Stein said as she was taking her home, "About that chewing gum, you must chew it but be careful not to swallow it."—"Oh, yes, I know," said the little girl. Miss Stein asked her how she knew, and she answered, "Oh, because when there was the last war my mother was a little girl and the American soldiers gave her chewing gum and all through this war my mother used to tell me about it." She sighed in rapture. "And now I have it."

ARAGON VICTORIOUS

More than anyone else, Louis Aragon is the poet of this war, as it was lost and won in western Europe. He is by no means the only war poet; in his own country, which enjoyed a poetic revival during the years of defeat, there are also Paul Eluard, Pierre-Jean Jouve, Jean Cassou, Henri Michaux, Loys Masson, Pierre Emmanuel, and Patrice de la Tour du Pin, to mention a few of the names that recur more than others. In England and America, it would be hard to count the poets in the armed forces, but most of them have written about the struggle in relation to themselves; in war as in peace they have continued taking their spiritual pulses. Aragon forgot himself in the struggle; he spoke for his invaded country. He is the one poet who has left a complete record of the wartime emotions that were felt in common, from the first shock of mobilization to the joy of liberated Paris.

As a poet, it was his good fortune to be French, that is, native of a country occupied by the Nazis, but one where they hoped to rule by fraud as well as force. They did not try to destroy French culture; nor did they imprison or execute most of the writers, as happened in Czechoslovakia and Poland. The poets continued to publish their work, such of it as passed the Vichy censorship. They also continued to revolt against the Germans and against their own semblance of a government; and thus, as poets, they had an advantage over the British and Americans who have been fighting the war in uniforms. The man in uniform feels that a responsibility has been lifted from his shoulders. It isn't his war, no matter how much he believes in it and how often he risks his life for victory; as always in the past, it is the generals' war and the soldiers' fight. But in France, in the early days of the Resistance, each man was fighting under his own orders, until he freely submitted himself to orders from his comrades. I remember that Aragon told me long ago, in the midst of his reaction from the other war, "An outlaw is braver than a soldier, because he acts for himself." In France, all the members of the Resistance were outlaws. Everything conspired to keep them from fighting: the press, the radio, the police, and their own self-interest. Throughout the country, men examined their consciences; and either they stayed safely at home or else they went back to war, not as soldiers in the beginning, but simply as men.

Poets write best as lonely men, as rebels. When they are speaking for a government or a ruling party—even if they regard it with utter devotion—their verse becomes formal, discreet, and stiff in the joints, like an old diplomat; or it avoids those qualities by assuming a false innocence, like that of Miss Millay's ballad about Lidice. The French poets of the Resistance had the advantage of speaking as individuals— that is one side of the picture—but they also acknowledged a social duty that poetry can assume only in times of confusion: against the efforts of their own government, they had to keep the spirit of freedom alive in their nation. This was a task that could not be performed by novels or essays or plays in the theatre (although some of them carried their secret messages) or speeches over the radio or articles in the newspapers (until the underground press was established); all those means of expression were closely censored. The poets discovered, however, that their own medium had opportunities not granted to the others; that, with its power of allusion, it could rouse emotions and lead toward courses of action scarcely to be hinted at in prose; that, poems being short, they could be copied and passed from hand to hand, even learned by heart, as Aragon's poems were learned and recited; that in short it could play the same role poetry had played in Homeric times and in the Middle Ages.

Poetry in England and the United States does not usually try to perform a social function, and fortunately does not have to perform it. The poet here, whether soldier or civilian, usually writes not only as an individual, but also as one opposed to the mass of his countrymen. When he says "I," he means specifically the "not-they," the not-as-other-men. Aragon as an individual spoke in his wartime poems for all patriotic Frenchmen: when he said "I," he also meant "we." And this was true even in the poems he wrote during the first months of idleness and skepticism at the front, when he declared again and again, "I am not one of theirs":

> I am not theirs because my human flesh
> Is not a pastry to be cut with the knife
> Because a river seeks and finds the sea
> Because my living needs a sister life.

He was not theirs, in short, because *they* (who might be either German or French) had become inhuman through believing themselves super-human. He was a man, like the other soldiers; and he spoke for them directly in their bewilderment, as he would also speak directly for the French nation in defeat. "For the French," said André Gide, whom Aragon would later attack—unjustly, I think—for his hesitations during the first year after the German invasion, "there are always, in every field (and so much the better), two poles, two tendencies, two parties; in our own field there is, on the one side, reflective poetry (I am using the word in its two senses of 'contemplative' and 'reflected as in a mirror') and, on the other side, direct poetry. . . . For all the splendors of cerebral poetry in France, it is from the other tendency, from direct poetry, that I am now expecting our renaissance: from the mood that inspired Aragon to write the poems in *Heartbreak*—" and he went on to quote the end of Aragon's "Unoccupied Zone," which was already famous in 1941:

> Hour after hour, without relief
> I sought an ill-remembered grief
> Until the September dawn
>
> When lying in your arms awake
> I heard one singing at daybreak
> Outside, an old French song
> Then knew my sorrow, branch and root
> Its music like a naked foot
> Troubled the pool where silence lay nightlong.

There is a fundamental simplicity about poems like this, in spite of their technical experiments, their involved rhyme schemes, their bold and sometimes obscure images. The emotion itself is always straight-forward. Aragon in his poems was giving back their old meaning to words like "love" and "courage" and "country." "Permit me to say in public," he wrote in one poem, "that the sun is the sun"—and it was as if he was also saying that death is death, that love is love, that France in defeat is still his country, and that liberty is not merely an orator's expression, but something worth risking one's life to restore. He wrote in "Christmas Roses," which is a tribute to the first men executed for their part in the Resistance:

> Noel, Noel! That faint sunrise
> Gave back to you, men of little faith,
> The love for which one willingly dies
> And the future that relives his death.

The war gave back to Aragon the world in which words have a real meaning, even the tritest of the words that describe human experiences. He was like a traveler returning after years to his own country-side, in which everything is familiar and yet has a different value, being seen with different eyes. That explains the effect, in his best poems, of a complex situation reduced, after years, to a statement as simple as that of the old Scotch ballads. He was the Border minstrel of this war.

Even Aragon's principal fault becomes a virtue in his wartime poetry. He writes easily, with apparently endless powers of invention, but sometimes also with deliberate negligence, with a willingness to follow the rhyme or the image wherever they lead him, with a tendency to repeat himself where he would refuse to copy others. He has a power of concentration that shames those of us who need quiet and leisure for their best work, or any work at all. Aragon works anywhere, at any hour and in any company. I have seen him writing in bed, propped on his left elbow; writing under the grape arbor while boys were noisily mowing the lawn; writing in a corner of a room that was full of people talking English and sometimes interrupting him with a question; he would answer it, in English, and go on writing French prose. That was in the early summer of 1939, when he was three-fourths of the way through a novel, *The Century Was Young*. The novel was still unfinished when, after his return to Paris, the newspaper he edited was suppressed on August 25. Aragon had a week of leisure before entering the army, on September 2. During that week, with the world going to pieces, he wrote the last hundred pages of his book. He had the proofs with him at Dunkerque, and made corrections in them while waiting to be evacuated.

For the poetry he wrote during the war, his special gift was necessary. There was no time for self-questioning, for writhing in the pains of composition; there was not much time to write at all, except for a man like Aragon who could do his work in barracks, in trains, in waiting rooms, or on the beach at Dunkerque. Unlike less naturally gifted poets, he was able to set down his impressions and emotions as they came, so that his six volumes of wartime poetry became a month-by-month record of the struggle: the boredom and loneliness of the "phony war"; the grotesque horror of the German invasion, like Breughel's conception of hell; the utter weight of defeat, under which Aragon was among the first to stand erect; then the impulse for reëxamining French history, to find the real strength of the nation; and the growing power of the Resistance, which at first he merely suggested in his poems, but later mirrored frankly, so that his work was forbidden by the Vichy censors and he turned to writing ballads of combat to be printed in the underground newspapers or smuggled across the border and published in Switzerland; and at last the frantic joy of "Paris, Paris, of herself liberated"—all of it is there, in Aragon's verse.

2

It was the war that made Aragon a poet again. He had written a quantity of verse in his younger days; and after his trip to Russia, about 1930, he had written one long poem, "Red Front," that led to his being given a sentence of five years in prison for insulting the French flag; but the sentence had been suspended and Aragon had plunged into politics, journalism, and social fiction. In 1939 he was the editor of *Ce Soir*, a left-wing afternoon newspaper with a circulation of almost half a million, and, besides his early books, he was the author of two long social novels with a rather wide sale and a generally favorable reception from the critics; a third novel, as I said, was almost finished.

Then, at the end of August, the newspaper was suppressed; the new novel was not exactly suppressed—it was too soon for that—but difficulties were put in the way of its publication; and the author, at the age of forty-two, was drafted into the army, where Military Intelligence was instructed to keep a careful watch on him. His double career in literature and journalism had come to a full stop.

He served through the "phony war" and the invasion of France as an "auxiliary doctor" (he had been graduated from medical school but had never taken his internship), and he ranked from beginning to end as an *adjutant*, roughly equivalent to an American warrant officer. At first he was punished for his political opinions by being assigned to a labor regiment composed chiefly of Czech and Spanish refugees, people not trusted to bear arms at the front but merely to dig fortifications. Later he managed to get himself transferred to a light motorized division, but, until the fighting began, he had very little to do. In his loneliness he began writing poetry again. It was poetry composed with an astonishing technical virtuosity; and also, what is more important, it expressed the bewilderment and the longing for home of the whole French army.

Aragon was finishing a poem ("The Interrupted Poem") on the early morning of May 10, 1940, when he received orders to join an armored detachment that was crossing the frontier into Belgium in advance of the main Allied forces. More than once during the campaign that followed, the detachment had to fight its way from behind the German lines. At last the whole division was surrounded, with the army to which it belonged; and it was only "by a pretty improbable piece of luck," as Aragon wrote in a letter to his friends the Josephsons, that it managed to join the English forces on the beach at Dunkerque. Its equipment had to be abandoned there. All that Aragon carried with him to England, he wrote in another letter, was his sleeping bag, a few dry biscuits, his raincoat, and the half-corrected proofs of his novel.*

---

*Meanwhile, the printer's type of the novel had been destroyed, apparently in a bombing raid. The book was later reset from the proofs that Aragon had carried with him through the Battle of France. Enough passages were deleted to meet the censor's objections, and the novel was published at last, in 1942. It was almost immediately suppressed by the Germans—but all that is another story.

His division returned to France after spending one night at Plymouth. It landed at Brest, received new equipment, and went back into the battle line at Vernon, on the lower Seine (where Louis and I had gone talking together in the long spring of 1923). From there it fought in the rear-guard of the retreating French armies until it had reached the country south of the Loire. Aragon was taken prisoner at Angoulême, on the last day of the fighting, but he escaped under fire with six automobiles and thirty men. He was demobilized at the end of July and, his wife having joined him, they spent three weeks together in a pink château in the Limousin. By that time he had received the Croix de Guerre, with a divisional citation, for his exploits in Belgium; a second Croix de Guerre, with an army citation, for the fighting on the Loire; and the Médaille Militaire, one of the two highest French decorations, for his escape from the Germans. Later this collection of medals would save him more than once from arrest by the Vichy police.

As for his poetic activity after the French armistice, it falls into three separate periods. First came the weeks that Louis and Elsa Aragon spent in the pink château and their four months in Carcassonne—the months, precisely, when French poets and their countrymen were stunned by the sudden collapse, as it then appeared, of a whole civilization; when they had no idea of what they could usefully do, either as writers or as patriots. During this period, Aragon wrote a long letter to Matthew and Hannah Josephson, at the end of which he said:

> In the Occupied Zone my books, like those of many other French writers, can no longer be sold, while in the Free Zone that question does not even arise, since all the printed copies are in Paris and the publisher is forbidden to ship them across the line of demarcation. Looking forward, I can see no possibility of earning my living as a writer; and it is even a question whether I can find any other sort of work. By being very careful with what remains of my army pay, I think we can live here in a small way until November 1. After that, who knows? . . .
>
> I am writing poems, and as long as the fighting lasted I was still able to publish them from time to time. I still write them, but I keep them for myself. Elsa, whose books are unobtainable like

mine, has just begun a long story, and I want her to finish it, because the beginning is wonderfully vivid. But it takes a great deal of courage to write without knowing what will happen to one's work. What a terrible road since the days we spent together! Note that the rest of this letter would be false to my meaning if you concluded from it that I have become pessimistic. I believe on the contrary that God moves in a mysterious way and that the gate is strait through which we must pass. In my country, even when it is unfortunate, even when it is crushed, I have a confidence that there is no way of expressing except by deeds; and there is nothing to change in what I told you there in your country house, of which I dream today as if it were some image of childhood or a scene from a novel. . . .

Your old friend (my hair is now completely white) who hasn't forgotten you.

Louis

The poems he was writing at the time were battle pieces like the "Tapestry of the Great Fear" and the "Song for a Barrel Organ"; or they were songs of France in defeat like "Richard II Forty" and "Richard Coeur-de-Lion" and "The Lilacs and the Roses"—all with the weight of emotion and the simplicity of old ballads, but with images drawn from our own age of total warfare. If he spoke of French roses, they were:

> Flowers that gave the lie to soldiers passing
> On wings of fear, a fear importunate as a breeze,
> And gave the lie to the lunatic push-bikes and the ironic
> Guns and the sorry rig of the refugees.

All these poems were written for himself, but Aragon showed them to other writers who had gathered in Carcassonne; copies passed from hand to hand. Somebody sent an imperfect copy of one poem to the literary supplement of Le Figaro, which was then being published in Lyons, in the Unoccupied Zone. "The Lilacs and the Roses" appeared in the issue of September 21, 1940 (and appeared again, with the author's corrections, in the issue of September 28). Many people expected that the newspaper would be fined or even suppressed for its temerity in printing a poem that said in simple words what everybody was feeling. The censor, however, had no objections to offer. Poems like those that Aragon was writing found protection in the ambiguous position of the Vichy government: they were patriotic and Vichy, too, claimed to be patriotic; they appealed to French traditions and Vichy was also appealing to them; they were the work, in Aragon's case, of a veteran three times decorated and Vichy was trying to conciliate the other veterans. The result was that more and more of Aragon's new poems appeared, in *Poésie 41* and other legally printed magazines; and many other French poets began to write in a similar vein.

That was the first winter of what Pierre Seghers, the editor of *Poésie*, would afterwards describe as the conspiracy of poets, *la conspiration des poètes*. Others, including Gide, spoke of a poetic renaissance, and they had good reasons for using the phrase, since poetry was receiving more attention than at any other period since the flowering of the Romantic movement. But the renaissance this time had a political or, to be more exact, a national basis. When writers discovered how much they could say in verse without having their work suppressed, and how carefully poems were being read, they turned away from prose; novelists became poets; former poets began writing verse again; new poets were discovered by the score. As Aragon said in the long letter that he wrote me, in English, after the liberation of France: "The new poetry was in fact a conspiracy among certain writers and poets, conscious and unconscious, to put into our literature the necessary patriotic flavor and express just what our masters wanted not to be told."

His poems of this second period were written slowly (he had more leisure during those months than afterward or before), with great formal inventiveness and technical finish, and with a wealth of historical allusions. He couldn't attack the Germans directly, but he could refer to the sorrows of France during the Hundred Years War, and his readers understood. His rebellion was more clearly expressed with every month that passed. After the Germans began shooting hostages, he could no longer express himself within the strict limits of "legal" literature. As the result of one angry poem, "X . . . Français," written to commemorate an engineer named Jacques Bonsergent, who had been executed for helping to organize the Resistance, all the French reviews were "advised" by Vichy not to print any more of Aragon's work. He continued writing for them, under a dozen different pseudonyms—and occasionally under his own name as well—but most of his poems were now printed either in Switzerland, after being smuggled across the border, or else in the newspapers of the underground. And the poet himself had to go underground, after the invasion of North Africa. He said in a letter from which I have quoted already: "When, on November 11, 1942, the Italians crossed the border and entered Nice, we left without regard to other considerations and went under the deep and pleasant cover of illegality."

In the same letter, after describing his work for the Resistance, he tried to give me a picture of France before the liberation. He said in English that keeps a French flavor:

> We had received orders *not* to do any local job, *not* to come in touch with local party members, and so on. But we couldn't, after a certain moment, keep from helping the people around us: because that last year you can't imagine what France was like. My God, it was a repayment for everything in life! And people can slander and chitchat and loathe us, but we have seen that, the heroic moment when everybody was ready at every moment to die for anybody, people they didn't even know, provided that they were against the common enemy. You must believe me . . . that it is by no means a manner of speech if I say that in those incredibly long and bloody months life became a song for all of us: and you know, in the best of songs there are certainly tears, but how beautiful the voice and the eyes of people appear when singing, they can't stop themselves crying!

In those days when life itself was a song, Aragon was still writing poems. He even wrote a very long poem, *Le Musée Grévin*, in which Laval, Hitler, Mussolini, and Pétain were presented as figures in a waxworks museum. First printed by Midnight Editions, the book-publishing house of the Resistance, *Le Musée Grévin* was reprinted a hundred times all over France, usually as a folded leaflet in very small type. Aragon also wrote, during this period, a number of songs and ballads for the French Partisans. These appeared in dozens of underground papers; then, after the liberation, they were collected and published in Paris as *Reveille in France* (*La Diane Française*).

Writing for his comrades in their own clandestine press, Aragon was at last free to say exactly what he felt about the foreign invaders and the traitors at home. But along with this privilege he had a duty: he had to make every line of verse contribute directly to the struggle. Space in the underground papers was precious, and any poem that appeared in them, or any poem printed as a leaflet and distributed at the risk of death, had to be written and judged by other standards than those of literature in the abstract. All the songs and ballads in *La Diane Française* show the exultant grief of those days when "everybody was ready at every moment to die for anybody." Many of them, but especially the "Ballad of One Who Sang at the Stake," enjoyed a popularity that poets might dream about here, but never achieve in these days when poetry is practiced as a private art. In the time of the maquis, they were learned by heart and recited at campfires; after the liberation, they were read from the stage of the Comédie Française; they were heard over the radio and even on phonograph records. . . . This sort of popularity makes us distrust them a little, as poems. There is no doubt that some of them will live for a long time: the "Prelude" and "Elsa at the Mirror" and "Christmas Roses" among others; but I should judge that the future will prefer the "legal" poems that Aragon wrote in the first days of defeat. In them the need for speaking his mind without violating the rules of the Vichy censor was like a new difficulty, a new convention superimposed on the old poetic conventions. The devices he found for meeting it gave his poems of that period more depth, more richness, more density than he could achieve in ballads where his whole meaning had to be clear at a first glance.

In all, Aragon managed to write and publish six books of poetry during the war, not counting the *Cantique à Elsa*, which was published in Algiers and later included in a longer volume. Of the others, only the first, *Heartbreak* (*Le Crève-Coeur*), was printed legally in France during the occupation; it was promptly suppressed by the Germans. *Les Yeux d'Elsa*, *Brocéliande*, and *En Français dans le Texte* all appeared in Switzerland; a few copies of each were smuggled across the border with the complicity of the French censor at Annemasse. The fifth volume was *Le Musée Grévin*, printed illegally by the Resistance; the sixth and last, which appeared in Paris after the liberation, was *La Diane Française*. Together the six books are a record of the wartime emotions of French soldiers and civilians—and of all those in Allied countries who were committed to the war—such as no other poet has even attempted to give. All of Aragon's virtues and even his faults conspired together to make the story complete. I know of nothing in English or American literature to compare with it, not even the record of the Civil War that Walt Whitman left in his *Drum-Taps*.

LIMOUSINES ON GRUB STREET
How Writers Earned Their Livings: 1940–46

A t the end of the 1930s, there was a boom in what was coming to be known as the literature business, and the boom has continued after the war. Most of our 11,806 professional authors—to borrow a figure from the 1940 census reports—are still insecure and underpaid; but those who achieved or blundered into popularity have been living like speculators in a bull market. Before the market crashes, let us trace the history of the boom and examine its effects on the profession of authorship.

The new era of best-sellers began as early as 1931, with the publication of Pearl Buck's first novel. *The Good Earth* stood at the top of the bookstore lists for two years, was reprinted many times at various prices, was translated into twenty languages, and had an American sale in all editions of probably more than a million copies, although the publisher has never released the exact figures. In 1933 and 1934, the best-seller was *Anthony Adverse*, first of the oversized historical romances. It had so wide a popular appeal that it became a sort of St. Christopher for the booksellers, lifting them on its back and carrying them through the slough of the Depression; its sale has now reached 1.2 million copies. In 1936 and 1937, the book was *Gone with the Wind*, with an American sale in the first ten years of 3.7 million copies; at home and abroad it has been the greatest publishing success of the century. All three of these novels had been issued to its subscribers by the Book of the Month Club, which, with its competitors, was changing the history of the book trade in America.

Essentially the book clubs are companies that carry on the business of selling books by mail to various types of readers. By 1946 there were twenty-six of the clubs, with 3.6 million subscribers scattered in all the towns and almost all the hamlets of the country. There were special clubs for Protestants, Catholics, radicals, children, executives, students of science, lovers of the classics, Sears Roebuck customers, and mystery fans; but two of the clubs that appealed to a general audience—the Book of the Month Club and the Literary Guild—were the oldest and by far the most successful.

The Book of the Month Club issued its first selection in April 1926; at the end of the first year it had 40,000 members. Its growth was steady even during the Depression, and phenomenal in the early wartime years; by 1943 it was setting a limit of 600,000 on its membership because of the paper shortage. In spite of difficulties with production, it was distributing nearly 300,000 copies, on the average, of the books it recommended, besides many other volumes ordered by its members from reviews in its monthly magazine; and it was then the third largest private customer of the Post Office Department, the first two being Sears Roebuck and Montgomery Ward.

Obviously the membership had learned to rely on the taste of the five judges who made its monthly selections. The judges never managed to choose the twelve best books of the year in point of literary merit—it is a question whether they tried to do so—but they almost always chose something of interest and they often took chances: that is, they voted for out-of-the-way books which, without their approval, would have had no chance for success. The growing popularity of non-fiction books was a phenomenon of the years after 1930. Partly it was explained by the support that many of them received from the Book of the Month Club.

The Literary Guild, which began to distribute books in 1927 after years of discussion and promotion, had a more uneven history. At first it grew as fast as its rival; then for some years it fell behind, as a result of choosing books that were either too difficult or, in some cases, simply too dull for its audience; there were times when it teetered on the edge of bankruptcy. After 1937 it began a period of rapid growth under a new editor, John Beecroft, who also made the monthly selections for two other large book clubs owned by the same publishing house: the Doubleday One Dollar Book Club and the Book League of America. But the Guild received his special attention; it overtook and passed the Book of the Month Club during the war, when it had a larger supply of paper; and by 1946 it had 1,250,000 members, as against 925,000 for its rival.

Paper stocks, however, were only part of the story. The more rapid growth of the Guild after 1937 was also the result of its having adopted an older, safer, and somewhat more cynical policy. Its selections were chiefly novels with a well-constructed plot that was easy to follow; books that Beecroft was certain its members would like. The bookstore audience liked them too; and it was largely owing to the influence of the Guild that sales of more than a million copies for historical romances and local-color novels once more became commonplace, as in the years before the First World War. Indeed, the best-selling novels of the new era—like *Captain from Castile* and *The Black Rose*—were almost on the same literary level as those of the period from 1900 to 1915; on the average they were a little better than *Freckles*, a little worse than Winston Churchill's *The Crisis*; neither better nor worse, but only franker in sexual matters, than *The Trail of the Lonesome Pine*.

The publishing industry as a whole was growing in the wartime years; after 1942 the production of books was limited, not by public demand, which seemed to have no end, but merely by the supply of paper and binding cloth and the time available on the printing presses. Magazines also enjoyed a period of wartime prosperity when they could sell as many copies as they could print, and print as many copies as their paper quota made possible. Yet all this time there were whole categories and age groups of writers who gained little or nothing whatever from the boom in the book and magazine trades.

Most of the younger men were in the Army; many women and older men were in war work that took all their energies. Poets and scholarly critics, if they had time for writing, learned that it had become harder than ever to find a publisher for books that wouldn't sell. Even the great majority of novelists and general essayists had little share in wartime profits. Lacking the art of salesmanship, or regarding its use as a dangerous temptation, they lived very much as before, on crumbs from a dozen different tables: now an advance from a publisher (who was likely to be more generous in wartime), now a story sold to a magazine, now a literary prize or fellowship (there were more of these than in the past), now an invitation to deliver a lecture or teach in a writers' summer school, now a book review or a manuscript to be reported on, now a few dollars for permission to reprint something of theirs in a textbook or anthology, now an invitation to spend a month or two writing at Yaddo or the MacDowell Colony—in general an irregular series of little windfalls that somehow kept them going while they waited to see whether the next book would pay for the publisher's advance on it and even yield them an actual royalty check. Meanwhile a few score or even hundreds of the most popular writers were earning money almost at the rate of war contractors.

If these were lucky enough to have a book taken as its sole monthly choice by one of the two largest book clubs, they each received, in 1946, an advance payment of $50,000; and there was the prospect of further payment from the club if the members liked their work—not to mention the royalties from bookstore sales, which were certain to be larger for club selections than for other books. Magazines as a class had not raised their top rates for thirty years, and the successful magazine writers of 1940 were being paid rather less than Jack London had received in 1910; but this was another situation that changed during the war. All money was "hot" in those days because of income and excess-profits taxes; and the magazines that were making profits subject to high taxation often shared part of the wealth with their collaborators by giving them higher fees, at a cost to themselves of about 10 percent.

The growth of reprint publishing had involved very little increase in the economic rewards of authorship. The various pocket books, for example, paid royalties of only one cent per copy, to be divided equally between the author and his original publisher; so that the author's share for an edition of 100,000 was only $500. On the other hand, the sale of foreign rights had begun to yield respectable sums; and the digest magazines paid from $4,000 to $10,000 or more for permission to make a condensed version of a popular novel.

Two young ladies, overheard by a reporter for *The New Yorker*, were discussing the latest number of *Omnibook*, a monthly devoted to book digests. "It takes five or six books and boils them down," said one of the ladies. "That way you can read them all in one evening." The other said, "I wouldn't like it. Seems to me it would just spoil the movie for you." The movie was not only more important for these young ladies; it was also the largest source of income for many writers. As much as $200,000 was paid for the motion-picture rights to successful books, and $300,000 for plays that ran only three weeks on Broadway. There is one case on record where a Hollywood producer paid $150,000 for a then unpublished first novel that the critics didn't like when it finally appeared.

There were also numerous instances where authors were defrauded by legal but palpably unfair contracts, and the Author's League was battling for and about the creation of new machinery to protect their rights. Meanwhile, successful writers were depending more and more on the advice (costing 10 percent of their net proceeds) of literary agents who were skilled in exploiting all the financial possibilities of a novel or an autobiographical story. The agents had greatly increased in number: a directory called *The Literary Marketplace* gave the names of eighty as being "among the most active in the field." A few of them were partnerships or corporations larger than the average publishing house.

With the new ramifications of the literature business, they needed all their skill. It was now theoretically possible for a single book to be first-serialized in a big-circulation magazine; then distributed by one of the two leading book clubs at the same time that it went on public sale; then sold to Hollywood for a large cash payment and a percentage of the future profits (spread over several years so as to lower the income surtax); then reviewed in the newspapers and magazines and over the radio—and even turned into a comic strip for publication in part of the Hearst press; then printed by one of the digest magazines in painless capsule form; then second-serialized in some of the newspapers (although this particular use of books was declining); then sold to an English publisher; then translated into as many as twenty foreign languages (with royalties to the author for all editions except those printed in Russia, China, Japan, and sometimes Holland); then chosen by a second book club, one that specializes in cheaper reprints; then reprinted for the general public in a series of editions at prices ranging downward from $1.98 to 25 cents, the sale of which would be vastly stimulated by the release of the motion picture, followed by a half-hour radio version of the Hollywood cinematization; while all the time the author was besieged for interviews, paid and unpaid personal appearances, lectures . . . and the great machine of exploitation rolled on and on, through wider circles of business enterprise, and literary values were forgotten somewhere over the horizon or in the past.

Besides commercialism, two other tendencies were transforming the literary world after 1930. To name each of them in a long word, they were institutionalization and collectivization.

Literary activities were coming more and more to be centered upon the institutions that were powerful enough to support them. The government itself was the largest of these and, in the days of the Federal Writers' Project, it had also shown signs of becoming the most influential. There was at one time talk of establishing a Bureau of Fine Arts with authority to undertake cultural projects and award prizes and fellowships. A conference held under official auspices in the autumn of 1941 resolved that the government had an interest in supporting the fine arts, including literature, that went beyond the measures it had already taken toward keeping artists and writers employed during the Depression. But our entrance into the war, and later the hostility of Congress and the change in government personnel, put an end to these plans. The only government support for literature after 1945 was through the State Department in the foreign field, and through the research programs maintained by the Library of Congress.

Many of the functions that might have been performed by a Bureau of Fine Arts were gradually taken over by the American universities. With their vast endowments and, in many cases, their support by state governments (in addition to help from the Carnegie and Rockefeller Foundations), they became the local centers of cultural activity. They maintained, generally speaking, the best American libraries for scholarly work. They offered extension courses and free lectures that took the place of the old-time chautauquas and lyceums. They became a refuge for the little-theatre movement, which was declining almost everywhere else except in summer resorts.

To their student bodies, they gave courses and seminars in creative writing, often with the help of well-known authors. Teaching and writing, in the early 1900s, had been two separate worlds. After 1940, however, it was no longer surprising to hear that a critic, an experimental poet, or even a successful novelist or biographer was on the faculty at Harvard, Minnesota, California, or any one of a dozen other universities. Some of these writers—and some of their brighter students—had their creative work published by the university presses.

The publishing trade had so far resisted the tendency toward concentration and amalgamation that had triumphed almost everywhere else in American society. A typical second-line publishing house, one that issued about thirty books a year, might start with a working capital of less than $200,000. It might consist of two partners, one of whom acted as senior editor, the other as sales manager; one or two junior editors; an advertising manager; four salesmen, who might also handle the books of another publisher as a sideline; and half a dozen secretaries, typists, and stock-room clerks. It was a small business, of the type that newspapers romanticize not only because it expresses the myth of individual enterprise, but also because it is disappearing from the commercial world.

Meanwhile the larger publishing houses were expanding—either horizontally, by adding new departments that specialized in reprints, textbooks, medical books, sporting books; or else vertically, by invading the retail book trade. Doubleday and Company had expanded in both directions. Besides a trade-book department, it had a large press under construction; it had four subsidiary companies that published various types of reprints; it owned four book clubs, including three of the largest; and it also operated an extensive chain of bookstores. Simon and Schuster controlled Pocket Books, Inc., the largest of the 25-cent reprint publishers; it had a share in the People's Book Club; it wholly owned the Venture Press, devoted to the work of new authors; and it had a fraternal relationship with the Marshall Field newspapers and projected magazines.

In many other fields connected with writing, the process of concentration had gone faster and farther. In the periodical field, for example, the big-circulation magazines had all become institutions employing hundreds of persons and possessing a sort of corporate personality. There was a tendency for magazines to be consolidated into chains:

these included the Luce chain, the Curtis chain, the Crowell-Collier chain, the Hearst chain, the McCall Corporation, and, in Chicago, the Smart group, not to mention a dozen corporate collections of popular all-fiction monthlies.

In motion pictures there were a few big producing companies each of which hired scores of writers, exactly as it hired actors or cameramen. In radio there were the four big networks, which earned their profits by selling time on the air to the not more than two hundred corporations that engaged in large-scale advertising. Radio writers had to hold the public's attention while remembering that their primary function was not to create characters or tell a story, but chiefly to sell soap.

More and more writers in all fields had ceased to be independent craftsmen and instead had become officials of public or private institutions. They worked for the federal government, they taught in universities, they wrote on contract for magazine corporations, they were hired by motion-picture producers or radio advertising agencies. They were sometimes very well paid; on the largest magazines they might earn salaries of as much as $25,000 a year (or even more, if they were among the top favorites of *Reader's Digest*); and there were a very few writers for the movies who earned $5,000 a week on short-term contracts. At the other end of the scale, writers hired or put under contract by the pulp-paper magazines might earn less than the rate for cub reporters under a Newspaper Guild contract. Lavishly paid or miserably paid, salaried writers as a class did honest work, the best that was possible in the circumstances, but the work wasn't their own. It had become collective to a degree never achieved in Russia, where collectivization is set forward as an ideal.

The Russians sometimes sent "shock brigades" of writers to report on a particular situation; at one time it was the industrial and agricultural progress of Tajikistan. The writers all made the same conducted tour; then afterwards each submitted his individual report. But American writers employed by an institution might not only be assigned to the same collective task; each of them might be expected to perform only part of it, like a single worker on the production line. In Hollywood, for example, it was a practice of some companies to set

three writers to work independently on the same story. The best features of their three versions would be combined, usually by a fourth
writer, and the completed script would then be subject to further
changes by the producer, the director, and the editor in the cutting
room (not to mention all the changes in emphasis that might be made
by the actors, the costumers, the scene designers, and the composers
of the musical score); till at last the film emerged as a vast collective
enterprise in which nobody could recognize more than a few scenes or
sounds as his own.

Writing for some magazines had become almost as purely a collective process: for example, an idea might be suggested by one of the
editors, adopted after a general conference of executives, assigned to a
researcher to gather the facts, then to a writer (or even two or three
writers in succession) to put them together, then again to one or more
editors to whip it into final shape. In the Luce magazines, most of the
articles were unsigned, for one good reason among others that it would
have been as difficult in some cases to assign them to any single authorship as it would have been to identify the man chiefly responsible
for the ten-millionth Chevrolet to move down the production line.

Even in fields where the process was less advanced, there was an in-
creasing amount of acknowledged or unacknowledged collaboration.
Hardly any play by a new author reached Broadway until it had been
worked over by a play doctor, who received half-credit for the result
and half the royalties. On Publishers' Row it was understood that most
books by war heroes, corporation executives, and government officials
were actually written by their literary ghosts. Sometimes a Hollywood
producer, instead of filming an original story by one of his own hired
hands, would pass along the plot to some needy novelist, with an advance payment and a promise of more if the book written to specifi-
cations was accepted by a reputable publisher and not too unfavorably
reviewed. Or again, a literary agent might invent the subject and even
the plot of a novel, might convince a magazine editor that it was just
what he wanted for a serial; and the editor might assign it to one of his
trusted writers, just as he would order a suit from his tailor.

Much of current American writing had come to represent, not a personal vision, but rather a trend, an imprint, or a decision taken at a
board of directors' meeting. There was now a much wider audience for

all writing (except some of the best) than there had ever been before, and there was a much larger body of writers trained to meet its demands. There had been a great elaboration in technique, so that American fiction in the 1940s was the most skillful written anywhere in the world. Yet there was also a greater timidity among the mass of writers, of the sort that develops in any bureaucratic situation; and there was a tendency to forget that, although a great book expresses a whole culture and hence has millions of collaborators, including persons long since dead, in another sense it must finally be written by one man alone in a room with his conscience and a stock of blank paper.

THE BATTLE OVER
EZRA POUND

The literary battle of the year is being fought over Ezra Pound and the Bollingen Award. Since the end of the Federal Arts Projects it is the only battle among and against the bookmen that has reached the floor of Congress or, as the cannon thundered, has forced an agency of the United States government to sue for peace.

Hostilities started late last winter with a statement by the Fellows of the Library of Congress. Under a grant from the Bollingen Foundation they were offering a $1,000 prize, which was to be awarded annually to the best new book of poems by an American citizen. They announced on February 23 that the first year's prize had gone to the *Pisan Cantos*, by Ezra Pound, who is a citizen under indictment for treason. Judged to be insane by a medical board, he has been confined in St. Elizabeths Hospital in Washington, D.C.

At first there were only mild skirmishes over the award. A few newspapers printed favorable editorials, while others were puzzled rather than angry; they wondered who were the Fellows of the Library of Congress and why they had chosen a book by a guaranteed-to-be-crazy poet who had given radio broadcasts for the enemy, like Axis Sally and Tokyo Rose. It was learned that the Fellows were an unpaid advisory group of poets and critics appointed by the Librarian of Congress; at present the group has fourteen members. Two of them, Karl Shapiro and Paul Green, announced that they hadn't voted for Pound's book and apparently there was one other vote against it, leaving it as the first choice of eleven Fellows. Dwight Macdonald, the editor of *Politics*, praised their decision for its freedom from prejudice; he called it "the brightest political act in a dark period." William Barrett dissented in *Partisan Review* on the ground that the form of a poem cannot be judged apart from its content. He quoted passages to show that the content of the *Pisan Cantos* was fascist and antisemitic. Three of the Fellows stated their various positions in the correspondence columns of the same magazine. The battle was dying away in scattered shots and letters to the editor when suddenly the *Saturday Review* marched in with fresh battalions, like Blücher at Waterloo.

In two long articles (*SR*, June 11 and 18) Robert Hillyer charged that the award to Pound was an insult to "our Christian war dead"— that was one of his phrases—besides being part of a far-flung conspiracy against American ways of life and literature. He did not state, but he took time and space to imply, that the conspirators included Paul Mellon, the financier; T. S. Eliot, the Nobel prizeman; and Dr. Carl G. Jung, the psychoanalyst, besides the Bollingen Foundation, the Pantheon Press, at least half the Fellows of the Library of Congress, all the poets who admire Pound or Eliot, all the "new critics," most of the literary quarterlies, and I don't know how many other persons and institutions. Their common aim, he said, was the seizure of power in the literary world, and beyond that "the mystical and cultural preparation for a new authoritarianism."

Those are big words and the editors of the *Saturday Review* supported them. In the same issue as the first of Hillyer's articles they printed a statement which, defying lightning and suits for libel, was doubly signed for the editorial board by Norman Cousins, Editor, and Harrison Smith, President. "The Bollingen Prize given to Ezra Pound will eventually set off a revolution of no mean dimensions," they prophesied. It has indeed set off a revolution in their correspondence columns, where hundreds of readers have leaped into print and combat.

This revolution by letters to the editor has been rich in patriotic slogans: "Up with the English classics!"—"Down with the cult of unintelligibility!"—"Down with the new criticism!"—"Down with the fascist dogs!"—"Down, down with expatriates!"—"Save our college girls from reading T. S. Eliot!" Even here in the Connecticut hills one hears the drums of combat interrupting the Yankee twang of the mowing machine; and it is hard for us not to join the cultured mob that is apparently getting ready to storm the Library of Congress, drive out the new authoritarians, and hang Eliot to the nearest, if any, lamp post. But another voice—perhaps that of the mowing machine—warns us to stop and see what the issues are before we begin to fight.

Is there any real conspiracy in the literary world to promote what Hillyer calls "a new authoritarianism"? Look as hard as I could, I found no signs of it; nor could I find many connections among the persons and institutions listed in Hillyer's two articles. Besides Ezra Pound there is one man on the list, one only, who may have been a fascist sympathizer at one time. It seems that Dr. Jung spoke well of Hitler, before 1938, but his American disciples insist that he afterward changed his mind. Incidentally there are few of these disciples and not one of them is a "new critic" or a Fellow of the Library of Congress.

Let us consider some of the others indicted by Hillyer as members of a conspiracy against the American way of life. Paul Mellon, the son of Andrew Mellon, is a public-spirited man who has done a great deal for American literature, chiefly through the Bollingen Foundation. I know several writers who have received grants from the Foundation and not one of them shows a trace of fascist thinking; they include the usual proportion of liberals, conservatives, and political bystanders. Although the Foundation gave money to the Library of Congress with which to make a poetry award, it did not know—nor did Paul Mellon know—that Pound was being considered for the first year's prize.

And the Pantheon Press: what malice or misinformation prompted Hillyer to drag it into his article as if into the prisoner's dock? It is a small publishing house founded by two refugees from Hitler and very favorably known for its editions of the European classics. By now it has received the apologies of the *Saturday Review*. The editors should also offer their apologies to T. S. Eliot. Hillyer implied that he exercised a malign influence over the other Fellows and persuaded them to give the award to Pound; whereas the truth is that he neither nominated the *Pisan Cantos* for the prize nor argued that it was the best book to choose; he merely cast one vote for it among eleven. Hillyer also called him "a disciple of Dr. Jung," an author whom Eliot has not read. His own political convictions are conservative, traditional, and not in the least totalitarian. He is a pluralist who believes that we owe our loyalties, not to the state alone, but also to church, class, region, family, and profession. He thinks it is a symptom of decay and a catastrophe in itself for the state to become all-powerful.

And what about the other Fellows of the Library? I have known most of them for years and respect them all as men and writers. It is ridiculous to charge them with antisemitism or with having fascist sympathies. Since the award was made I have talked with some of them; they said that Pound's politics were crazy and contemptible. One Fellow had read the text of Pound's broadcasts for the Italian government and thought that the poet, if he recovered his sanity, should be convicted of treason. "But that is a matter for the courts to decide," he said. "Our job wasn't to pass on the question of Pound's loyalty; we were giving a prize for a book of poems."

On account of statements like this the Fellows have been accused of advancing the false principle that art is entirely separate from life. Those with whom I talked insisted that they had no such intention. To paraphrase what some of them said—for I cannot remember the exact words—they felt that too many second-rate authors had been given prizes for expressing the right opinions. We criticize the Russians—and rightly—for making their poets follow the party line; yet recently some American critics have been treating our own poets in the same fashion, demanding that they be wholesome, popular, and patriotic. The Fellows insisted that there are other virtues in literary works than those of the good citizen or the government official. Originality, learning, sharpness of image, purity of phrase, and a strict literary conscience: these are virtues, too, and they are present in Pound's work along with his contemptible politics. By giving him the prize, the Fellows said, they were defending "that objective perception of value on which any civilized society must rest."

After listening to their arguments, I am certain that the Fellows were trying hard to perform their double duty as citizens and men of letters. It is silly to accuse them of weaving plots and harboring dire motives. The real questions about their choice are literary rather than political; or rather the literary and the political questions are so intermingled that by answering the first we also answer the second. What we should ask is whether, in giving their prize to the *Pisan Cantos*, the Fellows were choosing the right ground on which to defend the objective perception of value. Under the stated terms of the award, do Pound's last Cantos represent "the highest achievement of American poetry" during the year 1948? If they fail to represent that achievement, then the Fellows were wrong by definition and the great arguments about poetry and treason, form and content, the new poets and the new criticism can all be deferred to a better occasion.

So let us consider the book, the author, and the curious position he occupies in the history of art in our time. For some thirty years after 1907 Pound was an explorer, a precursor, a discoverer of new moods and manners and critical standards. He exerted a decisive influence on the work of several authors greater than himself, including Yeats, Eliot, and Hemingway. And he continued to write, write in various fashions, classical, medieval, Japanese, and Mandarin, until he finally patched together a multilingual style of his own and accumulated an imposing body of work—imposing in its bulk and in the brilliant phrases scattered through it like sunbeams in a fog; and yet how much of it will survive?

My friends keep praising his Mauberley poems, first published in 1920; and I read them again last week with a good deal of admiration, it is true, but also with the feeling that they had inspired better poems by Eliot and E. E. Cummings. There are fine lyrics scattered through the rest of his work from beginning to end; but he usually spoils the lyrics by some intrusive gesture of pedantry or self-assertion, like an actor who insists on taking his bows before the play has ended. Spoiled work: that is the phrase for most of Pound's poems and I think for all the *Cantos*; they are never cheap or easy, never lacking in new phrases, but they are spoiled—and spoiled by vices that are inseparable from the virtues of his poetry; spoiled like the man himself by arrogance, crotchets, self-indulgence, obsessive hatreds, contempt for ordinary persons, the inability to see the world in motion (everything in Pound's poems is frozen, as in a gallery of broken plaster casts), and finally by a lack of constructive power that keeps him from building his separate perceptions into unified works of art.

Arrogance, crotchets, and self-indulgence are also the faults that mark his brief political career. Since his personality is the same in all fields, it is hard to draw a distinction between his art and his life, between the form and the content of his work or between his poetry and his politics. I confess to being less excited than others by the public implications of his disloyalty. The *London Times Literary Supplement* wasn't altogether frivolous when it said that his worst crime wasn't his broadcasts for Mussolini but his translations from Sextus Propertius. The broadcasts were silly and ineffective. They did not succeed in persuading American soldiers to desert or malinger—the GI's weren't even amused by his thirty-year-old American slang—nor can I believe that his antisemitic outbursts caused the death of a single Jew among the millions who perished. This brilliantly gifted man who had failed to become another Propertius or Ovid failed again in the role of Coriolanus; the spoiled great poet was also a spoiled traitor, despised and laughed at by his foreign masters. After being arrested by his own countrymen he was sent to a mental hospital without being granted the dignity of a public trial. It was the perfect retribution, a spoiled punishment for a spoiled crime.

The *Pisan Cantos* is the weakest of his books, the most crotchety and maundering. It contains two almost-fine lyrics, both spoiled by pedantry, and a third lyric of twenty lines that belongs with the best verse of our time:

> The ant's a centaur in his dragon world.
> Pull down thy vanity, it is not man
> Made courage, or made order, or made grace,
>   Pull down thy vanity, I say pull down.
> Learn of the green world what can be thy place . . .

That is superb, but there is not enough of it to redeem a disordered book of disordered observations, an old man's mutterings. In American poetry 1948 was not distinguished, but still it was the year when William Carlos Williams published the second long volume of his *Paterson*. Archibald MacLeish had a new book of poems, *Actfive*, and Peter Viereck a very lively first book. It seems to me that the *Pisan Cantos* was the worst of several possible choices; but my chief grievance against the Fellows is that by giving a prize to Pound they forced him back into the limelight, thus destroying the symmetry and perfect justice of his fate.

Against Hillyer one is justified in having other and more serious grievances. For thirty years he has been a poet and professor involved in many of the literary and academic struggles of his time. He regards Eliot and W. H. Auden as his poetic rivals and he has attacked them often, in articles that revealed an obsessed rage. Some of the "new critics" have been his academic rivals, at Harvard and now at Kenyon College, and he has battled with them, too. It would seem that his two articles in the *Saturday Review* are an attempt to carry this private warfare into a national or international field where all the issues become inflated and falsified.

Let us put his articles to the semantic test of seeing what courses of action he was advising, and to whom.

To Congress he was saying quite plainly, "Investigate the Bollingen Award and force T. S. Eliot to resign as a Fellow of the Library." Representative Jacob K. Javits (Rep., N.Y.) had no sooner read the articles than he demanded such an investigation. Eliot hasn't been asked to resign, a demand which would be a grave discourtesy, and the investigation seems to have been canceled; but the mere threat of it has forced the Library of Congress to withdraw the Bollingen Award, as well as two other annual prizes it had offered, for prints and chamber music. Historically this withdrawal is almost the end of the effort started when Archibald MacLeish was Librarian, to create a living relationship between the Library and the artists and writers of our time. So far as Hillyer is responsible for the retreat, I do not think that he should be proud.

But he had messages for others besides congressmen and government officials. Thus, he was saying to Paul Mellon and other wealthy men who had made or thought of making grants to encourage American writing, "Be careful, save your money, the *Saturday Review* is watching you." The Rockefeller Foundation has helped two of the literary quarterlies to pay fair rates to their contributors. Hillyer was telling the Foundation, in effect, "These quarterlies print the 'new critics,' who don't like my work and I'm sure are tainted with fascism. Don't renew their grants when they expire." Many of the universities have been adding poets and critics to their faculties. Hillyer seemed to be warning their boards of trustees, "Make sure that the poets and critics haven't read Eliot or I guarantee that you'll get into trouble."

Writers are like doctors and priests and judges in that they have a double duty, to the public and to the values of their own profession. With his muttered threats and his charges of a vast conspiracy, Hillyer has been false to both obligations. He has misled the public about the nature of an argument among poets and critics, while he has harmed all writers in his attempt to punish a few. Today there is a war in which the battle over Ezra Pound is merely an episode. The little American republic of letters is under attack by pretty much the same forces as those to which the Russian writers have already yielded: that is, by the people who prefer slogans to poetry and national self-flattery to honest writing. Hillyer has gone over to the enemy, like Pound in another war. Worsted in a struggle among his colleagues and compatriots, he has appealed over their heads and under false colors to the great hostile empire of the Philistines.

GAMMON FOR DINNER

> Well, that Sunday Albert was home, they had
>   a hot gammon,
> And they asked me in to dinner, to get the
>   beauty of it hot—
> HURRY UP PLEASE ITS TIME.
>
> *The Waste Land*

The beauty of it hot. . . . I hate to write about my own adventures and misadventures, but this time I'll set them down, because they belong to the record of American life in our time.

L'affaire Cowley started in the usual fashion, with the usual charges of communism and hints of terrific revelations to follow. Keep the termites out of our universities! Save our college girls! Granted the tragic background of this age and the fear just below the surface of our daily lives, it is curious that so much of the foreground should be occupied by outrageous farces and by episodes copied (wham, bing, zowie) from the comic strips. I don't see why one should waste one's time answering charges that aren't half believed by the chargers. I don't see why anyone accused of Communist activities should flatter the accusers by trying to hide or apologize for anything in his past career. When I heard in 1949 that there were going to be political protests against my appointment as Walker-Ames visiting lecturer at the University of Washington, I sent a long letter to the university about the radical organization I had joined in the 1930s, when Hitler was the enemy. If those past affiliations, I said, "will prove embarrassing to the university, it would be wisest to call off our arrangement now, and fast. I have plenty to do this winter without crossing the continent and I have absolutely no wish to be a victim or a martyr."

The university wired back, "Emphatically desire that you come," and I took the westbound train, though with some fear I was making a blunder. On one point I needn't have worried. The first or political campaign against the visiting lecturer had been advertised with eight-column front-page headlines in the local newspapers, but before I reached Seattle it had pretty well collapsed. The charges weren't impressive in themselves, I clearly wasn't a Communist and, since I had put my past activities on record, the newspapers had nothing left to reveal. But just before I took the train a second attack had started, and although the public heard less about it than about the first or political attack, it proved to be much more serious.

The second or literary attack was based on the argument that the visiting lecturer was unfit to be heard by students at the University of Washington because he had written immoral poems. When I first heard the charge I thought it was preposterous. It was as if I was being given a course in British cookery: after a teatime dish of gooseberry fool they were serving me gammon for dinner: gammon in its secondary sense of "Humbug, deception; (int.) nonsense!"

The beauty of it hot. . . . I had been writing poems for thirty years and most of them had appeared in magazines of general circulation. To the best of my knowledge nobody had ever written a letter to the editor asserting that one of my poems was immoral. Many of them had been reprinted in various anthologies for school and college use. I hadn't ever heard that a teacher complained because her pupils were encouraged to read them. Most of the poems were collected in one or another of two volumes of verse I published, in 1929 and 1941. The press-clipping bureaus had supplied me with copies of all the reviews and I didn't remember one of them that used such words as immorality or indecency. When I heard that such words were being used in Seattle I was amazed and said that people who thought the poems were immoral must live at a very high altitude, where water boils at a low temperature. But that was before I learned how carefully the second attack had been planned and how secretly it had been carried out. There was a moment, they told me, when the attackers had been very close to success.

So far as I have been able to get behind the midnight cloak of anonymity and secrecy that surrounded the attack, here is the story of the battle that was nearly won by the wrong side.

With the political campaign against the visiting lecturer on the point of collapsing, some person or group decided that he or they could still win the holy war by digging a mine beneath the enemy trenches. As painful as the experience must have been for him, a certain gentleman decided or was deputed to dig his way through my books with pick and shovel and miner's lantern. The notion was that he would find seditious or subversive statements that could be used as high explosives to blow a breach in my walls, or breeches. There were of course no such statements to be found. But the gentleman who excavated my books—we might call him Albert because that isn't his name—discovered something else he thought could be used against me. Albert found a dirty word; to be more accurate he found eight or ten words he thought were dirty; and he hurried back to his office with these trophies from his travels underground (Rowley, Cowley, gammon and spinach).

Now he was ready to proceed with the attack. The first step, so I gather, was to ask his blushing stenographer to copy out the lines in which the dirty words occurred. The second step was to prepare a document—not a very long one—containing all the lines or stanzas from my poems which Albert regarded as being immoral or offensive. The third step was to distribute the document, under pledge of secrecy, to the officers of patriotic organizations and civic groups, including among others the American Legion, the Veterans of Foreign Wars, the Daughters of the American Revolution, the Council of Churches, and the Parent Teachers Association. The fourth and final step was to tip off the newspapers and ask them if they didn't want to get statements from the official persons who had seen the documents. The newspapers did, and a few but by no means all of the official persons were willing to make statements without giving the defense a chance to reply.

I don't know how and will probably never learn why Albert, as we have called the anonymous gentleman, went to such pains to make trouble for someone he had never seen. It would take more conceit than I possess to think that Malcolm Cowley was important enough to justify this planned campaign; and so I assume that the real aims were those of some local struggle for political preferment, in which the poisoned arrows directed at me were also supposed to hit some other target. Albert himself was running no risk. Staying in the background, discreetly masked, he was expecting patriotic and civic organizations to rush into the breach for him, scale the crumbling walls, and return to Albert with the head of the visiting lecturer.

And the scheme might have worked. The beauty of it was that there was only one defense against Albert's by now pretty famous document, which incidentally I have never been allowed to see. Friends on the university staff who have been permitted to steal a surreptitious glance at it tell me that it left its readers with the impression that *Blue Juniata* and *The Dry Season* combined in themselves all the outstanding qualities of Petronius, Aretino, Casanova, the Marquis de Sade, and the *Memoirs of Fanny Hill*. I find that very hard to believe, and yet I know that the method of quotation out of context can be used to misrepresent the opinions of anyone who ever published a line of verse or prose. Merely by leaving out the right words and replacing them with asterisks, even *Mother Goose* has been transformed into a collection of salacious poems.

The one defense against the anonymous gentleman's method of partial quotation and misquotation was to have people read the poems as a whole. For several days, however, that defense was impossible in the case of the visiting lecturer. Except for the library copies, which Albert kept hidden in his office, there was apparently not a single copy of *Blue Juniata* or *The Dry Season* to be found in Seattle; and to make the problem still more difficult, the books were out of print. Finally the university managed to find copies of both volumes at the University of California library. As soon as they had been read by Robert B. Heilman, the head of the English department, he was able to visit the various organizations circularized by the gentleman, read them the poems as a whole instead of quoting single lines, and convince them that the two books were not in the least immoral. Thanks to Mr. Heilman what might have been a tragic drama, with corpses, ended for me in good-natured comedy.

The gammon was too hot and Albert burned his fingers when he tried to eat with them. I have been told on good authority that he was scolded by some of the political powers in the state for actions that might have seriously damaged the university. For the moment Albert is quiet. The visiting lecturer is safely home in Connecticut, but the situation in retrospect seems to him rather less comic than it did in

Seattle. In spite of burning his fingers Albert found the effective method for attacking any writer who is asked to serve on a university staff: read his books, take a few words or phrases out of context, distribute them to the right organizations, and wham, bing, zowie! During the past few years there has been a movement toward bringing the academic world and the literary world closer together, but Albert's method could put a stop to that—unless every move toward suppression is fought as successfully as this recent one at the University of Washington. In our age of suspicion and intolerance we need more voices speaking for decency (not merely of language), good manners, and good sense. HURRY UP PLEASE ITS TIME.

SOME DANGERS TO AMERICAN WRITING

While reading the special number of the *London Times Literary Supplement* devoted to "American Writing: Its Independence and Vigour," I kept thinking of one subject that wasn't mentioned in a collection of thoughtful essays. Almost all the anonymous contributors spoke graciously, if they were English—or proudly, if they were Americans—about our literary achievements of the last fifty years. None of them made what should have been an obvious statement: that American writing, or at least American authorship, is now more precisely threatened than at any other time in the century.

An earlier situation has been reversed. We used to think that the literary present mightn't be brilliant, but that great things were surely on the way. Now we look backward instead of forward with assurance, to a brilliant period that began after the First World War. We suspect that the period is ending or has ended and our new uncertainties are about the future.

The uncertainties aren't caused by a feeling that the new generation is wanting in talent. One hears of many gifted writers now in their twenties or early thirties; the question is whether still younger writers—and readers too—are being trained to take their places. The question is also whether the talent will be strong enough to resist the dangers that threaten from several directions. At present the dangers are intermingled, but they might be distinguished as political, social, academic and (in the narrow sense) educational. I propose to discuss each of them briefly, without paying much attention to the hopeful tendencies that are also present. Sometimes it is useful to look at the darker side of a situation; at least we know then what we have to fight.

The political danger to American writing is connected with the loyalty crusade, which has led to some curious activities in or against the literary world. Since many of these have been reported at length in the press, I can be excused for not talking about such familiar matters as the purge of American overseas libraries, the investigations into private opinions and family relationships, the blacklisting of many writers by the entertainment industries, the often successful attempts to censor books (or rather authors, since the books are usually attacked without being read), the denials of passports to various writers, and the denials of visas to distinguished foreigners like Graham Greene. There are, however, some aspects of the loyalty crusade that haven't received enough attention.

It hasn't been sufficiently explained that finding and exposing subversives, or possible subversives, has become a flourishing new profession, one that employs thousands of ambitious men. How many thousands would be hard to say, but—counting all the government, semipublic, and private organizations in the field, not to mention the free-lance operatives—there must be many more investigators than there are open or secret Communists. The more suspects that each investigator finds, the better his chances for professional advancement.

The writing trade has become a favorite object of suspicion. Authors can be investigated without tedious travels and interviews, merely by going to the nearest public library. If authors have questionable opinions, they are likely to put them into books, and the books can be used against them after twenty or thirty years. The result is that authorship has become a dangerous profession for public servants and candidates for public office. Even the reading habit is sometimes regarded with suspicion, unless the reader confines himself to detective stories and the right magazines. There was a time when more books per capita were sold in Washington than in any other American city; that was before the loyalty crusade.

Besides discouraging some writers, and apparently many readers, the crusade has affected three or four specialized branches of American authorship. Radio and television writing has patently suffered from losing most of its few original craftsmen to the blacklist (while the others have learned to be cautious). Motion-picture writing has lately improved, but only after some years of abject dullness. The crusade has also affected American sociology, once a field for brilliant researches;

of recent years most sociologists have been writing about subjects guaranteed to be uncontroversial, in a style that seems deliberately calculated to frighten away the intelligent but unspecialized reader. That same reader is being given few books on international affairs, at a time when good ones are desperately needed. With a few exceptions, new books in the field seem to be more timid or conventional in their ideas than most of the "think books"—as we used to call them—that appeared in the thirties and forties.

The social danger to American writing is the atmosphere of anti-intellectualism that has spread over the country. In some of its aspects it is a product of the loyalty crusade and of the effort to discredit the New Deal. Politicians argue that the New Deal was a creation of the long-hairs, the do-gooders, the eggheads, that they tried to impose a foreign pattern on the country ("a blueprint for socialism"), that they were sympathetic with Russian aims, and that they should all be turned out of their jobs, whatever the jobs might be. Senator Jenner said in Congress, "Let them earn their living as dishwashers or ditch diggers."

We can take for granted that the President doesn't agree with Senator Jenner, but he too made a point of attacking "so-called intellectuals." Mr. Eisenhower or his speech writers must have been sure that the attack would be well received by his radio audience. That is the most disturbing feature of anti-intellectualism in the 1950s—not its manifestations in official life (as when the head of a government bureau is warned "not to hire too many Ph.D.'s"), but its popularity in the country at large.

Some of its effects are evident in television, where book and information programs have been disappearing one by one. Other effects are displayed in the public schools, which are the mirror of popular ideals for the next generation. Gifted pupils used to be pushed ahead by their teachers and admired by most of their classmates (though with an undertone of distrust). Now, in many schools, they are forbidden to make more progress than the duller members of their age groups; nobody skips a grade or gets left behind. They used to distinguish themselves by making high marks, but now, in many school systems, marks have been abolished. The bright pupil is made to feel ashamed of being a "brain." The new ideal is the all-around boy, universally liked, perhaps a little weak in grammar and general knowledge, but a good dancer and dater and salesman of himself.

In the pre-literary world, a special manifestation of this atmosphere is the decline of high-school journalism. Every big high school used to have its printed newspaper or literary magazine; often it had both. Now, in many big schools, there is no publication edited by students, not even a mimeographed bulletin; interest seems to be lacking, and sometimes ability. College literary magazines have also declined in importance; many of the monthlies have become quarterlies or yearbooks or have disappeared; some were suppressed by the college administration. At Harvard, which doesn't practice censorship, there used to be two literary magazines, one a fortnightly, which between them published some twenty-five issues in the college year; now there is one litarary magazine, Mother *Advocate*, which publishes six issues. As at many other colleges, young writers are losing the valuable experience of being published and read by their contemporaries.

The economic danger to American writing is the slow crisis in bookselling and publishing. Largely the crisis is due to the decline of the best-selling novel, which used to be the staple of the book trade. Most books lose money for their publishers, but novels with a sale of more than a hundred thousand copies in hard covers earn a large profit, which the publisher uses to support his other activities. There have been few novels since 1947 with a bookstore sale in the hundreds of thousands. Some novels have sold millions in softcover reprints, but they didn't yield much, comparatively speaking, to the original publishers, and they did nothing to support the bookstores.

I never expected to find myself writing in defense of best-selling novels. Formerly I pointed out that many of them were honest books, but that others were meretricious and helped to debauch the public taste. Now I remember that all of them, including *Forever Amber*, helped to support the writing profession at many levels. They attracted customers to the bookstores, and many of the customers also bought less popular books. They made it possible for publishers to subsidize young writers and issue many books of limited circulation. They paid for publishers' advertising, which helped to keep bookreview pages and scholarly magazines alive.

People have been talking about the decline of book reviewing, which is a noticeable phenomenon of the last two years. It isn't a decline in the talent or training or good will of individual reviewers; chiefly the phenomenon is economic. Publishers without best-sellers on their lists haven't been able to spend so much for advertising. Many newspapers and magazines, warned by their accounting departments, have begun to devote less space to books, besides getting rid of some reviewers and piling more work on the others. From an economic point of view, the literary profession is interdependent at all its levels. Serious and experimental books have been receiving less attention because best-sellers haven't been selling.

Unable to support themselves by writing books, many authors have been taking refuge in the universities, and that too might prove to be a danger to American writing. I would be the last to censure authors for earning their livings as best they can. University teaching is better than washing dishes or digging ditches or writing speeches for illiterate Congressmen; it is a respected and self-respecting profession that grants some leisure for literary work. The alliance between writing and teaching has produced some promising results, notably a new school of analytical criticism and a quantity of poems, many of which deserve to be more widely read. It has also produced many novels written with patient attention to critical principles. If I say that it is a danger, that is because I am thinking of what might happen if some present tendencies were carried to extremes—as everything seems to be carried in this country of extremes.

One tendency is for learning to be emphasized at the expense of invention and imagination. The scholar-writer turns his attention to the past. He analyzes Conrad and Joyce in order to explain how they produced their special effects and he learns how these can be reproduced in his own work and that of his students, but he is often less concerned with producing new effects—even though they may be needed to express his own sense of life. Another tendency is for criticism to assume a greater importance than fiction or poetry. Still another is for the scholar-writer to lose the sense of addressing a broad audience with varied types of experience; he begins to talk—as the sociologists and some of the new critics already do—in the narrow jargon of his craft. His novels, if he continues to write them, are likely to deal with narrow themes, so as not to betray his ignorance of the business world, the labor world, the political world. He lives and writes as part of a specialized bureaucracy.

But the greatest danger that threatens American writing is the decline of the reading habit, which has lately been especially noticeable in recruits to the armed forces and in new classes entering college. Among the many causes of the decline are illustrated comic books and television; we seem to be developing into a nation of lookers and listeners rather than readers. Perhaps a more central cause is the breakdown of public secondary education. Boys and girls are being graduated from high school without having been asked to read more than two or three paragraphs a week. Most of the less ambitious students—more than half of the senior class in some high schools—have never read a book from cover to cover.

But the decline in reading ability isn't confined to dullards and the indifferent. An Eastern university that chooses the best from a long list of candidates for admission gave a reading test to its students on two occasions, twenty-five years apart. The test showed that freshmen could read as well in 1925 as seniors in 1950. Other universities have found themselves teaching grammar, syntax, and remedial reading instead of literature. These are some aspects of a situation that has been disturbing not only the book trade but also magazine publishers and newspaper tycoons. It helps to explain why magazines are printing sensational stories about the American schools. One syndicated Sunday supplement has paid for an advertising campaign in favor of the written word, which "endures." It is as if the publisher were trying to delay the time at which writing and printing would cease to be the normal means of conveying ideas and sales messages.

The situation isn't so black as I have painted it. I have omitted all the hopeful elements, including the vitality of American writing and the ability it has shown to survive and develop in other hostile periods, such as the one that followed the Civil War. This country has always corrected its mistakes, often by going to the opposite extreme. Secondary education will be reformed once more; changes are already under way. The loyalty crusade will end some day, in spite of the individuals and institutions that would profit by extending it.

There is no assurance, however, that American writing will enter another brilliant period. Today for the first time we have to admit the possibility of a situation in which American writing would be confined to an elite of scholars, in which it would become as elaborate and dead as late-Roman writing, and in which the public would find its esthetic satisfactions in bang-bang gunsmoke on the television screen.

PART TWO

THE USABLE PAST

THE HAWTHORNES IN
PARADISE

There are only a few great love stories in American fiction, and there are fewer still in the lives of famous American writers. Nathaniel Hawthorne wrote one of the greatest, *The Scarlet Letter*. He also lived a story that deserves to be retold with all the new knowledge we can bring to bear on it—as long as there are lovers in New England; it was his courtship and conquest of Sophia Peabody. Unlike his first novel, the lived story was neither sinful nor tragic. Everything in the foreground was as softly glowing as a June morning in Salem, but there were shadows in the background and obstacles to be surmounted; among them were poverty, seemingly hopeless invalidism, conniving sisters, political intrigues, a silken temptress, a duel that might have been fought to the death, and inner problems more threatening than any of these. It was as if Hawthorne had needed to cut his way through a forest of thorns—some planted by himself—in order to reach the castle of Sleeping Beauty and waken her with a kiss, while, in the same moment, he wakened himself from a daylong nightmare.

When he first met Sophia, Hawthorne was thirty-three years old, and he had spent twelve of those years in a dreamlike seclusion. Day after day he sat alone in his room, writing or reading or merely watching a sunbeam as it bored through the blind and slowly traveled across the opposite wall. "For months together," he said long afterward, in a letter to the poet R. H. Stoddard, "I scarcely held human intercourse outside of my own family; seldom going out except at twilight, or only to take the nearest way to the most convenient solitude." He doubted whether twenty people in Salem even knew of his existence.

In remembering those years, Hawthorne sometimes pictured his solitude as being more nearly absolute than it had been. There were social moments even then. Every summer he took a long trip on his Manning uncles' stagecoach lines and "enjoyed as much of life," he said, "as other people do in the whole year's round." In Salem he made some whist-playing acquaintances and learned a little about the intricacies of Democratic party politics. He had a college friend, Horatio Bridge, of Augusta, Maine, to whom he wrote intimate letters, and Bridge was closely connected with two rising political figures, also Democrats and college friends of Hawthorne's, Congressman Jonathan Cilley of Maine, and Franklin Pierce, the junior senator from New Hampshire. All three were trying to advance Hawthorne's career, and Bridge had rescued him from complete obscurity by guaranteeing a publisher against loss and thereby inducing him to issue the first book with Hawthorne's name on it, *Twice-Told Tales.*

After the book appeared in the early spring of 1837, its author made some mild efforts to emerge into Salem society, where the young ladies admired him for his courtesy, his deep-set eyes—so blue they were almost black—and his air of having a secret life. He thought of marriage and even fancied himself in love that spring, as Romeo did before meeting Juliet, but his courtship of a still-unidentified woman was soon broken off. Hawthorne was beginning to fear that he would never be able to rejoin the world of living creatures. His true solitude was inward, not outward, and he had formed the habit of holding long conversations with himself, like a lonely child. His daylong nightmare was of falling into a morbid state of self-absorption that would make everything unreal in his eyes, even himself. "None have understood it," says one of his heroes, Gervayse Hastings of "The Christmas Banquet," who might be speaking for the author, "—not even those who experience the like. It is a chilliness—a want of earnestness—a feeling as if what should be my heart were a thing of vapor—a haunting perception of unreality! . . . All things, all persons . . . have been like shadows flickering on the wall." Then putting his hand on his heart, he says, "Mine—mine is the wretchedness! This cold heart . . ."

Sophia Amelia Peabody, five years younger than Hawthorne, never suffered from self-absorption or an icy heart, but she had a serious trouble of her own. A pretty rather than a beautiful woman, with innocent gray eyes set wide apart, a tiptilted nose, and a mischievous smile, she had beaux attending her whenever she appeared in society: the trouble was that she could seldom appear. When Sophia was fifteen, she had begun to suffer from violent headaches. Her possessive mother explained to her that suffering was woman's peculiar lot, having something to do with the sin of Eve. Her ineffectual father had her treated by half the doctors in Boston, who prescribed, among other remedies, laudanum, mercury, arsenic, hyoscyamus, homeopathy, and hypnotism, but still the headaches continued. Once as a desperate expedient she was sent to Cuba, where she spent two happy years on a plantation while her quiet sister Mary tutored the planter's children. Now, back in Salem with the family—where her headaches were always worse—she was spending half of each day in bed. Like all the Peabody women, she had a New England conscience and a firm belief in the True, the Beautiful, and the Transcendental. She also had a limited but genuine talent for painting. When she was strong enough, she worked hard at copying pictures—and the copies sold—or at painting romantic landscapes of her own.

Sophia had been cast by her family in a role from which it seemed unlikely that she would ever escape. Just as Elizabeth Peabody was the intellectual sister, already famous as an educational reformer, and Mary was the quiet sister who did most of the household chores, Sophia was the invalid sister, petted like a child and kept in an upstairs room. There were also three brothers, one of them married, but the Peabodys were a matriarchy and a sorority; nobody paid much attention to the Peabody men. It was written that when the mother died, Sophia would become the invalid aunt of her brother's children; she would support herself by painting lampshades and firescreens, while enduring her headaches with a brave smile. As for Hawthorne, his fate was written too; he would become the cranky New England bachelor, living in solitude and writing more and more nebulous stories about other lonely souls. But they saved each other, those two unhappy children. Each was the other's refuge, and they groped their way into each other's arms, where both found strength to face the world.

2

It was Elizabeth, the intellectual sister, who first brought them together, unthinkingly, in a moment of triumph for herself. She had long admired a group of stories, obviously by one author, that had been appearing anonymously in the annual editions of a gift book, *The Token*, and in the *New England Magazine*. Now she learned that the author was a Salem neighbor. Always eager to inspire a new genius, she made patient efforts to inveigle him into the Peabody house on Charter Street, with its square windows looking over an old burying ground where Peabodys and Hathornes—as the name used to be spelled— were sleeping almost side by side. She even took the bold step of paying several visits to the Hawthorne house on Herbert Street, known as "Castle Dismal," where nobody outside the family had dared to come for years.

Usually she was received by Hawthorne's younger sister, Louisa, who, Miss Peabody said disappointedly, was "quite like everybody else." The older sister, Elizabeth—usually called Ebe—was known with good reason as "the hermitess," but she finally consented to take a walk with her enterprising neighbor. Madam Hawthorne, the mother, stayed in her room as always, and Nathaniel was nowhere to be seen. He did, however, send Miss Peabody a presentation copy of his book, and she replied by suggesting some journalistic work that he had no intention of doing. Then, on the evening of November 11, 1837, came her moment of triumph. Elizabeth was sitting in the parlor, looking at a five-volume set of Flaxman's classical engravings that she had just been given by Professor Felton of Harvard, when she heard a great ring at the front door.

"There stood your father," she said half a century later in a letter to her nephew Julian Hawthorne, "in all the splendor of his young beauty and a hooded figure hanging on each arm." The figures were Louisa and Ebe. Miss Peabody bustled them into the parlor and set them to looking at Flaxman's illustrations for *The Iliad*. Then she ran upstairs to the invalid's room and said, "Oh, Sophia, Mr. Hawthorne and his sisters have come, and you never saw anything so splendid— he is handsomer than Lord Byron! You must get up and dress and come down. We have Flaxman too."

Sophia laughed and said, "I think it would be rather ridiculous to get up. If he has come once he will come again."

A few days later he came again, this time in the afternoon. "I summoned your mother," Miss Peabody said in the same letter, and she came down in her simple white wrapper, and glided in at the back door and sat down on the sofa. As I said, "My sister, Sophia—Mr. Hawthorne," he rose and looked at her—he did not realize how intently, and afterwards, as we went on talking, she would interpose frequently a remark in her low sweet voice. Every time she did so, he looked at her with the same intentness of interest. I was struck with it, and painfully. I thought, what if he should fall in love with her. . . .

Miss Peabody explained why that was a painful thought: it was because "I had heard her so often say, nothing would ever tempt her to marry, and inflict upon a husband the care of such a sufferer." But there was an unspoken reason too, for it is clear from other letters that Elizabeth Peabody wanted Nathaniel Hawthorne for herself. Whether she hoped to marry him we cannot be sure, but there is no question that she planned to become his spiritual guide, his literary counselor, his muse and Egeria.

Sophia had no such clear intentions. She told her children long afterward that Hawthorne's presence exerted a magnetic attraction on her from the beginning, and that she instinctively drew back in self-defense. The power she felt in him alarmed her; she did not understand what it meant. By degrees her resistance was overcome, and she came to realize that they had loved each other at first sight. . . . That was Sophia's story, and Hawthorne did not contradict her. There is some doubt, however, whether he told her about everything that happened during the early months of their acquaintance.

3

What followed their first meeting was a comedy of misunderstandings with undertones of tragedy. Hawthorne was supposed to be courting Elizabeth—Miss Peabody, as she was called outside the household: *the* Miss Peabody, as if she had no sisters. There was a correspondence between them. In one of her missives—and that is the proper word for them—she warned Hawthorne that her invalid sister would never marry. His answer has been lost, but Miss Peabody quoted him as saying, "Sophia is a rose to be worn in no man's bosom." Satisfied on this point, she advised him to study German, write books for children, and have no truck with Democratic politicians. She liked to think of him as an otherworldly genius who might save the soul of America, if only he would read the German philosophers in the original. Hawthorne obediently studied German, but he did not take kindly to advice about his personal affairs, and Miss Peabody went off to West Newton to live with her married brother. While she was there, Sophia wrote her a series of letters. Most of them mentioned Mr. Hawthorne, more and more warmly, but Sophia maintained the pretense that her interest in him was intellectual, or at most sisterly, and that he was still Elizabeth's suitor. Meanwhile Hawthorne himself was secretly involved with a Salem heiress.

The story of his involvement, and of the duel to which it nearly led, was told in some detail by Julian Hawthorne in his biography of his parents. Unfortunately Julian did not give names (except "Mary" and "Louis") or offer supporting evidence. Poor Julian, who was sometimes irresponsible, has never been trusted by scholars, and the result is that later biographers of Hawthorne either questioned the story or flatly rejected it. Norman Holmes Pearson of Yale, who was preparing a definitive edition of Hawthorne's letters, discovered an interesting document in the Morgan Library. He wrote an article about it for the *Essex Institute*'s quarterly, one for which other scholars stand in his debt. The article was a memorandum by Julian on a conversation with Miss Peabody, one in which she described the whole affair, giving names and circumstances and supporting Julian's story at almost every point. She even explained by implication why the principal figures in the story had to be anonymous. Two of them were still living in 1884, when Julian's book was published, and one of them was the widow of a president of Harvard.

Her name when Hawthorne knew her was Mary Crowninshield Silsbee, and she was the daughter of former United States Senator Nathaniel Silsbee, a great man in New England banking and shipping. Julian says that she was completely unscrupulous, but admits that she had "a certain kind of glancing beauty, slender, piquant, ophidian, Armida-like." Armida—in Tasso's *Jerusalem Delivered*—was a heathen sorceress, daughter of the king of Damascus, who lured the boldest of the Crusaders into her enchanted garden. Mary Silsbee exercised her lures on the brilliant young men she met in her travels between Salem and Washington. One of them was John Louis O'Sullivan of Washington, who was laying ambitious plans for a new magazine to be called the *Democratic Review*.

The young editor was a friend of Hawthorne's classmate Jonathan Cilley, the rising congressman from Maine. Cilley had given him a copy of *Twice-Told Tales* as soon as the book appeared. O'Sullivan was impressed by it and wrote to the author soliciting articles at the generous rate, for the time, of five dollars a page. He also told Miss Silsbee about Hawthorne. Fascinated by O'Sullivan's picture of a mysterious Salem genius, Armida at once determined, Julian says, "to add him to her museum of victims."

Her method of operation was to cast herself on Hawthorne's mercy by revealing what she told him were the secrets of her inmost soul. She read him long and extremely private passages from her diary—"all of which," Julian says, "were either entirely fictitious, or such bounteous embroideries on the bare basis of reality, as to give what was mean and sordid an appearance of beauty and a winning charm." Hawthorne, who had never considered the possibility that a Salem young lady might be a gratuitous liar, began to regard himself as Miss Silsbee's protector and champion. But he disappointed her by offering none of his own confidences in return.

She tried a new stratagem. Early in February 1838, she summoned Hawthorne to a private and mysterious interview. With a great deal of calculated reluctance she told him that his friend O'Sullivan, "presuming upon her innocence and guilelessness"—as Julian tells the story—"had been guilty of an attempt to practise the basest treachery upon her; and she passionately adjured Hawthorne, as her only confidential and trusted friend and protector, to champion her cause." Hawthorne promptly wrote a letter to O'Sullivan, then in Washington, and challenged him to a duel. The letter has disappeared, but there is another to Horatio Bridge written on February 8—possibly the same day—in which he speaks darkly of a rash step he has just taken.

O'Sullivan must have discussed the challenge with their friend Jonathan Cilley; then he wrote a candid and friendly letter to Hawthorne refusing the challenge. But he did more than that; he made a hurried trip to Salem and completely established his innocence of the charge against him. Although Hawthorne could scarcely bring himself to believe that Miss Silsbee had made an utter fool of him, he had to accept the evidence. In Miss Peabody's words, he called on Armida and "crushed her."

To this point the story had been a comedy, or even a farce, but it soon had a tragic sequel on the national scene. In 1838 the House of Representatives was equally divided between conservatives and radicals, not to mention the other division between southerners and northern antislavery men. Jonathan Cilley was a rising leader among the radical free-soil Democrats, and there are some indications that his political enemies had decided to get rid of him. On a flimsy pretext, he was challenged to a duel by a fire-eating southern congressman, William J. Graves of Kentucky. He was still hesitating whether to accept the challenge when somebody said to him—according to Julian's story—"If Hawthorne was so ready to fight a duel without stopping to ask questions, you certainly need not hesitate." Horatio Bridge denied this part of the story, but there is no doubt that Hawthorne considered himself partly responsible for what followed. The duel, fought with rifles at ninety yards, took place on the afternoon of February 24. After the first exchange of shots, and again after the second, Cilley's second tried to effect a reconciliation, but Graves and his second both declined. Cilley said "They thirst for my blood." On the third exchange, he was hit in the body and fell dying.

Hawthorne brooded over the duel for a long time. His memorial of Cilley, which was among the first of his many contributions to the *Democratic Review*, reads as if he were making atonement to the shade of his friend. In a somewhat later story, "The Christmas Banquet," from which I have quoted already, he describes a collection of the world's most miserable persons. One of them is

> a man of nice conscience, who bore a blood stain in his heart—the death of a fellow-creature—which, for his more exquisite torture, had chanced with such a peculiarity of circumstances, that he could not absolutely determine whether his will had entered into

the deed or not. Therefore, his whole life was spent in the agony of an inward trial for murder.

Julian's story would lead us to believe that Hawthorne, once again, was thinking of himself.

4

There were other causes for worry in those early months of 1838, when Hawthorne was still supposed to be courting Sophia's intellectual sister. One of the chief causes was Mary Silsbee, who refused to let him go. Miss Peabody's memorandum says that Mary somehow "managed to renew relations with him," and that she then offered to marry him as soon as he was earning $3,000 a year, a large income for the time. Hawthorne answered that he never expected to have so much. When his sister Ebe heard the story, she remarked—according to Miss Peabody—"that he would never marry at all, and that he would never *do* anything; that he was an ideal person." But Hawthorne did something to end the affair; he disappeared from Salem.

Before leaving town on July 23, he paid what was known as a take-leave call on Sophia. "He said he was not going to tell any one where he should be for the next three months," she told Elizabeth in a letter: "that he thought he should change his name, so that if he died no one would be able to find his gravestone. . . . I feel as if he were a born brother. I never, hardly, knew a person for whom I had such a full and at the same time perfectly quiet admiration." Then, suspecting that she had gone too far, she added, "I do not care about seeing him often: but I delight to remember that *he is*." It was as near as she could come to telling Elizabeth that she was already in love.

At the end of September when Hawthorne came back to Salem—from North Adams, his mysterious hiding place—Miss Silsbee had disappeared from his life. She had renewed her acquaintance with another suitor, now a widower of forty-nine with an income well beyond her minimum requirement; he was Jared Sparks, the editor of George Washington's papers, who would become president of Harvard. Hawthorne now had more time to spend at the house on Charter Street. He was entertained by whichever sister happened to be present, or by all three together, but it began to be noticed that his visits were longer if he found Sophia alone. One day she showed him an illustration she had drawn, in the Flaxman manner, for his story, "The Gentle Boy." It showed the boy asleep under the tree on which his Quaker father had been hanged.

"I want to know if this looks like your Ilbrahim," she said.

Hawthorne said, meaning every word, "He will never look otherwise to me."

Under the Peabody influence, he was becoming almost a social creature. There was a sort of literary club that met every week in one of the finest houses on Chestnut Street, where the Salem merchants lived. The house belonged to Miss Susan Burley, a wealthy spinster who liked to patronize the arts. Hawthorne was persuaded to attend some of Miss Burley's Saturday evenings—usually as an escort for Mary or Elizabeth, since the invalid sister was seldom allowed to venture into the night air. There was one particularly cold evening when Sophia insisted that she was going to Miss Burley's whether or not she was wanted. Hawthorne laughed and said she was not wanted: the cold would make her ill. "Meanwhile," Sophia reported in a letter, "I put on an incalculable quantity of clothes. Father kept remonstrating, but not violently, and I gently imploring. When I was ready, Mr. Hawthorne said he was glad I was going. . . . We walked quite fast, for I seemed stepping on air."

The evening at Miss Burley's marked a change in their relations. From that time Sophia began taking long walks with Mr. Hawthorne in spite of the winter gales. Elizabeth was busy with her affairs in Boston, and Mary, the quiet sister, looked on benevolently. Sophia never felt tired so long as she could hold Mr. Hawthorne's arm. It was during one of their walks, on a snowy day just before or after New Year's, 1839, that they confessed their love for each other. Clinging together like children frightened of being so happy, they exchanged promises that neither of them would break. They were married now "in the sight of God," as old-fashioned people used to say, and as Hawthorne soon told Sophia in slightly different words, but that was a secret they would keep to themselves for a long time to come.

5

In the middle of January Hawthorne went to work as a weigher and gauger for the Boston Custom House. It was a political appointment made by the collector of the port, who was George Bancroft, the historian. Hawthorne had been recommended to him by several influential persons, including Miss Peabody, who may have hoped to get him out of Salem. Bancroft justified the appointment to Washington by writing that Hawthorne was "the biographer of Cilley," and thus a deserving Democrat. Cilley again. . . . It was as if the college friend for whose death Hawthorne felt responsible had reached out of the grave to help him. Many other deserving Democrats had sought for the post, but it was not a sinecure, and he worked as hard as Jacob did for Rachel, while saving half his salary of $1,500 a year. Every other Saturday he took the cars to Salem and spent an evening with Sophia. On the Saturdays in Boston he sent her a long letter, sometimes written in daily installments.

"What a year the last has been!" he wrote on January 1, 1840. ". . . It has been the year of years—the year in which the flower of our life has bloomed out—the flower of our life and of our love, which we are to wear in our bosoms forever." Three days later he added,

> Dearest, I hope you have not found it impracticable to walk, though the atmosphere be so wintry. Did we walk together in any such weather, last winter? I believe we did. How strange, that such a flower as our affection should have blossomed amid snow and wintry winds—accompaniments which no poet or novelist, that I know of, has ever introduced into a love-tale. Nothing like our story was ever written—or ever will be—for we shall not feel inclined to make the public our confidant; but if it could be told, me-thinks it would be such as the angels might delight to hear.

As a matter of fact, Hawthorne wrote the story from day to day, in that series of heartfelt letters to Sophia, and the New England angels would delight to read them. It is true that the tone of them is sometimes too reverent for the worldly taste of our century. "I always feel," Hawthorne says in July 1839, "as if your letters were too sacred to be read in the midst of people, and (you will smile) I never read them without first washing my hands." We also smile, but in a different spirit from Sophia's. We feel a little uncomfortable on hearing the pet names with which he addresses her, almost all superlatives: "Dearissima," "mine ownest love," "Blessedest," "ownest Dove," "best, beautifullest, belovedest, blessingest of wives." It is confusing to find that he calls her "mine own wife," and himself "your husband" or "thy husband," for three years before the actual marriage. His use of "thee" and "thou" in all the letters written after March 1840, though it reveals his need for deeper intimacy of expression, still gives an archaic look to the writing. But the feelings expressed are not in the least archaic; they are those of a restrained but passionate man, truly in love for the first and last time, and gifted with an extraordinary talent for self-awareness.

Long afterward Sophia, then a widow, tried to delete the passion before she permitted the letters to be read by others. She scissored out some of the dangerous passages, and these are gone forever. Others she inked out carefully, and most of these have been restored by the efforts of Randall Stewart—the most trustworthy biographer of Hawthorne—and the staff of the Huntington Library. They show that Hawthorne was less of an other-worldly creature than Miss Peabody pictured him as being. "Mine own wife," he says in one of the inked-out passages (November 1839), "what a cold night this is going to be! How I am to keep warm, unless you nestle close, close into my bosom, I do not by any means understand—not but what I have clothes enough on my mattress—but a husband cannot be comfortably warm without his wife." There is so much talk of beds and bosoms that some have inferred, after reading the restored text, that Hawthorne and Sophia were lovers for a long time before their marriage—and most of these readers thought no worse of them. But the records show that this romantic notion has to be dismissed. Much as Hawthorne wanted Sophia, he also wanted to observe the scriptural laws of love. "Mr. Hawthorne's passions were under his feet," Miss Peabody quoted Sophia as saying. If he had made Sophia his mistress, he would have revered her less, and he would have despised himself.

"I have an awe of you," he wrote her, "that I never felt for anybody else. Awe is not the word, either, because it might imply something stern in you; whereas—but you must make it out for yourself. . . . I suppose I should have pretty much the same feeling if an angel were to come from Heaven and be my dearest friend. . . . And then it is singular, too," he added with his Salem obduracy, "that this awe (or whatever it is) does not prevent me from feeling that it is I who have charge of you, and that my Dove is to follow my guidance and do my bidding." He had no intention of submitting to the Peabody matriarchs. "And will not you rebel?" he asked. "Oh, no; because I possess the power to guide you only so far as I love you. My love gives me the right, and your love consents to it."

Sophia did not rebel, but the Peabodys were confirmed idealists where Hawthorne was a realist, and sometimes she tried gently to bring him round to their higher way of feeling. Once she refused to kiss him good night because she had smelled a cigar on his breath. Another time she made the mistake of urging him to hear the famous Father Taylor, who preached to the sailors. "Dearest," he said,

> I feel somewhat afraid to hear this divine Father Taylor, lest my sympathy with thy admiration of him should be colder and feebler than thou lookest for. Belovedest wife, our souls are in happiest unison; but we must not disquiet ourselves if every tone be not reechoed from one to the other—if every slightest shade be not reflected in the alternate mirror. . . . I forewarn thee, sweetest Dove, that thy husband is a most unmalleable man; thou art not to suppose, because his spirit answers to every touch of thine, that therefore every breeze, or even every whirlwind, can upturn him from his depths.

But this conflict of wills is a minor note of comedy in the letters. In time Sophia learned to yield almost joyfully, not so much to Hawthorne's unmalleable nature as to his love. It is love that is the central theme of the letters—unquestioning love, and beneath it the sense of almost delirious gratitude that both of them felt for having been rescued from death-in-life. Sophia refused to worry about her health. "If God intends us to marry," she said to Hawthorne, "He will let me be cured; if not, it will be a sign that it is not best." She depended on love as her physician, and imperceptibly, year by year, the headaches faded away. As for Hawthorne, he felt an even deeper gratitude for having been rescued from the unreal world of self-absorption in which he had feared to be imprisoned forever. "Indeed, we are but shadows," he wrote to Sophia, "—we are not endowed with real life, and all that seems most real about us is but the thinnest substance of a dream— till the heart is touched. That touch creates us—then we begin to be. . . ." In the same letter he said:

> Thou only hast taught me that I have a heart—thou only hast thrown a deep light downward, and upward, into my soul. Thou only hast revealed me to myself; for without thy aid, my best knowledge of myself would have been merely to know my own shadow—to watch it flickering on the wall, and mistake its fantasies for my own real actions. . . . Now, dearest, dost thou comprehend what thou hast done for me?

His four novels, beginning with *The Scarlet Letter*, were written after his marriage and written because Sophia was there to read them. Not only Nathaniel Hawthorne but the world at large owes the gentle Sophia more than can be expressed.

6

When Miss Peabody was told of the engagement, after more than a year, she took the news bravely. Her consolation was that having Hawthorne as a brother-in-law might be almost as rewarding as having him for a husband; she could still be his Egeria. Not yet knowing how unmalleable he was, she still thought of forging him into the shape of her dream. Meanwhile she offered to serve as a secret courier and forward his letters to Salem. With Sophia's health improving, it was Hawthorne's inability to support a wife—especially a delicate wife who needed a servant in the household—that now seemed to be the chief remaining obstacle to the marriage.

The post in the Boston Custom House did not solve the problem. It left him with little time alone or energy for writing, and he could not be sure of keeping it after the next election. Hawthorne resigned at the end of 1840, a few months before he would have been dismissed—as were almost all his colleagues—by the victorious Whigs. After some hesitation he took a rash step, partly at the urging of Miss Peabody. He invested his Custom House savings in George Ripley's new community for intellectual farmers: Brook Farm. It was the last time he would accept her high-minded advice.

The dream was that Hawthorne would support himself by working in the fields only a few hours each day, and only in the summer; then he could spend the winter writing stories. He and Sophia would live in a cottage to be built on some secluded spot. Having bought two shares of stock in the community at $500 each—later he would lend Ripley $400 more—he arrived at Brook Farm in an April snowstorm. Sophia paid him a visit at the end of May. "My life—how beautiful is Brook Farm!" she wrote him on her return. ". . . I do not desire to conceive of a greater felicity than living in a cottage, built on one of those lovely sites, with thee." But Hawthorne, after working for six weeks on the manure pile—or gold mine, as the Brook Farmers called it—was already disillusioned. "It is my opinion, dearest," he wrote on almost the same day, "that a man's soul may be buried and perish under a dung-heap or in a furrow of the field, just as well as under a pile of money." By the middle of August he had decided to leave Brook Farm. "Thou and I must form other plans for ourselves," he told Sophia; "for I can see few or no signs that Providence purposes to give us a home here. I am weary, weary, thrice weary of waiting so many ages. Yet what can be done? Whatever may be thy husband's gifts, he has not hitherto shown a single one that may avail to gather gold."

"Thy husband" and "mine own wife" were drawing closer to marriage, simply because they had exhausted their vast New England patience. "Words cannot tell," Sophia had written, "how immensely my spirit demands thee. Sometimes I almost lose my breath in a vast heaving toward thy heart." Hawthorne, now vegetating in Salem—while the Peabodys were in Boston, where Elizabeth had opened a bookshop—was looking desperately for any sort of literary work. In March 1842, he went to Albany to see John Louis O'Sullivan, who was again editing the *Democratic Review*. On the strength of the promises that O'Sullivan was always ready to make, Hawthorne decided to wait no longer; he would try to support a wife on what he could earn as a writer. It was a bold decision for an age when American writers were miserably paid and when Poe, his principal rival, had never earned as much as $1,000 in one year.

The wedding was set for the last day of June. During a visit to the Emersons, Miss Peabody found a home for the young couple; it was the Ripley house in Concord, where the parson used to live. Hawthorne could no longer defer telling his family about the engagement, after keeping it secret for three years. Now at last it became evident that there was and had always been another obstacle to his marriage.

The final obstacle was his older sister, Ebe the hermitess. She adored her handsome brother and clung to him as her only link with the world. The stratagem she found for keeping him was to insist that their mother would die of shock if she learned that he was marrying an invalid. Hawthorne loved his mother, though he had never been able to confide in her. This time he finally took the risk. "What you tell me is not a surprise to me," Madam Hawthorne said, ". . . and Sophia Peabody is the wife of all others whom I would have chosen for you." When Ebe had recovered from her fury at hearing the news, she wrote Sophia a frigid letter of congratulation.

> Your approaching union with my brother [she said] makes it incumbent upon me to offer you the assurance of my sincere desire for your mutual happiness. With regard to my sister and myself, I hope nothing will ever occur to render your future intercourse with us other than agreeable, particularly as it need not be so frequent or so close as to require more than reciprocal good will.

There would be, in fact, no intercourse with Ebe. She retired to a farmhouse in Beverly, where she spent the rest of her long life reading in her room and walking on the shore.

Three weeks before the date set for the wedding, Sophia terrified everyone by taking to her bed. There was talk of an indefinite postponement. Fortunately a new doctor explained that it was nothing unusual for a bride to run a fever, and so another date was chosen: Saturday morning, July 9. It was a few days after Hawthorne's thirty-eighth birthday, while Sophia was almost thirty-three. At the wedding in the parlor behind Miss Peabody's bookshop, there were only two guests outside the immediate family. It started to rain as the bride came down the stairs, but then the sun broke through the clouds and shone directly into the parlor. Hawthorne and Sophia stepped into a carriage and were driven across the Charles River, along the old road through Cambridge and Lexington, into the Land of Eden.

7

And so they lived happily ever after? They lived happily for a time, but as always it came to an end, and the lovers too. For Hawthorne after twenty years of marriage, the end was near when he went feebly pacing up and down the path his feet had worn along the hillside behind his Concord house, while he tried to plan a novel that refused to be written. For Sophia the end was a desolate widowhood without the man who, she never ceased to feel, "is my world and all the business of it." But the marriage was happy to the end, and at the beginning of it, during their stay at the Old Manse, they enjoyed something far beyond the capacity of most lovers to experience: three years of almost unalloyed delight.

On the morning after their first night in the Old Manse, Hawthorne wrote to his younger sister, Louisa, the one who was quite like everybody else. "Dear Louse," he said affectionately, "The execution took place yesterday. We made a christian end, and came straight to Paradise, where we abide at the present writing." Sophia had the same message for her mother, although she expressed it more ecstatically. "It is a perfect Eden round us," she said. "Everything is as fresh as in first June. We are Adam and Eve and see no persons round! The birds saluted us this morning with such gushes of rapture, that I thought they must know us and our happiness." The Hawthornes at thirty-eight and thirty-three were like children again—like children exploring a desert island that every day revealed new marvels. Their only fear was that a ship might come to rescue them. Once the great Margaret Fuller wrote them and suggested that another newly married couple, her sister Ellen and Ellery Channing, might board with them at the Manse. Hawthorne sent her a tactful letter of refusal. "Had it been proposed to Adam and Eve," he said, "to receive two angels into their

Paradise, *as boarders*, I doubt whether they would have been altogether pleased to consent." The Hawthornes were left happily alone with Sarah the maid and Pigwiggin the kitten.

They were exercising a talent that most New Englanders never acquire, that of living not in the past or in dreams of the future, but in the moment itself, as if they were already in heaven. Sophia wrote letters each morning or painted in her studio, while Hawthorne worked meditatively in the garden that Henry Thoreau had planted for them. In the afternoon they explored the countryside together or rowed on the quiet river, picking waterlilies. Hawthorne wrote in his journal,

> My life, at this time, is more like that of a boy, externally, than it has been since I was really a boy. It is usually supposed that the cares of life come with matrimony; but I seem to have cast off all care, and live with as much easy trust in Providence, as Adam could possibly have felt, before he had learned that there was a world beyond his Paradise.

Sometimes they ran footraces down the lane, which Sophia grandly called "the avenue." Sometimes in the evening she wound the music box and, forgetting her Puritan training, danced wildly for her lover. "You deserve John the Baptist's head," he teased her. In the records of that time—there are many of them, and all a delight to read—there is only one hint of anything like a quarrel. It arose when one of their walks led them to an unmown hayfield. Hawthorne, who had learned about haying at Brook Farm, told Sophia not to cross it and trample the grass. "This I did not like very well and I climbed the hill alone," Sophia wrote in the journal they were keeping together.

> We penetrated the pleasant gloom and sat down upon a carpet of dried pine leaves. Then I clasped him in my arms in the lovely shade, and we laid down a few moments on the bosom of dear Mother Earth. Oh, how sweet it was! And I told him I would not be so naughty again, and there was a very slight diamond shower without any thunder or lightning and we were happiest.

There was some thunder and lightning even during those three sunny years at the Old Manse. Sophia's mother and her sister Elizabeth had insisted that she must never bear children, but she longed for them ardently. One day in the first February she fell on the ice—where she had been sliding while Hawthorne skated round her in flashing circles—and suffered a miscarriage. When her first baby was born in March 1844, it lingered, as Hawthorne said, "ten dreadful hours on the threshold of life." It lived and the parents rejoiced, but now they had financial worries: O'Sullivan took years to pay for the stories he printed, and Ripley hadn't returned the money advanced to Brook Farm. There were weeks when Hawthorne was afraid to walk into Concord for the mail, lest he meet too many of his creditors. Sophia's love did not waver, then or for the rest of her life, nor did her trust in the wisdom and mercy of Providence. It had snatched her from invalidism and spinsterhood and transported her to Paradise. It had made her "as strong as a lion," she wrote to her sister Mary, "as elastic as India rubber, light as a bird, as happy as a queen might be," and it had given her a husband whose ardent love was as unwavering as her own. She was expressing in five words all her faith in Providence, and indeed all her experience of life, when she stood at the window in Hawthorne's study one April evening at sunset and wrote with her diamond ring on one of the tiny panes—for him to see, for the world to remember:

Man's accidents are God's purposes.

Sophia A. Hawthorne 1843

WALT WHITMAN'S
BURIED MASTERPIECE

The first edition of *Leaves of Grass*, as placed on sale July 4, 1855, bears little outside or inside resemblance to any of the later editions, which kept growing larger as Whitman added new poems. The original work is a thin folio about the size and shape of a block of typewriting paper. The binding is of dark-green pebbled cloth, and the title is stamped in gold, with the rustic letters sending down roots and sprouting above into leaves. Inside the binding are ninety-five printed pages, numbered iv–xii and 14–95. A prose introduction is set in double columns on the roman-numeraled pages, and the remaining text consists of twelve poems, as compared with 383 in the final or "Deathbed" edition. The first poem, later called "Song of Myself," is longer than the other eleven together. There is no table of contents, and none of the poems has a title.

Another calculated feature of the first edition is that the names of the author and the publisher—actually the same person—are omitted from the title page. Instead the opposite page contains a portrait: the engraved daguerreotype of a bearded man in his middle thirties, slouching under a wide-brimmed and high-crowned black felt hat that has "a rakish kind of slant," as the engraver said later, "like the mast of a schooner." His right hand is resting nonchalantly on his hip; the left is hidden in the pocket of his coarse-woven trousers. He wears no coat or waistcoat, and his shirt is thrown wide open at the collar to reveal a burly neck and the top of what seems to be a red-flannel undershirt. It is the portrait of a devil-may-care American workingman, one who might be taken as a somewhat idealized figure in almost any crowd.

His full name, though missing on the title page, appears twice in the first edition, but in different forms. On the copyright page we read, "*Entered according to Act of Congress in the year 1855, by* WALTER WHITMAN. . . ." On page 29, almost in the middle of the long first poem, we are introduced to "Walt Whitman, an American, one of the roughs, a kosmos." When a law-abiding citizen, even one of the roughs, changes his name even slightly, it is often because he wishes to assume a new personality. A reader might infer that *Walter* Whitman is the journeyman printer who had become a hack journalist, then a newspaper editor, before being lost to sight; whereas *Walt* Whitman is the workingman of the portrait and the putative author—but actual hero—of this extraordinary book.

No other book in the history of American letters was so completely an individual or do-it-yourself project. Not only did Whitman choose his idealized or dramatized self as subject of the book; not only did he create the new style in which it was written (working hard and intelligently to perfect the style over a period of six or seven years), but he also created the new personality of the proletarian bard who was supposed to have done the writing. When a manuscript of the poems was ready in the spring of 1855, Whitman's work was only beginning. He designed the book and arranged to have it printed at a job-printing shop in Booklyn. He set some of the type himself, not without making errors. He did his best to get the book distributed, with the lukewarm cooperation of his friends the Fowler brothers, whose specialty was not bookselling but water cures and phrenology. He was his own press agent and even volunteered as critic of the book, writing three—or a majority—of the favorable reviews it received.

In spite of his best efforts not many copies were sold, and the first edition has not been widely read, except in the special world of literary scholars. The author himself might have been forgotten, if it had not been for a single fortunate event. One copy—not in pebbly green cloth, but paperbound—had been sent to Emerson, who was the most widely respected American of letters and the man best qualified to understand what the new poet was saying. Emerson wrote a letter of heartfelt thanks. When the letter was printed in the New York *Tribune*—without the writer's permission—it amazed and horrified the little American republic of letters. Nobody agreed with Emerson except a few of the extreme Transcendentalists, notably Thoreau and Alcott.

Whitman was almost universally condemned, at least for the next ten years, but he would never again be merely a call in the midst of the crowd.

> Concord   21 July
> Masstts 1855

Dear Sir,

I am not blind to the worth of the wonderful gift of "Leaves of Grass." I find it the most extraordinary piece of wit & wisdom that America has yet contributed. I am very happy in reading it, as great power makes us happy. It meets the demand I am always making of what seemed the sterile & stingy Nature, as if too much handiwork or too much lymph in the temperament were making our western wits fat & mean. I give you joy of your free & brave thought. I have great joy in it. I find incomparable things said incomparably well, as they must be. I find the courage of treatment, which so delights us, & which large perception only can inspire. I greet you at the beginning of a great career, which yet must have had a long foreground somewhere, for such a start. I rubbed my eyes a little to see if this sunbeam were no illusion; but the solid sense of the book is a sober certainty. It has the best merits, namely, of fortifying & encouraging.

I did not know until I, last night, saw the book advertised in a newspaper, that I could trust the name as real & available for a post-office. I wish to see my benefactor, & have felt much like striking my tasks, & visiting New York to pay you my respects.

> R. W. Emerson

Mr. Walter Whitman.

Emerson was being impulsive for a Concord man, but he was also trying to make his phrases accurate. Later, disapproving of Whitman's conduct, he would change his mind about the "great career." He would not and could not feel that most of the poems written after 1855 contained "incomparable things said incomparably well." But his praise of the first edition was unqualified, and it tempts me to make some unqualified statements of my own, as of simple truths that should have been recognized long ago.

First statement: that the long opening poem, later miscalled "Song of Myself," is Whitman's greatest work, perhaps his one completely realized work, and one of the great poems of modern times. Second, that the other eleven poems of the first edition are not on the same level of realization, but nevertheless are examples of Whitman's freshest and boldest style. At least four of them—their titles in the Deathbed edition are "To Think of Time," "The Sleepers," "I Sing the Body Electric," and "There Was a Child Went Forth"—belong in any selection of his best poems. Third, that the text of the first edition is the purest text for "Song of Myself," since many of the later corrections were also corruptions of the style and concealments of the original meaning. Fourth, that it is likewise the best text for most of the other eleven poems, but especially for "The Sleepers"—that fantasia of the unconscious—and "I Sing the Body Electric." And a final statement: that the first edition is a unified work, unlike any later edition, that it gives us a different picture of Whitman's achievement, and that—considering its very small circulation through the years—it might be called the buried masterpiece of American writing.

All that remains is to document some of these statements, not point by point, but chiefly in relation to "Song of Myself."

2

One reason among others why "Song of Myself" has been widely misprized and misinterpreted, especially by scholars, is that they have paid a disproportionate share of attention to its sources in contemporary culture. Besides noting many parallels with Emerson, they have found that it reflected a number of popular works and spectacles. Among these are Italian opera (notably as sung at the Astor Place Theatre in the great season of 1852–1853, when "Alboni's great self" paid her long and only visit to New York); George Sand's novel, *The Countess of Rudolstadt*, which presented the figure of a wandering bard and prophet (as well as another of her novels, *The Journeyman Joiner*, in which the hero was a carpenter and a proletarian saint); Frances Wright's then famous defense of Epicurean philosophy, *A Few Days in Athens*; the Count de Volney's *Ruins*, predicting the final union of all religions; Dr. Abbott's Egyptian Museum, on Broadway; O. M. Mitchel's book, *A Course of Six Lectures on Astronomy*, as well as other writings on the subject; and a number of essays clipped from the English quarterly reviews, of which the poet seems to have been a faithful reader. All these works and shows had a discernible influence on Whitman, but when they are listed with others and discussed at length they lead to one of the misconceptions that are the professional weakness of scholars. They tempt us to conclude that "Song of Myself" was merely a journalist's report, inspired but uneven, of popular culture in the 1850s. It was something more than that, and something vastly different from any of its literary sources.

I might suggest that the real nature of the poem becomes clearer when it is considered in relation to quite another list of works, even though Whitman had probably read none of them in 1855. Most of them he could not have read, because they were not yet written, or not published, or not translated into English. That other list might include the *Bhagavad-Gita*, the *Upanishads*, Christopher Smart's long crazy inspired poem *Jubilate Agno*, Blake's prophetic books (not forgetting *The Marriage of Heaven and Hell*), Rimbaud's *Illuminations*, *The Chants of Maldoror*, and Nietzsche's *Thus Spake Zarathustra*, as well as *The Gospel of Sri Ramakrishna* and a compendious handbook, *The Philosophies of India*, by Heinrich Zimmer (New York, 1951). I am offering what might seem to be a curious list of titles, but its double purpose is easy to explain. "Song of Myself" should be judged, I think, as one of the great inspired (and sometimes insane) prophetic works that have appeared at intervals in the Western world, like *Jubilate Agno* (which is written in a biblical style sometimes suggesting Whitman's), like the *Illuminations*, like *Thus Spake Zarathustra*. But the system of doctrine suggested by the poem is more Eastern than Western, it includes notions like metempsychosis and karma, and it might almost be one of those *Philosophies of India* that Zimmer expounds at length.

What is extraordinary about this Eastern element is that Whitman, when he was writing the poems of the first edition, seems to have known little or nothing about Indian philosophy. It is more than doubtful that he had even read the *Bhagavad-Gita*, one of the few Indian works then available in translation. He does not refer to it in his notebooks of the early 1850s, where he mentions most of the books he was poring over. A year after the first edition was published, Thoreau went to see him in Brooklyn and told him that *Leaves of Grass* was "Wonderfully like the Orientals." Had Whitman read them? he asked. The poet answered, "No: tell me about them." He seems to have taken advantage of Thoreau's reading list, since words from the Sanskrit (notably "Maya" and "sudra") are used correctly in some of the poems written after 1858. They do not appear in "Song of Myself," in spite of the recognizably Indian ideas expressed in the poem, and I would hazard the guess that the ideas are not of literary derivation. It is true that they were vaguely in the air of the time and that Whitman may have breathed them in from the Transcendentalists or even from some of the English quarterly reviewers. It also seems possible, however, that he reinvented them for himself, after an experience similar to the one for which the Sanskrit word is samadhi, or absorption.

What it must have been was a mystical experience in the proper sense of the term. Dr. Richard Maurice Bucke, the most acute of Whitman's immediate disciples, believed that it took place on a June morning in 1853 or 1854. He also believed that it was repeated on other occasions, but neither these nor the original experience can be dated from Whitman's papers. On the other hand, his notebooks and manuscripts of the early 1850s are full of sidelong references to such an experience, and they suggest that it was essentially the same as the illuminations or ecstasies of earlier bards and prophets. Such ecstasies consist in a rapt feeling of union or identity with God (or the Soul, or Mankind, or the Cosmos), and a sense of ineffable joy leading to the conviction that the seer has been released from the limitations of space and time and has been granted a direct vision of truths impossible to express. As Whitman says in the famous fifth chant of "Song of Myself":

> Swiftly arose and spread around me the peace and joy and
> knowledge that pass all the art and argument of the earth;
> And I know that the hand of God is the elderhand of my own,
> And I know that the spirit of God is the eldest brother of my own,
> And that all the men ever born are also my brothers . . . and the
> women my sisters and lovers.

It is to be noted that there is no argument about the real occurrence of such ecstasies. They have been reported, sometimes in sharp detail, by men and women of many different nations, at many historical periods, and each report seems to bear a family resemblance to the others. Part of the resemblance is a feeling universally expressed by mystics that they have acquired a special sort of knowledge not learned from others, but directly revealed to the inner eye. This supposed knowledge has given independent rise to many systems of philosophy or cosmology, once again in many different cultures, and once again there is or should be no argument about one feature of almost all the systems or bodies of teaching: that they too have a family resemblance, like the experiences on which they are based. Indeed, they hold so many principles in common that it is possible for Aldous Huxley and others to group them all together as "the perennial philosophy."

The arguments, which will never end, are first about the nature of the mystical state—is it a form of self-hypnosis, is it a pathological condition to be induced by fasting, vigils, drugs, and other means of abusing the physical organism, or is it, as Whitman believed, the result of superabundant health and energy?—and then about the source and value of the philosophical notions to which it gives rise. Do these merely express the unconscious desires of the individual, and chiefly his sexual desires? Or, as Jungian psychologists like to suggest, are they derived from a racial or universally human unconscious? Are they revelations or hallucinations? Are they supreme doctrines, or are they heretical, false, and even satanic? They belong in the orthodox tradition of Indian philosophy. In Western Christianity, as also in Mohammedanism, the pure and self-consistent forms of mysticism are usually regarded as heresies, with the result that several of the medieval mystics were burned at the stake (though Theresa of Avila and John of the Cross found an orthodox interpretation for their visions and became saints).

Whitman cannot be called a Christian heretic, for the simple reason that he was not a Christian at any stage of his career, early or late. In some of the poems written after the Civil War, and in revisions of older poems made at the same time, he approached the Christian notion of a personal God, whom he invoked as the Elder Brother or the great

Camerado. But then he insisted—in another poem of the same period, "Chanting the Square Deific"—that God was not a trinity but a quaternity, and that one of his faces was the "sudra face" of Satan. In "Song of Myself" as originally written, God is neither a person nor, in the strict sense, even a being; God is an abstract principle of energy that is manifested in every living creature, as well as in "the grass that grows wherever the land is and the water is." In some ways this God of the first edition resembles Emerson's Oversoul, but he seems much closer to the Brahman of the *Upanishads*, the absolute, unchanging, all-enfolding Consciousness, the Divine Ground from which all things emanate and to which all living things may hope to return. And this Divine Ground is by no means the only conception that Whitman shared with Indian philosophers, in the days when he was writing "Song of Myself."

3

The poem is hardly at all concerned with American nationalism, political democracy, contemporary progress, or other social themes that are commonly associated with Whitman's work. The "incomparable things" that Emerson found in it are philosophical and religious principles. Its subject is a state of illumination induced by two (or three) separate moments of ecstasy. In more or less narrative sequence it describes those moments, their sequels in life, and the doctrines to which they give rise. The doctrines are not expounded by logical steps or supported by arguments; instead they are presented dramatically, that is, as the new convictions of a hero, and they are revealed by successive unfoldings of his states of mind.

The hero as pictured in the frontispiece—this hero named "I" or "Walt Whitman" in the text—should not be confused with the Whitman of daily life. He is, as I said, a dramatized or idealized figure, and he is put forward as a representative American workingman, but one who prefers to loaf and invite his soul. Thus, he is rough, sunburned, bearded; he cocks his hat as he pleases, indoors or out; but in the text of the first edition he has no local or family background, and he is deprived of strictly individual characteristics, with the exception of curiosity, boastfulness, and an abnormally developed sense of touch. His really distinguishing feature is that he has been granted a vision, as a result of which he has realized the potentialities latent in every American and indeed, he says, in every living person, even "the brutish koboo, called the ordure of humanity." This dramatization of the hero makes it possible for the living Whitman to exalt him—as he would not have ventured, at the time, to exalt himself—but also to poke mild fun at the hero for his gab and loitering, for his tall talk or "omnivorous words," and for sounding his barbaric yawp over the roofs of the world. The religious feeling in "Song of Myself" is counterpoised by a humor that takes the form of slangy and mischievous impudence or drawling Yankee self-ridicule.

There has been a good deal of discussion about the structure of the poem. In spite of revealing analyses made by a few Whitman scholars, notably Carl F. Strauch and James E. Miller, Jr., a feeling still seems to prevail that it has no structure properly speaking, that it is inspired but uneven, repetitive, and especially weak in its transitions from one theme to another. I suspect that much of this feeling may be due to Whitman's later changes in the text, including his arbitrary scheme, first introduced in the 1867 edition, of dividing the poem into fifty-two numbered paragraphs or chants. One is tempted to read the chants as if they were separate poems, thus overlooking the unity and flow of the work as a whole. It may also be, however, that most of the scholars have been looking for a geometrical pattern, such as can be found and diagramed in some of the later poems. If there is no such pattern in "Song of Myself," that is because the poem was written on a different principle, one much closer to the spirit of the Symbolists or even the Surrealists.

The true structure of the poem is not primarily logical but psychological, and is not a geometrical figure but a musical progression. As music "Song of Myself" is not a symphony with contrasting movements, nor is it an operatic work like "Out of the Cradle Endlessly Rocking," with an overture, arias, recitatives, and a finale. It comes closer to being a rhapsody or tone poem, one that modulates from theme to theme, often changing in key and tempo, falling into reveries and rising toward moments of climax, but always preserving its unity of feeling as it moves onward in a wavelike flow. It is a poem that bears the marks of having been conceived as a whole and written in one prolonged burst of inspiration, but its unity is also the result of conscious art, as can be seen from Whitman's corrections in the early manuscripts. He did not recognize all the bad lines, some of which survive in the printed text, but there is no line in the first edition that seems false to a single prevailing tone. There are passages weaker than others, but none without a place in the general scheme. The repetitions are always musical variations and amplifications. Some of the transitions seem abrupt when the poem is read as if it were an essay, but Whitman was not working in terms of "therefore" and "however." He preferred to let one image suggest another image, which in turn suggests a new statement of mood or doctrine. His themes modulate into one another by pure association, as in a waking dream, with the result that all his transitions seem instinctively right.

In spite of these oneiric elements, the form of the poem is something more than a forward movement in rising and subsiding waves of emotion. There is also a firm narrative structure, one that becomes easier to grasp when we start by dividing the poem into a number of parts or sequences. I think there are nine of these, but the exact number is not important; another critic might say there were seven (as Professor Miller does), or eight or ten. Some of the transitions are gradual, and in such cases it is hard to determine the exact line that ends one sequence and starts another. The essential point is that the parts, however defined, follow one another in irreversible order, like the beginning, middle, and end of any good narrative. My own outline, not necessarily final, would run as follows:

First sequence (chants 1–4): the poet or hero introduced to his audience. Learning and loafing at his ease, "observing a spear of summer grass," he presents himself as a man who lives outdoors and worships his own naked body, not the least part of which is vile. He is also in love with his deeper self or soul, but explains that it is not to be confused with his mere personality. His joyful contentment can be shared by you, the listener, "For every atom belonging to me as good belongs to you."

Second sequence (chant 5): the ecstasy. This consists in the rapt

union of the poet and his soul, and it is described—figuratively, on the
present occasion—in terms of sexual union. The poet now has a sense
of loving brotherhood with God and with all mankind. His eyes being
truly open for the first time, he sees that even the humblest objects
contain the infinite universe—

> And limitless are leaves stiff or drooping in the fields,
> And brown ants in little wells beneath them,
> And mossy scabs of the wormfence, and heaped stones, and elder
>   and mullen and pokeweed.

Third sequence (chants 6–19): the grass. Chant 6 starts with one of
Whitman's brilliant transitions. A child comes with both hands full
of those same leaves from the fields. "What is the grass?" the child
asks—and suddenly we are presented with the central image of the
poem, that is, the grass as symbolizing the miracle of common things
and the divinity (which implies both the equality and the immortality)
of ordinary persons. During the remainder of the sequence, the poet
observes men and women—and animals too—at their daily occupa-
tions. He is part of this life, he says, and even his thoughts are those
of all men in all ages and lands. There are two things to be noted about
the sequence, which contains some of Whitman's freshest lyrics. First,
the people with a few exceptions (such as the trapper and his bride) are
those whom Whitman has known all his life, while the scenes described at length are Manhattan streets and Long Island beaches or
countryside. Second, the poet merely roams, watches, and listens, like
a sort of Tiresias. The keynote of the sequence—as Professor Strauch
was the first to explain—is the two words "I observe."

Fourth sequence (chants 20–25): the poet in person. "Hankering,
gross, mystical, nude," he venerates himself as august and immortal,
but so, he says, is everyone else. He is the poet of the body and of the
soul, of night, earth, and sea, and of vice and feebleness as well as virtue, so that "many long dumb voices" speak through his lips, including those of slaves, prostitutes, even beetles rolling balls of dung. All
life to him is such a miracle of beauty that the sunrise would kill him
if he could not find expression for it—"If I could not now and always

send sunrise out of me." The sequence ends with a dialogue between the poet and his power of speech, during which the poet insists that his deeper self—"the best I am"—is beyond expression.

Fifth sequence (chants 26–29): ecstasy through the senses. Beginning with chant 26, the poem sets out in a new direction. The poet decides to be completely passive: "I think I will do nothing for a long time but listen." What he hears at first are quiet familiar sounds like the gossip of flames on the hearth and the bustle of growing wheat; but the sounds rise quickly to a higher pitch, becoming the matchless voice of a trained soprano, and he is plunged into an ecstasy of hearing, or rather of Being. Then he starts over again, still passively, with the sense of touch, and finds himself rising to the ecstasy of sexual union. This time the union is actual, not figurative, as can be seen from the much longer version of chant 29 preserved in an early notebook.

Sixth sequence (chants 30–38): the power of identification. After his first ecstasy, as presented in chant 5, the poet had acquired a sort of microscopic vision that enabled him to find infinite wonders in the smallest and most familiar things. The second ecstasy (or pair of ecstasies) has an entirely different effect, conferring as it does a sort of vision that is both telescopic and spiritual. The poet sees far into space and time; "afoot with my vision" he ranges over the continent and goes speeding through the heavens among tailed meteors. His secret is the power of identification. Since everything emanates from the universal soul, and since his own soul is of the same essence, he can identify himself with every object and with every person living or dead, heroic or criminal. Thus, he is massacred with the Texans at Goliad, he fights on the *Bonhomme Richard*, he dies on the cross, and he rises again as "one of an average unending procession." Whereas the keynote of the third sequence was "I observe," here it becomes "I am"—"I am a free companion"—"My voice is the wife's voice, the screech by the rail of the stairs"—"I am the man. . . . I suffered. . . . I was there."

Seventh sequence (chants 39–41): the superman. When Indian sages emerge from the state of samadhi or absorption, they often have the feeling of being omnipotent. It is so with the poet, who now feels gifted with superhuman powers. He is the universally beloved Answerer (chant 39), then the Healer, raising men from their deathbeds

(40), and then the Prophet (41) of a new religion that outbids "the old cautious hucksters" by announcing that men are divine and will eventually be gods.

Eighth sequence (chants 42–50): the sermon. "A call in the midst of the crowd" is the poet's voice, "orotund sweeping and final." He is about to offer a statement of the doctrines implied by the narrative (but note that his statement comes at the right point psychologically and plays its part in the narrative sequence). As strangers listen, he proclaims that society is full of injustice, but that the reality beneath it is deathless persons (chant 42); that he accepts and practices all religions, but looks beyond them to "what is untried and afterward" (43); that he and his listeners are the fruit of ages, and the seed of untold ages to be (44); that our final goal is appointed: "God will be there and wait till we come" (45); that he tramps a perpetual journey and longs for companions, to whom he will reveal a new world by washing the gum from their eyes—but each must then continue the journey alone (46); that he is the teacher of men who work in the open air (47); that he is not curious about God, but sees God everywhere, at every moment (48); that we shall all be reborn in different forms ("No doubt I have died myself ten thousand times before"); and that the evil in the world is like moonlight, a mere reflection of the sun (49). The end of the sermon (chant 50) is the hardest passage to interpret in the whole poem. I think, though I cannot be certain, that the poet is harking back to the period after one of his ten thousand deaths, when he slept and slept long before his next awakening. He seems to remember vague shapes, and he beseeches these Outlines, as he calls them, to let him reveal the "word unsaid." Then turning back to his audience, "It is not chaos or death," he says. "It is form and union and plan. . . . it is eternal life. . . . it is happiness."

Ninth sequence (chants 51–52): the poet's farewell. Having finished his sermon, the poet gets ready to depart, that is, to die and wait for another incarnation or "fold of the future," while still inviting others to follow. At the beginning of the poem he had been leaning and loafing at ease in the summer grass. Now, having rounded the circle, he bequeaths himself to the dirt "to grow from the grass I love." I do not see how any careful reader, unless blinded with preconceptions, could overlook the unity of the poem in tone and image and direction.

4

It is in the eighth sequence, which is a sermon, that Whitman gives us most of the doctrines suggested by his mystical experience, but they are also implied in the rest of the poem and indeed in the whole text of the first edition. Almost always he expresses them in the figurative and paradoxical language that prophets have used from the beginning. Now I should like to state them explicitly, even at the cost of some repetition.

Whitman believed when he was writing "Song of Myself"—and at later periods too, but with many changes in emphasis—that there is a distinction between one's mere personality and the deeper Self (or between ego and soul). He believed that the Self (or atman, to use a Sanskrit word) is of the same essence as the universal spirit (though he did not quite say it *is* the universal spirit, as Indian philosophers do in the phrase "Atman is Brahman"). He believed that true knowledge is to be acquired not through the senses or the intellect, but through union with the Self. At such moments of union (or "merge," as Whitman called it) the gum is washed from one's eyes (that is his own phrase), and one can read an infinite lesson in common things, discovering that a mouse, for example, "is miracle enough to stagger sextillions of infidels." This true knowledge is available to every man and woman, since each conceals a divine Self. Moreover, the divinity of all implies the perfect equality of all, the immortality of all, and the universal duty of loving one another.

Immortality for Whitman took the form of metempsychosis, and he believed that every individual will be reborn, usually but not always in a higher form. He had also worked out for himself something approaching the Indian notion of karma, which is the doctrine that actions performed during one incarnation determine the nature and fate of the individual during his next incarnation; the doctrine is emphatically if somewhat unclearly stated in a passage of his prose introduction that was later rewritten as a poem, "Song of Prudence." By means of metempsychosis and karma, we are all involved in a process of spiritual evolution that might be compared to natural evolution. Even the latter process, however, was not regarded by Whitman as strictly natural or material. He believed that animals have a rudimentary sort of soul ("They bring me tokens of myself"), and he hinted or surmised, without directly saying, that rocks, trees, and plants possess an identity, or "eidólon," that persists as they rise to higher states of being. The double process of evolution, natural and spiritual, can be traced for ages into the past, and he believed that it will continue for ages beyond ages. Still, it is not an eternal process, since it has an ultimate goal, which appears to be the reabsorption of all things into the Divine Ground.

Most of Whitman's doctrines, though by no means all of them, belong to the mainstream of Indian philosophy. In some respects he went against the stream. Unlike most of the Indian sages, for example, he was not a thoroughgoing idealist. He did not believe that the whole world of the senses, of desires, of birth and death, was only maya, illusion, nor did he hold that it was a sort of purgatory; instead he praised the world as real and joyful. He did not despise the body, but proclaimed that it was as miraculous as the soul. He was too good a citizen of the nineteenth century to surrender his faith in material progress as the necessary counterpart of spiritual progress. Although he yearned for ecstatic union with the soul or Oversoul, he did not try to achieve it by subjugating the senses, as advised by yogis and Buddhists alike; on the contrary, he thought the "merge" could also be achieved (as in chants 26–29) by a total surrender to the senses. These are important differences, but it must be remembered that Indian philosophy or theology is not such a unified structure as it appears to us from a distance. Whitman might have found Indian sages or gurus and even whole sects that agreed with one or another of his heterodoxies (perhaps excepting his belief in material progress). One is tempted to say that instead of being a Christian heretic, he was an Indian rebel and sectarian.

Sometimes he seems to be a Mahayana Buddhist, promising nirvana for all after countless reincarnations, and also sharing the belief of some Mahayana sects that the sexual act can serve as one of the sacraments. At other times he might be an older brother of Sri Ramakrishna (1836–1886), the nineteenth-century apostle of Tantric Brahmanism and of joyous affirmation. Although this priest of Kali, the Mother Goddess, refused to learn English, one finds him delivering some of Whitman's messages in—what is more surprising—the same tone of voice. Read, for example, this fairly typical passage from *The Gospel of Sri Ramakrishna*, while remembering that "Consciousness" is to be taken here as a synonym for Divinity:

> The Divine Mother revealed to me in the Kali temple that it was She who had become everything. She showed me that everything was full of Consciousness. The Image was Consciousness, the altar was Consciousness, the water-vessels were Consciousness, the door-sill was Consciousness, the marble floor was Consciousness— all was Consciousness. . . . I saw a wicked man in front of the Kali temple; but in him I saw the Power of the Divine Mother vibrating. That was why I fed a cat with the food that was to be offered to the Divine Mother.

Whitman expresses the same idea at the end of chant 48, and in the same half-playful fashion:

> Why should I wish to see God better than this day?
> I see something of God each hour of the twenty-four, and each moment then,
> In the faces of men and women I see God, and in my own face in the glass;
> I find letters from God dropped in the street, and every one is signed by God's name,
> And I leave them where they are, for I know that others will punctually come forever and ever.

Such parallels—and there are dozens that might be quoted—are more than accidental. They reveal a kinship in thinking and experience that can be of practical value to students of Whitman. Since the Indian mystical philosophies are elaborate structures, based on conceptions that have been shaped and defined by centuries of discussion, they help to explain Whitman's ideas at points in the first edition where he seems at first glance to be vague or self-contradictory. There is, for example, his unusual combination of realism—sometimes brutal realism—and serene optimism. Today he is usually praised for the first, blamed for the second (optimism being out of fashion), and blamed still more for the inconsistency he showed in denying the existence of evil. The usual jibe is that Whitman thought the universe was perfect and was getting better every day.

It is obvious, however, that he never meant to deny the existence of evil in himself or his era or his nation. He knew that it existed in his own family, where one of his brothers was a congenital idiot, another was a drunkard married to a streetwalker, and still another, who had caught "the bad disorder," later died of general paresis in an insane asylum. Whitman's doctrine implied that each of them would have an opportunity to avoid those misfortunes or punishments in another incarnation, where each would be rewarded for his good actions. The universe was an eternal becoming for Whitman, a process not a structure, and it had to be judged from the standpoint of eternity. After his mystical experience, which seemed to offer a vision of eternity, he had become convinced that evil existed only as part of a universally perfect design. That explains his combination of realism and optimism, which seems unusual only in our Western world. In India, Heinrich Zimmer says, "Philosophic theory, religious belief, and intuitive experience support each other . . . in the basic insight that, fundamentally, all is well. A supreme optimism prevails everywhere, in spite of the unromantic recognition that the universe of man's affairs is in the most imperfect state imaginable, one amounting practically to chaos."

Another point explained by Indian conceptions is the sort of democracy Whitman was preaching in "Song of Myself." There is no doubt that he was always a democrat politically—which is to say a Jacksonian Democrat, a Barnburner writing editorials against the Hunkers, a Free Soiler in sympathy, and then a liberal but not a radical Republican. He remained faithful to what he called "the good old cause" of liberty, equality, and fraternity, and he wrote two moving elegies for the European rebels of 1848. In "Song of Myself," however, he is not advocating rebellion or even reform. "To a drudge of the cottonfields," he says, "or emptier of privies I lean. . . . on his right cheek I put the family kiss"; but he offers nothing more than a kiss and an implied promise. What he preaches throughout the poem is not political but religious democracy, such as was practiced by the early Christians. Today it is practiced, at least in theory, by the Tantric sect, and we read in *Philosophies of India*:

> All beings and things are members of a single mystic family (*kula*). There is therefore no thought of caste within the Tantric holy "circles" (*cakra*). . . . Women as well as men are eligible not only to receive the highest initiation but also to confer it in the role of guru. . . . However, it must not be supposed that this indifference to the rules of caste implies any idea of revolution within the social sphere, as distinguished from the sphere of spiritual progress. The initiate returns to his post in society; for there too is the manifestation of Sakti. The world is affirmed, just as it is— neither renounced, as by an ascetic, nor corrected, as by a social reformer.

The promise that Whitman offers to the drudge of the cottonfields, the emptier of privies, and the prostitute draggling her shawl is that they too can set out with him on his perpetual journey—perhaps not in their present incarnations, but at least in some future life. And that leads to another footnote offered by the Indian philosophies: they explain what the poet meant by the Open Road. It starts as an actual road that winds through fields and cities, but Whitman is doing more than inviting us to shoulder our duds and go hiking along it. The real journey is toward spiritual vision, toward reunion with the Divine Ground; and thus the Open Road becomes Whitman's equivalent for all the other roads and paths and ways that appear in mystical teachings. It reminds us of the Noble Eightfold Path of the Buddhists, and the Taoist Way; it suggests both the *bhakti-marga* or "path of devotion" and the *karma-marga* or "path of sacrifice"; while it comes closer to being the "big ferry" of the Mahayana sect, in which there is room for every soul to cross to the farther shore. Whitman's conception, however, was even broader. He said one should know "the universe itself as a road, as many roads, as roads for traveling souls."

I am not pleading for the acceptance of Whitman's ideas or for any other form of mysticism, Eastern or Western. I am only suggesting that his ideas as expressed in "Song of Myself" were bolder and more coherent than is generally supposed, and philosophically a great deal more respectable.

5

But there is more to be said in judgment of Whitman and his work. It was a truly extraordinary achievement for him to rediscover the outlines of a whole philosophical system chiefly on the basis of his own mystical experience and with little help from his reading. Frances Wright's *A Few Days in Athens?* Volney's *Ruins? De Rerum Natura?* The novels of George Sand? There is hardly a hint of them in Whitman's fundamental thinking, although there is more than a hint of Emerson's Neoplatonism. But Emerson, who regarded himself as a teacher not a prophet, had nothing to do with notions like metempsychosis or karma or the universe pictured as a road for traveling souls. His temporary disciple felt that he had gone far beyond the teacher and was venturing into an unexplored continent of the Self. What does it matter that his sense of discovery was largely based on ignorance of the mystical tradition! It could still encourage him to make real discoveries in style and symbol, and it could arouse a feeling of release and exhilaration in his readers.

This aspect of "Song of Myself" becomes clearer when the poem is compared with another long work about the mystical experience, T. S. Eliot's *Four Quartets*. The works have more in common than Eliot has realized, but there is a fundamental difference that leads to many others. Eliot could never have made the mistake of thinking that his experience was the first of its kind. He knows the tradition thoroughly and can always dignify his personal memories with quotations or half-quotations from the *Bhagavad-Gita* (which he read long ago in Sanskrit), from John of the Cross, *The Cloud of Unknowing*, and the anchoret Juliana of Norwich. Using craftsmanship as well as learning, he has invented a rich structure for *Four Quartets*, so that it becomes a magnificent exercise in architectonics. What we miss in the poem may be simply the exhilaration that comes from a sense of discovery. Even in his mystical experience, Eliot cannot forget the lesson of caution he has learned from his studies. He knows that his eternal moment in the rose garden will last for a moment only. He knows that he must go back to his usual state of being, and then—

> Ridiculous the waste sad time
> Stretching before and after.

Disciplined as he is by tradition, Eliot makes few mistakes of any sort; nor does he encourage his disciples to make them (except sometimes the great mistake of shrinking into dryness and pedantry). Whitman, on the other hand, misleads as much as he inspires, and there is no doubt that he has had a fatal influence on some of his disciples. There is also no doubt that he was the first to be misled, and very soon after writing "Song of Myself." At that point his exhilarating pride of discovery began to change into humorless arrogance. If he had been as familiar with the mystical tradition as Eliot shows himself to be, Whitman would have been warned against the feeling of omnipotence that, as we have seen, often follows a mystical experience. We read in *Philosophies of India* that the adept reaches a point in his spiritual progress at which he becomes identified with the personal creator of the world illusion. "He feels," Dr. Zimmer continues, "that he is at one with the Supreme Lord, partaking of His virtues of omniscience and omnipotence. This, however, is a dangerous phase; for if he is to go to Brahman, the goal, he must realize that this inflation is only a subtle form of self-delusion. The candidate must conquer it, press beyond it, so that the anonymity of sheer being (*sat*), consciousness (*cit*), and bliss (*ananda*) may break upon him as the transpersonal essence of his actual Self."

Whitman, of course, had never heard of this purely anonymous or transpersonal state. Remaining for a long time in the dangerous phase of self-inflation (or "dilation," as he called it) and regarding himself as a God-inspired prophet, he kept looking about for other new doctrines to prophesy. The first of these he found was a rather bumptious American nationalism, which is already suggested in his prose introduction to the first edition of *Leaves of Grass* (written after the poems), but which becomes more explicit in the new poems of the second or 1856 edition. Also in the second edition, he announced himself in an open letter to Emerson ("Dear Master") as the prophet of unashamed sex. In

1857 he determined to become what he called a "wander speaker"—
"perhaps launching at the President, leading persons, Congressmen or
Judges of the Supreme Court . . . the greatest champion America ever
could know, yet holding no office or emolument whatever—but first
in the esteem of men and women." Soon afterward he dreamed of
founding a new religion, for which *Leaves of Grass*—expanded into 365
chapters or psalms, one to be read on each day of the year—would serve
as a holy testament. Preserved among his papers is a note to himself
that reads: "The Great Construction of the New Bible. Not to be di-
verted from the principal object—the main life work—the three
hundred and sixty-five. It ought to be ready in 1859." During those
years before the Civil War, Whitman was afflicted with megalomania
to such an extent that he was losing touch with the realities, or at least
the human possibilities, of American life.

At the same time he was making—if judged by the mystical tradition—another blunder against which the Indians might have
warned him. He had once been careful to distinguish the external self
or personality from the deeper Self that he was celebrating in his greatest poem. Now he forgot the distinction and began to celebrate
"myself" in the guise of a simple separate person—greater than other
persons, no longer standing aloof and unperturbed, but greedy for
praise and tortured with desires. This person, however, laid claim to
all the liberties and powers that Whitman had once ascribed to the
transpersonal Self. Anything that the person felt like saying was also
the right and inspired thing to say. Composing great poems was a simple matter. All the person had to do was permit Nature—*his* nature—
to speak "without check with original energy."

While dreaming his crazy dreams, Whitman continued to live with
his family in a little frame workingman's house in Brooklyn, where he
shared a bed with his idiot brother. Thoreau on his first visit noted that
the bed was unmade and that an unemptied chamberpot stood beneath
it. Other literary men described their meetings with Whitman in a
tone of fascinated horror that suggests the accounts of present-day visitors to North Beach or Big Sur or Venice West. Indeed, one cannot
help feeling that the Whitman of those days was a predecessor of the
beats: he had the beard, the untrimmed hair, and although his costume was different, it might be regarded as the 1860 equivalent of

sweatshirt and sandals. Some of his conduct also resembled that of the Beat Generation. He stayed out of the rat race, he avoided the squares (preferring the company of omnibus drivers and deck hands on the ferries); he was "real gone," he was "far out"; and he was writing poems in what Lawrence Lipton calls "the 'open,' free-swinging style that is prized in Beat Generation literature." Some of them should be read to loud music as a means of glossing over their faults and holding the listener's attention—not to the music of a jazz combo, like beat poetry, but perhaps to that of a regimental brass band.

A poet's conduct and his work are two ways of expressing the same habits of thinking. It was during those years just before the Civil War that Whitman first indulged himself in a whole collection of stylistic mannerisms. He had once planned to write in what he called "A perfectly transparent, plate-glassy style, artless, with no ornaments, or attempts at ornaments, for their own sake." He had planned to use "Common idioms and phrases—Yankeeisms and vulgarisms—cant expressions when very pat only." The effect he wanted to achieve was one of "Clearness, simplicity, no twistified or foggy sentences, at all— the most translucid clearness without variations"; and that was one of the effects he did achieve in the first edition, except in a few gangling passages and a few others where he was being deliberately hermetic. It was after 1855 that he began to cultivate his bad habits of speech— such, for example, as unnecessary or "poetic" inversions; as foreign words, often used incorrectly and without good reason (there had been only a few of them in "Song of Myself"); as ugly new words of his own coinage; as the "I" placed obtrusively at the end of a phrase ("No dainty dolce affettuoso I"); as the Quaker names for months and days, such as "Fourth-month" for April and "First-day" for Sunday (which might have been excusable if Whitman had been a Quaker); and as, worst of all, the interminable bald inventories that read like the names of parts and organs in an anatomical chart or like the index to a school geography. In the first edition he had broken most of the nineteenth-century rules for elegant writing, but now he was violating an older literary convention, that of simply being considerate of one's readers.

Whitman's beat period, however, proved to be only a transitory phase of a life that had several other phases. The best record of his attitude during the period is the greatly expanded text of the third or

1860 edition, which is an engaging and impressive book for all its extravagant gestures, and which, after the first, is the other vintage edition of his poems. Soon after it was published, the Civil War gave a new direction to Whitman's career. His war poems are disappointing, with three or four exceptions, but his unselfish service in army hospitals helped to establish him in still another personality, one he kept to the end: that of the good gray poet, and it was during the postwar years that he produced some of his most important work. Much of it shows that he was turning back toward the Eastern beliefs expressed in "Song of Myself." Perhaps the return was caused by another mystical experience, but although the supposition seems a likely one, the only evidence to support it consists of scattered passages in his two prose works of the time, *Democratic Vistas* and *Specimen Days*. We know, however, that he planned at the time to make "Passage to India" the title not merely of a long poem about the journey of the soul toward God, but of a whole volume "bridging the way," as he said, "from life to death."

The volume would be designed to stand beside *Leaves of Grass*, which he had come to regard as a finished work. Some of the poems he planned to put into the new book—"Proud Music of the Storm," "Prayer of Columbus," and most of all "Passage to India" itself—are truly admirable in conception and in their rich symphonic structure. The language, however, is more abstract and a great deal less vivid or Yankee than that of the first edition (besides retaining most of the mannerisms developed in his period of self-inflation). If he did have another mystical experience before writing the poems, it failed to give him the miraculously fresh vision of familiar people and objects that had followed his earlier illumination. As for the creed put forward in "Passage to India" and other poems of the same period, it is no longer purely mystical, being mixed with the ambiguous doctrine of male comradeship or "adhesiveness" that Whitman had first expressed in the "Calamus" poems of the 1860 edition, and mixed again with his still more recent doctrine of Personalism. The deeper Self is now identified with the personality (or eidólon, as he was beginning to call it). God Himself becomes personal (or four-personal, in "Chanting the Square Deific") and is addressed as the Older Brother of the soul.

Soon the notion of publishing a grand new book had to be put aside, as a result of the apoplectic stroke that Whitman suffered in January 1873. He lived nineteen years longer and wrote scores of poems, but most of them were occasional verses bearing a curious resemblance to his newspaper editorials of the 1840s. The only ambitious work he finished was "Dream of Columbus" (1874), which served as a dignified and moving peroration to his career. He retired to Camden, New Jersey, where he lived serenely and received a good many visitors, most of them his devoted followers, so that he presented the picture of an Indian guru surrounded by his *adhikanin* or disciples.

During the first years in Camden Whitman spent a good deal of time revising his early poems, in the hope of reshaping his extremely diversified work into an organic whole. Most of the revisions were designed to make his style more uniform, to bring his teaching up to date, or to gloss over the differences between what he had once said and what he now believed. "Do I contradict myself?" Once Whitman had asked the question defiantly, but now it worried him. He still regarded himself as a prophet, and a prophet's duty is to have been always right. It would have been better for his strictly poetic reputation if he had allowed the early illuminated Whitman to speak for himself, the bohemian or inflated Whitman to speak for himself, and the good gray poet to speak for himself, each in his separate fashion.

6

In the collection of variorum readings compiled long ago by Oscar Lovell Triggs, the revisions in "Song of Myself" occupy thirty pages. Triggs found that Whitman had changed the wording of all but five of the fifty-two chants into which he had finally divided the poem. In those five—chants, 9, 27, 28, 29, and 52—the only changes are in punctuation and spelling. Of course the division into numbered chants is an important change in itself and one that has proved to be convenient for students, though it has also proved misleading.

A still more important change is in the title. By virtue of the image that holds the poem together, its title should be "Leaves of Grass," but Whitman had transferred this phrase to the book as a whole. In the first edition, the frontispiece partly takes the place of a title, since readers are being asked to interpret the poem as the testament of the idealized American workingman whom it portrays. In the second or 1856 edition, there is a title in words: "A Poem of Walt Whitman, an American." That is an awkward but accurate phrase, if we regard Walt (not Walter) Whitman as the name of the idealized figure. Beginning with the third or 1860 edition, the poem was called simply "Walt Whitman"—not so accurate a title any longer, if we remember that the name was by now completely identified with the living poet. It was not until 1881 that the poem became "Song of Myself," a phrase that I think is completely false to its original intention. "Myself" is "my personality," and Whitman had originally been writing about a not-myself, a representative figure who, by achieving union with his transpersonal soul, had realized the possibilities latent in every man and woman.

In the first edition the poet-hero presents himself, as I said, without a hint of his local or family background; he is simply "Walt Whitman, an American, one of the roughs, a kosmos." That is exactly how he should be presented, since he is speaking for all Americans and indeed for all humanity. In later editions he acquires a personal background by virtue of his complete identification with the author. As "Walt Whitman, a kosmos, of Manhattan the son," he becomes a strictly localized divinity (while ceasing to imply that each of the roughs contains in himself the entire universe). There are other changes in the same direction. In 1881 Whitman took eight lines from "Starting from Paumanok," which was written in his beat days, and inserted them at the end of the first chant. Four of the new lines are:

> My tongue, every atom of my blood, form'd from this soil, this air,
> Born here of parents born here from parents the same, and their
> parents the same,
> I, now thirty-seven years old in perfect health begin,
> Hoping to cease not till death.

He was actually thirty-four or -five when he started to write the poem, and thirty-six when it was published—but what does it matter about his age or health or his determination to cease not till death? The real point is that if he insists on presenting himself as a proud descendant of the early settlers, he can no longer presume to speak for first-generation Americans; nor can he claim to be "Not merely of the New World but of Africa, Europe or Asia. . . . a wandering savage," as he had done in the original text. He has gained an identity at the cost of ceasing to be universally representative.

There is a significant change in the first line of the poem, the addition (in 1881) of three words I have put in italics: "I celebrate myself, *and sing myself*." At first one feels that "celebrate" and "sing" are synonyms, and that the new phrase has been added partly to balance the line and partly in obedience to Whitman's old-age habit of never saying in three words what might be said in six. But the truth is that "sing" introduces a new theme into the text. In the first edition the poet-hero had "celebrated" himself by telling what he saw and did and believed. He had spoken compulsively and without self-consciousness. In the late editions, however, he also "sings"—which in Whitman's jargon means "writes a song about"—himself. When he observes the miraculous world about him, it is no longer for the pure joy of seeing, as in the first edition, but also with the intention of collecting material; he is "Absorbing all to myself and for this song." This new habit of his becomes particularly obtrusive at the beginning of chant 26. Here, in the original version, the poet-hero had been preparing to demonstrate that by merely listening, in a state of complete passivity, he could be swept forward into an ecstasy of hearing. He had said in the first two lines:

> I think I will do nothing for a long time but listen,
> And accrue what I hear into myself. . . . and let sounds
>   contribute toward me.

Only four words of the second line were changed in 1881, but they were important for the meaning. The new line reads (with my italics):

> *To* accrue what I hear into *this song, to* let sounds
>   contribute toward *it*.

"To" implies purpose here: "in order to." If the poet is consciously trying to hear sounds that will enrich the texture of his song, he is no longer being passive, and the effect on the reader of the passage that follows is seriously weakened.

The good gray poet must have been abashed by many gestures of his earlier myself. "Washes and razors for foofoos. . . . for me freckles and a bristling beard." One can be certain that such a line would go; the wonder is that it survived until 1881. "Where the laughing gull scoots by the slappy shore and laughs her near-human laugh." The word "slappy" gives color to the line, and it was the one word to be omitted, in this case as early as 1856. There is no space to offer more than this bare suggestion of all the gay impudence and vivid Yankee-isms that were excised from later editions. I am more interested at present in apparently minor revisions that change the meaning of the poem. Among them are the phrases that introduce his accounts of the Goliad massacre in Texas (chant 34) and of the sea fight between the *Serapis* and the *Bonhomme Richard* (chants 35 and 36). In the first edition these two accounts are offered as further examples of the power of identification. The poet-hero *is* one of the murdered Texans—perhaps the "youth not seventeen years old"—and he *is* one of the sailors on the *Bonhomme Richard,* just as he had already been the mother condemned for a witch and the hounded slave that flagged in the race. By 1867, however, Whitman felt he should offer explanations. He inserted a line at the beginning of chant 34, "Now I tell what I knew in Texas in my early youth," thus falsifying his own biography, and he inserted another line at the end of the first stanza of chant 35, besides two words, which I have italicized, in the first line of the following stanza:

> List to the yarn, as my grandmother's father the sailor
>   told it to me.

> Our foe was no skulk in his ship I tell you (*said he,*)

The result is that these great examples of the poet-hero's ability to identify himself with all creatures, living or dead, are reduced in one case to a story told long ago in Texas, in the other to an old sailor's yarn—"said he"—and thereby lose their reason for being part of the poem. Whitman can no longer say about them, "I am the man. . . . I suffered. . . . I was there." In both cases it would seem, however, that he was not so much concealing what he once meant to say as, on this occasion, honestly forgetting it.

I have been talking about the revisions only in "Song of Myself," but some of the same statements could be made about the final text of the other eleven poems in the first edition. Since these poems are less important, the revisions in them seem less objectionable. "Song of the Answerer" and "Who Learns My Lesson Complete?" were improved, even greatly improved, by the omission from each of tasteless lines and a feeble ending. "Great Are the Myths," a still weaker poem, disappeared after 1876 without being missed. On the other hand, two of the best poems suffered most from revision: "The Sleepers" by losing a passage (lines 60–70) that starts with adolescent sex and ends in surrealism, and "I Sing the Body Electric" by the addition of a final section that is not in the least electric, being merely a long anatomical catalogue.

In another sense, however, all the poems have suffered, even those in which the revision was wisely handled. Most of them had been composed at the same time, in the same furious burst of inspiration; the only exceptions seem to be the two political poems, "Europe the 72d and 73d Years of These States," written in 1850—it was Whitman's first successful experiment in free verse—and "A Boston Ballad," written in June 1854. The other poems all have something to do with his state of mystical illumination; they explain one another, strengthen one another, and are further strengthened by being printed after "Song of Myself," since they amplify some of the same themes. In the text of the Deathbed edition, ten of them are scattered among six of the "clusters" into which the book was finally divided, while "Song of Myself" is paired with the vastly inflated "Starting from Paumanok." It is as if a close family of brothers had been assigned to separate branches of the armed forces, with the result that each of them lost something of his personality without contributing much to his new group. In the first edition everything belongs together and everything helps to exhibit

Whitman at his best, Whitman at his freshest in vision and boldest in language, Whitman transformed by a new experience, so that he wanders among familiar objects and finds that each of them has become a miracle. One can read the book today with something of the amazement and the gratitude for its great power that Emerson felt when reading it more than a century ago.

HEMINGWAY AT MIDNIGHT

When Ernest Hemingway's first books appeared, they seemed to be a transcription of the real world, new because they were accurate and because the world in those days was also new. With his insistence on "presenting things truly," he seemed to be a writer in the naturalistic tradition (for all his technical experiments); and the professors of American literature, when they got round to mentioning his books in their surveys, treated him as if he were the Dreiser of the lost generation, or perhaps the fruit of a deplorable misalliance between Dreiser and Jack London. Going back to his work in 1944, you perceive his kinship with a wholly different group of novelists, let us say with Poe and Hawthorne and Melville: the haunted and nocturnal writers, the men who dealt in images that were symbols of an inner world.

On the face of it, his method is not in the least like theirs. He doesn't lead us into castles ready to collapse with age, or into very old New England houses, or embark with us on the search for a whale that is also the white spirit of evil; instead he tells the stories he has lived or heard, against the background of countries he has seen. But, you reflect on reading his books again, these are curious stories that he has chosen from his wider experience, and these countries are presented in a strangely mortuary light. In no other writer of our time can you find such a profusion of corpses: dead women in the rain; dead soldiers bloated in their uniforms and surrounded by torn papers; sunken liners full of bodies that float past the closed portholes. In no other writer can you find so many suffering animals: mules with their forelegs broken drowning in shallow water off the quai at Smyrna; gored horses in the bullring; wounded hyenas first snapping at their own entrails and then eating them with relish. And morally wounded people who also devour themselves: punch-drunk boxers, soldiers with battle fatigue, veterans crazy with "the old rale," lesbians, nymphomaniacs, bullfighters who have lost their nerve, men who lie awake all night while their brains get to racing "like a flywheel with the weight gone"—here are visions as terrifying as those of "The Pit and the Pendulum," even though most of them are copied from life; here are nightmares at noonday, accurately described, pictured without the romantic mist, but having the nature of obsessions or hypnagogic visions between sleep and waking.

And, going back to them, you find a waking-dreamlike quality even in stories that deal with pleasant or commonplace aspects of the world. Take for example "Big Two-Hearted River," printed in his first American collection of stories, *In Our Time*. Here the plot, or foreground of the plot, is simply a fishing trip in the northern peninsula of Michigan. Nick Adams, who is Hemingway's earliest and most personal hero, gets off the train at an abandoned sawmill town; he crosses burned-over land, makes camp, eats his supper and goes to sleep; in the morning he looks for bait, finds grasshoppers under a log, hooks a big trout and loses it, catches two other trout, then sits on the bank in the shadow and eats his lunch very slowly while watching the stream; he decides to do no more fishing that day. There is nothing else in the story, apparently; nothing but a collection of sharp sensory details, so that you smell or hear or touch or see everything that exists near Big Two-Hearted River; and you even taste Nick Adams' supper of beans and spaghetti. "All good books are alike," Hemingway later said, "in that they are truer than if they had really happened and after you are finished reading one you will feel that all that happened to you and afterwards it all belongs to you: the good and the bad, the ecstasy, the remorse and sorrow, the people and the places and how the weather was." This story belongs to the reader, but apparently it is lacking in ecstasy, remorse, and sorrow; there are no people in it except Nick Adams; apparently there is nothing but "the places and how the weather was."

But Hemingway's stories are most of them continued, in the sense that he has a habit of returning to the same themes, each time making them a little clearer—to himself, I think, as well as to others. His work has an emotional consistency, as if all of it moved on the same stream of experience. A few years after writing "Big Two-Hearted River," he wrote another story that casts a retrospective light on his fishing trip (much as *A Farewell to Arms* helps to explain the background of Jake Barnes and Lady Brett, in *The Sun Also Rises*). The second story, "Now I Lay Me," deals with an American volunteer in the Italian army who isn't named but who might easily be Nick Adams. He is afraid to sleep at night because, so he says, "I had been living for a long time with the knowledge that if I ever shut my eyes in the dark and let myself go, my soul would go out of my body. I had been that way for a long time, ever since I had been blown up at night and felt it go out of me and go off and then come back." And the soldier continues:

> I had different ways of occupying myself while I lay awake. I would think of a trout stream I had fished along when I was a boy and fish its whole length very carefully in my mind; fishing very carefully under all the logs, all the turns of the bank, the deep holes and the clear shallow stretches, sometimes catching trout and sometimes losing them. I would stop fishing at noon to eat my lunch; sometimes on a log over the stream; sometimes on a high bank under a tree, and I always ate my lunch very slowly and watched the stream below me while I ate. . . . Some nights too I made up streams, and some of them were very exciting, and it was like being awake and dreaming. Some of those streams I still remember and think that I have fished in them, and they are confused with streams I really know.

After reading this passage, we have a somewhat different attitude toward the earlier story. The river described in it remains completely real for us; but also—like those other streams the soldier invented during the night—it has the quality of a waking dream. Although the events in the foreground are described with superb accuracy, and for their own sake, we now perceive what we probably missed at a first reading: that there are shadows in the background and that part of the story takes place in an inner world. We notice that Nick Adams regards his fishing trip as an escape, either from a nightmare or from realities that have become a nightmare. Sometimes his mind starts to work, even here in the wilderness; but "he knew he could choke it because he was tired enough," and he can safely fall asleep. "Nick felt happy," the author says more than once. "He felt he had left everything behind, the need for thinking, the need to write, other needs. It was all back of him." He lives as if in an enchanted country. There is a faint suggestion of old legends: all the stories of boys with cruel stepmothers who wandered off into the forest, where the trees sheltered them and the birds brought them food. There is even a condition laid on Nick's happiness, just as in many fairy tales, where the hero must not wind a certain horn or open a certain door. Nick must not follow the river down into the swamp. "In the swamp the banks were bare, the big cedars came together overhead, the sun did not come through, except in patches; in the fast deep water, in the half light, the fishing would be tragic. In the swamp fishing was a tragic adventure. Nick did not want it. He did not want to go down the stream any further today."

Now, I question whether this shadowy background of "Big Two-Hearted River" was deliberately sketched in by the author, or whether it was more than half-consciously present in his mind. In those days Hemingway was trying to write with complete objectivity; he was trying, as he afterwards said, "to put down what really happened in action; what the actual things were which produced the emotion that you experienced." But the emotion was often more personal and more complicated than he suspected at the time (though he might afterwards define it more clearly); and the "actual things" were presented so vividly in his stories that they became, for the reader, something more than "what really happened in action"; they also became metaphors or symbols. Many poems have the same double effect; and Hemingway's stories are often close to poetry.

Years later he began to make a deliberate use of symbolism (as in "The Snows of Kilimanjaro"), together with other literary devices that he had avoided in his earlier work. He even began to talk about the possibility of writing what he called fourth-dimensional prose. "The reason everyone now tries to avoid it," he says in Green Hills of Africa, "to deny that it is important, to make it seem vain to try to do it, is because it is so difficult. Too many factors must combine to make it possible."

"What is this now?" asks Kandisky, the Austrian in leather breeches who likes to lead the life of the mind. And the author explains:

> "The kind of writing that can be done. How far prose can be carried if anyone is serious enough and has luck. There is a fourth and fifth dimension that can be gotten."
> "You believe it?"
> "I know it."
> "And if a writer can get this?"
> "Then nothing else matters. It is more important than anything else he can do. The chances are, of course, that he will fail. But there is a chance that he succeeds."
> "But that is poetry you are talking about."
> "No. It is much more difficult than poetry. It is a prose that has never been written. But it can be written, without tricks and without cheating. With nothing that will go bad afterwards."

Now, I don't know exactly what Hemingway means by prose with "a fourth and fifth dimension." It would seem to me that any good prose has four dimensions, in the sense of being a solid object that moves through time; whereas the fifth dimension is a mystical or meaningless figure of speech. But without understanding his choice of words, I do know that Hemingway's prose at its best gives a sense of depth and of moving forward on different levels that is lacking in even the best of his imitators, as it is in almost all the other novelists of our time. Moreover, I have at least a vague notion of how this quality in his work can be explained.

2

Considering his laborious apprenticeship and the masters with whom he chose to study (including Pound and Gertrude Stein); considering his theories of writing, which he has often discussed, and how they have developed with the years; considering their subtle and increasingly conscious application, as well as the complicated personality they serve to express, it is a little surprising to find that Hemingway is almost always described as a primitive. Yet the word really applies to him, if it is used in what might be called its anthropological sense. The anthropologists tell us that many of the so-called primitive peoples have an extremely elaborate system of beliefs, calling for the almost continual performance of rites and ceremonies; even their drunken orgies are ruled by tradition. Some of the forest-dwelling tribes believe that every rock or tree or animal has an indwelling spirit. When they kill an animal or chop down a tree, they must beg its forgiveness, repeating a formula of propitiation; otherwise its spirit would haunt them. Living briefly in a world of hostile forces, they preserve themselves—so they believe—only by the exercise of magic lore.

There is something of the same atmosphere in Hemingway's work. His heroes live in a world that is like a hostile forest, full of unseen dangers, not to mention the nightmares that haunt their sleep. Death spies on them from behind every tree. Their only chance for safety lies in the faithful observance of customs they invent for themselves. In an early story like "Big Two-Hearted River," you notice that Nick Adams does everything very slowly, not wishing "to rush his sensations any"; and he pays so much attention to the meaning and rightness of each gesture that his life alone in the wilderness becomes a succession of little ceremonies. "Another hopper poked his face out of the bottle. His antennae wavered. Nick took him by the head and held him while he threaded the hook under his chin, down through his thorax and into the last segments of his abdomen. The grasshopper took hold of the hook with his front feet, spitting tobacco juice on it." The grasshopper is playing its own part in a ritual; so too is the trout that swallows it, then bends the rod in jerks as it pumps against the current. The whole fishing trip, instead of being a mere escape, might be regarded as an incantation, a spell to banish evil spirits. And there are other magical ceremonies in Hemingway's work, besides those connected with fishing and hunting and drinking. Without too much difficulty we can recognize rites of animal sacrifice (as in *Death in the Afternoon*), of sexual union (in *For Whom the Bell Tolls*), of self-immolation (in "The Snows of Kilimanjaro"), of conversion (in "To Have and Have Not"), and of symbolic death and rebirth (in the Caporetto passage of *A Farewell to*

Arms). When one of Hemingway's characters violates his own standards or the just laws of the tribe (as Ole Andreson has done in "The Killers"), he waits for death as stolidly as an Indian.

Memories of the Indians he knew in his boyhood play an important part in Hemingway's work: they reappear in *The Torrents of Spring* and in several of his shorter stories. Robert Jordan, in *For Whom the Bell Tolls*, compares his own exploits to Indian warfare, and he strengthens himself during his last moments by thinking about his grandfather, an old Indian fighter. *In Our Time*, Hemingway's first book of stories, starts by telling how Nick Adams' father is called to attend an Indian woman who has been in labor for two days. The woman lies screaming in a bunkhouse, while her husband, with a badly injured foot, lies in the bunk above her smoking his pipe. Dr. Adams performs a Caesarean section without anesthetic, then sews up the wound with fishing leaders. When the operation is finished, he looks at the husband in the upper bunk and finds that he is dead; unable to bear his wife's pain, he has turned his face to the wall and cut his throat. A story Nick Adams later tells is of Trudy Gilby, the Indian girl with whom he used to go squirrel shooting and who, under the big hemlock trees, "did first what no one has ever done better." Most of Hemingway's heroines are in the image of Trudy; they have the obedience to their lovers and the sexual morals of Indian girls. His heroes suffer without complaining and, in one way or another, they destroy themselves like the Indian husband.

But Hemingway feels an even closer kinship with the Spaniards, because they retain a primitive dignity in giving and accepting death. Even when their dignity is transformed into a blind lust for killing, as sometimes happened during their civil war, they continue to hold his respect. Agustín, in *For Whom the Bell Tolls*, sees four of Franco's cavalrymen and breaks out into a sweat that is not the sweat of fear. "When I saw those four there," he says, "and thought that we might kill them I was like a mare in the corral waiting for the stallion." And Robert Jordan thinks to himself: "We do it coldly but they do not, nor ever have. It is their extra sacrament. Their old one that they had before the new religion came from the far end of the Mediterranean, the one they have never abandoned but only suppressed and hidden to bring it out again in wars and inquisitions." Hemingway himself seems to have a feeling for half-forgotten sacraments; his cast of mind is pre-Christian and pre-logical.

Sometimes his stories come close to being adaptations of ancient myths. His first novel, for example, deals in different terms with the same legend that T. S. Eliot was not so much presenting as concealing in *The Waste Land*. When we turn to Eliot's explanatory notes, then read the scholarly work to which they refer as a principal source—*From Ritual to Romance*, by Jessie L. Weston—we learn that his poem is largely based on the legend of the Fisher King. The legend tells how the king was wounded in the loins and how he lay wasting in his bed while his whole kingdom became unfruitful; there was thunder but no rain; the rivers dried up, the flocks had no increase, and the women bore no children. *The Sun Also Rises* presents the same situation in terms of Paris after the First World War. It is a less despairing book than critics like to think, with their moral conviction that drinkers and fornicators are necessarily unhappy; at times the story is gay, friendly, even exuberant; but the hero (who is also a fisherman) has been wounded like the Fisher King, and he lives in a world that is absolutely sterile. I don't mean to imply that Hemingway owes any debt to *The Waste Land*. He had read the poem, which he liked at first, and the notes that followed it, which he didn't like at all; I doubt very much that he bothered to look at Jessie L. Weston's book. He said in 1924, when he was writing about the death of Joseph Conrad: "If I knew that by grinding Mr. Eliot into a fine dry powder and sprinkling that powder over Mr. Conrad's grave, Mr. Conrad would shortly appear, looking very annoyed at the forced return, and commence writing, I would leave for London early tomorrow morning with a sausage grinder." And yet when he wrote his first novel, he dealt with the same legend that Eliot had discovered by scholarship; recovering it for himself, I think, by a sort of instinct for legendary situations.

And it is this instinct for legends, for sacraments, for rituals, for symbols appealing to buried hopes and fears, that helps to explain the power of Hemingway's work and his vast superiority over his imitators. The imitators have learned all his mannerisms as a writer, and in some cases they can tell a story even better than Hemingway himself; but they tell only the story; they communicate with the reader on only one level of experience. Hemingway does more than that. Most of us are also primitive in a sense, for all the machinery that surrounds our lives. We have our private rituals, our little superstitions, our symbols and fears and nightmares; and Hemingway reminds us unconsciously of the hidden worlds in which we live. Reading his best work, we are a little like Nick Adams looking down from the railroad bridge at the trout in "Big Two-Hearted River": "many trout in deep, fast-moving water, slightly distorted as he watched far down through the glassy convex surface of the pool, its surface pushing and swelling smooth against the resistance of the log-driven piles of the bridge. At the bottom of the pool were the big trout. Nick did not see them at first. Then he saw them at the bottom of the pool, big trout looking to hold themselves on the gravel bottom in a varying mist of gravel and sand."

3

During the last few years it has become the fashion to reprimand Hemingway and to point out how much better his work would be (with its undoubted power) if only he were a little more virtuous or reasonable or optimistic, or if he revealed the proper attitude toward progress and democracy. Critics like Maurice Coindreau (in French) and Bernard DeVoto have abused him without bothering to understand what he plainly says, much less what he suggests or implies. Even Maxwell Geismar, who is one of the few professors with a natural feeling for literary values, would like to make him completely over. "What a marvelous teacher Hemingway is," he exclaims, "with all the restrictions of temperament and environment which so far define his work! What could he not show us of living as well as dying, of the positives in our being as well as the destroying forces, of 'grace under pressure' and the grace we need with no pressures, of ordinary life-giving actions along with those superb last gestures of doomed exiles!" Or, to put the matter more plainly, what a great writer Hemingway would be, in Geismar's opinion, if he combined his own work with equal parts of Trollope and Emerson.

And the critics have some justice on their side. It is true that Hemingway has seldom been an affirmative writer; it is true that most of his work is narrow and violent and generally preoccupied with death.

But the critics, although they might conceivably change him for the worse, are quite unable to change him for the better. He is one of the novelists who write, not as they should or would, but as they must. Like Poe and Hawthorne and Melville, he listens to his personal demon, which might also be called his intuition or his sense of life. If he listened to the critics instead, he might indeed come to resemble Trollope or Emerson, but the resemblance would be only on the surface and, as he sometimes says of writing that tried hard to meet public requirements, it would all go bad afterwards. Some of his own writing has gone bad, but surprisingly little of it. By now he has earned the right to be taken for what he is, with his great faults and greater virtues; with his narrowness, his power, his always open eyes, his stubborn, chip-on-the-shoulder honesty, his nightmares, his rituals for escaping them, and his sense of an inner and an outer world that for twenty years were moving together toward the same disaster. *

---

*Since this introduction to the *Portable Hemingway* (1944) has become a subject of controversy, it is reprinted here without changes, except for the omission of one paragraph (at the beginning of Section 2, on page 173). The paragraph summarized Hemingway's early life and it was based—it had to be based—on printed sources available at the time. One of these was *Who's Who*, which, in ten or more editions, gave his birth date as 1898 instead of 1899. There were gross errors in all the other printed sources. I learned in later years that most of the errors could be traced back to Hemingway, who liked to embroider stories about himself. He also was given to making honest and sometimes damaging confessions, not only in letters written late at night but in his fiction as well. "Complicated" is the one word for his character. He nursed grudges and could be, so people said of him, "as mean as cat piss," yet he was in many ways a vastly appealing person.   M.C., 1984

IN DEFENSE OF THE
1920s

No other period in American literature has been denounced more vehemently and persistently than the 1920s. Not to mention the early attacks against *This Side of Paradise* in 1920 and against *Three Soldiers* in 1921, there were the professorial insults of the Humanists and, all through the Depression, the continued jeers of the proletarian critics. These were followed, after the beginning of the Second World War, by the exhortations of MacLeish as a reformed poet lecturing his comrades in sin, and by the anathemas of Van Wyck Brooks, who spoke as a moralist deeply concerned for the future of literature and his country; both were threatened, he believed, by roving bands of unrepentant writers. Still other voices joined in. The attacks were made by men of different literary and political faiths, who invoked a mixture of conservative, radical, reactionary, and liberal-democratic standards; but in general they brought forward the same charges: that the literature of the 1920s was superficial, immoral, negative, and had failed to depict the healthier side of American life.

Bernard DeVoto restates and magnifies these accusations. In his new book, *The Literary Fallacy*, he asserts that the authors of the 1920s were "ignorant, inaccurate or foolish—or frivolous or corrupt." They completely misunderstood the society of their time—which, he says, "was rugged, lively, and vital; but literature became increasingly debilitated, capricious, querulous and irrelevant." And DeVoto ends by saying:

> Never in any country or any age had writers so misrepresented their culture, never had they been so unanimously wrong. Never had writers been so completely separated from the experiences that alone give life and validity to literature. And therefore, because separation from the sources of life makes despair, never had liter-

ature been so despairing, and because false writing makes trivial writing, never had literature been so trivial. . . . Seeking for a phrase which will convey the quality of that literature, history may sum it up as the Age of Ignominy.

But you wonder, reading his book, how it came about that such an ignorant, foolish, debilitated, querulous, trivial, and utterly ignominious literature has managed to survive this series of attacks. Why do young writers still imitate Wolfe or Crane or Fitzgerald, in preference to Willa Cather and Robert Frost? Why do flyers back from New Guinea and Australian war correspondents in the Middle East write novels in Hemingway's early manner? Might it be that the continuing attacks against those writers are another testimony to their life and power? Even Bernard DeVoto, who belabors them from any convenient angle; who is now a sociological critic, now a wise anthropologist, now a historian, now a moralist, now (briefly and inadvertently) an esthetician, now radical, now conservative, now speaking in behalf of the American scholar and now rallying the crowd against him— even DeVoto proclaims the vigor and art of these writers by his need to use all weapons against them.

In his attacks, he is not always careful to preserve the appearance of consistency and fairness. Thus, he indicts *The Flowering of New England* and *New England: Indian Summer* on two principal counts: that they fail to consider national affairs or the opening of the frontier, and that they neglect economic trends "in showing us the delicacies of minds absorbed in the fascinating task of writing books." Forgetting that the two works together were planned as a literary history of New England, he insists on judging them as a social and cultural history of the nation at large. In his second chapter, he condemns writers for their careless use of the word "fascist." "Except in a small number of cases," he says, and with good reason, ". . . the epithet 'fascist' applied by writers to one another has meant one or the other of two things. It has meant either 'I disagree with him' or 'He does not like my books.' " In his fourth chapter, however, he forgets this wise observation in his rage at Hemingway. "From the beginning up to now," he says, "both implicitly and explicitly, with a vindictive belligerence, Mr. Hemingway has always attacked the life of the mind, the life of the spirit and the shared social experience of mankind. . . . It is a short step from thinking of the mob to thinking of the wolf pack, from the praise of instinct to war against reason, from art's vision of man as contemptible to dictatorship's vision of men as slaves." In other words, Hemingway is a short step from being a fascist. Either DeVoto disagrees with him or he doesn't like DeVoto's books.

A graver fault than this unfairness or inconsistency—of which I could give many other examples—is the author's failure to define his subject strictly in his own mind. He says that his book is an examination, "reasonably detailed but far from complete, of certain ideas, dogmas and conclusions which appear and reappear in much American literature of the 1920s, particularly in the work of writers who were then widely held to be most characteristic of the time and most expressive of its spirit." Elsewhere he mentions these writers by name: they are H. L. Mencken (born in 1880), Sinclair Lewis (1885), Ernest Hemingway (1899), John Dos Passos (1896), William Faulkner (1897), Thomas Wolfe (1900), T. S. Eliot (1888), and Van Wyck Brooks (1886). Most of these men belonged to one of two different categories. Either they were the writers who *dominated* the 1920s (along with Dreiser, Anderson, Cabell, and Hergesheimer) or else they were the men who *appeared* in the 1920s, existed as a group in opposition to the dominant trends, and did their best work in the following decade. Brooks was the one exception. He detested the 1920s and, for a time, he wrote nothing whatever; all his best work was done before and after the period that DeVoto claims to be treating. When he collects the faults of two hostile generations while neglecting their virtues, the result is an interesting amalgam of literary crimes, but it bears little resemblance to what actually happened in American letters.

The principal crime of which DeVoto accuses both generations together is that of indulging in what he calls "the literary fallacy." This he defines as, "essentially, the belief that literature is the measure of culture." But in that case, why confine himself to the 1920s, considering that writers of all ages have held a similar belief? And why confine himself to literature? There is also an agricultural fallacy, which consists in believing that agriculture is the measure of culture. There is a plumbing fallacy: that bathrooms are the measure of culture. At all times men have sought to glorify their own professions; you might almost call it the human fallacy. It is a pardonable failing, and it causes less damage than might be expected, considering that human culture is a unity, something that can be approached and penetrated from almost any angle; men often start from such different fields as fiction, agriculture, science, and even plumbing to reach the same truths about life as a whole. There is also a critic's fallacy, however, and it is somewhat less innocent than the others we have mentioned. It consists in projecting an imaginary purpose for works of literature, quite different from the actual purposes of their authors, and then condemning the authors jointly and separately because they failed to achieve it. DeVoto writes as if to illustrate that fallacy. He takes for granted that the authors of the 1920s should all have been cultural historians and should all have depicted American civilization as DeVoto now sees it; then he charges them with offering only a false or fragmentary picture. Quoting Emerson, he orders them back from their special interests to "the meal in the firkin, the milk in the pan."

But when I came to reread "The American Scholar," I found that Emerson's words had a different application from the one that DeVoto was trying to give them. They were a plea, not for writing great treatises on American civilization based on years of study in the library, but rather for understanding our immediate surroundings. "What would we really know the meaning of?" Emerson asked. "The meal in the firkin; the milk in the pan; the ballad in the street; the news of the boat; the glance of the eye; the form and gait of the body; show me the ultimate reason of these matters . . . and the world lies no longer a dull miscellany and lumber-room, but has form and order; there is no trifle, there is no puzzle, but one design unites and animates the farthest pinnacle and the lowest trench." He was saying almost what Hemingway said at the end of *Death in the Afternoon*: "Let those who want to [do so] change the world, if you can get to see it clear and as a whole. Then any part you make will represent the whole if it's truly made." There is no sign in this quotation—although there are a few signs elsewhere—of the violent anti-intellectualism that DeVoto imputes to Hemingway. There is every sign of an intellectual purpose he shared with other members of his generation: to deal only with the parts of the world they knew best, in the conviction that those parts would reveal the whole world. They hated eloquence, even of Emerson's homely sort; but instinctively they agreed with him that "one design unites and animates the farthest pinnacle and the lowest trench."

Hemingway, for example, didn't write about America the Vastly Beautiful, as DeVoto would have liked him to do; he wrote about the Michigan woods, about Paris cafés and fighting on the Isonzo and bull-fights in Spain; these were his meal in the firkin and his milk in the pan. Faulkner wrote about a single Mississippi county in book after book dealing with hundreds of different characters; by now he has composed what is our nearest approach to a *comédie humaine*. Fitzgerald wrote about his wealthy neighbors on Long Island and the Riviera, investing them with a false glamor and carefully explaining its falsity. Wolfe wrote badly at times, worse than any other American author of distinction, but he also gave us the poetry of the adolescent who feels infinite possibilities in himself and sets out from a back-country town to conquer the world—or rather, his part of the world. All these authors wrote about parts of the world; Dos Passos and Hart Crane were the only exceptions, the only men of their generation who tried to deal with America as a whole. Crane's attempt was a failure—as a whole; but he is marvelous in his treatment of specific scenes: the Brooklyn Bridge, the subways, the Mississippi. Dos Passos wrote from the special view of the traveler, the man who continually meets new people, hears their stories briefly, and travels on. That too was a part of the world: a cross-section taken horizontally rather than in depth.

The parts of America that appear in their novels and poems are not in general the smiling parts, the broad farmlands, the big Sunday dinners after coming home from church, the bouncing optimism that Mr. DeVoto finds everywhere. As a matter of fact, these authors were rebelling against another picture of American life that was dominant and accepted, that was preached in the churches, proclaimed at Rotary luncheons and romanticized by *The Saturday Evening Post*. Nobody was misled by them at the time they were writing: if anybody wanted the antidote to Dos Passos, let us say, he could find it in every magazine at his dentist's office and almost every novel in the loan library at the corner drugstore. But a curious thing has happened in the intervening years. The orthodox, optimistic, forward-looking literature of the

1920s has disappeared so completely that DeVoto doesn't even remember it. The literature of the rebels and renegades has survived and has come to be taken as a complete picture of the period. It had the strength to live.

Today it is time for us to see these authors in perspective, with their great faults—which are not always the faults DeVoto imputes to them—set beside their greater virtues; their lack of broad vision set beside their power in depicting what was close at hand; their injustice to certain phases of American life set beside their emotional depth and lyricism. It is much too soon to assign them their separate ranks, and I should question whether any of them will ever be placed on the same level as Emerson or Thoreau or Melville; yet together (and with a dozen contemporaries almost equally gifted) they represent a great period in American letters, the greatest since Concord in the 1850s. To them and to their critics I would apply what Gide said recently about Victor Hugo, after mentioning his faults one after another: "But instead of demanding qualities from people that we could easily find elsewhere, should we not take them for what they are: the titans for titans, the dwarfs for dwarfs, and the pedants who attack Hugo for fools?"

THE MIDDLE-AMERICAN
PROSE STYLE

A t the very end of *Wars I Have Seen*, Gertrude Stein descends from the great problems of war and peace, on which her remarks are sometimes rather silly, to a smaller but no less complicated problem on which she can speak with authority. Briefly it is the growth of a specifically American style in speech and writing. "There is one thing," she says, "one has to remember about America, it had a certain difficulty in proving itself American which no other nation has ever had." She believes that the difficulty was in essence linguistic:

> The trouble of course is or was that by the time America became itself everybody or very nearly everybody could read and write and so the language . . . instead of changing as it did in countries where nobody knew how to read and write while the language was being formed, the American language instead of changing remained English, long after the Americans in their nature their habits their feelings their pleasures and their pains had nothing to do with England.
>
> So the only way the Americans could change their language was by choosing words which they liked better than other words, by putting the words next to each other in a different way than the English way, by shoving the language around until at last now the job is done, we use the same words as the English do but the words say an entirely different thing.

Miss Stein shows very little interest here in the new words that originated in this country. She says, "We use the same words as the English do," thus dismissing in one phrase the subject to which Sir William Craigie and his collaborators have devoted the four big volumes of their *Dictionary of American English on Historical Principles*.

H. L. Mencken's subject, in *The American Language*, is also the special words that Americans use. In this otherwise complete and endlessly interesting work, he has almost nothing to say about sentence structure, position of accented words, length of phrase, choice *among* correct words, and other habits of speech that distinguish an American from an Englishman, even when both of them might defend their separate usages by referring to the same grammars and the same dictionaries.

Miss Stein, on the other hand, is chiefly concerned with these questions of style. She thinks that the American language consists not so much in the words themselves as in the different way that Americans have of putting English words together. As if to prove her point—though almost any other passage in her latest book, *Wars I Have Seen*, would illustrate it almost as well—she has written the two quoted paragraphs, in which every word is from *The Oxford Dictionary*, in which only one phrase ("different way than") is by English standards a grammatical error, yet in which the whole effect is un-English. And she says, "At last now the job is done," with the air of dedicating a native monument that she has helped to build.

In one sense, though Miss Stein does not say so, the job was partly done a long time ago. It would seem from the records that Americans had at least a standard dialect, if not a spoken language of their own, many years before they had an independent government. As early as 1735, an Englishman in Georgia was complaining of what he called the "barbarous English" of the older settlers. In 1754 a London journalist suggested that a glossary of Americanisms would soon be in order. Two years later Samuel Johnson reviewed a book of essays published in Philadelphia. He said that it was written "with such elegance as the subject admits, tho' not without some mixture of the American dialect," which he described as "a tract of corruption."

These early British comments, with others, are quoted by Mr. Mencken in the first section of *The American Language*. The second and third sections are devoted to British abuse of American morals, manners, and politics, but especially of American speech, during the fifty years that followed the Revolution. It was in the midst of this British counteroffensive that Sydney Smith asked his famous series of questions: "In the four quarters of the globe, who reads an American book?

or goes to an American play? or looks at an American picture or statue? . . ." Still harsher things were said by Southey, the Poet Laureate, and a host of minor journalists, till Americans came to believe that the whole campaign was subsidized by the Foreign Office. But the point that concerns us here is its effect on the prose style of American writers.

It had, in reality, two effects that contradicted each other. British abuse made some writers excessively self-conscious in matters of style and set them trying to write a purer English than their colleagues across the water. In this aim Washington Irving succeeded so well that his *Sketch Book* would be used, for more than a century, as a first reader for students of the English language all over the world. Whitman, on the other hand, reacted by trying to make his style more American, more cosmopolitan—he declared that "The best of America is the best cosmopolitanism"—and decidedly less English. He said in the lecture he called "An American Primer": "Ten thousand native idiomatic sounds are growing, or are today already grown, out of which vast numbers could be used by American writers, with meaning and effect—words that would be welcomed by the nation, being of the national blood—words that would give that taste of identity and locality which is so dear in literature." Once in a conversation with Horace Traubel, he described *Leaves of Grass* as "only a language experiment."

But although Whitman's style was rich in American and cosmopolitan words—and even richer in Whitmanisms—it was not the style that would be adopted as their own by young American poets and novelists of the following century. That style had a different source, in literature and geography, and it might be useful to trace its history in brief.

2

Many American novels of the last twenty years, especially those by young men, are written in an exaggeratedly simple style, full of "ands," "all rights," and "anyways," full of accurate notes about the physical actions of the characters and flat statements about the way they felt. Book reviewers call it "the Hemingway style." Literary historians explain that it began as a combination of what Hemingway learned from Gertrude Stein and Sherwood Anderson with his oral memory of Midwestern speech. The truth is that it goes back much farther into the American past.

It began long ago as an attempt to reproduce the actual words and intonations of the American frontiersmen. Its earliest appearance was in humorous writing, and notably in the great collection of tales that gathered round David Crockett, the congressman from the cane-brakes. Robert Montgomery Bird, of Philadelphia, was possibly the first to use something like the real language of frontiersmen in the dialogue of a novel: *Nick of the Woods*, published in 1837. Mark Twain, of Missouri, was the first to write a whole book and a serious book in the new style: of course it was *Huckleberry Finn*.

It was published in 1884, with an introductory note explaining that several dialects were used in it: "the Missouri Negro dialect; the extremist form of the backwoods Southern dialect; the ordinary 'Pike County' dialect; and four modified versions of the last." All the dialects are exactly rendered, when the characters start talking, but that isn't the important feature of the book, even from the standpoint of style. Its importance there is that Huck tells the story in his own words and that, besides being a modified version of the Pike County dialect, those words are also a literary medium capable of being used for many different effects: not only backwoods humor but also pity and terror and the majestic sweep of the river. Ernest Hemingway would say, many years later: "All modern American literature comes from one book by Mark Twain called 'Huckleberry Finn.' . . . There was nothing before. There has been nothing as good since."

There has been, however, a further development of this Mid-American style as a literary language. In a sense, Mark Twain had apologized for using it, by putting it into the mouth of an illiterate hero; it was not at all his own manner of speech. The next step was for an educated author to write the style when talking in his own person. That was the step taken by Gertrude Stein in her first book, *Three Lives*. No publisher would accept the manuscript and she had to pay for having it printed; but the printer hesitated to do the work, even when payment of his charges was guaranteed. He sent an emissary to Miss Stein in Paris, to learn whether she was really illiterate. "You see," her visitor said hesitantly, "the director of the Grafton Press is under the impression that perhaps your knowledge of English . . ."—"But I am an American," said Gertrude Stein, as if that explained her whole manner of writing.

Unlike most of her later books, *Three Lives* told a recognizable story—three stories, in fact—and it had a clearly recognizable effect on Sherwood Anderson, who read it in his Chicago days and wrote in praise of the author. Miss Stein was a teacher and critic of Hemingway's, at the time when he was "trying to learn to write," as he said, "commencing with the simplest things"; and Anderson was one of his early, fervent, and brief admirations. Hemingway did not learn his style from them—even at first it was largely his own invention—but Miss Stein in particular encouraged him to write a strictly Midwestern prose.

It was widely imitated from the beginning. Before his first books were published in New York, there were young Americans in Paris writing and talking and even walking like Hemingway. Before his own stories were being accepted by magazines of general circulation, several of his followers had found their way into the *Saturday Evening Post*. Now, after twenty years, his influence is continuing to spread. Almost all the war novels by correspondents and fighting men are written in something that approaches Hemingway's early manner.

I have sketched this long development very briefly, mentioning only a few of the crucial books and authors. To illustrate the story, let me give a series of five quotations, extending over more than a century:

1. Old Tiger and Brutus were sitting upon the edge of the water, whining because they couldn't git over; and I had a mighty good dog named Carlow,—he was standing in the water ready to swim; and I observed as the water passed by him it was right red,—he was mighty badly cut. When I come to notice my other dogs they were all right bloody, and it made me so mad that I harked 'em on, and determined to kill the bear.

I hardly spoke to 'em before there was a general plunge and each of my dogs just formed a streak going straight across. I watched 'em till they got out on the bank, when they all shook themselves, old Carlow opened, and off they all started. The water was right red where my dogs jumped in, and I loved 'em so much it made me mighty sorry.

Sketches and Eccentricities of
Col. David Crockett of West Tennessee,
1833.

2. I was powerful glad to get away from the feuds, and so was Jim to get away from the swamp. We said there warn't no home like a raft, after all. Other places do seem so cramped up and smothery, but a raft don't. You feel mighty free and easy and comfortable on a raft.

The Adventures of Huckleberry Finn,
by Mark Twain, 1884.

3. Jeff had never spoken to her at all about it. It just seemed as if it were well understood between them that nobody should know that they were so much together. It was as if it were agreed between them, that they should be alone by themselves always, and so they would work out together what they meant by what they were always saying to each other.

Three Lives,
by Gertrude Stein, 1908.

4. As the shadow of the kingfisher moved up the stream, a big trout shot upstream in a long angle, then lost his shadow as he came through the surface of the water, caught the sun, and then, as he went back into the stream under the surface, his shadow seemed to float down the stream with the current, unresisting, to his post under the bridge where he tightened facing up into the current.

Nick's heart tightened as the trout moved. He felt all the old feeling.

In Our Time,
by Ernest Hemingway, 1925.

5. They did not break into a run. Their happiness was terrifying; they walked slowly toward their women. . . . The women ran toward the men. There was equal happiness on both sides, it

just happened that most of the men knew their women would be there, whereas some of the women were not sure that their men would be there. That was the difference.

A Bell for Adano,
by John Hersey, 1944.

Even without dates or signatures, the casual reader of these five passages would assume that they were written by five different authors; yet he would also notice, I think, that they belong to the same prose tradition. Essentially it is a Midwestern style, but it is something more than a dialect, and it does not depend for its effect on misspellings or on violations of English grammar. If all the errors were edited out of the earlier passsages; if Davy Crockett said "get" instead of "git" and Huck Finn said "wasn't any" instead of "warn't no"; if all the words listed as Americanisms were changed to their English equivalents, these five quotations would still be American by virtue of the accents, the pauses, the fashion in which words are put together.

All five authors, from the unknown journalist who listened to Davy Crockett's stories and tried to set them down in their original form to the war correspondent who wrote a novel based on what he saw in Sicily (and made his Sicilian villagers talk like John Steinbeck's *paisanos*), reveal the same underlying attitude toward their material. They all have the same habit of making flat assertions about their emotional reactions ("It made me mighty sorry," "You feel mighty free and easy and comfortable on a raft," "He felt all the old feeling") that come after a series of violent physical images and therefore give the effect of understatement. Hemingway didn't invent that trick, any more than Crockett did; it was always part of the Midwestern tradition in story telling.

Neither did Gertrude Stein invent the trick of repeating the same word in several sentences, so that it gives a keynote to the paragraph. Crockett found the trick instinctively: notice his repetition of "water" and "right red." Mark Twain used the word "raft" as keynote of the quoted sentences, which, by the way, have been echoed hundreds of times in contemporary writing. Hemingway used the words "stream" and "current" and "tightened." Most writers of standard English prose keep looking for synonyms, in order not to repeat the same words over and over. This Midwestern style, on the other hand, is based on a pattern of repetitions.

Here are a few of its other characteristics, as revealed in the quoted passages:

1. The words are simple in themselves, taken from common speech, and the authors make no effort to avoid a long succession of monosyllables. The "phrase"—that is, the group of words—tends to be rather longer than in standard English, and the accent or changed tone of voice falls on the last word in each group, almost as in French. Thus: "As the shadow of the *kingfisher* moved up the *stream*, a big trout shot upstream in a long *angle*, then lost his shadow as he came through the surface of the *water*. . . ."

2. The sentence structure is generally looser than in standard English, with a number of simple statements connected by "and" or "but" or "when."

3. Most of these authors show a fondness for intensifying adverbs and adverbial expressions: "mighty," "right," "powerful," "just," "so," "at all." This, by the way, has always been a characteristic of American as a spoken language.

4. Some of the authors make an excessive use of present participles and participial tenses to give the effect of continued action: "they were always saying," "tightened facing up," etc.

5. All of them tend to avoid abstract nouns; instead they use relative clauses to convey the same ideas. This tendency is especially clear in the passage from Gertrude Stein: she does not say "their meaning," but "what they meant"; she does not say "their conversation," but "what they were always saying to each other."

Some day I should like to see a more systematic analysis of this style that American novelists now seem to learn in the cradle. And some day I should like to see its development traced through the fiction of the last twenty years. It was certainly Hemingway who made it popular, but some of his contemporaries (including Fitzgerald and Dos Passos, but not Thomas Wolfe) seem to have approached it independently. It began to run riot among the novelists who appeared a little later than Hemingway, including Steinbeck and Saroyan and Raymond Chandler. Curiously it has never gained a hold in contemporary poetry: Carl

Sandburg's early experiments in the American language were widely read but had comparatively few imitators. The poets, most of them, write a tortured but late-classical English. The novelists try with more or less success to speak United States.

AIDGARPO

When George Soule, my senior colleague on *The New Republic*, made a tour of the Soviet Union some years ago, he was invited to attend a meeting of the Georgian poets in Tiflis. They sat at a big round table drinking toasts in Caucasian wine. Then for a moment they fell silent while the translator said to George, "The poets want to know why Americans don't appreciate their own great poet Aidgarpo."

"Who?" said George.

"Aidgarpo," said the translator, putting the accent on the second syllable to rhyme with Harpo.

"Oh . . . I see. We call him Edgar Allan Poe. He is, well, he isn't sentimental enough to satisfy most Americans."

George was looking for a simple answer that wouldn't lead to arguments. He must have found the right one, for the poets went on to other topics, after drinking a formal toast to Aidgar Al*lan*po. Really to explain why Poe has a greater reputation in Europe, and beyond the borders of Europe, than he has in his own country would have taken George all afternoon, and even then the Soviet poets mightn't have understood.

Had he tried to be accurate, he could have begun by saying that, in one sense, Poe *is* appreciated in the United States; that he is more widely read than any other author of what we now describe as our classical period;* that he is also more widely imitated; that there have been more editions of Poe, more biographies and critical studies, than of his New England contemporaries. He could have mentioned the Poe cottages, the Poe houses, the Poe shrines maintained in cities where he lived, as well as the collections assembled at great expense by the bibliophiles who specialize in Poe material.

He would have been forced to add, however, that almost all this ap-

*This was still true in 1945.

preciation or commemoration is of the wrong sort. The readers of Poe
are usually of high-school age or mentality. The imitations of Poe are
in the pulp-paper magazines. The editions of Poe, with a few exceptions (fortunately including the present one-volume selection by
Philip Van Doren Stern), are carelessly put together; and they are embellished with some of the worst copper engravings in all the history
of romantic bad taste. The rhapsodies on Poe are mostly by third-rate
critics. The biographies are often much better; but the very first of
them, by Rufus Wilmot Griswold, was malicious to the point of criminal libel, and it was almost a hundred years before Griswold's forger-
ies were exposed. For most Americans, Poe and his work have been lost
in a theatrical legend. In order to find again what he really wrote, and
to judge it at something like its true value, we have to dig for it under
an accumulated mass of sentimental valentines, poison-pen letters,
high-school notebooks, and ladies' lace handkerchiefs wet with tears.
And having finally disinterred his remains, we are likely to find something else than our ideal of the great American writer.

For example, we find—as George Soule might have explained to the
Soviet poets—that Poe is not at all in the main current of American
literature; not even in one of the minor currents. One can trace a line
that runs from Hawthorne to Henry James to T. S. Eliot, and thence
to most of the poets writing today. One can trace another line that runs
from the frontier humorists to Mark Twain, and thence to Hemingway
and all his imitators. One can trace the history of naturalism in the
American novel and of Whitmanism in American poetry; but Poe
stands off to the side. Like other American authors, he had his predecessors and his disciples, but the former were rather obscure figures,
like Charles Brockden Brown for the tales and Thomas Holley Chivers
for the later poems; while the disciples in America were horror-story
fictioneers or jingle-bell poets; in any case, men who played no part in
the history of American writing.

Not only was his work outside the main current of our literature; it
also stood apart from American life. For this reason, the purely sociological critics have had a hard time dealing with Poe; they have been
unable to find more than minor connections between the man and his
milieu. They found, it is true, that he regarded himself as a member
of the Virginia slave-holding gentry, and mirrored the beliefs of that

class when he touched on social or political topics; but they also had to admit that he touched on such topics rarely. They found that his formal style had something to do with the ideals of chivalry surviving in the South. They found that he conducted his own Civil War against the New England critics. But having made these observations, they left their readers with the feeling that everything important about Poe was still to be explained.

There are, however, two aspects of his work, both neglected by the sociological critics, that are nevertheless completely of his time and nation. Living in the great age of American invention and the first age of American showmanship, he distinguished himself in both fields.

In all his critical work, he revealed a mechanistic attitude toward literature. A story or a poem, he believed, was essentially a machine for producing an "effect," that is, for arousing a given emotion in its readers. In explaining how he wrote "The Raven," he says: "It is my design to render it manifest that no one point in its composition is referable either to accident or intuition—that the work proceeded, step by step, to its completion with the precision and rigid consequence of a mathematical problem." Again, in *Marginalia*, he defines the ideal plot as "that from which no component atom can be removed, and in which none of the component atoms can be displaced, without ruin to the whole." The definition would also apply to an efficient machine, which can produce its effect without any excess parts or wasted motions. In some ways Poe resembled the half-crazed inventors of his time, working in poverty to discover, let us say, a process for vulcanizing rubber—and dying in poverty after the discovery was made—much more than he resembled any other American writer. His hatred of plagiarism, expressed so often in his criticisms, was exactly the attitude of an inventor toward those who infringe his patents.

In his eagerness to create effects, Poe was a showman too; and he was not always nice in his choice of materials. Like the stage manager of a company touring the provinces, he made the best of what was at hand; if buckram had to serve for silk brocade, glass for jewels, and bombast for emotion, why should he care, so long as the audience was properly impressed? The American audience of his time was not distinguished for its taste, yet all his effects had to be measured by its reactions; and he had to compete for its attention with elocutionists, travelers from the Holy Land, and the freaks in Barnum's Museum. All this explains the cheapness or vulgarity for which Poe has often been blamed, and with reason; but his critics have usually neglected to say that the quality is completely absent from his early stories and poems. He did his best work in the years when the audience had scarcely heard of him.

He lived in a period when most American writers were dilettantes, with Irving, Cooper, and N. P. Willis almost the only exceptions; and yet he worked hard to establish professional standards of authorship. He wrote and lobbied for an international copyright law; he defended his colleagues against the British critics. In his own writing, however, he showed no interest in using American speech or even in portraying the American background. Long afterward critics went through his work looking for native landscapes. They found a few of these: Sullivan's Island, near Charleston, in "The Gold Bug" and glimpses of Westchester County in "Landor's Cottage"; the hills near Charlottesville, Virginia, in "A Tale of the Ragged Mountains," and the Richmond waterfront in the first episode of *Arthur Gordon Pym.* But the critics, if they were honest, had to admit that he usually described the landscapes of an inner world, which were as formless and colorless as the background of a dream. The places he mentioned were remembered from his reading more often than from his actual travels; he liked to situate his stories in "some large, old, decaying city near the Rhine," or in "an abbey, which I shall not name, in one of the wildest and least frequented portions of fair England." But the real setting of all his work was a book-lined chamber, anywhere, in which Poe sat dreaming. He was describing his own case when he wrote, at the beginning of "Berenice":

> The recollections of my earliest years are connected with that chamber, and with its volumes—of which I will say no more. Here died my mother. Herein was I born. . . . Thus awaking from the long night of what seemed, but was not, nonentity, at once into the very regions of fairyland—into a palace of imagination—into the wild dominions of monastic thought and erudition—it is not singular that I gazed around me with a startled and ardent eye—that I loitered away my boyhood in books, and dissipated my youth in revery; but it *is* singular that as years rolled

away, and the noon of manhood found me still in the mansion of my fathers—it *is* wonderful what stagnation there fell upon the springs of my life—wonderful how total an inversion took place in the character of my commonest thought. The realities of the world affected me as visions, and as visions only, while the wild ideas of the land of dreams became, in turn—not the material of my every-day existence—but in very deed that existence utterly and solely in itself.

The library was his birthplace as an author; it was the imagined scene of his mother's death and of his own betrothal (which he also regarded as a *betrayal* of his dead mother); it was the real setting of his visions; in brief, it was his fatherland. No wonder, then—as George Soule might have explained to the Soviet poets—that Poe has always seemed a little foreign to American critics; no wonder that his work "carries well" into foreign languages—*qu'il porte bien*, as the French say of a wine that loses none of its flavor when exported. His stories deal with emotions that are intense and unusual, but almost never localized; they can be understood just as well by the French or the Russians as they were understood by his Virginia neighbors. His sentence structure is logical, his vocabulary is somewhat abstract, and he uses very few of the homely words that have no equivalents in other languages. His work in general is an ideal subject for translation.

He had the good luck, moreover, to find the ideal translator. When Charles Baudelaire was a young man of twenty-five—the year was either 1846 or 1847 and Poe was still living—he happened to run across some fragments of Poe's work, probably the earliest French versions of one or two magazine pieces. At once Baudelaire felt "a singular commotion," as he said many years later in a letter to his friend Armand Fraisse. "Since Poe's complete works were not collected in a uniform edition until after his death," he continued, "I had patience enough to be friendly with Americans living in Paris, so that I could ask them to lend me files of the magazines that Poe had edited. And then I found, believe me if you will, poems and stories that already existed in my mind, but in vague, confused and disorderly fashion; Poe had been able to put them together and bring them to perfection." Baudelaire had possessed some knowledge of English since his school days, but now he studied it again, as preparation for translating the stories. He continued working on them till 1865, just before his last illness. Much of his own critical work and several of his later poems were influenced by Poe; for example, there is one fine poem, "La Voix," that is clearly based on the passage I quoted from "Berenice."

In his translations, Baudelaire was extremely accurate; he tried to follow Poe's sentence structure and even his curious system of punctuation, with dashes where other writers would use commas. Yet his taste was better than Poe's, and often, without changing the sense, he found a less ornate word or a simpler construction. Moreover, he translated only what he regarded as the essential Poe: forty-three of the tales as against sixty-eight in American editions, besides *Eureka* and three of the shorter essays. He omitted most of the space-filling journalism; and the result is that Poe, in Baudelaire's translation, stands clear of the rubbish with which his grave has been encumbered. Reading Poe in French, one can see his importance in the history of European and world literature. He stands at the exact beginning of the doctrine of art for art's sake (or life for art's sake); he stands at the exact point of transition between the Gothic romance, set in a haunted German castle, and that modern type of story in which the terror, as Poe said, "is not of Germany, but of the soul"; and he also stands at the exact point where Romantic poetry is transformed into Symbolist poetry. Poe, in fact, was the first to state the doctrines that French poets—and after them English, German, Russian, and even American poets—would continue to develop for a hundred years after his death.

Even the English and American poets learned those doctrines indirectly through Baudelaire rather than directly from Poe. Baudelaire was a less original thinker, but he was a much greater poet; and not the least of his poetic creations was the mythical figure of an American writer, which grew bigger and mistier as it traveled eastward—until it crossed the high mountains that divide Europe from Asia, and the Georgian poets at their meeting in Tiflis drank a toast to Aidgarpo.

JAMES THURBER'S WORLD
AND WORDS

I. HIS WORLD

There are two ways to review the selected writings and drawings of James Thurber. The wrong way, I think, is to be deeply impressed by the fact that Thurber is a funny man and try to match his book with a funny review, making great use of exaggeration and overstatements, which you have been taught to regard as the essence of American humor. The other and somewhat revolutionary method is the one I should like to follow. It consists in reviewing his book exactly as if it were the work of any other skillful and serious American writer.

The Thurber Carnival contains thirty-three of his "pieces," a general term to describe his stories, almost-stories, light essays and autobiographical sketches. All but one of them first appeared in *The New Yorker*. Most of them have also appeared in one or another of his earlier volumes, but the first six were previously uncollected. In addition to the pieces, there is *My Life and Hard Times,* complete with illustrations; and the selection ends with 125 pages of Thurber's drawings. These suffer from being reduced to a maximum width of four inches; they sometimes lose the effect of movement and part of the detail gets blurred (as note "Zero Hour—Connecticut" and "Gettysburg" on pages 366–67); but it is good to have so many of them together, even if we have to look at them through a reading glass. The pieces are intact, and they are just as funny or sad or frightening as when we read them the first time.

Most of them might have been written to illustrate the difference between wit and humor. Wit, says the *Shorter Oxford*, is "that quality of speech or writing which consists in the apt association of thought and expression, calculated to surprise by its unexpectedness; later always with ref. to the utterance of brilliant or sparkling things in an amusing way." Humor, says *Webster's Collegiate*, "implies, commonly, broader human sympathies than wit, and a more kindly sense of the incongruous, often blended with pathos." There is not much wit in Thurber's writing, although there is plently of it in his conversation. Occasionally in a story he permits himself a relatively brilliant or sparkling metaphor—he says, for example, "This midsummer Saturday had got off to a sulky start, and now, at three in the afternoon, it sat, sticky and restive, on our laps"; but for the most part he confines himself to the almost businesslike description of incongruous situations that are often blended with pathos.

He doesn't always bother to be funny. Eight of the pieces, by my count, are quite serious in effect and intention, and several of the others balance on the edge between farce and disaster, like a clown on a very high trapeze. Four of them—all funny ones—end with the murder of the hero, and two—both serious—end with his natural death (one of the last heroes is a dog). Four others end with dreams of killing or being killed, and two with the hero of one and the villainess of the other reduced to raving madness. There are fifteen pieces—almost half the selections in the book—that are largely based on nightmares, hallucinations, or elaborate and cruel practical jokes. Entering Thurber's middle-class world is like wandering into a psychiatric ward and not being quite sure whether you are a visitor or an inmate. The author himself bustles around in a white jacket, but sometimes he stops to say in a pleasant, matter-of-fact voice, "You know, they don't suspect. They think I'm a doctor."

He writes so naturally and conversationally that it is hard to realize how much work goes into his stories. His art is in fact extremely conscious and is based on a wide knowledge of contemporary writing. In a letter to Fred B. Millett, written in 1939, Thurber listed some of his favorite authors: Henry James first of all, then Conrad Aiken, Hemingway, Fitzgerald, Edmund Wilson, and Willa Cather, among others. The list would indicate, he said, "that I like the perfectly done, the well ordered, as against the sprawling chunk of life. . . . I also owe a debt to E. B. White . . . whose perfect clarity of expression is it seems to me equaled by very few and surpassed by simply nobody. . . . I came to *The New Yorker* a writer of journalese and it was my study of White's writing, I think, that helped me to straighten out my prose so that people could see what it meant." Besides learning to write with an easy flow and coherence that very few authors achieve, he also learned to omit everything inessential, including the winks, the rib-nudgings, and the philosophical remarks of older American humorists. He achieves a sort of costly simplicity, like that of well-tailored clothes or good conversation.

Within his fixed limits of length and sympathy and subject, one feels almost nothing but admiration for Thurber's work; one's only regret is that he hasn't made the limits broader. Other things being equal, a good long story is better than a good short one; and most of Thurber's begin and end within 3,000 words, a convenient length for *The New Yorker*. Most of his characters are upper-middle-class couples from the upper Middle West, who have moved to New York, prospered financially, and bought or rented houses in Connecticut. His favorite subject is their domestic quarrels, which he portrayed in a famous series of drawings, here reproduced, as "The War Between Men and Women."

Henry James in his time was also impressed by the conflict between American business or professional men and their wives. In *The American Scene*, he described it as "a queer deep split or chasm between the two stages of personal polish, the two levels of the conversible state, at which the sexes have arrived." It was the wives who had reached what he regarded as the much higher level. "Nothing," he said, "is more concomitantly striking than the fact that the women, over the land—allowing for every element of exception—appear to be of a markedly finer texture than the men." He recommended the subject to the painter of manners, and Thurber has adopted it as his own. When he describes the split or chasm, however, it is as if each of the sexes had crossed to the opposite side. The women in his stories are hard, logical, aggressive; they have all the virtues and vices that James assigned to businessmen. The husbands, on the other hand, are widely read, dreamy, introspective; they are helpless without their wives, but at the same time they try to escape into an imagined world of men. Thus Walter Mitty, driving the family car, pictures himself as the commander of a huge, hurtling eight-engined navy hydroplane. He imagines the crew looking up and grinning as a storm beats against the wings. "The Old Man'll get us through," they say to one another. "The Old Man ain't afraid of Hell!" . . . "Not so fast! You're driving too fast," says Mrs. Mitty; and the hydroplane of Walter Mitty's dream comes hurtling down.

Almost all of Thurber's heroes are dreamers and escapists, even when they are happily married. The author defends them in his illustrated "Fables for Our Times." The moral of one fable is, "Who flies afar from the sphere of our sorrow is here today and here tomorrow"; of another, "Run, don't walk, to the nearest desert island." In his autobiographical sketches, Thurber describes two easy methods for escaping into a fantastic world: by sound and by sight. The first method consists in misunderstanding or misinterpreting words and phrases. Thus, he hears a station agent repeating time and again over the telephone, "Conductor Reagan on the 142 has the lady the office was asking about"; and soon, brooding over the sentence, he imagines himself among silky, desperate spies. On another occasion his maid, who always mispronounces words, comes to his study and says, "They are here with the reeves." His hired man, who has the same bad habit, tells him, "I go hunt grotches in de voods," and again, "We go to the garrick now and become warbs." The servants are referring to wreaths and crotches and wasps in the garret; but before Thurber succeeds in unraveling their remarks, they have sent him wandering off into surrealist landscapes that he compares, at one point, to the secret world of Salvador Dali.

His other means of escape is simply by taking off his glasses. Because his vision is defective, the whole world thereupon assumes a different shape for him. On one such occasion, so he says, "I saw the Cuban flag flying over a national bank, I saw a gay old lady with a gray parasol walk right through the side of a truck, I saw a cat roll across a street in a small striped barrel, I saw bridges rise lazily into the air, like balloons." Reading these lines, and the rest of "The Admiral on the Wheel," one can scarcely help thinking of a famous passage from Rimbaud's "Alchemy of the Word":

> I habituated myself to simple hallucination: I would see quite honestly a mosque instead of a factory, a school of drummers composed of angels, barouches on the roads of the sky, a drawing-room at the bottom of a lake: monsters, mysteries; the announcement of a musical comedy would cause horrors to rise before me.

Then I explained my magical sophistries by the hallucination of words!

I ended by finding sacred the disorder of my mind.

There is in fact a curious similarity between one type of fantastic American humor and the current in European poetry that is represented in various phases by Rimbaud and Lautréamont, by expressionism, dadaism, and surrealism. None of these schools has flourished here (although surrealism now has more disciples than the others possessed), and I think the reason may be that our sense of rightness is offended when we hear a young man proclaiming that he has a wild, satanic imagination whose disorder he finds sacred, and then describing his dreams. But the truth is that we enjoy fantasy much more than the French; and we gladly listen to the same type of dreams when they are described by Thurber in a matter-of-fact voice and with a self-deprecatory air.

2 . HIS WORDS

Aesop's animals are Greek citizens, and those of La Fontaine are French peasants or noblemen, with the lion as *Le Grand Monarque*. It is only proper that Thurber's animals should be the mirrors of a new society that seems to consist of college-bred Americans with more bright gadgets than they need and with more neuroses than they can afford.

I suspect that most of them were born in Columbus, Ohio, like the author, and that they have followed him into the Connecticut jungle where they feel at home: lions and lemmings, toads and tigers, wolves and gaudy young wolfesses, all of them busy at their avocations of driving too fast, drinking too much if they are males, worrying about the children if they are mothers, and getting into family arguments. These are usually won by the females, who have the inborn advantage of knowing exactly what they want, which is everything.

In the first of the new fables, two almost shapeless creatures crawl out of the sea at the almost beginning of time. The male feels uneasy in the new environment and globs back into the water (the verb "to glob" is one of Thurber's many inventions), but the female goes flobbering almost imperceptibly toward the scrubby brown growth beyond the sand, while dreaming of things that will later become rose-point lace, taffeta, and jewelry. A couple of eons later, the male feels lonely and comes flobbering after her. And the moral of the story? "Let us ponder this basic fact about the human: Ahead of every man, not behind him, is a woman."

Often in the fables we find the sexes joined in single or wedded combat. A grizzly bear comes home from a month-long bender after a Christmas party to find that his wife has filled the house with lamps that emit an odor of pine cones, chairs that bounce him up and down, cigarette boxes that can't be opened, and supersafety matches that won't light. He smashes the furniture, throws the gadgets out of the window, and goes roaring away with the most attractive of the unmarried female bears, one named Honey. Moral: "Nowadays most men lead lives of noisy desperation." In another fable Proudfoot the tiger is consistently rude to his wife, who rebels one night. Next morning the cubs, male and female, tumble eagerly downstairs while calling to their mother, "What can we do?" She tells them, "You can go in the parlor and play with your father. He's the tiger rug just in front of the fireplace." Moral: "Never be mean to a tiger's wife, especially if you're the tiger."

Though he reports a number of these bloody skirmishes, there is a softer note in many of Thurber's latest communiqués about the war between men and women. He is no longer the stern male patriot that he was in the days when he drew a woman's face on the dragon waiting to devour a timid St. George. As a good moralist, he warns each woman not to be a bragdowdy (in Thurber's definition, a woman who admits, often proudly, that she has let herself go—a frumpess); a hug-moppet (an overaffectionate old woman, a bunnytalker); a starefrock (a woman who stares another woman up and down—hence, a rude female, a hobbledehoyden); or an interfering busybody. "Thou shalt not convert thy neighbor's wife," he tells her, "nor yet louse up thy neighbor's life."

But he also warns each man—here or in other recent work—not to be a snatchkiss (Thurber's word for a kitchen lover); a smugbottle (a man, usually American, who boasts of his knowledge of wines—a fuss-grape); or a growp (like Proudfoot the tiger, who kept snarling "Growp," by which he actually meant, "I hope the cubs grow up to be xylophone players or major generals").

Perhaps Thurber thinks of himself as having risen above the hurly-burly, *au dessus de la mêlée*.

At sixty-one, almost sixty-two, he is becoming more inventive in his language but more traditional in his wisdom. The fables find new ways of telling us that all is vanity, that beauty is no more fleeting than ugliness, and that misery loves company but can't always find it. Some of the morals are: "The noblest study of mankind is Man, says Man"; "Where most of us end up there is no knowing, but the hellbent get where they are going"; "It is wiser to be hendubious than cocksure"; "This is the posture of fortune's slave: one foot in the gravy, one foot in the grave"; "You can't very well be the king of beasts if there aren't any"—this for a story of total war in the jungle; and "A word to the wise is not sufficient if it doesn't make any sense," for a fable about the chaos of the English language.

This last has become what is probably his favorite subject of warning. The animals in his fables, like the persons in his stories, are always misunderstanding one another and jumping to fatal conclusions. "Get it right," he tells them, "or leave it alone. The conclusion you jump to may be your own." He also says, "We live, man and worm, in a time when almost everything can mean almost anything, for this is the age of gobbledygook, doubletalk, and gudda." Consulting *The Thurber Album*, one learns that gudda, a language spoken in the environs of Columbus, Ohio, is so named for the word that most frequently pops up in it. The word is a verb of possession ("I gudda horse"), of necessity ("I gudda get a horse"), and of futurity ("I'm gudda get a horse tmawra"). Thurber still talks like a man from Columbus—that is, fast and through his nose—but he never uses gudda except when he is doing impersonations. His effort through most of a long career has been to write lucid, correct, and expensively simple English.

I should hesitate to say that his prose is the best now being written in this country. Other things being equal, the best prose would be that which was most effective in presenting the boldest subjects. Except in his fables, where he can touch them lightly, Thurber has always avoided bold subjects like war and revolution, love and death; he prefers to write about the domestic confusions of people whose sedentary lives are not too different from his own. It isn't a very complicated society that he presents, or one with a rich fabric of inherited values, or one in which men and women are destroyed by their splendid passions. His most ambitious hero is Walter Mitty, who has his visions of glory while buying puppy biscuits. His tragic lover (in "The Evening's at Seven") goes back to a *table d'hôte* dinner at his hotel and, in token of a shattered life, orders consommé instead of clam chowder.

Comedy is his chosen field, and his range of effects is deliberately limited, but within that range there is nobody who writes better than Thurber, that is, more clearly and flexibly, with a deeper feeling for the genius of the language and the value of words.

He tries never to intone or be solemn. "Humor," he once wrote in a letter to me, "cannot afford the ornaments and indulgences of fine writing, the extravagance of consciousness-streaming, or lower-case unpunctuation meanderings. There is a sound saying in the theater: 'You can't play comedy in the dark.' I saw Jed Harris and Billy Rose trying to disprove this one night in Philadelphia twenty-five years ago when they put on an eight-minute Don Marquis skit in absolute darkness: the sounds of voices, glasses, and the cash register of an old-time beer saloon. People fell asleep, or began coughing, or counting their change, or whispering to their neighbors, or reading their programs with pencil flashlights. Comedy has to be done *en clair*. You can't blunt the edge of wit or the point of satire with obscurity."

In his effort to be absolutely clear, he pays so much attention to the meaning and color of words that he speaks of them almost as if they had personalities to be cultivated or avoided. "What could be worse than 'eroticize'?" he asked in another letter. "It is one of those great big words, or tortured synonyms, with which psychiatry has infected the language, so that a page of type sometimes looks like a parade of Jack Johnsons wearing solid gold teeth and green carnations in the lapels of their electric-blue morning suits." He prefers the familiar words that would be used in conversation without a self-conscious pause. His art consists in arranging them so that they give the impression of standing cleanly and separately on the page, each in its place like stones in a well-built wall.

That impression is not an easy one to achieve, and Thurber takes endless pains with his stories. He spent fifty working days on "The Secret Life of Walter Mitty," which is four thousand words long. By contrast he did a whole book of fifty drawings, *The Last Flower*, in two hours of an otherwise idle evening. He has often explained to art critics that he draws for relaxation, as others doodle at the telephone. He never redraws, but he continually rewrites. Last year he told an interviewer that one of his stories—"The Train on Track Six," still unpublished—had been rewritten fifteen times from beginning to end. "There must have been close to 240,000 words in all the manuscripts put together," he said, "and I must have spent two thousand hours working at it. Yet the finished version can't be more than twenty thousand words."

His gradual loss of eyesight, now almost total, once threatened to put an end to his work. As early as 1941 he found that he could no longer distinguish the keys of a typewriter. When a series of painful operations failed to restore his vision, he took to writing with a black crayon on yellow copy paper. But his one eye kept growing weaker—the other had been lost in a boyhood accident—and his handwriting larger in compensation, until twenty words filled a page and a hundred used up the crayon. Nobody except his wife and his secretary could decipher what he had written.

Then slowly he trained himself to give dictation. It was harder for him than for most writers, because so much of his work depends on his finding exactly the right word and using it in exactly the right place, but at last he found a practical system that he follows most of the time. He spends the morning turning over the text in his mind, moving words around like a woman redecorating the living room, and then in the afternoon he calls in a secretary. The system would be impos- sible without his remarkable memory. Sometimes he remembers, word for word, three complete versions of the same story.

His loss of vision has had an effect on his style that will be noted by almost every reader of his new fables. All the sound effects have been intensified, as if one sense had developed at the cost of another, and the language is full of onomatopoeia and alliteration. "The caves of ocean bear no gems," one studious lemming reflects as all the others plunge into the water, "but only soggy glub and great gobs of mucky gump." Man tells the dinosaur, in one of the best fables, "You are one of God's moderately amusing early experiments . . . an excellent example of Jehovah's jejune juvenilia." There are puns too, like "Monstrosity is the behemother of extinction," and there are rhymes not only in the morals but scattered through the text, so that whole passages could be printed as verse.

But this preoccupation with words, with their sound, sense, and arrangement into patterns, has affected more than the style of the fables. It is also transforming the imagination of the author, who seems to be presenting us with a completely verbalized universe. The only conceivable end for the inhabitants of such a universe would be mass suicide resulting from complete verbal confusion; and that is exactly how Thurber pictures them as ending, in the fable about lemmings which also ends the collection.

It seems that a single excited lemming started the exodus by crying "Fire!" when he saw the rising sun. Hundreds followed him toward the ocean, then thousands, each shouting a different message of fear or exultation. "It's a pleasure jaunt!" squeaked an elderly female lemming. "A treasure hunt!" echoed a male who had been up all night; "Full many a gem of purest ray serene the dark unfathomed caves of ocean bear." His daughter heard only the last word and shouted, "It's a bear! Go it!" Others among the fleeing thousands shouted "Goats!" and "Ghosts!" until there were almost as many different alarms as there were fugitives. Then they all plunged into the seas, and that was the end of the lemmings.

Symbolically it was also the end of mankind as only Thurber could have imagined it: not with a bang, not with a whimper, but in a universal confusion of voices and meanings.

PROLEGOMENA TO
KENNETH BURKE

I. DRAMATISM

It is hard for me to write about *A Rhetoric of Motives* because the author is my oldest friend. I first met Kenneth Burke when I was three years old and he was four. At that time my father was the Burkes' family physician and he took my mother and me along with him in the buggy when making one of his visits. Mother used to tell me that I went around the parlor touching everything in my reach while Kenneth followed apprehensively repeating, "Don't touch. Mustn't." One is always tempted to read meanings and patterns into those childhood stories and it is true that in our high-school days I was more venturesome than Kenneth, getting into more scrapes, but afterwards our relations were reversed. As a critic he has been the one who went touching everything from floor to chandelier, while at times I have scolded him by letter for not observing the critical rules handed down by the Elders.

By touching and asking questions and taking nothing for granted he has come to be one of the few truly speculative thinkers of our time. It is not a time that encourages speculation; we have begun to speak wistfully of the past; there is a general longing for certainty or security and meanwhile our few explorations, whether intellectual or geographical, are usually made by organized groups. Even dissent, so far as it is related to Communism or anti-Communism, has become an organized and bureaucratized activity. Burke belongs to an older line, that of the individual seekers after truth; one thinks of William James and his father, too; of C. S. Peirce, John Jay Chapman, and perhaps of Thorstein Veblen more than the others.

I speak of Veblen because he had the same concern with hidden social motives, but I doubt that Burke would like to be compared with him. "Veblen," he says in the *Rhetoric*, "treads cumbrously. And his terminology of motives is far too limited in scope; hence, at every step in his exploration, important modifiers would be needed, before we could have a version of human motives equal to the depths at which the ways of persuasion . . . must really operate." Burke's terminology is wider in scope and permits a deeper reading of human motives. Where Veblen tends to simplify or cheapen a situation, Burke likes to reveal the complexity of motives lying behind it. Where Veblen is critical and even corrosive, Burke is more often admiring. "See how vastly ingenious men are in hiding their follies," he seems to be saying; and he accepts the follies as a condition of the social environment.

Yet he has in common with Veblen a bent of mind that is revealed in his use of a special vocabulary. Veblen had a special vocabulary, too; it was different from Burke's, but it was invented for the same general purposes, one of which was to cast new light on a subject by describing it in terms borrowed from a strikingly different subject; thus, he discussed the American leisure class as if he were an ethnologist writing about the Polynesians. Burke often uses the same method; he calls it "perspective by incongruity."

Veblen began his career as a student of philosophy, but his interest in human relations soon led him into sociology and economics. Burke started from literary criticism and always circles back to it; his critical essays are as fruitful—or one might rather call them seedful—as any written in our time; but I think it is an error to approach him as a critic primarily. In his latest books one finds that his interest in human relations is leading him more and more toward general philosophy, where Veblen began.

A Rhetoric of Motives, the very latest, is the second volume of a trilogy which will be devoted to the strategies of human expression and communication. In the first volume—*A Grammar of Motives* (1945)— he had offered a general statement of principles (the "grammar" of the title was used in the sense of "elements," as one might say "a grammar of painting"). Burke held that there were five elements involved in any statement about human motives; they were act, scene, agent, agency, and purpose. His theory was that every philosophical school had laid a special emphasis on one of the five; thus, materialism emphasized the *scene*; idealism, the *agent*; pragmatism, the *agency* or instrument; and mysticism, the ultimate *purpose*. Burke himself showed more sympathy with Aquinas, who, he said, was "dramatistic" in his method and who conceived of existence as an *act*.

Having defined his terms in the first volume, Burke goes forward in the second to discuss language as the medium of human relations. "Rhetoric" in Burke's sense is a very broad term; he seems to define it—though never in exactly these words—as the study of the linguistic and symbolic means by which human beings try to influence one another. Thus, it includes the traditional rhetoric, to which he devotes some interesting chapters, but it also includes topics that are usually regarded as lying in the province of the anthropologists or the economists or the Freudian psychologists. At one point he criticizes the Freudians for "concealing the nature of exclusive social relations behind inclusive terms for sexual relations." He promises that in the last volume of the trilogy, which will be *A Symbolic of Motives*, he will analyze Freud's work to show "how many logical and dialectical principles are, by his own account, involved in the operations of the dream."

In books like the *Grammar* and the *Rhetoric* we begin to see the outlines of a philosophical system on the grand scale, something that Veblen never attempted. The system starts with the definition that *man is a symbol-using animal*, and from this it branches out in all directions. In the sense that it is a humanistic or man-centered system it must always remain partial; it does not attempt to deal with the extra-human world of matter and energy. In another sense and within its fixed limits, the system promises to be complete. Already it has its own methodology (called "dramatism"), its own aesthetics (based on the principle that works of art are symbolic actions), its logic and dialectics, its ethics (or picture of the good life), and even its metaphysics, which Burke prefers to describe as a meta-rhetoric.

Burke has a reputation for being difficult to read and one must admit that it is partly deserved—while adding the proviso that most Americans, including our college graduates, have been so corrupted by skimming through their newspapers and half-listening to the radio that they find any reading difficult if it deals, even in the simplest fashion, with general ideas. In so far as the difficulty can be ascribed to the author's presentation of a subject, and not to the subject itself or to the audience, I think it is largely a matter of Burke's special vocabulary, which has to be learned like a new language.

He is looking for terms that will cast new light on old situations and he finds them in unexpected places. Sometimes they are colloquial phrases like "moving in on," "slipping out from under," "cashing in," or "being driven into a corner," to which he gives a philosophical meaning. Sometimes they are technical terms that he borrows from anthropology or sociology or semantics. Sometimes they are the words of Greek philosophers or theologians carried over into English; in the present volume I noted, among others, "eristic," "chiliastic," "heuristic," "eschatology," "noetic." It is a good idea to have a big dictionary at hand when reading him for the first time.

Besides a special terminology, Burke also has habits of thought that make him hard to follow. He is a dialectician who is always trying to reconcile opposites by finding that they have a common source. Give him two apparently hostile terms like poetry and propaganda, art and economics, speech and action, and immediately he looks beneath them for the common ground on which they stand. Where the Marxian dialectic moves forward in time from the conflict of thesis and antithesis to their subsequent resolution or synthesis—and always emphasizes the conflict—the Burkean dialectic moves backwards from conflicting effects to harmonious causes. It is a dialectic of reconciliation or peacemaking and not of war. At the same time it gives a backward or spiral movement to his current of thought, so that sometimes the beginning of a book is its logical ending and we have to read the last chapter before fully understanding the first.

The point I want to make is that, with a little attention, we finally understand all the chapters. Burke is one of the authors who write to be read twice, and if we give his work that second reading most of our difficulties are cleared away. A second reading is like a second journey through a recently discovered mountain pass; the trail is marked now and we no longer get lost in ravines that end at the base of a cliff. There are, it is true, a few sentences that have to be walked around like boulders in the path; but most of the second journey is easy and we make it with a sense of exhilaration, as if we had suddenly learned to be at home in a strange country. What Burke teaches us on the journey is how to interpret human experience, including literary experience, as a series of ritual dramas: initiations, penances, rebirths, and castings out of scapegoats. We learn his lesson and, when we come down out of the mountains, we discern a new richness in our favorite books and a new eventfulness in the landscape of our familiar lives.

2. HIS FIRST LAW OF AESTHETICS

A small press in Los Altos, California, is republishing Kenneth Burke's early books and has started with *Counter-Statement* (1931), which was his first collection of critical writing. I doubt that there is an American author of our time whose out-of-print books offer more reasons for putting them back on display. Moreover, the right beginning has been made, since *Counter-Statement* introduces many of the ideas that would be developed in Burke's later writing, where they aren't always easy to follow. Sometimes that is because the ideas are difficult in themselves, but more often it is because they come forward in such variety and profusion, jostling one another on the page, that the reader is first exhilarated, then bewildered, as on his first visit to a crowded and vaguely foreign city. More simply conceived and simply written, *Counter-Statement* will give him a sense of direction.

Although the book consists of seven essays that seem to deal with unrelated subjects, most of the essays are explanations or applications of the same critical principle. It is a principle that Burke discovered for himself when reading *Hamlet* and observing the complicated fashion in which Shakespeare prepared his audience for the appearance of the ghost. Wasn't this psychological manipulation of the audience the true *form* of the passage and indeed of the play as a whole? "Form in literature," Burke wrote, "is an arousing and fulfillment of desires. A work has form in so far as one part of it leads a reader to anticipate another part, to be gratified by the sequence." From that principle might follow a new system of aesthetics.

A first deduction from the principle is that works of art, from the formal point of view, might be regarded as complicated and sensitive machines for producing *effects* in the minds of their audience. But as soon as we make this deduction and find ourselves using the familiar word "effects," it becomes apparent that Burke's principle is not so completely new as it has seemed. "Effect," in the singular, was the favorite critical term of Edgar Allan Poe and he too regarded the work of literature as a sort of machine that operated on the emotions of the reader.

In "The Philosophy of Composition" Poe explained step by step how he had written "The Raven" to produce a certain single effect in the mind of the reader. Baudelaire greatly admired his explanation and translated it into French, though he hinted that it was not completely honest. "But after all," he said, "a little charlatanism is always permitted to genius, and is even proper to it. . . ." Mallarmé, not disturbed by the question of charlatanism, studied English so that he could read Poe in the original. His exploration of new poetic techniques was inspired by Poe's critical writing. In a first letter to Mallarmé the young Paul Valéry described himself as being "deeply infused with the profound doctrines of the great E. A. Poe—perhaps the subtlest artist of this century."

It is curious to note that Poe's doctrine of "effect," which depends on communication with the reader, was adopted by the French symbolist poets who were most esoteric and least concerned with communication. But the doctrine also had its influence on American writers who were more concerned with having their work understood. Hemingway, writing of his apprentice years, hints at a similar conception of what a story should do. "I was trying to write then," he says at the beginning of *Death in the Afternoon*, "and I found the greatest difficulty . . . was to put down what really happened in action; what the actual things were which produced the emotion that you experienced." If he found "the sequence of motion and fact" that had produced the emotion in himself, and set down the sequence in its pure outlines, his story would produce the same emotion in the reader. Once again the story was regarded as a machine for producing a certain single effect. With such examples before us we can see that Burke's definition of form in literature as "an arousing and fulfillment of desires" was based on the theory and practice of other writers for at least a century. His originality lay in making the definition so simple and direct, so much like a scientific law, that it became a basis for research into the mechanics of literary appeal.

In *Counter-Statement* and still more in his later books, Burke has contributed widely to that research by helping to reveal the hidden complexities of our language. There are scores of linguistic and stylistic questions on which he has cast new light: for example, he has written on the mimetic value of sounds; on inadvertent puns that betray an author's intentions; on "clusters" of images that do the same; on the naming of characters and how the names sometimes determine the characters; on the part played in poems by the poet's conception of the social hierarchy; on rituals of death and rebirth, or of the casting out of devils, that often appear in naturalistic novels; and on the dramatic devices that conceal themselves even in business documents and statistical tables. He calls his method "dramatism" and defines it as "a perspective that, being developed from the analysis of drama, treats language and thought primarily as modes of action." One can see how the method developed from the principle first announced in *Counter-Statement*.

In the critical field, dramatism has the great virtue of finding complexities in any work it singles out for attention, and of making the work more interesting than it had seemed on a casual reading. The new or intrinsic or ontological critics owe a considerable debt to Burke and his linguistic researches. But his method as they apply it to the analysis of texts—and even as Burke himself applies it—has the weakness of not providing us with critical judgments or standards of value.

In making this statement I continue an old argument with Burke, whose answer has always been that he isn't primarily a critic. He started from literary criticism (after writing two books of fiction), he has provided us with many brilliant examples of the critic's art; and yet the most brilliant of all the examples is possibly his essay on *Mein Kampf*, in which he explains Hitler's strategies of persuasion. In other words the quality of his attention does not depend on the literary greatness of his subject; and when his literary subject happens to be a great one, as in another brilliant essay, on "Venus and Adonis," he may not even discuss the qualities that make it a masterpiece. He is more interested in mechanisms of appeal, as in the Hitler essay, and in the disguises of social attitudes, as in the "Venus and Adonis." We could, however, go further and say that his real subject is man as a symbol-using animal. Since that is his definition of man—"specifically the symbol-using animal"—the subject leads him into a survey of all human activities that involve speech, and even of wordless activities that have a symbolic value. Instead of being a critic he is primarily a speculative philosopher, as ingenious and full of insights as any we now possess.

SOCIOLOGICAL HABIT PATTERNS IN LINGUISTIC TRANSMOGRIFICATION

I have a friend who started as a poet and then decided to take a post-graduate degree in sociology. For his doctoral dissertation he combined his two interests by writing on the social psychology of poets. He had visited poets by the dozen, asking each of them a graded series of questions, and his conclusions from the interviews were modest and useful, though reported in what seemed to me a barbarous jargon. After reading the dissertation I wrote and scolded him. "You have such a fine sense of the poet's craft," I said, "that you shouldn't have allowed the sociologists to seduce you into writing their professional slang—or at least that's my judgmental response to your role selection."

My friend didn't write to defend himself; he waited until we met again. Then dropping his voice, he said: "I knew my dissertation was badly written, but I had to get my degree. If I had written it in English, Professor Blank"—he mentioned a rather distinguished name—"would have rejected it. He would have said it was merely belletristic."

From that time I began to study the verbal folkways of the sociologists. I read what they call "the literature." A few sociologists write the best English they are capable of writing, and I suspect that they are the best men in the field. There is no mystery about them. If they go wrong, their mistakes can be seen and corrected. Others, however—and a vast majority—write in a language that has to be learned almost like Esperanto. It has a private vocabulary which, in addition to strictly sociological terms, includes new words for the commonest actions, feelings, and circumstances. It has the beginnings of a new grammar and syntax, much inferior to English grammar in force and precision. So far as it has an effect on standard English, the effect is largely pernicious.

Sometimes it misleads the sociologists themselves, by making them think they are profoundly scientific at points where they are merely being verbose. I can illustrate by trying a simple exercise in translation, that is, by expressing an idea first in English and then seeing what it looks like in the language of sociology.

An example that comes to hand is the central idea of an article by Norman E. Green, printed in the February 1956 issue of the *American Sociological Review*. In English his argument might read as follows: "Rich people live in big houses set farther apart than those of poor people. By looking at an aerial photograph of any American city, we can distinguish the richer from the poorer neighborhoods."

I won't have to labor over a sociological expression of the same idea because Mr. Green has saved me the trouble. Here is part of his contribution to comparative linguistics. "In effect, it was hypothesized," he says—a sociologist must never say "I assumed," much less "I guessed"—"that certain physical data categories including housing types and densities, land use characteristics, and ecological location"—not just "location," mind you, but "ecological location," which is almost equivalent to locational location—"constitute a scalable content area. This could be called a continuum of residential desirability. Likewise, it was hypothesized that several social data categories, describing the same census tracts, and referring generally to the social stratification system of the city, would also be scalable. This scale could be called a continuum of socio-economic status. Thirdly, it was hypothesized that there would be a high positive correlation between the scale type on each continuum."

Here, after ninety-four words, Mr. Green is stating, or concealing, an assumption with which most laymen would have started, that rich people live in good neighborhoods. He is now almost ready for his deduction, or snapper:

> This relationship would define certain linkages between the social and physical structure of the city. It would also provide a precise

definition of the commonalities among several spatial distributions. By the same token, the correlation between the residential desirability scale and the continuum of socio-economic status would provide an estimate of the predictive value of aerial photographic data relative to the social ecology of the city.

Mr. Green has used 160 words—counting "socio-economic" as only one—to express an idea that a layman would have stated in thirty-three. As a matter of fact, he has used many more than 160 words, since the whole article is an elaboration of this one thesis. Whatever may be the virtues of the sociological style—or Socspeak, as George Orwell might have called it—it is not specifically designed to save ink and paper. Let us briefly examine some of its other characteristics.

A layman's first impression of sociological prose, as compared with English prose, is that it contains a very large proportion of abstract words, most of them built on Greek or Latin roots. Often—as in the example just quoted—they are used to inflate or transmogrify a meaning that could be clearly expressed in shorter words surviving from King Alfred's time.

These Old English or Anglo-Saxon words are in number less than one-tenth of the entries in the largest dictionaries. But they are the names of everyday objects, attributes, and actions, and they are also the pronouns, the auxiliary verbs, and most of the prepositions and conjunctions, so that they form the grammatical structure of the language. The result is that most novelists use six Anglo-Saxon words for every one derived from French, Latin, or Greek, and that is probably close to the percentage that would be found in spoken English.

For comparison or contrast, I counted derivations in the passage quoted from *American Sociological Review*, which is a typical example of "the literature." No less than forty-nine per cent of Mr. Green's prose consists of words from foreign or classical languages. By this standard of measurement, his article is more abstruse than most textbooks of advanced chemistry and higher mathematics, which are said to contain only forty per cent of such words.

In addition to being abstruse, the language of the sociologists is also rich in neologisms. Apparently they like nothing better than inventing a word, deforming a word, or using a technical word in a strange context. Among their favorite nouns are "ambit," "extensity" (for "extent"), "scapegoating," "socializee," "ethnicity," "directionality," "cathexis," "affect" (for "feeling"), "maturation" (for both "maturing" and "maturity"), and "commonalities" (for "points in common"). Among their favorite adjectives are "processual," "prestigeful," and "insightful"—which last is insightful to murder—and perhaps their favorite adverb is "minimally," which seems to mean "in some measure." Their maximal pleasure seems to lie in making new combinations of nouns and adjectives and nouns used as adjectives, until the reader feels that he is picking his way through a field of huge boulders, lost among "universalistic-specific achievement patterns" and "complementary role-expectation-sanction systems," as he struggles vainly toward "ego-integrative action orientation," guided only by "orientation to improvement of the gratification-deprivation balance of the actor"—which last is Professor Talcott Parsons's rather involved way of saying "the pleasure principle."

But Professor Parsons, head of the Sociology Department at Harvard, is not the only delinquent recidivist, convicted time and again of corrupting the language. Among sociologists in general there is a criminal fondness for using complicated terms when there are simple ones available. A child says "Do it again," a teacher says "Repeat the exercise," but the sociologist says "It was determined to replicate the investigation." Instead of saying two things are alike or similar, as a layman would do, the sociologist describes them as being either isomorphic or homologous. Instead of saying that they are different, he calls them allotropic. Every form of leadership or influence is called a hegemony.

A sociologist never cuts anything in half or divides it in two like a layman. Instead he dichotomizes it, bifurcates it, subjects it to a process of binary fission, or restructures it in a dyadic conformation—around polar foci.

So far I have been dealing with the vocabulary of sociologists, but their private language has a grammar too, and one that should be the subject of intensive research by the staff of a very well-endowed foundation. I have space to mention only a few of its more striking features.

The first of these is the preponderance of nouns over all the other parts of speech. Nouns are used in hyphenated pairs or dyads, and sometimes in triads, tetrads, and pentads. Nouns are used as adjectives without change of form, and they are often used as verbs, with or without the suffix "-ize." The sociological language is gritty with nouns, like sanded sugar.

On the other hand, it is poor in pronouns. The singular pronoun of the first person has entirely disappeared, except in case histories, for the sociologist never comes forward as "I." Sometimes he refers to himself as "the author" or "the investigator," or as "many sociologists," or even as "the best sociologists," when he is advancing a debatable opinion. On rare occasions he calls himself "we," like Queen Elizabeth speaking from the throne, but he usually avoids any personal form and writes as if he were a force of nature.

The second-personal pronoun has also disappeared, for the sociologist pretends to be speaking not to living persons but merely for the record. Masculine and feminine pronouns of the third person are used with parsimony, and most sociologists prefer to say "the subject," or "X _____," or "the interviewee," where a layman would use the simple "he" or "she." As for the neuter pronoun of the third person, it survives chiefly as the impersonal subject of a passive verb. "It was hypothesized," we read, or "It was found to be the case." Found by *whom?*

The neglect and debasement of the verb is another striking feature of "the literature." The sociologist likes to reduce a transitive verb to an intransitive, so that he speaks of people's adapting, adjusting, transferring, relating, and identifying, with no more of a grammatical object than if they were coming or going. He seldom uses transitive verbs of action, like "break," "injure," "help," and "adore." Instead he uses verbs of relation, verbs which imply that one series of nouns and adjectives, used as the compound subject of a sentence, is larger or smaller than, dominant over, subordinate to, causative of, or resultant from another series of nouns and adjectives.

Considering this degradation of the verb, I have wondered how one of Julius Caesar's boasts could be translated into Socspeak. What Caesar wrote was *"Veni, vidi, vici"*—only three words, all of them verbs. The English translation is in six words: "I came, I saw, I conquered," and three of the words are first-personal pronouns, which the sociologist is taught to avoid. I suspect that he would have to write: "Upon the advent of the investigator, his hegemony became minimally coextensive with the areal unit rendered visible by his successive displacements in space."

The whole sad situation leads me to dream of a vast allegorical painting called "The Triumph of the Nouns." It would depict a chariot of victory drawn by the other conquered parts of speech—the adverbs and adjectives still robust, if yoked and harnessed; the prepositions bloated and pale; the conjunctions tortured; the pronouns reduced to sexless skeletons; the verbs dichotomized and feebly tottering—while behind them, arrogant, overfed, roseate, spilling over the triumphal car, would be the company of nouns in Roman togas and Greek chitons, adorned with laurel branches and flowering hegemonies.

THE LIMITS OF THE
NOVEL

R ecently I undertook to write the introduction to a paperback anthology of a new sort, compiled with more than the usual care by
Robert Terrall. *From the Great Novels* is the title, and the book will consist of passages selected from 28 novels beginning with *Don Quixote*;
not all the others are great ones but at least they are famous and worth
rereading. Of course there is no passage, however well chosen, that
could stand for the novel from which it is taken. Mr. Terrall's book
has the advantage, however, of bringing together three centuries of fiction as if in a sample assortment of masterworks. By presenting a very
broad picture, it might lead to some general reflections on the history
and future of the novel.

A novel might be defined as a long but unified story, designed to be
read at more than one sitting, that deals with a group of lifelike characters in a plausible situation and leads to a change in their relationship. Key words in the definition are *group* and *change*. The first implies
that the novelist is presenting some sort of social order, no matter how
small or intimate, while the second implies that the order is not quite
the same at the beginning of the novel as it will be at the end; how the
change came about is the story. Two other words, *lifelike* and *plausible*,
suggest a difference between the novel and the romance, which is an
older form demanding more credulity from its somewhat less sophisticated readers.

Within the broad limits of this definition, the novelist is granted
liberties of every sort that can be imagined. He may deal with any subject (provided it is *one* subject), with any setting on the terrestrial
globe (or beyond it, in heaven or hell or outer space), and with any
group of characters belonging to any historical period or time of life.

To mention four common types of novels, his book may be "The
Adventures of—" or "The Courtship of—" or "The Education of—"

or "The Rise (or Fall) of—,"and the dashes might stand for the names of any conceivable heroes or heroines. Again the hero may be a group of persons—for example, a family (as in hundreds of novels), an army platoon (as in *The Naked and the Dead*), a ship's company (as in *Mister Roberts*), a city (as in *Sironia, Texas*), or even a nation during thirty years (as in Dos Passos' three-volume *U.S.A.*). The style may be courtly or colloquial, or anything between those extremes, and it may be used to enforce any sort of lesson, solemn or cynical, or no lesson at all. In general the novelist is compelled to meet only two stipulations beyond those already stated, but he must meet them on pain of early death for his book. He must present characters in whom the reader can believe, and he must create a mood of expectancy.

Considering the simplicity of these requirements, with the scope they offer to inventive writers, and considering the powerful appeal of the novel to many types of readers, we are inclined to forget that it is a comparatively new form of literature. One reason for its late appearance is suggested by a phrase in our definition: "designed to be read." Epic and ballad poetry, which preceded the novel, was designed to be recited in noble houses or sung at a cottage hearth. Even the romance, which was popular in the ancient world and during the Renaissance, was allied to the art of telling stories aloud. Its readers—or listeners— would tolerate any sort of improbabilities and any wanderings into pleasant by-paths so long as the storyteller kept them interested from one moment to another; they were not concerned with the shape of the story as a whole. Before the true novel could appear, there had to be a large body of literate persons with money to buy books, and with something else that seems to develop at a rather late stage of culture: a self-conscious interest in the social behavior of others like themselves. Moreover, the books that portrayed such behavior had to be available; in other words, there had to be authors, publishers, booksellers, libraries, a reading-matter industry with many branches.

All this might explain why not a single novel survives from ancient times, among scores of Greek and Latin romances. Scholars are generally agreed that the *Satyricon* of Petronius—if we had the whole work instead of scattered passages—might prove to be a novel in the modern sense, and there may have been others like it. The oldest novel of which we have a complete text is *The Tale of Genji*, written in Japan during the eleventh century.

In Western Europe—as also in China—the invention of the novel followed by more than a hundred years the invention of printing with movable type. Scholars like to say that *Don Quixote*, half of which was published in 1604, is the first Western example of the new form. The first French novel, and still one of the greatest, is *The Princess of Clèves* (1678); and most critics hold that the first English novel is Richardson's *Pamela* (1740), which was widely imitated in Europe, although some would make a prior claim for *Robinson Crusoe* or *Moll Flanders*.

A hundred years after *Pamela*, the novel had clearly replaced the stage play as a central medium, one that attracted ambitious writers of every nation with a message to deliver or a story to tell. All sorts of material was pressed into the new universal mold. If the same writers had lived in another age, some of them would have been epic or didactic poets or preachers or pamphleteers, but one suspects that most of them would have been playwrights. The nineteenth-century Shakespeares were Dickens, Balzac, and Tolstoy. After another hundred years the novel remains by far the most popular form with writers and the public at large. If that position is threatened, it is more by the new electronic arts—and still more by inner developments in the art of fiction—than it is by any other system of arranging written words.

Customarily we are told that the novel is a middle-class form of literature, and that is largely true as regards its origins, but the passages collected in Mr. Terrall's book would suggest that it is not primarily middle-class in its interests. These twenty-eight novelists seem to do best with characters from the lower ranks of society, and second best with noblemen; some of their most effective scenes are those in which nobles and peasants confront each other (as on the battlefield of Waterloo, when the young Marchesino del Dongo is saved by a *vivandière*). Our novelists seem to take less interest in the middle classes, and sometimes write about them with strained attention but also with an air of distaste, as if they had first scrubbed their hands and had the nurse pull on a pair of rubber gloves. That is Flaubert's attitude in *Madame Bovary*, and it helps to explain why one great novel is admired and imitated more than it is loved.

There is another generality to be made from the selections in this volume. Although all but one of the novelists are men, they are fascinated by their women characters and in many cases make them more vivid than those of their own sex. That is already true of Cervantes when he describes the night his hero spent at an inn; the unforgettable character in that episode is Maritornes, the hunch-backed, ill-smelling, open-hearted serving wench. In the same way Fielding's Lady Booby—not to mention Mrs. Slipslop—and Thomas Mann's Egyptian princess have more life than the two Josephs they are trying to corrupt; they join hands across the centuries with Moll Flanders, Valérie Marneffe, Emma Bovary, Anna Karenina, and Molly Bloom. The talent of a great novelist is in large part a talent for creating passionately living women.

But the great novelists have other points of resemblance; it is as if they all revealed features inherited from one enduring race. Not only do they deal with the same subjects in their vastly different fashions— and that is only to be expected, since their underlying subject is always the pity, absurdity, and richness of human life—but they also reveal a surprising number of connections between one novelist and another. Often the connection is within the same decade and the same national literature. Melville—to mention only one example—had written the first draft of a novel about whaling, incidentally while reading Shakespeare's tragedies. Then he met Hawthorne, read his stories, and completely rewrote the novel to incorporate the "blackness" he admired in them; it was only in this second version—so the scholars have come to believe—that he presented Captain Ahab and his search for the white whale.

Sometimes, however, the influence of a great novelist is exercised from one language to another, even at a distance of centuries. Thus Cervantes: we find definite traces of his work in Fielding and Sterne, Manzoni, Dostoevski (*The Idiot*), and even Jaroslav Hašek; the good soldier Schweik is a late though by no means the last reincarnation of Sancho Panza. Defoe, Scott, and Flaubert, among others, were examples for all countries. But the enduring influence on the novel—at least on great novels—comes from outside the field of prose fiction: it was Shakespeare who inspired Scott, Manzoni, Dickens, Hugo, Balzac, Stendhal, Melville, and Tolstoy (even though the last ended by convincing himself that *Uncle Tom's Cabin* was greater than *Hamlet*).

In our own time and country the Shakespearian note reappears in Wolfe and Faulkner, some of whose characters speak in Elizabethan blank verse. What most of the earlier great novelists acquired from Shakespeare was a sense of freedom and power and an overmastering dream, that of depicting all the human passions carried to their utmost intensity. It is to be noted that Shakespeare had less effect on novelists of the second or third rank. Apparently a writer has to reach a certain level of vision before he can undergo that influence without succumbing under it.

Among the novelists of our own time, Thomas Mann—and Gide to a lesser extent—look back to Goethe; Hemingway looks back to Stendhal and Mark Twain; Dreiser to Balzac (more than to Zola), Faulkner also to Balzac (as well as Shakespeare), and Somerset Maugham to Racine—not for immediate models, but rather for secret inspiration and springs of courage. The great men recognize one another at a distance, as if they were raised to such a height that they could neglect the intervening crowd of little men. Baudelaire described his favorite painters as *Les Phares*, the beacons, "burning on a thousand citadels," and the great novelists are beacons too, sending their long beams of light across the plain.

Yet for all their acknowledged kinship, they are rivals in a lofty way, almost like feudal barons in their separate strongholds. They make visits of state and exchange compliments without swearing fealty. The new novelists say to the older ones, "You have built your castles and marked off your domains. Admiring your achievements, I leave them to you and press beyond the frontier to conquer a domain of my own." They must always do more, go farther, and that explains why the novel is a dynamic form, never remaining the same from one generation to another.

During the last three centuries it has made an almost continual but disorderly progress not in one direction but in all directions, and always toward the extreme limit of any particular tendency. Thus we have, to mention a few examples, the limit of scientific naturalism in Zola (though later writers would outdo him in mere brutality), the limit of middle-class sociological realism in *Babbitt*, and the limit of invaded privacy—or so it would seem—in Molly Bloom's inner monologue. Joyce himself would go deeper into the psyche, by merging thoughts into dreams, and in *Finnegans Wake* he would also reach the limit of difficulty, for any book intended to be read and understood.

The limit of externality was reached in Hemingway's early stories (Gertrude Stein had overpassed the limit), and that of controlled fantasy was probably reached in Kafka; at least one suspects that anything more fantastic than *The Castle* would not be a novel. The limit of conscious vision was reached in Henry James, and something like the limit, for ordinary readers, of writing directed by the subconscious in William Faulkner; the limit of intricate formal structure in Thomas Mann; the limit of historical scope in *War and Peace*; that of geographical scope in *U.S.A.* The limit of minute analysis was reached in the nine volumes of *Remembrance of Things Past*, and quite possibly the limit of sheer bulk for any novel conceived as an architectural unit. Jules Romains tried to outdistance Proust by writing a novel in thirty volumes, but, like Hemingway's old fisherman, he "went out too far"; after the first sixteen volumes he lost command of the material, and very few readers followed him to the end.

It is as if each of the greater authors had said, "I have traced a road to the end; no farther in this direction." There are other roads, of course, and some of the new writers will find them. Yet a question that suggests itself is whether the new roads will lead into territory as rich for the novelist as the roads already built, and whether they will be as rewarding for readers to follow. That is the inner development in the novel which seems to threaten its central position in Western literature. It keeps moving toward limits, as if by decree, yet the more it approaches them, the less hold it may have on the great body of literate persons who made the novel possible.

EMMA BOVARY AND
HER AMERICAN AVATARS

Among the many famous novels of the nineteenth century, it is
Madame Bovary that has exerted by far the greatest influence on
the history of literature. That is not at all the same as calling it the
greatest novel. If asked to name the greatest, most critics would choose
War and Peace, with its tremendous scope, although there would be
some votes cast for *The Red and the Black*, for *The Brothers Karamazov*,
and for one or two of Dickens' works; critics like to differ among themselves. They might agree, however, that Flaubert's first and best
novel, while pitched in a lower key than any of the others, has had a
deeper and apparently more lasting effect on the writing of fiction.

Its influence, which can be traced in different directions, is based
on several features of the novel. Among them I shall name only three,
beginning with the character of the heroine. Emma Bovary on her first
appearance was a totally new figure in literature, but the author had
pieced her together from a number of models in life. First there was a
farmer's daughter whom the Flauberts had often heard about; she had
married a country doctor, spent his money on her lovers, and committed suicide when she found that her dreams led only to hopeless
debts. Then there was Mme. Pradier, wife of a sculptor who divorced
her for infidelity; there was Flaubert's neglected mistress, Louise Colet,
who was furious when she read the book and found that the author had
made a double use of her; and most of all there was Flaubert himself,
who projected his passions and romantic fancies into poor Emma's
heart. He used to tell his curious readers, "*I* am Madame Bovary."

"Everything one invents is true, you may be perfectly sure of that,"
he said to Louise Colet in one of the marvelous letters* he wrote her

*Many of them are included in that excellent volume, *The Selected Letters of
Gustave Flaubert*, translated and edited by Francis Steegmuller.

while the novel was creeping ahead. ". . . after reaching a certain point," he continued, "one no longer makes any mistakes about the things of the soul. My poor Bovary, without a doubt, is suffering and weeping at this very instant in twenty villages of France." She was weeping in cities too, as Flaubert discovered when his book appeared. People everywhere kept asking him, "Is it Madame So-and-so you were writing about?" Young women identified themselves with Emma, and one of them, having recognized her own emotions, wrote the author to say that she had wept all day and stayed awake all night after reading a single installment of the novel. Life was imitating art— or, to be more exact, an aspect of life was being recognized for the first time because an artist had reinvented it.

Soon Emma returned to literature, under many different names. Novels about her were written not only in France but all over Europe. In 1889 she crossed the Atlantic and appeared in New Orleans. That was in *The Awakening*, long a forgotten novel by Kate Chopin that reveals an almost Flaubertian talent for structure and language. But the public was not prepared to read about an American Bovary, and Mrs. Chopin was so crushed by hostile reviews that she did not dare to write another book. It was by no means the end of Emma's American story. Broken and harnessed like a livery horse she reappeared in 1920 as the heroine of *Main Street*, and this time she found a new public that could sympathize with her frustrations. In 1923 she played the part of Marian Forrester in what I think is the all-around best of Willa Cather's novels, *A Lost Lady*. In 1949 she was called Grace Tate, and her adulteries were the subject of John O'Hara's *A Rage to Live*. In 1957 she was Marjorie Penrose, once again *By Love Possessed*; and these are only the most brilliant of her American avatars. Starting as a village innocent, Emma had traveled farther and risen higher than in her wildest dreams. She had become one of those lasting archetypes that people the literary imagination.

Meanwhile the novel to which she gave her name had been exerting its influence through other channels, as the result of qualities that had little to do with the nature of the heroine. The author's willingness to write about drab scenes and ordinary, even repulsive, persons; the almost scientific accuracy with which he presented them; his obstinate disregard of polite sentiments and moral precepts; his attitude toward the characters, which always seemed to be that of the dispassionate observer; his refusal to express his own emotions or ever to pass judgment—all this represented only one side of Flaubert's personality as an artist, but nevertheless it caused him to be regarded as a forerunner, almost a founder, of the Naturalistic school that dominated French fiction after the Franco-Prussian War. Zola studied him, Daudet admired him, Maupassant was proud to be called his disciple. Later their methods—especially Zola's—were imported to America by Frank Norris, and still later the Naturalistic school was represented here by Dos Passos, Steinbeck, Farrell, O'Hara, Marquand, and many other novelists—all of them, in a sense, grandchildren of Flaubert, though he might not have cared to recognize all of his descendants.

But the deeper influence of *Madame Bovary* depends not so much on the characters, including the heroine, or on the author's attitude toward his material, as it does on the form of the novel, and depends not so much on the perfected form as on the methods by which it was achieved. In other words, that influence goes back to the actual writing of *Madame Bovary*, a process that demanded, in this case, a daylong and yearlong sacrifice of the author's personality; of love, comfort, health, and everything else that did not contribute to producing a few more pages worthy of being saved from his uncompromising rejection of the second-rate. Flaubert, said Henry James, "was born a novelist, grew up, lived, died a novelist, breathing, feeling, thinking, speaking, performing every operation of life, only as that votary." By dint of his "obstinate rigor," in Leonardo's phrase, he became a sort of guardian angel or father image to the novelists who succeeded him; and that explains why this childless man was so often invoked as "Papa Flaubert."

To Henry James, who remembered reading an installment of *Madame Bovary* in a Paris hotel when he was only thirteen, he became a sort of wayward but still protecting father, one of whom he said, ". . . we practice our industry, so many of us, at relatively little cost just *because* poor Flaubert, producing the most expensive fictions ever written, so handsomely paid for it." To lesser novelists he became a different sort of father, preaching a stern code they found it impossible to observe; a reproachful saint, a holy icon looking down from the wall at their artistic sins. The best of the younger novelists tried to learn his lessons and work in his spirit, but with a different end in view: not that of writing another *Bovary*, but that of producing a work as different from it as *Bovary* had been from any earlier novel. The real successors in fiction to Flaubert's greatest work were three books that appeared, in three different languages, shortly after the First World War: *Remembrance of Things Past*, *The Magic Mountain*, which was closest to *Bovary* in method, and Joyce's *Ulysses*, which was closest in spirit. Said Ezra Pound, who had also studied the lessons of Flaubert, "The best criticism of any work, to my mind the only criticism of any work of art that is of any permanent or even moderately durable value, comes from the creative writer or artist who does the next job. . . . Joyce has taken up the art of writing where Flaubert left it."

But if Joyce has gone beyond him, in a sense, it does not mean that *Madame Bovary* has been superseded. It continues to stand as a perfect work, unique of its kind; as one of the few novels for which no other can be substituted; as the work that must be read if we are to understand what has happened in fiction during the last hundred years.

It seems to me that Flaubert's originality resulted from the sweeping nature of the demands he made upon himself. When writing *Madame Bovary* he stood ready to answer for everything. Novelists before his time had been satisfied to excel in some particular respect; they had brought their characters to life, or had kept their stories moving, or had accurately depicted some environment, or had given their books a balanced structure, or in some cases had labored over their prose; but in meeting two or three of the requirements that might be made of an ideal novel, they had usually neglected the others. Flaubert was determined to meet all the common requirements, at any expense of time, and he even invented new ones of his own. He would never analyze his characters as Balzac liked to do, but instead would make them reveal themselves in action. He would omit every detail and every word that did not advance the story. Then came the most difficult of his new requirements: he would write the novel in apparently simple prose that had the authority and consistency of verse. "A good prose sentence," he told Louise Colet, "should be like a good line of poetry—*unchangeable*, just as rhythmic, just as sonorous."

It was the effort to write such prose that kept him at his desk from early in the afternoon until long after midnight. Every sentence must have a different structure from that of the preceding sentence. Repetitions must be avoided, especially those involving common words like "of," "but," "for," "all," and "however." There must be no hint of anything approaching a rhyme. To guard against mistakes, he read every line aloud to his friend Louis Bouilhet, who came to see him on Sundays; they tested the rhythm first of the sentences, then of the paragraphs. Sometimes the friend advised him to throw a whole chapter away. "There are moments," Flaubert said in a letter to his mistress, "when it all makes me want to die like a dog. Ah—I shall know the pangs of art before it is finished."

But the book moved ahead, sometimes by only a page a week, sometimes by three or four, and once he reported a triumphant eight pages. He was held to the task partly by his Norman stubbornness, partly by a faith that I think he was the first to call the religion of art. It was not only a creed for him but also a stern rule of conduct. "Art is vast enough," he told Louise, "to take complete possession of a man. To divert anything from it is almost a crime; it is a sin against the Idea, a dereliction of duty." It was in art, moreover, that he found the only hope of survival after death; survival not for himself, but for the work to which he was consecrating his life. "I remember how my heart throbbed," he said in another letter, written years afterwards, "and what violent pleasure I experienced, when I looked at one of the walls of the Acropolis, a wall that is completely bare. . . . Well, I wonder whether a book, quite apart from what it says, cannot produce the same effect. In a work whose parts fit precisely, whose surface is polished, and which is a harmonious whole, is there not an intrinsic virtue, a kind of divine force, something as eternal as a principle?"

The book he finished in 1856, after working on it for nearly five years without a vacation, has that sort of perdurability. It survives because it is fitted together chapter by chapter like polished blocks of marble; because there is nothing false in it, and because the builder's pitiless chisel has left nothing weak to be worn away. Other books, vastly more popular at the time—*The Wandering Jew, The Last Days of Pompeii*—have been carried off to the attics of country houses. Most of

Scott's novels have become unreadable, like almost all of Cooper and even some famous novels of our own century; they were too loosely built to endure a change in the climate of feeling. *Madame Bovary* is as living as the day it was written.

AMERICAN FICTION ON THE ANALYST'S COUCH

An always vigorous and prolific critic, Leslie A. Fiedler has written one of the most ambitious surveys of our literature (*Love and Death in the American Novel*) since Vernon L. Parrington's *Main Currents in American Thought*. Besides their size and scope, the two works have one other resemblance and one only: each of them expounds a single doctrine. Parrington believed that the two main currents were populism (in the broadest sense) and realism; he was ready to dismiss everything else in American literature as either noxious or "merely belletristic." Fiedler's doctrine is very different and requires some explanation.

To state it briefly—in other words, unfairly—he believes that American fiction started at a time when it might have followed either one of two European traditions: that of the sentimental novel, as developed by Samuel Richardson and his French imitators, or that of the gothic novel as invented by Horace Walpole. The sentimental novel, at its best, deals with the real world and creates characters by analyzing them. The gothic novel deals with an imagined world and simply *projects* characters, making them embodiments of the novelist's inner desires and fears. Its reality, like its power, depends on the unconscious truth of the story it tells.

The sentimental novel has never flourished in America, except on bestseller lists. That is partly because our social conventions prevented any honest depiction of adult love, and partly because the novelists themselves were not emotionally mature, all having suffered from the Oedipus complex and all—without exception, by Fiedler's doctrine—having been afraid of sexual responsibilities. The disappearance of love as a subject left a vacuum that was filled with images of flight, pursuit, violence, and death, in other words, with the gothic element in fiction. It was Charles Brockden Brown, never known to a wide public but admired by his fellow writers, who naturalized the gothic novel by taking it out of haunted castles and placing it in the American wilderness. Hawthorne, Poe, Melville, Mark Twain, and Faulkner have all told variations of the gothic legend, which has become—so Fiedler insists—the great and only tradition of the American novel. Anyone who departs from it falls into optimism and commercialism or incurs the eternal damnation of being middlebrow.

All this sounds pretty extreme or double-domed as a thesis. To be absolutely fair, I want to record my belief that much of it is accurate, especially with the qualifications—though never enough of these—that Fiedler introduces into his discussion. It is true, for example, that much of the best American fiction—more than we like to admit—has been pessimistic, rebellious, and melodramatic. It is true that adult love has played an amazingly small part in it and that our best novelists have portrayed a disappointingly small number of complete and convincing women. It is also true that some of the novelists have been "duplicitous"—to borrow one of Fiedler's overworked words—in the sense of writing innocent stories that conceal some pretty murky relationships among the principal characters.

There are other illuminating points in the discussion (many of them borrowed from D. H. Lawrence or from Gershom Legman, the author of a brilliantly biased pamphlet called *Love and Death*). Women in American novels, Fiedler says—following Lawrence—are often presented in pairs, one bright, the other dark, so that the blonde represents unassailable virtue and the brunette is a picture of untamed passion. The blonde is almost always the heroine until our own century, and then she becomes selfish, vindictive, frigid—in a word, the enemy.

A great deal of American fiction, Fiedler says, has been an escape from a society under female domination into an imagined world of male companionship. Much of it has revealed a fear of darker races, which represent wild Nature; and the hero of the novel is often involved in some close relation with an Indian, a Polynesian, or a Negro (Chingachgook in *The Last of the Mohicans*, Queequeg in *Moby-Dick*, Nigger Jim in *Huckleberry Finn*, and Sam Fathers in *The Bear*). Fiedler wants us to believe that this relation is "a homoerotic fable," and he adduces a great deal of evidence—sometimes persuasive, sometimes based on a misreading of the text—in favor of his special interpretation.

For months to come his book will be the subject of after-dinner arguments, especially if the kids have been sent to bed. I shall be taking a negative stand in some of the discussions. Therefore I should like to record a few reasons why I think that Fiedler's doctrine and his critical method, in spite of their yielding many illuminations, are narrow, oversimplified, and leave us with a needlessly bleak picture of writers and writing in America.

My first complaint about his loosely Freudian method, with its emphasis on love and death, *eros* and *thanatos*, is that it doesn't provide a standard for choosing the best works or a means of revealing their superiority to lesser works. The method works superbly with inspired but slapdash authors like Charles Brockden Brown. It works with fourth-rate or fifth-rate novels like Mrs. Rowson's *Charlotte Temple* and George Lippard's *The Monks of Monk Hall*, which are of merely symptomatic interest.

It works pretty well with some of our best authors, including Hawthorne, Melville, and Faulkner, but not necessarily with their best novels; for example, Fiedler has fresher things to say about Melville's deplorable nightmare, *Pierre*, than about *Moby-Dick*; nightmares are more Freudian. It doesn't work at all with a whole galaxy of novelists whom Fiedler dismisses as "middlebrow": William Dean Howells, Edith Wharton, Willa Cather, Sinclair Lewis, James Gould Cozzens, or anyone else who tries to present normal Americans. Three of those five names aren't even listed in a long index. The method also works badly with Henry James, whom Fiedler apparently would like to dismiss, but doesn't quite dare.

A second complaint would be that the Freudian or—to invent a word—erotothanastistic method disregards the special nature of literary works and two, at least, among the principal aims of novelists. It treats the novel as a mere expression of the author's unconscious desires. It never admits that novels are *structures* of language, or that the author spends most of his time perfecting both the language and the structure so as to give his book a lasting life independent of himself. Besides those dark fears of love and death that Fiedler discusses at such length, the writing of a novel expresses two fundamental human passions: the desire to create something with a life of its own and the longing for immortality.

A third objection to the Freudian method of criticism is that it introduces a new vocabulary as a means of reinterpreting almost everything in terms of sexual pathology. For what we used to regard as endearing qualities, it finds phrases intended to shock and degrade. I have thought at times of compiling a dictionary of Freudian synonyms for the use of college freshmen. Here are a few of the phrases guaranteed to impress young instructors:

Never say friendship; say "innocent homosexuality." Never say curiosity; say "voyeurism," or refer to the curious man as a "castrated peeper." Instead of mourning for the dead, refer to "necrophilia." Instead of self-awareness, speak of "narcissism." Remember that fun and games do not exist in the Freudian world except as "the symbolic enactment of sado-masochistic desires." Remember that family affection is merely "a repressed incestuous longing" and that chastity is "the morbid fear of full genital development." A tomboy is a "transvestite" and a writer is—what?

A gifted American writer is (or reveals or represents) almost all these Freudian things, if we agree with Fiedler. The more gifted he is the more deplorable are his lapses from what seems to be the Fiedlerian ideal of responsible genitality. But what if he does somehow become fully mature, wise, temperate, successfully married? Then he suffers the worst fate of all; he is condemned to be a "middlebrow" or even, compounding the punishment, an "upper middlebrow." The author can't win, ever, by Fiedler's standard of judgment. Only the critic can win; only the critic can pry into secret places without being a voyeur, can make deliberately shocking statements without being an exhibitionist, can torture authors without being a sadist, and can dance on their mutilated bodies without being accused of necrophilia.

But does he really enjoy great literature? The question somehow remains, with another question to which it leads: whether the critic's punishment, ordained by an inscrutable Providence, isn't that he should be forced to consort, at least in libraries, with authors whom he pities and despises, while reading so many books that fill him with revulsion. There is more in American fiction, much more, than Fiedler has been able to find.

ON BEING GENIUSES
TOGETHER

I. SHAKESPEARE AND COMPANY

When a young American went to Paris in the early 1920s, the chances are that he wouldn't stop to unpack his suitcase at the wonderfully cheap little Left Bank hotel that his friends were sure to have told him about. It was always a different hotel, but always the same café, and the young man would go straight to the terrace of the Dôme, where he would stay until the lights went out in the small morning hours. The following afternoon he would cross the Luxembourg Gardens and visit Shakespeare and Company, which was the other American center in Paris: banned drinks in the first, banned books in the second. The Dôme was not only for drinking but for gossip, high jinks, business opportunities, and meeting friends to have dinner with. Shakespeare and Company was for looking at the titles of books, browsing among the little magazines, and perhaps exchanging a few charmed words with the brilliant new people who wrote for them.

Shakespeare and Company was also "Miss Beach," as we called her in those days before everything had gotten to be so chummy. Miss Beach was a wisp of a woman with a determined chin, a mouth always on the point of curving into a sympathetic smile, and sparkling, almost glittering, dark eyes. Her central characteristic was a passionately unselfish interest in new writing. If we said we were writers, she was always glad to see us, even if we couldn't afford to buy books from her or enroll ourselves as subscribers to her lending library.

Reading her memoirs, we are once again reminded that everybody in the new world of American letters went to see Miss Beach. First there were Gertrude Stein and Ezra Pound, who couldn't bear each other; then Sherwood Anderson, Hemingway in bandages, Fitzgerald tipsy in the afternoon, MacLeish, Cummings, Dos Passos freshly arrived from Bagdad, Thornton Wilder behind his huge round spectacles; then later Allen Tate, Nathanael West, Katherine Anne Porter— all the writers soon to be famous, all the editors of little exiled magazines, and the new composers too, such as George Antheil and Virgil Thomson, together with a clutch of young painters and various coveys of Smith and Vassar graduates. They came to Miss Beach with their aspirations and worries, and they stayed hoping to catch a glimpse of James Joyce behind his dark glasses, twirling an ashplant as he crossed the rue de l'Odéon. Joyce was the one literary god of the 1920s—the others were only demigods—and Miss Beach was his prophet and publisher.

For me the truly fascinating chapters of *Shakespeare and Company* are those in which this publisher describes her most unbusinesslike relations with her author and divinity. Joyce accepted favors and demanded services as if he were not a person but a sanctified cause. It was, he seemed to be saying, a privilege to devote one's life to the cause, and those who paid his debts for him were sure to be rewarded in heaven. Miss Beach agreed with him. Admiring and almost worshiping his work, she invested all the profits of her bookshop, begged all the money she could from relatives, and mortgaged all her credit in publishing *Ulysses*. Joyce kept pushing her closer to bankruptcy by making more and more corrections in proof. When the book finally appeared on his fortieth birthday—February 2, 1922—it was a monument to the genius and patience of the author, but also to the self-sacrificing devotion of its publisher.

Although Joyce occupied a central position in the affairs of Shakespeare and Company, he is only one figure in this crowded book of memoirs. It is never better than in those last chapters in which Sylvia—by now we all know her well enough to call her Sylvia—is dealing with her life in occupied Paris and with the heroism of her friends in the Resistance. She says nothing about her own courage, which was tested more than once. She tells us, however, that when the Germans threatened to confiscate her books, she stripped the shop bare, moving everything upstairs to her wonderfully crowded apartment. On the day of the Liberation, Hemingway appeared in the rue de l'Odéon with a whole caravan of jeeps. The caravan stopped in front of what had been Shakespeare and Company. "Sylvia!" he shouted over and over in his deep voice, and soon the whole street had taken up his joyful call. I think it is time for us all to cry "Sylvia! Sylvia!"

2. THOSE PARIS YEARS

"This memoir," Kay Boyle says in presenting the chapters about her own life that she has included in this new edition of *Being Geniuses Together*, "is part of a dialogue that I have never ceased having with Robert McAlmon." But what was McAlmon's part in this dialogue that started forty-five years ago and did not cease with his lonely death in 1956? And who in the world, younger readers will ask—in fact have already asked me when I told them about the book—was Robert McAlmon?

Scottish by descent, born in Kansas and raised in South Dakota, McAlmon blew into Paris like a wind from the prairies. That was in 1921, the year when scores of young Americans came storming into the Montparnasse cafes, all bent on having a hell of a good time before they utterly transformed, or so they hoped, the world of art and letters. Ford Madox Ford, who enjoyed their company—so long as they pretended to believe his stories—compared them to a herd of stampeding Herefords.

McAlmon was more like a wild Cayuse or its rider. He wore a broad-brimmed hat that wasn't like a cowboy's, but that still made him look as if he had galloped into town on a Saturday afternoon to spend what he had earned in a month by riding the range. He sang Western songs and had enough of a cowboy's energy to carry him through nights of drinking and dancing. He also had self-confidence, a winning smile, and what seemed to the rest of us a generous supply of money, derived from his incredible marriage to the poet Bryher, only daughter of Sir John Ellerman, the shipping magnate.

In 1921 many people thought that McAlmon was destined to have a more brilliant career than any of the other young expatriates. He wrote more and faster than the others, from what seemed to be a richer store of early experiences. He quickly met everyone who counted in the literary world, beginning with Eliot, Pound, and Joyce (who was his favorite drinking companion); and he met each of them as an equal—or secretly more than an equal, since he measured them all against an ideal picture of his own talent and found most of them wanting.

His intimacy with men of genius did not keep him from being generous to younger and needier writers, and it was partly to help them gain recognition that he founded Contact Editions. Though a very small house, with two partners and no employees, by 1929 it had published the work of several famous or soon-to-be-famous authors—Hemingway (his first two booklets), Pound, W. C. Williams, Mary Butts, H. D., Robert M. Coates, and Gertrude Stein—as well as seven books of poetry and fiction by Robert McAlmon.

When did everything start to go sour? By 1929 some of the young writers he encouraged—and chiefly Hemingway, whom he regarded as a rival—were leaving him far behind. His marriage had ended; his money was running out; he had given up his publishing house; and, though he was working fast on several books, they seemed likely to remain in manuscript. There were friends of his who insisted—so Kay Boyle reports—"that McAlmon had been exploited, neglected, deceived, and imitated beyond recognition, but anyway preyed on by the vultures of the writing world."

McAlmon seemed to share that opinion, and he did not bear his sorrows like a Christian. When he came to write his memoirs of the 1920s—that is, the original text of *Being Geniuses Together*—he passed so many harsh judgments on famous men, and offered so many reports of their disgraceful behavior, that one is tempted to regard the book as McAlmon's revenge on almost all the writers he had known.

Being Geniuses Together was written in Paris in 1934 and was published four years later in London. There was no American edition at the time, partly because the 1920s were then out of fashion, but chiefly because the text fell short of the brilliant title. For all its faults, however, the book was rich in anecdotes and scathing judgments; it was soon to be rifled by others who wrote about those Paris years as they came back into vogue, and after McAlmon's death the copies that appeared on the rare-book market brought a higher price from sale to sale.

It was the last of his manuscripts to be published during his lifetime, and McAlmon was to spend the next twenty years as a solitary and embittered man. But what was the reason for the spectacular neglect from which he suffered? One cannot explain it by talking about "vultures," of which the writing world contains no larger share than the business world, in spite of its being even more bitterly competitive. From what I have read of McAlmon's work, I should hazard what might be the true cause of his failure: that he never in his life wrote so much as a memorable sentence. Phrases, yes, like "being geniuses together," but there were not many of these, and they marked the limit of his skill with words.

Though he lived in a society composed of geniuses and would-be geniuses, he refused to accept instruction. Ezra Pound once offered indirectly to criticize his poems, a service that Pound had already performed for Yeats and Eliot (not to mention Hemingway, who learned from him what to omit). McAlmon's comment is that Ezra "will be the pedagogue, yearning for pupils to instruct, and I, whether I write well or badly, have my idea of how I want to do it." He was radically unteachable. He could not even learn from his own mistakes, since he seldom bothered to correct them.

Always he wrote at top speed in the effort to set down "what happened"; always he used the first and easiest words that occurred to him, and the result is that his writing never improved; over the years it slowly lost its original freshness. In 1928 Slater Brown, a man who has always loved good prose, summed up what most of the expatriates felt about McAlmon's work:

> I would rather live in Oregon and pack salmon
> Than live in Nice and write like Robert McAlmon.

The couplet was printed in the magazine *transition* and was often spoken aloud in Montparnasse cafes. After forty years Miss Boyle is still indignant about it. She was one of the desperately poor young writers helped by McAlmon, and she has remained one of his defenders, in a select company that also includes Katherine Anne Porter and Ezra Pound. Partly as a gesture of loyalty, she decided some years ago to prepare a new edition of his book. She revised and shortened the text (McAlmon's work always cries for emendation); she consulted the original typescript and restored some passages deleted by the English publisher; then she nearly doubled the length of the book by recounting her own adventures in chapters that are printed alternately with his. By her choice of emphasis, however, McAlmon remains the central figure, and he even acquires a dignity of failure that had been lacking in the story as told solely by himself.

At the same time Miss Boyle's chapters reveal by contrast, and without her intending them to do so, the fact that McAlmon never mastered the craft of writing. Miss Boyle, on the other hand, was bound to the craft like a medieval apprentice. Burdened or blessed as she was by the lack of a college education, she was determined to learn from any book that would teach her. One grim winter in Le Havre, when she was trying to write in a kitchen festooned with wet laundry (of her own laundering), the book was Rebecca West's *The Judge*, which she had saved pennies to buy at a secondhand bookstall.

"I read it as a textbook," she says, "studying the shape of the sentences, looking up in the ragged dictionary the words I was not sure of. . . . All that mattered to me was that she was a woman, and that she had written a novel, a very long novel, which is what I was seeking to do." McAlmon, even as a very young man, would have been ashamed to study anyone or anything as a model; he read books to judge them, most often with a hostile and contemptuous eye. His story when set beside Kay Boyle's reminds one of Hogarth's twin fables of the idle and the industrious apprentice.

But a deeper contrast between the two authors is also revealed in this new edition of *Being Geniuses Together*. It arises from the different answers they have found to an old question: whether a writer, in Conrad Aiken's phrase, should "give himself away." McAlmon's answer is negative. He is candid about other people, sometimes to the point of being spiteful, but he tells us little about his feelings and almost nothing about his intimate life. Miss Boyle is sometimes less than candid about others, since she wants to protect them, but she "gives herself away" by speaking frankly of her worst follies.

Thus, she tells us how she left her first husband to live with Ernest Walsh, the editor of *This Quarter*, when Walsh was dying of consumption, how she bore him a posthumous child, and how Walsh's former Mrs. Maecenas paid for her confinement. She tells how she yielded to self-pity during one summer in Paris and took more lovers than she can now remember, while hating them all and trying to punish herself. By placing the facts on record, without boasting or sniveling, she achieves a sort of selflessness. Apparently she agrees with Conrad Aiken's feeling "that this was one of the responsibilities of a writer—that he should take off the mask."

McAlmon leaves his mask in place, and it is only in Miss Boyle's chapters that we catch a glimpse of the despairing face behind it. Once he burst out to her, after a crazy, boring party at Harry Crosby's summer place: "I'm fed up with whatever it is I'm carrying around inside this skin, rattling around inside these bones!" He struck his chest violently with his fist—so she reports—and his face was hard as stone. "Don't care about me!" he shouted. "Stop it, will you? Let the God-damned pieces fall apart!" There is nothing in his own chapters like that moment of self-revelation.

Yet his memoir is full of entertaining stories about the misdeeds of the great, and I have to report that this collaboration—posthumous in McAlmon's case—has proved amazingly successful. It gives us pictures of two lives—and many surrounding lives—from different angles, as if they had been taken with a stereoscopic camera. Thereby it gives us an impression of depth and substantiality that have been lacking in other memoirs of Paris in the 1920s, and notably in McAlmon's original story.

3. WE HAD SUCH GOOD TIMES

I am reviewing a book published in 1970 that has received very little notice in this country. So far I have not met an American who has read it. In Canada, where the author, John Glassco, is respected in literary circles, it is on sale in some but not all of the larger bookstores: *Memoirs of Montparnasse*. The title calls to mind a whole genre of books, by Hemingway, Gertrude Stein, Henry Miller, Kay Boyle, and fourteen more authors, at a hasty count, all more or less acquainted with each other and all except Miller given to dropping the same names. The author of one book reappears as a derided character in another, while the reader grumbles, "Are you here again?" But Glassco's book, published from a manuscript nearly forty years old, is fresher and truer to the moment than the others, as well as being more novelistic and, in a sense, legendary.

The others—again with an exception for *Tropic of Cancer*—were written long after the events they colored with various shades of repentance, resentment, and nostalgia. Glassco was writing on the very scene, then soon after leaving it, so that events baldly happen instead of being reconstructed. He is a poet, not a novelist, but he has an instinct for telling stories and his life enforced on him a paradigmatic plot. He becomes such another *exemplum* as Scott Fitzgerald, but with an important distinction. Fitzgerald made his experience seem representative by regarding himself as a figure in history. Glassco regards himself as a figure in literature or legend: he is young Tom Rakewell in *The Rake's Progress*; he is Faust tempted by Mephistopheles; and toward the end he is Keats's knight-at-arms: "Oh what can ail thee, man-at-arms, alone and palelee loitering?" Mrs. Quayle misquotes in a husky Boston whisper when she finds him alone in a bar on the rue du Montparnasse. She looks at him with "the fixed, mindless stare of a predatory bird" and we recognize her as *la belle Dame sans Merci*. Mephistopheles appears as Serge Kirilenko, "an off-white Russian photographer" looking prosperous in an astrakhan cap and an overcoat with a fur collar. The author himself, while playing Faust and knight-at-arms, remains a precocious Canadian boy with a sharp eye and an accurate ear.

But the story. . . . John Glassco—"Buffy," as everyone learned to call him—came to Montparnasse in February 1928, very late in its occupation by transatlantic writers and hangers-on of the arts, but with advantages over most of the early colonists. He was younger, only eighteen; he had read more books—chiefly the English and French Decadents, but with a background in the classics; he spoke French passably well; he had good manners and an exquisite lack of moral preconceptions. Also he had an allowance from his father of $100 a month, on which he proposed to live and support his friend Graeme Taylor, who was trying to write the great Canadian novel. "The first thing we found was that with the franc at four cents we were much richer than in Montreal," Buffy says. "I don't think the rate of exchange is always given its proper importance as an element in the charm of Paris."

Buffy met everybody. Elderly men of letters—George Moore, Frank Harris, Ford Madox Ford—were impressed by his familiarity with their work and pictured him as a renewal of themselves at eighteen. Old dikes, young whores, apprentice lesbians, transvestites, painted aunties, nymphomaniacs all looked at his fresh, unstubbled cheeks, his blond pompadour, his slim body, and crowded round him shouting, so I imagine, "Meat! Meat!" as cannibals used to shout when going into battle. Buffy smiled and let it be known that he was writing his memoirs. He even started them, although, he says, "It was more fun to play at being a writer." But writing was fun, too, especially when his first chapter was printed in *This Quarter* and one of his surrealist poems was accepted by *transition*. On Bastille Day he rode through Paris in an open taxi, while "the city swam in a haze of heat and happiness. The driver was one of the best, and as he raced down the boulevards, blowing his horn like a berserk elephant, I had an experience of absolute ecstasy."

Paris, however, was becoming unbearably hot and also difficult in other ways, since Buffy's father had reduced his allowance to $50 a month. Robert McAlmon, the bitter homosexual novelist, took the two Canadians to Nice, where living was cheaper. There they met Stanley, a simple-minded earth goddess from Winnipeg, and shared her favors as well as her allowance, which was larger than Buffy's. When Stanley moved in with them, McAlmon moved out. They spent the winter of 1928–29 "sunk in greed, sloth, and sensuality," Buffy says, "the three most amiable vices in the catalogue." Then the landlord began padding their bills, money ran short, and they skipped off, leaving behind a trunk weighted down with Buffy's coonskin coat.

Everything turned bad from that moment. Their new flat in Paris had bedbugs. Stanley left them for a solicitous English girl, whom she described as "a very down-to-earth person—really basic and sincere." In the summer Graeme Taylor heard that his father was dying and the consulate paid his way to Montreal. Then Buffy's father, outraged by the chapter of memoirs in *This Quarter*, cut off the rest of his allowance. His friends advised him to follow Taylor home; "The party's over," they said. He couldn't accept their sound advice because he was doubly in love: with Paris and with Mrs. Quayle. A few days later he found that she had given him gonorrhea.

The experience kept them apart, even after both had cured themselves by leading ascetic lives, but it also created a bond between them. Meanwhile, with most of his American friends driven out of the Quarter by the Wall Street crash, Buffy had to find means of supporting himself. He had come to think that Paris was a great machine for stimulating all the senses; now he was forced to see it from the underside, as one of the operatives who were miserably paid to keep the machine going. Already he had written a pornographic book—in French—and the publisher had tried to cheat him out of his fee. He had typed manuscripts for Richard Le Gallienne in his dotage and the Dayang Muda of Sarawak, without being paid in cash. At the instance of Serge Kirilenko, he had earned a thousand francs by posing with two whores for filthy postcards. He had indulged in an orgy of writing poems until his money was gone and he was evicted from his room. Now, on the last warm night of November, he slept under the Pont Neuf after arguing for his place with a drunken beggar. The weather turned cold next morning. In a little bar he ran into Kirilenko, who suggested this time that he become a stud for prosperous old maids and widows. A businesswoman would provide the bedroom, for half the proceeds, and would recommend him to her clients as "a healthy, clean, affectionate and reliable young Canadian."

"Then shall I put you on her little list?" Kirilenko asked. "You will find the employment rather tedious, perhaps, but more rewarding than poetry."

Buffy says that homeless, cold, and hungry he made the classic response: "You might as well."

He lived for some weeks as a prostitute, with a sense of degradation, but McAlmon came back to Paris and rescued him; McAlmon had a generous side that redeemed his bitterness. They gave a big party together for a Negro theatrical troupe, the Blackbirds. Mrs. Quayle reappeared at the party and, as in Keats's poem, Buffy was borne away to her elfin grot—in this case a luxurious apartment near the Etoile. There he spent the winter as her privileged slave without ever going back to Montparnasse. On one occasion he searched for his poems, stored at the bottom of a trunk, but they had disappeared. "I looked them all over and burnt them," Mrs. Quayle explained. "They were quite unworthy of you, my lovely child."

The story breaks off at this point, two years after Glassco arrived in Paris, but there is a brief note to explain what happened afterward. Mrs. Quayle took her lovely child to Majorca, where she owned a villa. After a time she found another lover and moved him into the villa. Glassco began spitting blood. Mrs. Quayle bundled him off to the American Hospital in Neuilly, where the surgeons collapsed one of his lungs. A more radical treatment, thoracoplasty, was then advised, and the patient went back to Montreal. While waiting for the second operation, from which he was told that he had an even chance for survival, he worked feverishly to complete his memoirs. He had calculated the time he would need and set up a schedule, but the operation was moved forward a week, leaving the last two chapters unwritten. Yes, Glassco survived, but he never went back to the book.

It was published last year with very few changes, the author says, except in names like that of *la belle Dame sans Merci*. We should be grateful for having it in the original state. Besides embodying a fable, it presents the most accurate picture of Montparnasse that I have seen; this is the way it was. The book also explains, if only by implication, why so many persons have written memoirs of that time and place. Things have changed in Montparnasse as elsewhere, and the new generation cannot recapture that immense heedlessness, that belief in art—when there was time for it—or that energy and greed in the pursuit of pleasure. It was an age of Yes that the memoirists remember in the age of No. "Yes," they all seem to say even when bitching or apologizing or recounting disasters, "we had such good times."

PART OF A
CENTURY

The twentieth century started badly for American writers. In going over the literary records of the early 1900s, one senses a mood of discouragement that contrasts with the bounce and rebelliousness of the preceding decade. The 1890s had been a time of little magazines and avant-garde publishers, of new critical journals, of the first American little theater, and also of contending literary doctrines. Besides the established realists and local colorists—and besides the best-selling romantic novelists, whom all the younger men despised—there were also naturalists, impressionists, symbolists, decadents, high-minded socialists, Harvard poets (an impressively gifted group), and at least one Veritist, capitalized, in the person of Hamlin Garland, who invented the term. There was talent, there was conviction, there was almost everything, in fact, except a sympathetic audience for honest or experimental writing. The lack of an audience proved fatal, and by the end of the decade all this activity had been swept out of sight by what *The Bookman* described, at the time, as a "sudden onrush of ideality and romance which arose like a fresh sweet wind to clear the literary atmosphere. In this resistless new movement toward light and hope and peace," *The Bookman* continued, "those black books were cast aside and forgotten."

It is curious to note how writers can be discouraged by a resistless movement toward light, hope, and ideality. Soon the little magazines vanished with the groups that supported them, and the avant-garde publishers went bankrupt after losing most of their authors. The fact is that many of the rebel authors, and most of their leaders, had died shortly after the turn of the century, stricken in their early prime as if by some contagious blight. Among the careers that suddenly ended were those of Stephen Crane, Frank Norris, Lafcadio Hearn, Trumbull Stickney (the most original of the Harvard poets), James A. Herne (once known as the American Ibsen), and Kate Chopin of New Orleans, who had tried to write an American *Madame Bovary*. There were only a few survivors of this tragic generation. Among them Theodore Dreiser suffered a prolonged breakdown after *Sister Carrie* was treated by its publisher and its critics as a scandal to be hushed up; he would publish no fiction for ten years. Edwin Arlington Robinson was on the edge of succumbing to drink and disheartenment. Hamlin Garland, who also survived, had lost his early convictions; step by step he was going over to the enemy.

The enemy was of course the Genteel Tradition, which held that no book should be published unless it was a "decent" work that could "safely" be placed on the center table in the parlor and read by proper young girls. "It is the 'young girl' and the family center table," Frank Norris once complained, "that determine the standard of the American short story." He might also have said that they determined the standard of American novels, plays, essays, and poetry. Although his complaint was made in the 1890s, there was no improvement during the early 1900s, when in fact the Genteel Tradition seemed more oppressive than ever. Mark Twain deferred to it, during those years, by reserving most of what he regarded as his serious work for posthumous publication. Edith Wharton was bolder, being encouraged by her wealth and her social position, but she found it more congenial to live in Europe. Some interesting books were written at home by the muckraking journalists, but they were not intended to be permanent. One might say of the decade that almost all the lasting works it produced were either written in Europe (as note Henry James's major novels and the first books of younger writers like Ezra Pound and Gertrude Stein) or else were privately circulated, as was *The Education of Henry Adams*.

One might also say that American universities neglected one of their duties during this period—and in fact as late as 1930—by paying almost no attention to American authors, living or dead. They looked fixedly across the Atlantic. When they offered courses in comparative literature, the comparisons were among the authors of Britain, France, Germany, Spain, Italy, and sometimes Russia or Scandinavia. American literature was mentioned, if at all, as a rather disappointing and altogether colonial branch of English literature, so that undergraduates might easily have gained the impression that writing was an exclusively European art. There was indeed a break, about this time, in the whole tradition of American writing, and I think the universities helped to produce it by thus abolishing our literary past.

Writers of the new century would be condemned or privileged to start over from the beginning, as if nobody on this continent had ever practiced the art of making books. As a matter of fact, groups of young writers made several fresh starts, first in the 1910s, then in the 1920s, and then again in the 1930s, each time with a different conception of what they should do. I am not proposing to offer a history of twentieth-century American literature in capsule form. All I am trying to find is a rough sort of historical pattern, and I might start by dividing the century into segments of about ten years each. The division happens to be more than a matter of convenience. By historical accident almost every decade of our recent literature seems to possess a mood and manner of its own, as if writers had been working with their eyes on the calendar.

Once I thought of comparing the earlier—but not the later—decades to the early stages of a New England year. The 1890s, for example, would be a sort of January thaw in which the sap began to rise before the weather turned cold again. The ten years after 1900 would be a long March freeze. But winter doesn't last forever, even in New Hampshire, and the 1910s would be a sunny week in April, with flowers bursting forth under the bare trees. Some of the flowers had bloomed earlier and had miraculously survived under the snow: I am thinking here of Dreiser and Robinson, both of whom were rediscovered at the beginning of the decade. Soon there were younger rebels to bear them company, and notably there was a straggling but impressive parade of poets: Frost, Sandburg, Jeffers, Millay, Lindsay, Masters, Aiken, and Eliot, with Amy Lowell twirling a cigar like a drum major's baton as she tried to keep them all in step. But there were also new novelists (Cather, Anderson, Lewis), there was at last an admired playwright (Eugene O'Neill), there were brilliant radical journalists (Randolph Bourne, John Reed), and there were critics like Mencken and Van Wyck Brooks, who spoke for the younger men. Brooks in particular played almost the same part in this second renaissance that

Emerson had played in the thirties and forties of the preceding century.

In the 1910s there was at last an audience for serious writing, even of a sort not intended for the family center table, and there were also new ways of reaching the audience: new magazines, new publishers, and a profusion of little theaters. It is hard to characterize the extremely varied work of the writers who appeared in the decade. One can say that, with traditions broken, they seemed to owe an extremely small debt to American writers of the preceding century. One can say that they were generally critical in tone—critical, that is, of American life and institutions—but that most of them were moved by an essentially patriotic impulse. They wanted to produce books that would be worthy of this vast and still new country, by virtue of their scope, their newness, and their honesty. Hence, their emphasis was on subject matter, and they paid less than the proper attention to the structure and texture of their writing. There were some notable exceptions to this rule—among them Eliot, Frost, and Cather—but in general the writers of the 1910 generation were not models of skilled craftsmanship or of discriminating taste. It was a weakness that would lead to another change in the direction of American letters.

The change became evident in the course of the following decade. There is no good seasonal analogy for the 1920s, but perhaps one could call them a second spring that followed the cold rains of wartime and of the postwar reaction. Once again young writers were starting over from the beginning, with little regard for tradition and without even knowing, in most cases, that such a thing existed in America. They went abroad to write, or many of them did; and even those like William Faulkner who stayed mostly at home were deeply affected by European and chiefly French ideals of the literary life. The tradition to which most of their work belongs is ultimately that of Gustave Flaubert, with his belief that writing was more important than living and his addiction to the "quaint mania," as he called it, of wearing himself out in pursuit of the perfect phrase and the unchangeable paragraph. But Proust and Joyce, Pound and Eliot, are writers in the same line, and they all served as models for the work of what became known as the Lost Generation.

Here the most familiar names are those of Faulkner, Hemingway, Fitzgerald, Wolfe, Dos Passos, and Katherine Anne Porter among the novelists, of Cummings, Crane, and Tate among the poets, and of Edmund Wilson among the critics. It is difficult, once again, to characterize the writers of a whole literary period. One might say, however, that their general emphasis was on form rather than subject matter, with the result that they produced better finished and more complicated works than did most of their immediate predecessors. One might also say that the works—except for those of Dos Passos— are distinguished by intensity and depth rather than by any broad vision of the nation or the world.

Their lack of social vision came to be regarded as an inexcusable weakness and something close to a hanging crime by the young writers who appeared in the early Depression years. A new period was beginning, and it is one for which there is no seasonal comparison. One is tempted to call it a frost in June, if one thinks about the sorrows of the unemployed, but the literary atmosphere of the early years was anything but frosty or discouraged. The young writers of the 1930s were passionately convinced that they could help in their own way to end poverty and change the world. Rejecting all their predecessors except Whitman and Dreiser and John Reed, they started over once again, as the writers of the teens and twenties had done, and they moved in a new direction. At first they called themselves proletarian or revolutionary writers and then, after 1935, social realists. They were primarily concerned neither with form nor, except in appearance, with subject matter. They believed, it is true, that novels and poems should deal with the workers, or proletariat, but their real emphasis was on doctrine. If a book presented the right sort of doctrine—preferably one connected with the inevitable downfall of capitalism, or the triumph of the workers, or the crusade against fascism—they were willing to salute it as a good or sometimes as a great work.

Actually the decade was rich in literary works, but not many of the great or merely good ones were produced by these doctrinal writers. Their poetry was deplorable, and so was most of their prose. The main currents of the time are represented for me by three big novels, all written by somewhat older men. Dos Passos's *U.S.A.* is, among other things, an attack on monopoly capitalism, written around the thesis that human values are destroyed by the inevitable concentration of wealth in a few hands. "Yes, we are two nations," the author says at last, referring to the rich and the poor; and he finds no hope for decent ordinary people whether they choose to be radical or conservative. *The Grapes of Wrath* was almost the last of the proletarian novels, and it is the only one out of hundreds that is read today. Unlike *U.S.A.* it is a hopeful book, expressing the spirit of the decade as a whole; it assumes that the workers will triumph when they learn to unite. *For Whom the Bell Tolls*, published in 1940, is the one masterly American novel that deals with the anti-fascist crusade. Its hero sacrifices himself for a cause and thereby wins a respite from time and mortality; in the seventy hours before death he lives as full a life as he might have lived in seventy years. But the author and his readers know that the cause of the Spanish Republic was a lost one and that the hero's sacrifice was wasted. The decade of hope was ending in despair and disillusionment.

Our simple pattern of changing decades is obscured after 1940. Partly that is because the war was an interregnum in the literary world; young writers were busy in uniform, and everybody was waiting for them to come home and express themselves in completely new books. When the war novels began to appear by scores and then by hundreds, they mostly proved disappointing, at least to those who had been hoping for revelations. Some of them had brute power, of the sort possessed by *The Naked and the Dead* or *From Here to Eternity*, but it did not seem to be under the author's control. Though most of the other war novels were honest and surprisingly craftsmanlike, they added more to our knowledge of how soldiers felt and acted than they did to American literature.

It was not fiction by younger writers that flourished in the postwar years and almost as late as 1960; rather it was criticism that became a field of dicovery where new methods were applied and old masterpieces were reinterpreted. The principal labor, however, was one of consolidation. For the first time critics surveyed American writing of the twentieth century in relation to what had gone before. Universities joined in the work—in fact most of the critics were now professors, as were many of the new poets—and it was conducted on a grand scale. What emerged from the survey was a demonstration that American literature was more consistent and more unified than anyone had suspected in the past. Almost every existing current or tendency could be followed back into the nineteenth century, and some, it was shown, had started in colonial days. There was something in common between Hawthorne and Faulkner, for example, as there was between Whitman and Hart Crane; and Hemingway's best work was written in a mid-American prose style that was traced back through Mark Twain to the old Southwestern humorists. In the same way the social realists of the 1930s had points of resemblance with the muckraking novelists of the early 1900s, and the 1920s repeated the 1890s on a grander scale.

And the 1960s? By the beginning of the decade it was clear that there would be a reaction against the academic tradition in criticism and poetry. Once again young writers were rebelling against their predecessors, and they were speaking of themselves as "alienated" or "disaffiliated," or simply as "beat." There was even a growing body of poetry and fiction written from a new point of view. It was the work of writers who had started over from the beginning, but that was what their predecessors had done, and it was part of an American pattern too.

PART THREE

ASSESSMENTS
AND
RETROSPECTIONS

JOSEPH MITCHELL: THE GRAMMAR OF FACTS

In his own somewhat narrow field, which is that of depicting curious characters, Joseph Mitchell is the best reporter in the country. Some of his favorite subjects are Bowery angels, barflies, small-time Broadway sports, coffeepot poets, and Calypso singers. He writes about them with more sympathy and factual precision than you will find in the recent biographies of any famous authors or statesmen. In his new book, *McSorley's Wonderful Saloon*, there is not a trace of condescension. He says in an author's note, after explaining that these portraits were first written for *The New Yorker*, "The people in a number of the stories are of the kind that many writers have recently got into the habit of referring to as 'the little people.' I regard this phrase as patronizing and repulsive. There are no little people in this book. They are as big as you are, whoever you are."

They are in fact as big as life, because they are shown in perspective against their proper backgrounds. Mitchell's collection of portraits is the exact opposite of the books that choose an important subject, but are hastily written and have nothing much to say. These books, which form the bulk of current writing, always make you feel as if you had paid for looking into the wrong end of a telescope. Mitchell, on the other hand, likes to start with an unimportant hero, but he collects all the facts about him, arranges them to give the desired effects, and usually ends by describing the customs of a whole community.

Commodore Dutch, the subject of one portrait, "is a brassy little man who has made a living for the last forty years by giving an annual ball for the benefit of himself." Mitchell doesn't try to present him as anything more than a barroom scrounger; but in telling the story of his career, he also gives a picture of New York sporting life since the days of Big Tim Sullivan. The story called "King of the Gypsies" is even better. It sets out to describe Cockeye Johnny Nikanov, the spokesman or king of thirty-eight gypsy families, but it soon becomes a Gibbon's decline and fall of the American gypsies; and it ends with an apocalyptic vision that is not only comic but also, in its proper context, more imaginative than anything to be found in recent novels. "I just can't wait for the blow-up of the whole entire world," says Cock-eye Johnny. "It's going to bust wide open any day now, ask any gypsy, and I don't give a D-double-damn if it does." Still another portrait, that of my old friend Joe Gould, has for its background "the cafeterias, diners, barrooms, and dumps of Greenwich Village." Here the method is exactly that of the early Renaissance painters who, when depicting a rich landowner, liked to open a window and show the peasants working in the vineyards and olive fields of his estate.

Mitchell himself has a curious background for a man who specializes in genre pictures of metropolitan life. He was born on a cotton and tobacco farm in the North Carolina lowlands, not far from the Little Pee Dee River. As a boy he fished for blue bream in the swamps, hoed corn, and chopped cotton in his bare feet. He still likes to go barefoot in his New York apartment, although the rug doesn't feel as cool and springy as the soil of a cornfield after a light rain. At the University of North Carolina, he wrote for the college paper and had a story accepted for publication in the third edition of "The American Caravan"—the same volume that contained the first published work of Erskine Caldwell and Robert Cantwell. It was a story in which the hero whispered to the cold winds, "Would to find a wine as wild as the boar is wild in the swamp deep in winter." He fell in love with a field woman, but you never heard her name or saw her face; in fact you weren't quite sure whether she was white or colored. Everything in the story was twilight, mood, and strong lyrical feeling.

In the stories that Mitchell has been writing during the last few years, everything is action, factual statement, and direct quotation. There are no moods or mysteries, no wraithlike women, and no intrusions by the author, who now pretends to be merely a recording device. A good example of his behavioristic writing is the first paragraph of a portrait called "Mazie":

A bossy, yellow-haired blonde named Mazie P. Gordon is a celebrity on the Bowery. In the nickel-a-drink saloons and in the all-night restaurants which specialize in pig snouts and cabbage at a dime a platter, she is known by her first name. . . . She has a wry but genuine fondness for bums and is undoubtedly acquainted with more of them than any other person in the city. Each day she gives them between five and fifteen dollars in small change, which is a lot of money on the Bowery. "In my time I been as free with my dimes as old John D. himself," she says. Mazie has presided for twenty-one years over the ticket cage of the Venice Theatre, at 209 Park Row, a few doors west of Chatham Square, where the Bowery begins.

Mazie is a character who, allowing for a distance of three thousand miles and a hundred years, might have come straight out of Dickens. Almost all the subjects of Mitchell's portraits are essentially Dickens people, and therefore it is interesting to compare this paragraph with another in which Dickens introduces two of his favorite characters:

Mr. and Mrs. Veneering were bran-new people in a bran-new house in a bran-new quarter of London. Everything about the Veneerings was spick and span new. All their furniture was new, all their friends were new, all their servants were new, their plate was new, their carriage was new, their harness was new, they themselves were new, they were as newly married as was lawfully compatible with their having a bran-new baby, and if they had set up a great-grandfather, he would have come home in matting from the Pantechnicon, without a scratch upon him, French polished to the crown of his head.

After Dickens hit upon the phrase "bran-new" to describe the Veneerings—if he had been an American, he would have said "brand-new," which is etymologically sounder—everything else was a rhetorical development out of this one idea. None of it was observed or recorded, except possibly the baby; it was all the product of Dickens' inexhaustible verve. If Mitchell had been writing the paragraph, he would have started by saying, "The Veneerings were newly rich people with a brand-new baby"; then he would have gone on to tell how much they paid for their house, where they bought their furniture, and the sort of polish used by their three housemaids to make it shine. The style would be businesslike and completely unobtrusive.

I am tempted to wonder whether this *New Yorker* method isn't typical of our age and whether we haven't entered a period when even authorship has become an impersonal and collective undertaking. In Mitchell's factual writing, it is hard not to see an image of the factual lives we lead, under the dictatorship of numbers, statistical averages, and mass movements. Yet perhaps this impression of Mitchell is merely superficial. Reading some of his portraits a second time, you catch an emotion beneath them that curiously resembles Dickens': a continual wonder at the sights and sounds of a big city, a continual devouring interest in all the strange people who live there, a continual impulse to burst into praise of kind hearts and good food and down with hypocrisy. Unlike Dickens, he represses this lyrical impulse, but it controls his selection of details. You might say that he tries—often successfully—to achieve the same effects with the grammar of hard facts that Dickens achieved with the rhetoric of imagination.

MENCKEN AND
MARK TWAIN

In describing his childhood, H. L. Mencken devotes several pages to his discovery of *Huckleberry Finn*, which he calls "probably the most stupendous event of my whole life. . . . If I undertook to tell you the effect it had upon me my talk would sound frantic, and even delirious. I had not gone further than the first incomparable chapter before I realized, child though I was"—he was nine years old—"that I had entered a domain of new and gorgeous wonders, and thereafter I pressed steadily on to the last word." He also read everything else by Mark Twain that he could find in the house, but *Huckleberry Finn* was the book to which he returned time and again; he tells us that he read it at least once a year until he was forty, and twenty years later he went through it once more, finding it as magnificent as ever.

After reading his three books of memoirs, you feel that Mark Twain must have been the decisive influence in forming both his style and his literary picture of himself. All his life he has been, not a Connecticut Yankee but something quite similar, a Baltimore bourgeois at the court of ideas, eager to strip them of their romantic armor. All his life he has been rephrasing and modernizing the rather innocent bitterness of Mark Twain's later years. And there must have been times when he regarded himself as another Huck Finn—the bad boy at Sunday school, the bad boy at political conventions, the bad boy of literary criticism and highbrow magazines. If that is the case, however, you have to imagine that Huck was really the son of Judge Thatcher, and that no matter how many jokes he played or how many stretchers he told, he never really defied the standards of the owning classes. This was a Huck Finn who came home for supper every night and slept in his own bed.

Grown old, he likes to boast of his brass-bound and copper-riveted conservatism. He achieved it honestly, by direct descent and right of primogeniture. His father, August Mencken, was a prosperous cigar manufacturer who believed that all mankind "was divided into two great races: those who paid their bills and those who didn't. The former were virtuous," says his oldest son, "despite any evidence that could be adduced to the contrary; the latter were unanimously and incurably scoundrels." Father August was a kindly man in his own household, but he was convinced that working people belonged to the scoundrelly race; and his favorite story was of the trick by which he drove the Baltimore cigar-makers' union into bankruptcy. Young Mencken acquired his father's ideas along with his father's taste for good St. Louis beer and strong-smelling Pennsylvania tobacco. His first job was in his father's nonunion factory.

He says of himself, "I was a larva of the comfortable and complacent bourgeoisie, though I was quite unaware of the fact until I was along in my teens, and had begun to read indignant books. To belong to that great order of mankind is vaguely discreditable today, but I still maintain my dues-paying membership in it, and continue to believe that it was and is authentically human." One of his bourgeois traits is what he calls "a kind of caginess that has dissuaded me, at all stages of my life, from attempting enterprises clearly beyond my power." Another trait, derived partly from his background but more from within himself, is a strict honesty that is not confined to financial matters. There were times when he could have sold just a little of his independence or just a few of his personal convictions for very stiff prices, but he always refused these offers even when they were disguised as opportunities to improve the world. The master shoemaker stuck to his last.

Still another of the bourgeois traits he reveals is contempt and even hatred for all the people living on the wrong side of the tracks. He is very funny on the subject of their faults and misfortunes, but after a while the reader tires of his humor and begins to feel that there is too much gleeful malice in his stories of Negroes beaten over the head and skilled workingmen arrested because it was time to paint and repair the city jail. In his newspaper days he rather enjoyed being present at hangings—"I found the work light and instructive," he says, without bothering to pretend that he pitied the men who were dying. It is not that Mencken is cruel by temperament. When he was editing *The American Mercury* there were dozens of stories about his kindness to young writers, and everybody knows that he is devoted to his friends. He seems to feel, however, that only the bourgeoisie is authentically human. The rest of mankind belongs to a subhuman species whose members can best be described as bucks and wenches, blackamoors, apes, simians, anthropoids, and stumblebums. These are some of Mencken's favorite words, and his use of them reveals a defect that is not so much of the heart as of the imagination. He simply cannot believe that people outside the middle classes are worth the trouble of trying to understand them.

If anybody wonders why he seems a much smaller figure than Mark Twain, and less important in the history of American letters, I think we are not far from the answer. Except in point of imagination, Mencken comes close to his earliest model and sometimes even surpasses him. He is much more at home in the world of ideas than Mark Twain ever learned to be. He never makes Twain's enormous blunders in taste—not because his own taste is extremely good, but because it is always on the same level. He is a marvelous story-teller, even when he hasn't much of a story to tell, as in several chapters of his latest book. His style is one that other writers admire and hundreds of them used to imitate. They never did more than a botched job, because the original was completely suited to his own personality—picturesque, clear, self-satisfied, and never attempting anything beyond its power. It reduces the universe to something within four walls—something simple, boisterous, but not disorderly—let us say a middle-class Munich beerhall in the good days of Wilhelm II. Mark Twain always sweeps you outside; and the raft floats down the river into the mist; and each village it passes is a separate world, full of the human misery, cowardice, and kindness that Mencken claims to despise.

Indeed, if he had written *Huckleberry Finn*, it would have been a very different book. Huck himself, coming from a shiftless family, could scarcely have been the principal character. Nigger Jim would merely have been a stupid, good-natured blackamoor. The real heroes would have been the King and the Duke, who royally defrauded the yokels on both banks of the river and thereby proved Mencken's thesis about human rascality. The book would have ended with both of them preparing for greater exploits in Washington. It would have made a hilarious story, but no little boy would have read it word by word and have found at the end that his life had been forever transformed.

AUDEN EDITS AUDEN

Wystan Hugh Auden, born in 1907, is the most influential English or American poet of his generation. "English *and* American," I might as well have written, for he has lived in this country since 1938 and has taken to using a half-American idiom in his verse. One critic said: "It's just as if we had sent T. S. Eliot to England before the other war on a lend-lease arrangement. Now, with Auden, we are being repaid in kind."

Besides writing poems and essays and editing anthologies, such as his recent selections from Tennyson, Auden has been teaching at Swarthmore, a coeducational Quaker college near Philadelphia. (In England he had taught in a boys' school.) He was classified as 4-F after his draft examination, but last month he went back to Europe temporarily as one of the civilian members of a War Department mission. He didn't wait to read the—in general—highly complimentary reviews of his *Collected Poetry*, which had appeared just a few days before his departure.

For all its faults of selection and arrangement—and I'll talk about them later—the *Collected Poetry* confirms one's impression that Auden is among the great technical masters of English verse. Nobody else since Tennyson and Swinburne has shown such skill in handling rhymes, alliteration, and complicated metrical patterns. Nobody else has devoted so much studious attention to the problems of his craft.

He studies all the masters from earliest times and tries to reproduce their qualities. In his verse one can trace the influence of William Langland, who wrote *The Vision of Piers Plowman* in the late fourteenth century. One also can trace the influence of Skelton, Shakespeare, Donne, Dryden, Blake, Byron, Hölderlin, Hopkins, Yeats, Eliot, Marianne Moore, and the anonymous author of "Frankie and Johnny." Yet nobody could mistake a poem by Auden for the work of any other living or dead poet, including his own imitators on both sides of the Atlantic.

He is a master of the artificial forms of verse, French, Provençal, and Italian. He is especially good at sonnets in unconventional meters, but he also writes ballades, villanelles, sestinas, *terza rima*, and *canzoni* with the same easy grace.

Hardest of all these forms is the sestina, which contains six stanzas of six lines each, with a three-line envoi. The repetition of six words in an intricate pattern takes the place of rhyme. The *Encyclopaedia Britannica* talks about "the innumerable and terrible difficulties of the sestina," but they don't appall Auden. He writes sestinas as easily as if they were limericks, and I suppose that he could, on demand, write limericks as grave and musical as sestinas.

Most of the great verse technicians are not distinguished thinkers: like Swinburne, they are content to say that love is fleeting and even the weariest river winds somewhere safe to sea. Auden is an exception to the rule. His ideas are as complicated as his verse forms, and they are much more difficult for a critic to summarize. Once he published 87 pages of notes to explain the source and application of the ideas in one of his longer poems, the "New Year Letter." I enjoyed the notes almost as much as the poem, and had even more difficulty understanding them.

Perhaps the central idea in his work, from the beginning, is that of a psychosocial parallelism. In other words, he believes that evil and violence can be found in each man's heart as well as in the social world. Throughout our lives we keep repeating the patterns we learned to follow in the nursery; that is, we keep rebelling against or yielding to the commands of a stern father. We are all of us, Auden says:

> Lost in a haunted wood,
> Children afraid of the night
> Who have never been happy or good.

Sometimes Auden's verse has a prophetic quality. By looking at the conflicts in the human heart, he has been able to foresee—or, let us say, to forebode—the conflicts in the social world. Thus, in the early 1930s he wrote poems about the abandoned factories of northern England that could be applied just as well to the bombed cities of Europe today. They were war poems appearing ten years before their time. His

"New Year Letter," which dates from 1940, predicts that even the men of good will, *les hommes de bonne volonté*, would be infected by the Nazi mentality and might end by imitating their enemies. He says, in a memorable passage that suggests the death of Mussolini:

> It lures us all; even the best,
> *Les hommes de bonne volonté*, feel
> Their politics perhaps unreal
> And all they have believed untrue;
> Are tempted to surrender to
> The grand apocalyptic dream
> In which the persecutors scream
> As on the evil Aryan lives
> Descends the night of the long knives;
> The bleeding tyrant dragged through all
> The ashes of his capitol.

But there is more to be said about *The Collected Poetry of W. H. Auden*, and it is not so pleasant a task as listing his accomplishments. Editorial judgment is apparently not one of them. In compiling this new book, with its 466 pages, he has made it either too long or too short to serve his readers as a substitute for the ten other books he has published here since 1934.

It is too long if we had hoped to find in it only his best work, his witnessed and notarized claims to survival. It is too short, on the other hand, to display the scope of his talent by including poems in all his amazingly varied moods and manners: lyrical, philosophical, elegiac, narrative, dramatic, gay, nonsensical, savage, and solemn. The poet says in a short introductory note that tries to explain his standard of choice:

> In the eyes of every author, I fancy, his own past work falls into four classes. First, the pure rubbish which he regrets ever having conceived: second—for him the most painful—the good ideas which his incompetence or impatience prevent from coming to much . . . third, the pieces he has nothing against except their lack of importance: these must inevitably form the bulk of any col-

lection since, were he to limit it to the fourth class alone, to those poems for which he is honestly grateful, his volume would be depressingly slim.

The present collection is padded out with too many poems of the third class he mentions. When Auden writes them, they are by no means third-class poems, but they do have faults besides their lack of importance. In this merely respectable work, he shows a weakness for abstraction, for personified qualities like Fear and Mediocrity (with capital letters), for nouns of Latin derivation, and for lazy, colorless verbs. In general he gives us too many intellectualized metaphors and not enough sensual images. Sometimes he falls into a sort of euphuism or gongorism: for example, in a poem called "Autumn 1940," where he says:

> And many who have shared our conduct will add
> Their pinches of detritus to the
> Nutritive chain of determined being.

He means that many of his English schoolmates will be killed by German bombs, but he hides the idea under abstract words. The result of all these mannerisms is a sort of grayness that spreads through the book like fog through the London streets, hiding the sense of what he says and sometimes stealing away the color from his best poems, if they happen to stand between two dull ones. It would have been better to let the best poems stand alone, in a volume shorter than this, but by no means depressingly slim.

Or again, Auden as the editor of his own work might have followed exactly the opposite course. He might have compiled a longer book, including not only the poems based on good ideas that he thinks never came to much, but also a few of the other poems that he now regards as pure rubbish. At the very least, they would have provided a setting for his more serious work, like the small buildings that surround a cathedral. And the fact is that many of these buildings are handsomer than Auden himself believes. Like many other poets—Yeats, for example—he is a harsh judge of his own early writing. Sometimes he forgets poetic laws and condemns a poem for political or religious or purely personal reasons.

Missing from the present collection are all the poems addressed to several of his early friends: some of them were good poems and, I hope, good friends. Missing are the poems or passages in which he spoke disrespectfully of the established church. In "On This Island" he had described the English cathedrals as "Luxury liners laden with souls,/ Holding to the east their hulls of stone," but now you look in vain for these lines or any like them. Missing, too, are all but the vaguest of his revolutionary poems, and all but the mildest of his satires directed against the British upper classes.

That isn't because he has changed his class loyalties and gone over to the Tories. He still hopes for a better society but, having become a devout Christian, he tries to achieve it by changing the hearts of individuals. He now says: "O all too easily we blame,/The politicians for our shame." He thinks that our own selfish irresponsibility explains the shortcomings of Churchill and Stalin and even, to some extent, the crimes of Hitler.

His satires must now impress him as being narrow and one-sided, as being aimed at a class when they should be directed, through individuals, at humanity as a whole. I won't argue about the political rightness or wrongness of his new opinions but the satires were good as poems, and I am sorry to see them go. His revolutionary verse—for example, some of the choruses in "The Dance of Death"—was livelier and stronger than the philosophical meditations that have taken its place in the present volume.

Nor is this the end of my complaints against a collection that, for all its faults, is as important as any of recent years. Besides omitting poems that are better than he thinks, Auden has arranged the others in a helter-skelter fashion, without regard for subject-matter or chronology. A poem called "1929," written in that year, is printed just after a fine sonnet called "Hongkong 1938" and just before a birthday poem written so recently that it appears for the first time in any book. The reader is given no chance to trace the changes in Auden's ideas or the development of his style.

Moreover, the poems themselves lose part of their effect through lack of a proper background. This may be merely a personal impression, but I confirmed it to my own satisfaction by turning back to earlier volumes, including *Another Time* and *On This Island*. I found that the good poems seemed more impressive there, even when—as usually happened—they had been reprinted in the *Collected Poetry* without a changed word. In their original setting, they stood like trees with roots. In the new book, they seemed merely to have lodged, like tumbleweeds.

THE LAST FLIGHT FROM
MAIN STREET

When Sinclair Lewis died in Rome on January 10, 1951, just before his sixty-sixth birthday, he had published twenty-one novels over a period of thirty-seven years. He left behind him the corrected proofs of a twenty-second novel, *World So Wide* (Random House), as a sort of epilogue to his career. It is unfortunate for his reputation that *World So Wide* is possibly the weakest of all his books. I say "weakest," not "worst," because there is little in *World So Wide* that is actively bad in the fashion of *The Prodigal Parents,* or in the different fashion of *The Man Who Knew Coolidge.* It is a pleasant and trifling story of which the chief fault is that, as a novel, it was never really written and doesn't quite exist.

It is the story of a year in the life of Hayden Chart, a successful young architect from Newlife (read Denver, Colo.). When Hayden's objectionable wife is killed in an automobile accident, he leaves his office in charge of a partner and goes wandering through the "world so wide" like a college boy on summer vacation. In Florence he meets Sam Dodsworth, from an earlier Lewis novel, and falls in love with Dr. Olivia Lomond, an assistant professor in history at the University of Winnemac.

Week after week Hayden stays in Florence instead of continuing his travels. Olivia proves to be not so cool and cloistered as she had seemed. Dr. Lorenzo Lundsgard appears, with plans to produce historical motion pictures and with a big expense account from Cornucopia Films. There are descriptions of Florentine churches and restaurants and accounts of cocktail parties in the American colony. There is also some mild suspense: Will Hayden marry Olivia, who is obviously the wrong woman for him? Will Lundsgard succeed in his aim of becoming a Fascist leader among American scholars? Will Hayden succumb to the easy ways of Florence and become a permanent expatriate? In the last chapter all the questions are answered a little too briskly and Hayden and his bride (who isn't Olivia) start back for Newlife by way of India and Ceylon.

The reappearance of Sam Dodsworth in the story is the key to its real nature. Hayden Chart is simply a younger Dodsworth, and Dr. Olivia Lomond, after starting out to be a new character, becomes a childishly scheming and unfaithful woman like Dodsworth's first wife. *World So Wide* is *Dodsworth* retold in half the number of words, with half the expenditure of imagination and curiosity. I couldn't find any feature in which it marked an advance over the earlier novel.

Reading it I remembered a sentence in an old essay by Van Wyck Brooks, "The Literary Life in America," published in 1921. "Our writers," Brooks said, "all but universally lack the power of growth, the endurance that enables one to continue to produce personal work after the freshness of youth has gone." *World So Wide* is an example that would seem to support Brooks's statement, but there are writers contemporary with Lewis who could be used as arguments on the other side; Brooks himself is one of them. T. S. Eliot, Willa Cather, and Eugene O'Neill have all shown a power of growth from one work to another.

Even Dreiser, who never learned to write better than he did in his first book, *Sister Carrie*, and whose later novels, except *An American Tragedy*, were all of them massive disappointments—even the Old Unteachable showed a sort of growth at the end and wrote the last chapter of his last novel, *The Bulwark*, on what was for him a completely new emotional level. He made his peace with the fathers and rounded out his story. On the other hand, Sherwood Anderson—and after him Thomas Wolfe—stood frantically still. They burst on our vision and amazed us, but then they simply kept bursting like Roman candles, with no surprises after the first pink star.

Lewis was different from any of the others and showed the power of growth for exactly eleven years of his career as a novelist. His work had the trajectory of a rocket in the sky: up, up, up, from *Our Mr. Wrenn* (1914) through *The Job* (1917) to *Main Street* (1920); then leveling off a little but still rising through *Babbitt* (1922) to its highest point in *Arrowsmith* (1925); then sinking, not too rapidly at first, through *El-*

mer Gantry (1927) and *Dodsworth* (1929); then down, down, down, in the books of his later years.

In reality the descending curve of the rocket wasn't quite so steep as its rise and there were little peaks in it, as if new stores of powder had been ignited. Lewis was an effective pamphleteer, though not a far-sighted prophet or a wise politician, in *It Can't Happen Here* (1935), and he was a bold campaigner against race prejudice in *Kingsblood Royal* (1947). In the former he was afraid, in the latter he was angry, and in both cases the emotion lent fire to the writing. *Cass Timberlane* (1945) was deeply felt on a more intimate level and was perhaps the best of his later books. *Kingsblood Royal* was the most popular, with a sale in all editions of 1,497,000 copies.

Even in these three novels, which stand far above the others he wrote after 1930, one observes a flagging power of invention; instead of creating new characters he was, for the most part, reintroducing the old ones under different names. A worse fault was that he had ceased to listen to anyone but himself. His early novels had been faithful transcripts of middle-class Midwestern speech. That speech has changed in the last thirty years, has learned new words and adopted new mannerisms, but Sinclair Lewis's characters in *World So Wide* talk almost exactly like those in *Main Street* and *Babbitt*. The result is that they sound like survivors from a vanished world, like people just emerging from orphanages and prisons where they had listened for thirty years to nothing but tape recordings of Lewis novels.

That is the case against his later work—or part of the case—and yet I started by thinking of this article as a defense of Sinclair Lewis. The truth is that I do not believe his permanent reputation will rest on anything he has written since 1930. All his later work will be swept aside, and perhaps the sooner the better for his fame. It would be a grave mistake, however, to undervalue what he wrote and what he did in his early days.

In 1920 he had a chance that American writers have seldom received. The success of *Main Street* not only gave him more money than he had dreamed of, but it also made him the acknowledged center of a whole galaxy of gifted writers, the leader, so to speak, of a new generation. Looking back on his career I think he deserves credit for accepting the responsibility as well as the privileges of his new situation. He didn't write easy books after *Main Street*. He laid out for himself an extensive plan of work: he would invent the state of Winnemac, more typical than any real state in the Union, and in one book after another he would describe the representative activities of its inhabitants, until he had completed a wide survey of American society.

He carried the project forward in a series of four big novels, each of which must have been harder for him to write than the one that came before it. Meanwhile he acted as a sort of spokesman for his generation of American writers and took what seems to us now the right side in most of the disputes he entered. He also made a point of helping writers younger than himself. To some of them he gave money—acting as a sort of private and informal Guggenheim Foundation—while to all of them he gave their full share of praise.

It was not at all an accident that Sinclair Lewis was the first American to receive the Nobel Prize for Literature. He had done more than any other American of his time to make our literature known in Europe; and when the Swedish Academy, which awards the prize, at last decided that our literature deserved official recognition, Lewis was the writer to whom it naturally turned. In his acceptance speech, on December 10, 1930, he spoke for a whole generation of American writers and ended by saluting the younger writers who would succeed him.

That was the high point of his career, but I think we have been placing too much emphasis on the slow decline that followed. The truth is that most writers decline at some time or another. Writing is normally a hazardous profession and those who retain the power of growth from year to year are the fortunate exceptions. The real task of critics is not to explain the decline in each case, but rather to explain the height and nature of the achievement from which it started. In the case of Sinclair Lewis they still have much to explain.

JAMES T. FARRELL:
TIME OBLITERATED

James T. Farrell's new novel, *Yet Other Waters*, is decidedly not one of his best, but it has an historically important subject—the Communist movement among writers in the middle 1930s—and it is the final volume of a trilogy. At this halting point in the author's career, there is something to be said about his achievements and shortcomings as a novelist and about the rather unusual purpose that lies behind them.

Farrell's first major work was the Studs Lonigan trilogy (1932–35), which was the life story of a Chicago Irish boy ruined by his environment. Revulsion and rebellion against the environment have never been expressed more powerfully, at greater length, in an American novel. The next major work was the Danny O'Neill tetralogy (1936–43), about a sensitive boy who lives in the same neighborhood, in worse conditions,and yet keeps faith with himself. Danny isn't a very interesting hero—we have read about too many others like him—but his desperately poor family is treated with a sympathy that is new in Farrell, and once more the narrative builds up to scenes of agonized revulsion.

The first volume of the present trilogy was *Bernard Carr*, published in 1946. It is named for the hero, a young writer who might be an older Danny O'Neill, while his public adventures—I don't know anything about the private life—are almost exactly those of James T. Farrell. Bernard escapes from Chicago for a summer in New York, where he writes his first story, sells advertising for the Telephone Red Book, and falls in love with a married woman. In the second volume, *The Road Between*, he marries a Chicago undertaker's daughter and takes her to Paris, where she has a stillborn child. He also launches himself on his career as a novelist.

Yet Other Waters starts in the spring of 1935, when Bernard is twenty-nine years old and has written four successful books, one of which has been sold to the movies. He is happy to be making money and is proud of his wife and their new baby. At this point he is drawn hesitatingly into the Communist movement, after getting himself arrested for picketing a department store. He takes part in the first American Writers' Congress, but offends the group that is running the congress and isn't named to the executive committee. At a drunken dance held to raise funds for the *New Masses*, he meets a long-legged, expensive-looking girl, a Communist camp follower, who invites him to come to bed with her. Instead he visits his family in Chicago and learns that his mother is dying of cancer.

On his return to New York he watches the Communists break up a meeting that the Socialists had called to commemorate the Austrian revolution and afterward hears them tell lies about what had happened. It is a decisive experience and leads him to desert the Communists. His flirtation with them had been paralleled by a brief love affair with the expensive-legged girl; he now quarrels with her and is reunited with his wife, who is having another baby. The Communist claque ruins the sale of his new novel, although it is the best he has written. At the end of the trilogy Bernard feels that he has finished his education. He says to himself, "I'll go on struggling," then looks at his wife and adds: "We'll go on."

Most of the characters in the novel seem to be copied from actual persons and many of them can be identified by anyone who consults the printed records of the first American Writers' Congress. They are identified, however, by the parts they played or the speeches they delivered, not by their looks or gestures or personalities. Rather than being characters in fiction, imagined and brought to life, they seem to be figures in the author's memory, rendered indistinct by the passage of time.

Bernard's relatives are treated more understandingly, especially his simple, pious mother (so much like Villon's mother in the ballade), and the description of her first visit to a doctor is possibly the best single passage that Farrell has written. On the other hand, Bernard himself is less vivid than he was in the first volume of the trilogy, before the sharp edges of his temper had been sandpapered down by success. Almost everyone else in the novel keeps telling him that he is a true artist and the white hope of American letters, but he says and does very little to confirm their judgment. When we are given samples of his inner thoughts, they prove to be commonplace, badly expressed and lacking in the self-awareness that one expects of any distinguished writer.

As a study of the 1930s, the chief weakness of the novel is that it devotes little attention to ideas, even though they played a decisive part in the situation that Farrell is trying to remember. I don't mean the sort of ideas that an author puts forward as his own, transforming the story into an argument, but the other ideas that guide his separate characters and bring them into conflict. Without the ideas the conflict loses most of its historical meaning and becomes hardly more than a personal squabble.

Something dangerously close to that happens in Farrell's novel. Almost the only reason he gives why so many of his characters had become converts or fellow travelers of Communism is that they thought it was "good" for writers, in the sense of giving them new subjects, a new audience, and a chance to work in Hollywood, while they feared that quarreling with the Party would get them unfavorable reviews and deprive them of their share in the future. All their actions seem to be dictated by vanity, fear, and the herd instinct. With some that was doubtless the full story, but there are other cases on record where the effective lure of Communism was the opportunity it seemed to offer for disinterested service. The convert started with ideas of how to create a happier world, made an unselfish commitment, and ended in corruption or disillusionment; that was the drama of the period, which might be regarded as a tragedy or a comedy, depending on one's point of view. Farrell gives us some accurate pictures of Communist methods, but, by leaving out the ideas, he reduces the drama to a solemn farce.

The faults of the novel are not to be explained by lack of talent, since the talent has been displayed in other books. They seem to be connected with a method or purpose or theory of art which has been consistently followed in Farrell's work, although it produced much more interesting results when applied to boys on the South Side of Chicago than it does now when applied to an older hero in a more complicated environment that calls for something more than simple rejection. Farrell himself has said that his purpose is, "stated generally, to re-create a sense of American life as I have seen it, and as I have reflected upon and evaluated it." The statement is all too general: how and why does one re-create a sense of American life?

There is a partial answer to these questions at the very beginning of the present trilogy. In the first chapter Bernard is sitting in the New York Public Library and trying to write his first story, while he stares desperately at the clock. We soon learn that the clock is his enemy and that writing this story about his own past is Bernard's only weapon of defense:

> Behind the clock, Time was now continuing its deadly work. It was a quarter after ten on this June morning, June, 1927. And all of the past was nothing, gone. The past was locked in books and stored in shelves in this very building. But he must work. He must lock something of his own past in words that would one day be stored on library shelves. Someday, other young men would come here and read books written by Bernard Carr, and they, they too, would brood and fume and fight with Time, and then they would think of him. Poignantly, they would see him as one of the rare dead men who had won his war against Time.

That seems to express Bernard's central purpose, which does not change as he grows older. All through the trilogy he is described in the process of writing stories and novels—with haste and urgency, as if fighting against time—and always the process is defined as one of remembering his own past. He sits at his typewriter and remembers "how, as a boy, and even more so in his adolescence, he had resented the fact that he'd been nursed at his mother's breasts. . . . All these feelings of his past must go into the novel." Again he tries to recall "other details and more of what he had thought and felt on that evening. . . . This was all so far away now. It was gone. He was bringing it back in memory, re-creating it in words—all the fears and hopes, all that hungering and dreaming for love." He never seems to think of rearranging the past; instead he tries to set it down exactly. "Bernard remembered Elsie Cavanagh in a red sweater. In the story, "Richard Clarke remembered a girl named Elsie in a red sweater." After reading dozens of such passages, one comes to feel that Farrell's life work, including his fourteen novels and his eight volumes of short stories, is not a work of invention or combination or construction, as with other novelists, but an immense labor of recollection.

In this country, no one else but Thomas Wolfe has remembered his past so obsessively, in so many long novels. Turning to France, however, we find the infinitely greater example of Marcel Proust, and it helps to define Farrell's work by contrast. Proust explains in the last volume of *Remembrance of Things Past* that he is trying to recapture the small, completely personal and often mistaken impressions which, in spite of their triviality or falseness, bring back an experience in its entirety (just as the taste of a little cake dipped in lime-blossom tea brings back his whole childhood). Farrell gives us few such impressions; instead he tries to catalogue all the factual details of a scene as he remembers it. That is a method condemned by Proust in advance.

There is, however, a more essential difference between Farrell's project and Proust's, based on their strikingly different attitudes toward their experiences. Proust was bent on recapturing time for the joy of possessing it. "The only true paradise," he said, "is the paradise we have lost." Farrell—if his autobiographical heroes are speaking for him—wants to recapture time in order to destroy it. That is what Bernard Carr is saying when he admits to himself "that he still had not escaped from the past. But he would! If necessary, he would write so that he would mangle and tear that past to ribbons and throw it away like something he had destroyed." In the same way Danny O'Neill promises himself that "he would drive this neighborhood and all his memories of it out of his consciousness with a book." Danny and Bernard Carr—and Farrell himself—are like patients on a psychoanalyst's couch, bringing up the details of a traumatic experience one after another, day after day, so as to banish the effects of the experience and make it possible for them to live in the present.

It is a purpose that can produce impressive novels—and Farrell has written them—but the novels must deal with special types of subject matter. In *Yet Other Waters* he has ventured out of what seems to be his proper field. He is treating an historical subject without displaying a sense of history, and with a technique that is aimed at the total obliteration of the past.

THE WORLD OF
JAMES GOULD COZZENS

"Love conquers all—*amor vincit omnia*, said the gold scroll in a curve beneath the dial of the old French gilt clock." Those are the first words of James Gould Cozzens's new book, published nine years after *Guard of Honor*, which is still the most thoughtful, the most brilliantly organized, and the best-written of all the American novels that deal with World War II. *By Love Possessed*, which deals with another grand theme, is not so brilliant or faultlessly written, but it goes deeper into human motives. Although one hesitates to call it quite the best of Cozzens's twelve novels—the first of them was written in 1924, the year he came of age—it promises to be the most widely read.

The clock with its motto plays a brief but conspicuous part in the story. At the beginning it strikes three; then two days later, on the last page of the novel, after a wild simultaneity of comic and tragic misadventures, the clock strikes four—as if to indicate that human lives continue their brief span, even if all their prospects have changed. The motto suggests—as does the title—that the book has love for its theme. As a matter of fact it presents us with many types of love, conjugal and parental, puppy, adulterous, and sacred, besides self-love, ambition, love of one's good repute, and simple lust. Its real theme, however, is the mischief caused when any sort of passion, uncontrolled by reason or custom, intrudes into human affairs. Cozzens has written something rare in fiction, a long, rich, and complicated novel not so much about love as against it.

The scene is a town in the Delaware Valley not fifty miles, I should judge, from the farm where Cozzens has spent most of his life since leaving college. He stays near home, in body as in spirit, and tries to recreate, so he says, "the things I have seen"; fortunately he has a sharp eye for character and a talent for making recombinations. What he recreates for us is a small but intensely living world, crowded with people of all ages and many social positions, from janitors to judges and tarts to clergymen. For each of them he remembers the right gestures and the right turns of speech, but he seems most interested in the inner lives of prosperous old-line Americans, particularly if they are conscious of their standing in society and of the duties it involves. Today Cozzens is one of the very few serious novelists who speak for this important group.

"I am more or less illiberal," he said in one of the infrequent interviews he has given, "and strongly antipathetic to all political and social movements. I was brought up an Episcopalian, and where I live the landed gentry are Republican. I do not understand music, I am little interested in art, and the theatre seems tiresome to me. My literary preferences are for writers who take the trouble to write well." The words seem to be spoken in a cool eighteenth-century voice, by a man who is closer in spirit to Samuel Johnson than he is to Samuel Beckett.

The hero of *By Love Possessed* is fifty-four years old, like Cozzens this summer, and at times he speaks in the same eighteenth-century manner. Arthur Winner, Junior, to give him his full name, is a successful lawyer, happily married, known for his kindness, wisdom, and integrity. He tries to be a man of reason, like his respected father, but he lives in a more illogical world where all his neighbors are swayed by passion. For the two days of the story they give him no peace; they besiege his office, they keep his telephones ringing, they summon him to church or court, they park their cars in his driveway and call him outside, they fling their arms around his neck, they pound at the screen door of his country house or stride in while fingering a pistol; and all of them—even the man with the pistol—are pleading out of the depths for his advice or merely his sympathy.

They are all possessed by love, as if by a daemon. There is only Arthur Winner who, sustained by the memory of his father and the good advice of a legal partner, seems able to resist the daemon and remain to some extent the man of reason, the still center of the storms that rage around him.

All that has come to be an expected pattern in Cozzens's novels. It is not an easy pattern, not anything that could be taught in English 298 and learned by bright students, so that they in turn could write

The Just and the Unjust or *Men and Brethren*, let alone *Guard of Honor*.
It takes for granted a broad knowledge of human nature and human
institutions. It takes for granted an easy style to read, which is almost
always a hard one to write, besides an unusual degree of patience, so
that the pattern, once applied to a new set of events, can be carried out
in its smallest details. It takes for granted a degree of professional responsibility that few young writers even try to acquire; Cozzens would
no more twist a character to meet the demands of his plot than he
would lie about or steal from his Delaware Valley neighbors. Nevertheless it *is* a pattern, almost a formula, and it has reappeared in one
novel after another.

There is a lawyer, young or old, or a staff officer or a clergyman
deeply involved in the lives of his parishioners. There is a climax in his
career, a period of two or three days during which hell breaks loose;
men die in accidents, women commit suicide, friends of the family
commit sexual crimes, his closest associates betray him through pure
irresponsibility; and meanwhile the hero tries to do his best for everyone, succeeding in some cases, failing in others, always questioning
his own motives and talent, yet somehow surviving by force of character. "Every day is a miracle," says old Judge Coates in *The Just and
the Unjust*, speaking as if for the author in all his novels. "The world
gets up in the morning and is fed and goes to work, and in the evening
it comes home and is fed again and perhaps has a little amusement and
goes to sleep. To make that possible, so much has to be done by so
many people that, on the face of it, it is impossible. Well, every day
we do it; and every day, come hell, come high water, we're going to
have to go on doing it as well as we can."

That has always been Cozzens's feeling about life, and it is expressed
once again in the new novel. This time, however, there are two important changes in his fictional pattern. His style used to be as clear as
a mountain brook; now it has become a little weedgrown and murky,
like the same stream when it wanders through a meadow. He may have
come to feel, as many do in middle age, that life is even more complicated than he had once believed and that the truth does not lie so
much in direct statements as it does in qualifications and parentheses.
Often he uses too many of these, like the later Henry James, and there
are times, especially when he is speaking of love, that he seems to

stammer a little, as if with embarrassment. The stammer, if we can call it that, adds an emotional quality to his writing that had once seemed to be lacking.

The other change is in the fortunes of the hero. Formerly the Cozzens hero came through his trials with a little more wisdom and humility than he had at the beginning, but otherwise untouched. He retained his emotional detachment, and it made us feel as readers that we had merely witnessed an experience instead of having lived it. Arthur Winner doesn't get off so easily. He is forced to admit what he had tried to put out of his mind: that he too had been possessed by love and had once betrayed his closest friend. Even worse, he discovers that he in turn has been betrayed, and in such a fashion that he will have to sacrifice his little fortune and his personal integrity to preserve his reputation. Dressed in the morning coat and striped trousers he had worn that morning as an usher in church, he stands in his office bewildered, feeling that the world around him had "come to a halt, to an end, had dissolved, had withdrawn in space, leaving him on a point of rock, the last living man." It is, so far, the most directly moving moment in any of Cozzens's novels.

But they are good novels all of them, so good that there is no living writer who couldn't learn lessons from them. Cozzens, who avoids literary society, has for years been a presence in the background, a little mysterious, often discussed and praised, but never so widely read as he deserves to be. With this new book it seems likely that he will be recognized for what he is, one of the country's truly distinguished novelists.

(*The following is the speech that Malcolm Cowley delivered at the presentation of the William Dean Howells Medal to James Gould Cozzens by the American Academy of Arts and Letters in 1961.*)

The Howells Medal of the Academy is awarded once every five years to a distinguished work of American fiction. This year the lustral honor is being paid to a very distinguished work that has been more disputed over and dissected than any other novel of the period beginning with 1955.

By Love Possessed, published in June 1957, had the early misfortune to be greeted with almost unanimous praise. The physical laws that govern literary opinion are such that anyone might have predicted the sequel; six months later the praise was answered with an equally vehement chorus of abuse. Except when this second chorus, or antistrophe, happened to deal with the debatable question of Mr. Cozzens's style, it was hardly at all concerned with standards. Chiefly the novel was attacked for what it seemed to suggest in terms of political doctrines, group loyalties, ethical standards, and the struggle between new and old tendencies in American society.

On all these public or personal questions, the Academy as a body has never taken a stand. Its award of the Howells Medal to James Gould Cozzens does not, I am sure, imply its approval or disapproval of his voting record, which he tells us is Republican, or his choice of characters, which seems to reveal a sympathy with the prosperous Anglo-Saxon segment of the population, or the religious faith of his hero, which is a rather detached Episcopalianism, or even his personal scale of values, with its eighteenth-century distrust of unbridled emotions and its emphasis on understanding and enduring the world that exists. The Academy is honoring a literary work, not a body of correct opinion.

In the field of literature proper, the award does not imply that the Academy would recommend as a universal practice Mr. Cozzens's method of constructing a novel, which consists in telling an essentially simple fable that observes the classical unities of time, place, and action, while extending the scope of the book by introducing scores of characters and projecting their lives far into the past. The award might imply, however, that nobody has practiced that particular method with more painstaking craftsmanship or a broader uderstanding of human relations in all their blundering complexity. Reread after three years, *By Love Possessed* appears to be a solid and lasting and, to his fellow novelists, an enviably difficult achievement, that is, a very long novel presenting the events of exactly forty-nine hours as seen through the eyes of a single character, with a whole community involved in a diversity of incidents, and yet with every incident maintaining a single tone, contributing to a single theme, and with the end of the book foreshadowed in its beginning. The Howells Medal is being awarded to a man who, all controversy aside, is the greatest architect in contemporary American fiction.

JOHN P. MARQUAND:
SOCIOLOGIST

A ny new Marquand novel—including *Women and Thomas Harrow*—will be a solidly constructed book of around 500 pages. Its hero will be a member, or about to become a member, of what C. Wright Mills calls "the power elite." In one of the early chapters he will encounter a crisis that promises to determine his future career. While the crisis develops swiftly, in a very few days, there will be something that reminds him of his past, and he will go over it step by step from the beginning; every Marquand hero has a filing-cabinet memory. Then, back in the present after a digression of more than 200 pages, he will realize that it is too late for him to choose another career or another personality or to recapture his first love. What he has been will decide what he has to be. The only answer to the crisis is to do the best he can in the old familiar way.

In offering this generalized synopsis, I run the risk of making Marquand's later novels seem more uniform than they are in reality. Each has a different content. If almost all of them are cast in the same mold, that is because the mold is not what interests him essentially. Marquand is a highly skilled fictional engineer, but since *The Late George Apley* (1937) he hasn't thought it necessary to exercise his talent for invention, at least in a major fashion.

Minor inventions abound in his later work—for example, the Harvard class biographies that Harry Pulham sets out to collect (in *H. M. Pulham, Esquire*), and the business trip to Charlie Gray's boyhood home (in *Point of No Return*), and the cover story for *Time* (in *Melville Goodwin, USA*) as a result of which the general calls his life to attention and marches it past us in review—but these are merely devices for introducing the necessary return to the past. They are, so to speak, new forms stamped into the body shell of the novel, but under them the power plant remains the same—and why should it be changed, considering that it has always served the author's essential purposes?

I suspect that those purposes are, first, to tell a story that will hold the continuous attention of a great many readers—sometimes of millions—and, second, to study some familiar but imperfectly known aspect of social life in the Northeastern seaboard states. Marquand is first of all a professional entertainer, and one of the best, but he is also something more than an amateur sociologist. His studies of social stratification in Newburyport, Mass.—not at all disguised as "Clyde" in several of his novels—are less systematic but show a deeper understanding of motives than the standard sociological study made by W. Lloyd Warner and associates, in *Yankee City*. His picture of the power elite is more finely accurate than C. Wright Mills's broader study.

As a sociologist, Marquand follows the method of creating—not copying from life—a leading figure in some profession, and then of exposing him to a series of representative situations, so that we end by feeling that we are familiar with one segment of American society. His novels differ from one another in the same way that professions differ; hidden in each of them is the sound principle that professions shape character. Thus, he seems to be saying that a two-star general, after thirty-five years in the Army, is an essentially different person from a banker, who in turn is different from an industrialist or a news commentator. All of them fall in love, all of them struggle to get ahead, but they do so in different fashions, since every professional field has its own standards of behavior.

Besides having this diversity of subject-matter, Marquand's later novels also differ in their quality as fiction; and the latest of all—*Women and Thomas Harrow*—is hardly one of the best. In the social terminology that Marquand used to apply to people in Clyde, it belongs in the lower-middle stratum of his serious fiction—somewhere above *Sincerely, Willis Wayde*, which is upper-lower, but well below *Melville Goodwin, USA* (middle-upper), and even farther from *Point of No Return*, which stands alone in the upper-upper class.

It is the story of two days in the life of a famous playwright, who has come back to Clyde after thirty years and has bought one of its handsome Federal houses. On the morning of the first day, Tom Harrow learns that he has lost his entire fortune, including the house in Clyde and the exquisitely chosen furniture that makes it look like a stage setting for *Berkeley Square*. In the afternoon, he finishes the third act of his new play.

Late at night, after a battle with his latest wife, who is a shrew, and a dinner party that couldn't be avoided, he sits alone in the library reviewing his early triumphs and dreaming of his first wife, whom he has never ceased to love. (This time the flashback of 235 pages is the most absorbing part of the story.) On the following day, he meets his first wife again, finds that she loves him still, but refuses the suggestion of a double divorce and remarriage. No matter how hopeless his present situation may be, he will carry on.

It is a good story as Marquand tells it—he always tells that story well—and the background of theatrical life is sharply recorded. If the book as a whole is less persuasive than some of his other novels, it is not because the author shows any sign of flagging energy but rather because of a technical device he has adopted in order to prove that his hero is truly a playwright. The mark of a playwright—so Marquand seems to be saying—is that he judges every scene, even the most intimate, as if it were being acted on a stage. Thus, we find Tom Harrow having thoughts like these:

> Her voice stopped. When Emily [his latest wife] was on the stage, her timing had left much to be desired; but occasionally she knew when to stop, and this was a correct moment, when everything was hanging in dramatic balance.

> It was time to go, and it was delightful to see that Rhoda [his first wife] had picked up her gloves. The last speech made a good curtain for some kind of act, and indeed the whole conversation had its own dramatic proportion.

From beginning to end, the book is full of such remarks. Even in the last tragic scene with Rhoda, when Tom abandons hope of seeing her again, "I wish you wouldn't always speak lines," she says, "but I suppose you can't help it." Suddenly we become aware that Tom, even here, has been speaking lines instead of pouring out his emotion or holding it back; he is still on the stage. And so in the book as a whole: it is shrewdly observed, it has maturity and wisdom, but—except in the long flashback—we watch the actors without forgetting they are actors or ever quite sharing their emotions.

FLEM SNOPES GETS HIS COMEUPPANCE

" "This book," William Faulkner says in a brief introductory note to *The Mansion*, "is the final chapter of, and the summation of, a work conceived and begun in 1925." That must have been one of the years when the still almost unpublished author, living by odd jobs in Oxford, Miss., used to visit Phil Stone in his law office and talk about many things, including modern literature and the ruin of the South. A fancy that amused both of them was that Mississippi was being ravaged by a tribe named Snopes, all born without a conscience, who had appeared from nowhere and burrowed through the land like rats or moles. Faulkner invented a series of wild stories about the rapacity of the Snopes clan. After being enjoyed over cold whiskey toddies, the stories were typed and sent to magazines, but they always came back.

Later, when Faulkner had become the notorious author of *Sanctuary*, a few of the stories were published, in some cases by the same magazines that had rejected them. Still later, in 1940, a whole group of published and unpublished stories about the coming of the Snopeses was fitted together into one of his most remarkable books, *The Hamlet*. One might say that its parts—including the famous *Spotted Horses*—are greater than the whole, but the whole has a grandness of outline too. It tells how Flem Snopes, the son of a barn-burning tenant farmer, appears in the hamlet of Frenchman's Bend; how he is followed by a devouring horde of his kinfolk; and how—for a price—he marries Eula Varner, the fabulously beautiful and just a little pregnant daughter of the local magnate. Having robbed or swindled everyone in the community—even V. K. Ratliff, the shrewdest of them all—he moves on to the conquest of Jefferson, the county seat, still gray-faced, lumpish and taciturn, still chewing tobacco "until the suption is out of it."

Faulkner's readers waited seventeen years for what they were told would be the second volume of a Snopes trilogy. In *The Town* (1957)

Flem starts his new career as half owner of a dingy lunchroom, with Eula frying steaks behind the counter. Soon the Mayor of Jefferson, dashing Major de Spain, becomes her lover. Flem says nothing and reaps his reward; he is made superintendent of the municipal power plant, then vice president of the Merchants and Farmers Bank. Other Snopeses invade the town, year after year. Most of them are thieves or swindlers, but Flem is studying how to be respectable. At a carefully chosen moment he threatens to expose his wife's liaison. Eula commits suicide, Major de Spain leaves town, and Flem becomes president of the bank that Colonel Sartoris had founded; the rats have driven the eagles from their nests.

The Town is more tightly constructed than The Hamlet; perhaps it is more of a novel, but it is less of a book to be read with admiring wonder. Part of the story is told by a painfully wise lawyer, Gavin Stevens, who manages to hide its simple outlines in a mist of grandiloquence and moral quibbling. The rest of it is told by Gavin's nephew Chick Mallison, or by his friend V. K. Ratliff, both affected by this lawyer's bad habits of speech. The Snopeses are now less endearingly loathsome than they had seemed in Frenchman's Bend. On the whole this second volume of the trilogy is Faulkner's dullest work in thirty years.

I am happy to report that the final volume is vastly better, at least in part. Like its predecessors, The Mansion has a simple and dramatic outline. Flem Snopes, now living in Major de Spain's antebellum mansion, has become so powerful that nobody belonging to the old Jefferson families can punish him for the evil he has done. But he has to be punished, in the fictional world that Faulkner has created, for one of the author's deepest beliefs is in the reality of a just Providence. The instrument of Providence must be another Snopes, and that is the essential story: how Mink Snopes, in 1908, had been provoked into committing a murder; how Flem had failed to come to his cousin's defense and then, fearing Mink's resentment, had tricked him into attempting to escape from the penitentiary, so that his sentence was doubled; how Mink persisted in what had become his one purpose in life; how he was pardoned after thirty-eight years, chiefly by the efforts of Flem's stepdaughter, Linda Snopes, who hoped he would avenge her mother's suicide; how he somehow made his way to Jefferson, and into the mansion, and what happened when Mink and Flem came face to face.

There is a great deal in the book that is not essential; chiefly this has to do with Linda's vain love for Gavin Stevens, her adventures in New York, and her attempts to educate the Negroes. Some of the motivation is weak (why didn't Gavin marry her?), and we are allowed to forget that Flem is purely evil, so that our distaste for him is mingled with more pity than Faulkner meant to arouse. Once again Gavin Stevens confuses part of the story in the telling, with the wrong sort of help from Chick Mallison and V. K. Ratliff. But whenever Mink Snopes appears, Faulkner's writing rises to a very high level—not quite so high as in *Spotted Horses* or *The Old Man*, but above almost everything else that is being written. *The Mansion* is a necessary book for his readers, who will find that one part of his Yoknapatawpha County saga, the Snopes part, has been definitely finished.

In its completed form the Snopes trilogy reveals both the marvelous qualities and the limitations of Faulkner as an epic poet in prose. We can see now that Yoknapatawpha County, for all its human richness, is something less than a world in itself; too many elements are weak or missing. Faulkner is not one of the novelists who can carry out a plan with the certainty that every detail will be consistent and that no scene or character will fall below a given standard of execution. He does lay plans and works to carry them out, but essentially he depends on his imagination or demon and there are times when the demon proves sulky or silent.

It seems to me that the demon is most obedient, or most in command, when Faulkner is telling stories about men or beasts who fulfilled their destinies. Old Ben, the hero of *The Bear*, was destined to be vainly pursued year after year, and Sam Fathers was destined to die when Ben was killed. The convict hero of *The Old Man* was destined to make his way back to the penitentiary against the power of the Mississippi in flood. Joe Christmas was born to be lynched and accepted his special doom, as Flem Snopes accepted another. Faulkner's best stories are all of them, in Isak Dinesen's phrase, anecdotes of destiny.

The demon is also in command when Faulkner is celebrating the Mississippi earth, whether this be the black soil of the Delta—where

he tells us that cotton grows man-high in the cracks of the pavement—
or the gullied red clay of the uplands, or the sand hills sparsely covered /
with sassafras and persimmon. Nobody in our time has written better
about the soil and the seasons, or about the men who depend on both
for the privilege of merely living; that is the strength of *The Hamlet*.
When Faulkner moves too far from the soil, his demon becomes re-
calcitrant, and the author himself reveals a less delicate sense of human
values. It is one of his limitations as a novelist that his wealthy towns-
people tend to become either knights or dragons; quixotic knights like
Gavin Stevens (who lacks a Sancho Panza) or dragons sometimes made
of pasteboard, like Flem Snopes in most of *The Mansion*.

And so it has to be Faulkner's portrait of Flem's cousin Mink, a
countryman, that gives a heroic touch to this latest novel. Mink has
changed in the course of patiently working out his destiny. When we
first met him in *The Hamlet*, he was a poisonous creature, a cotton-
mouth snake that struck without warning. Now we learn that he has
a true feeling for the soil, unique among the Snopeses, and in Faulkner's created world no man with such a feeling can be entirely bad. It
is Mink who obeys what he thinks are the commands of Old Moster,
his name for God, by ridding the world of a monster. Then he lies
down on the Mississippi earth, where he is "equal to any," the author
tell us, "good as any, brave as any . . . right on up to the very top itself
among the shining phantoms and dreams which are the milestones of
the long human recording."

WILLA CATHER'S VALUES

The Landscape and the Looking Glass is the longest book that is likely to be written about Willa Cather for many years, though not the most comprehensive. John H. Randall 3d, who teaches at Wellesley, is primarily concerned with only one aspect of his chosen author. He doesn't say much about her life story, since other writers have told as much as she wished to be known. More regrettably he fails to deal with Miss Cather's literary methods, except in a sidelong fashion. His real subject is her ideas—social, political, historical—and especially her moral philosophy, which he calls her "search for value."

In exploring this relatively narrow field, he shows a massive patience and a commendable zeal. He discusses each of her novels at length, retelling the plot and quoting what he regards as the significant passages. He passes all the characters in review. He examines the choice of incidents, the use of images, and tries to show what both imply in terms of ideology. Sometimes he ventures on shaky ground—for example, in his notion that *Sapphira and the Slave Girl* can be explained as a pious return to Protestantism—but most of his statements about Miss Cather's beliefs are documented and unassailable. To mention a few:

She was an unreconstructed individualist, a sister-in-art to the robber barons. Although she had a strong sense of duty, she felt no obligation to society as a whole. The only groups with which she sympathized were family units, and later the church as an extended family. She believed in the all-importance of the personal will: "The history of every country," she said in *O Pioneers!*, "begins in the heart of a man or a woman," and usually in a very young heart. Like an imperious child, she wanted this country to follow her desires. When the country went off in another direction, after World War I, she simply retired from the struggle, for she hated conflicts of any sort. In her later years she was always seeking a refuge—first in art, then in memories of her childhood, and finally in the distant past.

This is the picture of her mind that Mr. Randall presents at length, and he wants us to think it is damning. Indeed, he keeps scolding Miss Cather as if she were a Wellesley sophomore who had submitted a group of unwanted and unsatisfactory themes. He seems to feel they have wasted his time, and so he keeps making resentful comments in the margins. With some hesitation, he gives a B+ to O Pioneers!, which is the first of her mature novels. He says it is the only one in which she sometimes approached what he regards as a properly tragic vision of the world. All the later novels, he thinks, "embody an outlook on life so distorted and falsified as to be practically worthless as an interpretation of human experience."

Thus, in My Antonia, Miss Cather is being "dishonest and evasive," while "willfully failing to see life steadily and as a whole." In The Professor's House she gives signs of "intellectual and artistic bankruptcy." Mr. Randall is determined to be candid, even at the cost of seeming to be a prig. In Death Comes for the Archbishop, he says: "The portrayal of her ecclesiastical heroes fails to take into account the fact that religious calling demands the continuous subordination of the lower self to the higher self. . . . Although religious in spots, the book is only intermittently Catholic at best." The fact is that Miss Cather never achieved "esthetic and emotional maturity." "It was perfectly predictable that Willa Cather would hate the New Deal."

Mr. Randall is too young to have been a New Dealer, but he shows himself to be more civic-minded than Harry Hopkins in his prime. Wholly occupied with exposing malefactions against society, he seldom lets the defendant speak for herself, as she does admirably in her two critical volumes, Not Under Forty and the posthumous Willa Cather on Writing, and the rest of us might listen to what she said.

Miss Cather believed that the true author doesn't choose a subject, but merely accepts it, in accordance with his particular nature. A subject, she liked to say, quoting her older friend Sarah Orne Jewett, is "the thing that teases the mind over and over for years, and at last gets itself rightly put down on paper." If a writer is to achieve "anything noble, anything enduring, it must be by giving himself absolutely to his material."

That is a point she made time and again: the form of a novel grows out of the subject instead of being imposed on the subject. "It is a common fallacy," she said, "that a writer, if he is talented enough" can improve upon his subject-matter, by "using his 'imagination' upon it and twisting it to suit his purpose. The truth is that by such a process (which is not imaginative at all!) he can at best produce only a brilliant sham, which, like a badly built and pretentious house, looks poor and shabby in a few years."

The artist's real problem is not how to change his material but how to simplify it, "finding what conventions of form and what detail one can do without and yet preserve the spirit of the whole—so that all that one has suppressed and cut away is there to the reader's consciousness as much as if it were in type on the page."

Those were some of Miss Cather's literary principles, and she thought they were more important than the social and ethical and political ideas to which Mr. Randall devotes a long and overdocumented book. Her social ideas changed with the years, becoming always more conservative (and narrower and more regrettable). In literature, however, she was faithful to herself, to her ideal of good writing and to each of the subjects that teased her mind.

> The artist [she said] spends a lifetime in loving the things that haunt him, . . . in trying to get these conceptions down on paper exactly as they are to him and not in conventional poses supposed to reveal their character; trying this method and that, as a painter tries different lightings and different attitudes with his subject to catch the one that presents it more suggestively than any other. And at the end of a lifetime he emerges with much that is more or less happy experimenting, and comparatively little that is the very flower of himself and of his genius.

Miss Cather emerged with a number of books—nineteen, counting the two posthumous volumes—each of which is different from all the others and most of which, though written with her absolute integrity, might be classified as more or less happy experiments. But at least three books—*My Antonia*, *A Lost Lady*, and *Death Comes for the Arch-*

bishop—are the very flower of her genius. There aren't many authors of whom we can say that three of their works are contributions to the small permanent body of American literature.

At this point I venture a remark about her writing that, with variations, might be applied to a few other talented authors. Those three masterpieces—and her remaining work as well, if in a lesser measure—did perform services to American society even if Miss Cather was seldom conscious of having social intentions. For one example, she humanized the land itself, the wide, gently rolling, but savage land of her girlhood, endowing it with folk memories and warm associations. She celebrated the pioneers, not so much the Anglos among them as the Central Europeans and especially the Czechs, giving them a place they deserved in her American gallery of heroes and wonders. Not a Catholic herself, she rendered the poetry of the Church, giving that too a place in her gallery. She made her readers feel that culture is all of a piece, depending almost as much on gardens and kitchens as on classrooms and concert halls. All these are social lessons, not painted on the text but woven into the fabric. Let us not forget that Miss Cather's integrity as an artist was also, in its way, a social lesson.

What if Mr. Randall—he wasn't born then, but what if some other civic-minded critic had managed to gain Miss Cather's ear in 1922 or thereabouts when she thought that the world broke in two? What if he had persuaded her, deaf as she usually was to arguments, that she was wrong about the world and wrong to trust her instincts?—that she should write stories full of dramatic conflicts, revealing the misery of the human condition as well as its splendor; that social relations were more important than individual relations; that she herself should become "adjusted" and "emotionally mature" by accepting the world as it is instead of dreaming about the past—what then?

She would have written different books, and Mr. Randall might have praised them for their ideology, but I doubt that he would have written about them at such great length. Although there is nothing in his own system of criticism by which to test the judgment, I think he would have felt obscurely that those other books were no longer true to her nature or her subjects and that they were all a brilliant sham, "which, like a badly built and pretentious house, looks poor and shabby in a few years."

Mr. Randall, who doesn't like Willa Cather, has chosen the wrong subject, like many critics before him. He is like an overambitious marksman on the target range. He judges the distance; he tests the wind; he adjusts his sights; he tightens the strap; he aims with infinite patience; then, gently squeezing the trigger, he sends bullet after bullet into the bullseye—only to find, when he looks up for approbation, that he has been aiming all the time at the wrong target.

DREISER:
GENIUS IN THE RAW

Perhaps I should be satisfied with the result of Mr. Swanberg's clearly diligent and scholarly labors.

There is an immense mass of Dreiser material, and the new biographer has made full use of it. He has studied the great Dreiser collection at the University of Pennsylvania. He has examined the other collections and has read all the available Dreiser letters. He has profited from the help of Robert H. Elias, the author of what has been until now the standard life. "Dr. Elias," he says, "not only told me his own Dreiser recollections but gave me the use of his invaluable notes and letters, which appear frequently in my text—a generosity," he rightly adds, "that still astonishes me."

Many others have been of hardly less assistance. As a man of transparent honesty. Mr. Swanberg has gained the confidence of Dreiser's surviving friends, besides that of his niece, who is the only representative in the second generation of what had been a family of ten brothers and sisters. He has talked to many of Dreiser's mistresses, who told him enlightening stories (though some of them asked him to change their names in the book). After collecting enough information to fill a library shelf, he has arranged the gist of it in strictly chronological order and has written a single volume as long and as crowded with details of behavior as a Dreiser novel. It promises to stand for years as the authoritative biography.

And yet—

I found it rather hard to read and, in the end, disappointing. Such an experience with the book suggests a question. Might there not be something faulty in Mr. Swanberg's behavioristic method, or at least in his use of the method to present the extraordinary sort of person that Dreiser was?

I note that the biographer is full of good intentions toward his subject—if sometimes unable to repress his impatience—and that his admiration for Dreiser's novels seems greater than my own. Yet I also note that the hero of his story seems meaner, smaller, and less deserving of sympathy than I suspect that Dreiser was in life. Something essential is missing from the book. We find in it Dreiser's love affairs, not the interminable list of them, but more than a sufficient sampling. We find his business dealings, sometimes less than strictly honest; we find his public and private squabbles, his income-tax returns, his childish cunning, his massive ingratitude—in short, his deeds if not his dreams: But do we find Dreiser himself? There is something in him elusive, almost ungraspable—though one finds it revealed in his books more than in his outer life—and it is the quality that gives him stature in spite of his transgressions. Mr. Swanberg has failed to do more than briefly and intermittently suggest it.

I would venture that the missing quality is Dreiser's genius.

Dreiser is the clearest example in American literature, and perhaps in American life, of a man who possessed genius in its raw state, genius almost completely unfortified and unrefined by talent. He is our great primitive, compared with whom even Whitman seems overcivilized. Possibly Dreiser had more genius than any other American writer of our century, and it was not genius in the sense of mere inspiration or a miraculous waterfall of words. It was rather a vision of life that controlled the tone of his works, their choice of detail, their treatment of character, and their massing of events toward an inevitable climax—in short, that gave them power. But there are other elements of writing—for example, taste, learning, logic, grammar, style in a narrow meaning of the word, and a sense of proportion—which properly belong in the sphere of talent. At the edge of it Dreiser's genius halted.

It is true that he showed talent of a sort in the magazine world, when editing other people's manuscripts. But he was unwilling or unable to edit his own novels. Having produced his works of genius, he depended on other persons—Arthur Henry, Floyd Dell, James T. Farrell, Louise Campbell, Sally Kusell, Marguerite Tjader Harris, sometimes a whole crew of admiring women—to revise them into shape for publication. He accepted their emendations without pride, but also without gratitude, as if their work was a tribute paid to his genius. As for talent in the handicraft of writing—and at most times in the art of life—he had less of it than any other recognized author.

That lack of talent or simple competence in Dreiser is impressed on us many times in the present narrative, as are also his lapses in literary and personal behavior. Sometimes it seems that Mr. Swanberg's method leads him to talk of little else but Dreiser's faults. In consulting the index of 32 pages, I found that one of the long subheadings under "Dreiser, Theodore" is devoted to "His Traits, Habits, Activities." Only one of the traits is given a eulogistic name, "Artistic integrity," which, by the way, I am inclined to question. It was not Dreiser, but only his genius when it seized hold of him, that had artistic integrity.

The other traits, almost all with dyslogistic names, include "Sex worship" (18 entries), "Hypochondria," "Naivete," "Superstitions," "Mood fluctuations" (from manic to depressive), "Deep fear of poverty" (another term for miserliness), "Fixation on clothing," "Suspiciousness," "Rudeness," "Furtiveness," "Lack of writing discipline," "Lack of taste," "Drinking habits" (compulsive in his later years), and "Attitude toward Jews," which was a peasant's attitude, compounded of distrust and envy. Each of those undesirable traits is followed by at least two lines of page numbers, as a sign that it is illustrated in the text by many documented reports of his behavior.

This prolonged attention to the unhappier sides of Dreiser's character may have a curious effect on Mr. Swanberg's readers. They may come to feel immersed in the novelist's daily affairs, as if confined for life in a most unpleasant household. Everything around them is ugly. Everyone is embarrassing and continually embarrassed. The master of the house is mean and half-demented. The others resent and despise him secretly, yet pay him a reluctant homage. There are whines, slaps, howls, smells, domestic treacheries, and everything happens as if in a stale atmosphere, in rooms where the windows are never opened. At length the reader revolts, even though he does not question Mr. Swanberg's accuracy in presenting the facts about his subject's behavior. The truth remains, however, that Dreiser possessed—or was possessed by—his inexplicable genius, and that part of it consisted precisely in his gift for transforming his daily life, and ours, by opening unexpected windows.

I might illustrate from Dreiser's memories of his early years as reported in *Dawn*, a book that gives me more pleasure to reread than I can honestly confess to finding in his novels. It was during the summer before his sixteenth birthday that Dreiser came to Chicago alone, with three or four dollars in his pocket. At less than her usual price of two dollars, a kind-hearted landlady rented him a room on West Madison Street, then a middle-class neighborhood. "I washed my face and brushed my hair," Dreiser says, "then knelt down by the window— because I could hang farther out by doing so—and looked out. East and west, for miles, as it seemed to me, was a double row of gas lamps already flaring in the dusk, and behind them the lighted faces of shops." It was raining, but the street was full of people. While Dreiser was kneeling at the windowsill, the voice of Chicago spoke to him. "I am the soul of a million people," it said. ". . . I am the pulsing urge of the universe! You are a part of me, I of you! All that life or hope is or can be or do, this I am, and it is here before you! Take of it! Live, live, satisfy your heart! Strive to be what you wish to be now while you are young and of it! Reflect its fire, its tang, its color, its greatness! Be, be wonderful or strong or great if you will, but be!"

Dreiser obeyed the voice, as always in his fumbling, incompetent fashion. He tried to *be*; and meanwhile he tramped the streets looking for work. Mr. Swanberg tells us about the inefficient search and about the job he found in the filthy kitchen of a Levantine restaurant. He makes us feel that Dreiser was unqualified even for pearl-diving, besides having too little perseverance to hold on to the job when nothing else was available. Always those faults of character! But Mr. Swanberg does not mention the voice, though it would speak to Dreiser many times in his life—even as late as the year before his death, when he was finishing that flawed but somehow deeply moving novel, *The Bulwark*.

The voice, with the immense hunger it roused in him and all the visions it evoked through opened windows, was that of Dreiser's genius. Of course I am writing figuratively, but Dreiser felt when creating his best scenes (and sometimes when paying court to a temporarily adored woman) that someone or something greater than himself was standing over him and speaking. That greater presence— that power to clothe in dreams an age and a culture—is what Mr. Swanberg fails to suggest. In his biography the voice is silent.

Those questions as they relate to the Ashley Case are the theme of *The Eighth Day*. Wilder tells us about the adventures of John Ashley in Chile, where he dodges the "rat catchers"; about young Sophie Ashley and how she saves the rest of the household at the cost of her sanity; about the swift rise of Roger Ashley in Chicago journalism; and then about the earlier background of the Ashleys and of Eustacia Lansing, wife of the murdered man. In the course of these rapidly moving stories he introduces dozens of characters from all levels of society, including the saintly and the picaresque. He moves backward and forward in time as if all the stories were threads in a historical tapestry. At the end of the novel Roger Ashley visits a saintly old man and finds him "gazing intently at the homemade rug at his feet."

> . . . Roger's eyes followed his. It had been woven long ago, but a complex mazelike design in brown and black could still be distinguished.
>
> "Mr. Ashley, kindly lift that rug and turn it over."
>
> Roger did so. No figure could be traced on the reverse. It presented a mass of knots and of frayed and dangling threads. With a gesture of the hand the Deacon directed Roger to replace it.
>
> "You are a newspaperman in Chicago. Your sister is a singer there. Your mother conducts a boardinghouse in Coaltown. Your father is in some distant country. Those are the threads and knots of human life. You cannot see the design."

Silence. There are no final answers to the questions. There are only the illuminations we have found by the way, with the author's comments on human destinies, and the pleasure of reading—I almost said "of hearing," since Wilder writes for the ear—a skillfully told and well invented story.

The Eighth Day reminds one distantly of Wilder's most popular novel, *The Bridge of San Luis Rey* (1927), which also was concerned with chance and destiny. I can find in it no resemblance to any other novel of the past 100 years. Most of the others imitate reality, or offer us dreams to be substituted for reality, but Wilder has neither of these aims. Instead of imitating or evading, he *illustrates*, and he thus goes back to an older tradition in fiction. What *The Eighth Day* most resem-

THORNTON WILDER:
A UNIQUE CASE

In the early summer of 1902 John Barrington Ashley of Coaltown, a small mining center in southern Illinois, was tried for the murder of Breckenridge Lansing, also of Coaltown. He was found guilty and sentenced to death. Five days later, at one in the morning of Thursday, July 22, he escaped from his guards on the train that was carrying him to his execution.

That is the beginning of Thornton Wilder's sixth and longest novel, the first he has published in nearly twenty years. Although the words are printed here without quotation marks, they are the author's words, not mine. In taking notes for this review I tried to paraphrase several of his statements, including those in his opening paragraph, but I found in each case that the paraphrase was longer than the original. Wilder has a way of choosing the necessary facts and of stating them in the simplest and briefest fashion. The facts may be prosaic, but his statements are as hard to change as a finished line of poetry.

Where the reviewer can't paraphrase, at least he can delete and summarize: John Ashley, though tracked to South America, was not recaptured. Five years after his escape, another man confessed to the murder, but Ashley never reappeared. Meanwhile two of his four children had launched themselves, and the youngest was preparing to launch herself, on careers that would make them international figures. They would soon become—I must start quoting again—"the object of that particularly clamorous form of celebrity that surrounds those who are both ridiculed and admired, adored and hated. . . . So it was that as early as 1910 and 1911 people began to study the records of the Ashley Case and to ask questions—frivolous or thoughtful questions—about John and Beata Ashley and their children, about Coaltown, about those old teasers Heredity and Environment, about gifts and talents, and destiny and chance."

bles, though on a wider scale, is the *contes philosophiques* of Voltaire, each of which was written to illustrate a principle; its style is like that of *Candide, or Optimism*, though its substance is closer to that of *Zadig, or Destiny*. John Ashley is indeed a sort of Zadig, in both his ingenuity and his misfortunes. Though he never rises to high rank, as Zadig finally rises, his broken career paves the way for the glorious careers of his children.

In writing *Zadig* Voltaire had in mind *The Arabian Nights*, and Wilder also goes back to that still earlier tradition. One is tempted to picture him as a long-robed storyteller in some oriental marketplace. He does not reproduce the life around him in his tales; rather he invents and combines the sort of happenings that will attract a circle of listeners. If the happenings are amazing or touched with the miraculous, why, so much the better; they will be illustrations of the religious faith to which he adheres. Sufism, Taoism, Brahmanism, Zen, all have their cycles of stories. Wilder's faith would be hard to define, but it seems to include both Eastern and Western elements, combined in almost the same proportion that one finds in Thoreau, whom he greatly admires, and Emerson. On that side he goes back to an earlier American day, but he is more sophisticated than any of the Transcendentalists. Though some of the happenings he invents are close to being impossible, he uses his wide experience of the world to adorn them with realistic details and thus to make them plausible.

He is, in other words, an extremely complicated writer under his mask of simplicity. More and more I feel that his work has not received the close attention it deserves—from the critics, that is; the academies and the public have always been generous. Wilder has been awarded half-a-dozen gold medals, including that of the National Institute, and ten or more honorary degrees. Three of his plays have been enormously successful, and two of them won Pulitzer Prizes (besides his first Pulitzer for *San Luis Rey*). *Our Town* (1938), after its long run on Broadway, became the most popular play of the century in amateur theaters; until recently it was being performed somewhere in the world, and often in several places simultaneously, on every night of every year. That helps to explain the neglect of Wilder by literary critics, who are inclined to feel that such popularity must be only too well deserved.

Another reason why critics have failed to discuss his work is that it cannot be placed in any category that includes the work of other contemporary writers. Born in 1897, Wilder belongs to the same age group as Faulkner, Hemingway, Fitzgerald, Hart Crane, and Edmund Wilson, but it would be hard to name qualities that he shares with any of these, or with their successors. His work is untimely in a spectacular fashion. Indeed, he comes close to denying the existence of time when he denies its essential attribute, which is that of being irreversible. "It is only in appearance that time is a river," he says. "It is rather a vast landscape and it is the eye of the beholder that moves." Since human nature is unchanging, anything that once happened might happen again. "There are no Golden Ages and no Dark Ages. There is the oceanlike monotony of the generations of men under the alternations of fair and foul weather."

That same comparison of humanity with the unchanging ocean can be found in Emerson, who says, "Society is a wave. The wave moves onward, but the water of which it is composed does not." There are many Emersonian notes in Wilder's novels, though they do not appear to be echoes. One of them is the habit passed on to his characters, of speaking in aphorisms. Thus, a character says in *The Eighth Day*, "Suffering is like money, Mr. Tolland. It circulates from hand to hand. We pass on what we take in." The style there is Emerson's, and elsewhere many of the ideas are close to his. One example is Wilder's belief in the influence exerted by heroes of the sort that Emerson calls Representative Men. John Ashley and his children are such heroes; they bear, as it were, a sign on their foreheads; and Wilder leads us to infer that perhaps a change is coming at last; that these are the new men and women of the Eighth Day.

He likes to write about the Ashleys; they arouse his narrative verve and his gift for inventing new situations; but he is not blind to their faults. In one of his comments on them, he seems to be making a wry statement about himself. "Readers recognized his voice," he says of young Roger, the newspaperman, ". . . reasonable without being argumentative, earnest without being ponderous, and always brief. It was the voice of ethical persuasion. Finally his admirers and enemies found relief in the formula that he was 'old-fashioned.' He seemed to speak for the America of one's grandparents." I do not know what place Wilder's work will occupy in the America of our great-grandchildren. I do know that it is different from anyone else's work—as is proved once again by *The Eighth Day*—and that our present literature would be appreciably poorer without that earnest but never ponderous voice.

EDITING ELIOT

I should hesitate to say that *The Waste Land* was the greatest poem of the twentieth century, even the greatest in English. Other works might claim that distinction, but none of their authors has had as much effect as Eliot on almost all the gifted poets who followed him. After the early hostility, then the imitations by the hundred, then the endless pouring forth of scholarly commentaries, it has become evident that the publication of *The Waste Land* in 1922 was an event, in poetry, like the taking of the Bastille; nothing afterward was the same.

Many years ago we heard from Eliot himself that the book as published wasn't the whole poem as he had written it. He had showed the manuscript to his friend and mentor Ezra Pound, and on Pound's advice he had omitted much of it, perhaps a third of the original lines. His candid statement raised a number of questions. Would the omitted passages cast light on the somewhat ambiguous meaning and nature of the poem? How much of its final effect was owed to Pound? In the light of such permanent judgments as we can hazard, were Pound's deletions and changes the right ones to make?

It seemed that the questions would never be answered, the manuscript having vanished. But in 1968, two years after the poet's death, it reappeared—that is a long story in itself—as part of the Berg Collection at the New York Public Library. It has now been published in facsimile, with a transcript on facing pages and with a helpful introduction and notes by the poet's widow: in all a masterly job of editing and bookmaking. Once more the publication is an event, but of a different order: not in the art of poetry, but in the world of literary scholarship.

Mrs. Eliot's introduction casts new light on the poet's early years in England and on the circumstances in which *The Waste Land* was written and given to the public. What transpires from her factual account is that Eliot was an obviously gifted young man, well liked by London literary society and by his superiors at Lloyds Bank, where he worked eight hours a day; outwardly self-possessed, but inwardly troubled. He was overwhelmed by financial worries, by the illness of his first wife—already a semi-invalid—and by the frustrated desire "to write a long poem I have had on my mind for a long time." All this had conspired to give him an intense hatred for contemporary life and—as the poem was to show—a hope for personal redemption.

By the autumn of 1921 he was threatened with a complete breakdown. A specialist ordered him to "go away *at once* for three months quite alone, not exert my mind at all, and follow his strict rules for every hour of the day." The bank gave him a leave of absence, with pay. After a month at the seashore, he went to Lausanne to consult another specialist, and it was there, during the two following months, that he wrote most of *The Waste Land*. In other words, the poem is much more subjective, much more a personal lament, than its early critics suspected (exception made for Conrad Aiken, who wrote a searching and brilliant review). "It is a commonplace," Eliot was to say in a passage about Pascal which, as he later confessed, applied to his own experience at Lausanne,

> that some forms of illness are extremely favorable, not only to religious illumination, but to artistic and literary composition. A piece of writing meditated, apparently without progress for months or years, may suddenly take shape and word; and in this state long passages may be produced which require little or no retouch.

But do those forms of illness also sharpen the critical faculties? Eliot was worried about the general form of the draft he had written, and on his way back to London he stopped in Paris to consult with Ezra Pound. Together they spent several days going over the manuscript, and Pound's contribution is revealed page by page in the present facsimile.

I admit to doubts before reading it. Pound, I know, is often a superb critic, but with blind spots and a habit of applying his principles as if with a fireman's axe. He abhors general statements in poetry, and even personal statements when they are baldly expressed. He has wit, but little taste for humor. He owns to an ingrained prejudice against iambic pentameter, the traditional meter of English poetry. He has a high disdain for repetitive patterns of any sort and excises every word that does not sharpen an image, even when the omission violates the meter and destroys the rhyme scheme. Essentially what he admires is a succession of discrete images, each presented in the fewest possible words and having no relation with other images, as if they were all fragments of a broken mirror. His greatest weakness as a critic (and in his own poems as well) may be his lack of feeling for architectural form: centeredness, balance, completeness. Perhaps this has to do with another and more essential weakness, his lack of feeling for sequence in general, whether logical or temporal. He disdains to tell stories.

Remembering those crotchets, I was intensely curious to see Pound's comments on the original draft of *The Waste Land*. Was it possible, I wondered, that he had stricken out passages essential to the meaning of the poem?—that the draft might even be better, in the light of permanent standards, than the poem as Pound finally approved it? But, no, it was no better, as I found before reading to the end. Pound had gone straight to the weakest lines and passages in Eliot's draft, and, except in one instance, there can be little doubt that he was right to delete them.

Besides separate lines and stanzas through which he slashed with a fountain pen, there are three major deletions: (1) Fifty-four lines at the beginning of the poem were omitted, in this case by Eliot himself, though he may have been following one of Pound's suggestions. (2) A passage of eighty-nine lines, mostly in couplets, was omitted at the beginning of "The Fire Sermon." Pound "induced me," Eliot later wrote,

> to destroy what I thought an excellent set of couplets, for, said he, "Pope has done this so well that you cannot do it better, and if you mean this as a burlesque, you had better suppress it, for you cannot parody Pope unless you can write better verse than Pope—and you can't."

(3) The fourth section of the poem, "Death by Water," originally consisted of ninety-three lines. On Pound's advice, Eliot omitted all but the last ten, those dealing with Phlebas, the drowned Phoenician

sailor. The earlier lines of "Death by Water" make up the only omitted passage that arouses doubt and even regret. One can guess why Pound insisted on deleting it. The first twelve lines are a general invocation to sailors, and we remember that Pound detested general statements in poetry. The seventy-one lines that follow are a consecutive story: A Gloucester fishing schooner sets out for the Eastern banks, encounters all sorts of disasters, and finally, in a gale, is driven beyond the last of the northern islands and wrecked on the polar ice. Eliot, with the passion for literary models that he shared with Pound, had based it on the Ulysses canto (xxvi) of the *Inferno*, which he once described as "a well-told seaman's yarn." Pound, as I said, had a high disdain for story-telling.

Actually there are weak lines in the draft of the passage, but Eliot himself would have amended them, and the story as a whole contributes to the general design of *The Waste Land*. It also reveals something we should probably have missed without it: that *The Waste Land* is close in spirit to *The Rime of the Ancient Mariner*, being another great poem of guilt and redemption. When the shipwreck has been omitted and the whole section reduced to the ten lines about drowned Phlebas, *The Waste Land* loses something in proportion and balance; these were not qualities that Pound admired.

Elsewhere, however, his editing was brilliant, as in the famous passage about the typist seduced by the small house-agent's clerk. Eliot had written the passage as a separate poem of seventeen stanzas or sixty-eight lines, all strictly rhymed; the measure was the same as that of his Sweeney poems, and there was the same contrast between classical mythology—the scene is observed and reported by Tiresias—and contemporary squalor. Pound went over it with his fountain pen, drawing lines through words that offended him, whether or not they were necessary for the rhyme scheme, crossing out whole stanzas, and making severe comments in the margin. In the end he reduced the seventeen rhymed stanzas to forty-two lines, largely unrhymed, a masterpiece of economy and precision that has stamped itself on the literary imagination as the archetypal seduction of its time.

The fact remains that *The Waste Land* is definitely Eliot's work. Pound could never have written it, for all his stern theories and for all his fanatical devotion to language; he lacked Eliot's depth of revulsion and his Christian hope of salvation. In a negative way, however, Pound collaborated in the poem by deleting or discouraging some sides of Eliot's talent: the lyrical side with its delight in strong rhythms like those of "Prufrock"; the skilled rhymer's side that sometimes brought him close to Cole Porter; the narrative side that might have set him to writing ballads; and the intensity of feeling that sometimes betrayed him into writing awkward lines. By suppressing or concealing those sides, Pound encouraged the world to think of Eliot as an artist who always "moved on," like Picasso or Pound himself, from one phase to another. By canceling the weaker lines, he reinforced our notion of Eliot as the supreme dandy in verse, the man who printed few poems, but perfect ones full of felicities. Thus, Pound played a great part in creating the Eliot image. If this deeply troubled and sometimes uncertain young man became the arbiter of poetic elegancies, that was mostly due to himself, but some of it, at least, was Pound's doing.

JOHN O'HARA:
HE WROTE HONESTLY
AND WELL

Finis Farr is an experienced journalist but not, to put it charitably, a great biographer. He is not even a good biographer when his subject is a literary figure—in this case John O'Hara—since he does not feel qualified to make any but the most perfunctory judgments of literary merit. Many of the judgments are expressed in numerals: so many pages in the novel, so many copies sold in hard cover, so many paperback printings, so many dollars, count them, for the movie rights. He jots the figures down almost as if he were keeping records for the Internal Revenue Service.

That is not his only weakness as a biographer. He does not achieve any psychological depth—though he is good on the special psychology of the American Irish—and he offers no clear vision of the social background that O'Hara observed with lifelong care. Farr himself is much better at gathering material—with the generous help he received from O'Hara's family—than he is at putting it together. Nevertheless, the material he presents is so rich, and so much of it consists of O'Hara's picturesque, quirky, self-revealing letters, that one follows the disordered story with fascination and ends by feeling that one has lived with an extraordinary person.

John O'Hara was born in 1905 in Pottsville, Pa., the town called Gibbsville in his novels; it is a financial and trading center for the southern anthracite belt. He was not from the wrong side of the tracks, as some have assumed; his father was a respected and rather autocratic physician bent on "traveling in life first class," as he told his family. The eight children were brought up like a nobleman's heirs. Each of them had a pony and a pony cart, except for John, the oldest, who rode at the head of the procession on his own handsome saddle horse. Like his brothers and sisters, John was educated in private schools, and two of these advised him not to come back. He kept getting into scrapes, partly to show defiance of his rigidly moral father, whom he resented and deeply admired. At a third boarding school, conducted by the Vincentian fathers, he was named valedictorian of his class and then got drunk on the night before commencement. He thereby lost his diploma and his last real chance of getting into Yale, a boyhood dream.

When John was twenty the father died, leaving behind him less than a nobleman's estate; his safe-deposit box was crammed with worthless German marks. The son had been working for the *Pottsville Journal*, and he stayed on the paper for two more years, meanwhile acquiring a thorough knowledge of the Schuylkill County underworld. He moved on to Chicago, where he starved while looking for a job in winter without an overcoat. New York: he reached the big town as a boy of twenty-three, shy but with an ingratiating self-confidence. People kept finding jobs for him, and O'Hara kept losing them; he simply could not get up in the morning. He spent his nights in midtown speakeasies and became known as a booze fighter almost before he became known as a writer. But he kept writing doggedly, and soon *The New Yorker* was printing his little pieces in every other issue. In 1934, at the age of twenty-nine, he published the novel that made him famous, *Appointment in Samarra*. Its success was a victory over his father's ghost.

Nineteen years later, in August 1953, O'Hara was rushed to Medical Center on the point of death from a bleeding ulcer. Having saved his life with massive blood transfusions, the doctors told him what he must do to continue living. Soon afterward he wrote to his close friend Pat Outerbridge, "—yes, I am going to be up there on the cart with you. . . . My chief trouble is that the body resists booze, and if I take too much of it I'm liable to fall over dead. A hell of a way for booze to treat me after I've been so kind to it. I used to watch [W. C.] Fields put away the Martinis at Paramount, and say to myself, 'that's what I want to be when I get big.' Well, I almost made it."

O'Hara stayed on the cart without once climbing down. Unlike another friend, Scott Fitzgerald, he had not become a true alcoholic, but there had been two obsessive pursuits in his life before 1953, and drinking was one of them. Now, with the bottle pushed aside, he turned wholly to his other obsession, writing. Every night he retired to his study, drew shut the heavy curtains, read over what he had written the night before, then wrote from shortly after midnight to shortly before dawn. Sometimes his wife could hear his voice raised when he spoke a few lines of dialogue to make sure that he had caught the proper rhythm. She reported that, when the work was going well, the hum of his Remington Noiseless typewriter was like muffled drumming. Each finished page was laid face down on a neat pile that grew higher from night to night. When he reached the last page, a novel was practically ready for the printer, for he did not bother with second drafts or major revisions. His manuscripts contained only minor corrections—"pencil work," as he called them.

His last novel, *The Ewings*, was finished in February 1970, and four days later he started *The Second Ewings*. Though his health was failing, he kept at work compulsively. "I want to flood the world with my writing," he told his stepdaughter-in-law one afternoon in April when she asked him what he wanted to do next. That night he started work as before, but stopped when he felt pains in his chest and his left arm. He described the symptoms to his wife, went to bed early for him, and died in his sleep. Still in the typewriter, under a plastic cover, was page 74 of *The Second Ewings*.

He had written too much, as it is easy to say in retrospect; there are in all 32 books, including 15 novels, some of them immensely long, 14 volumes of short and long stories, two collections of columns for magazines and newspapers, and one book containing five plays. In the end his output of words outran his considerable power of invention. Almost any novel by O'Hara—except *Appointment* and *The Farmers Hotel*—is much like almost any of the others. He presented more than a thousand characters—so his biographer informs us—but many of these are O'Hara types, beautifully machined and interchangeable. They could never have justified a Nobel Prize, the honor for which he yearned, and yet he remains a novelist of stature, as well as being a magnificent story writer.

Much of his work deals with what he called The Region: that part of the anthracite belt lying south of a line drawn from Harrisburg to Wilkes-Barre to Reading. He was particularly interested in the leading families of The Region. His novels traced their rise to power after the Civil War and imagined the private events—most often adulteries—that marked their decline. I have always mentally classified O'Hara with two other novelists, Marquand and Cozzens, as social historians of the American upper bourgeoisie. O'Hara is more unsparing than Marquand; he has sharper ears and a long memory; but he seems to have less of a sociological framework for his rich material. As compared with Cozzens, he displays less interest in making each book a unified and balanced structure, a work of art in itself. Cozzens is an architect in fiction; O'Hara is a sort of hydraulic engineer with a primary interest in flow, not form.

What happens next? is the question he had to answer every night. He tried to carry the reader along, as in a canoe without paddles on a river with pools and rapids. "I want to control the reader as much as I can," he explained in a letter to William Maxwell of *The New Yorker*, "and I make the effort in all sorts of ways. . . . There are times when I want to slow down the reader, almost imperceptibly, but slow him down. . . . I can do it for a greater length of time with a big block of type, like the Caporetto retreat"—of course in *A Farewell to Arms*; here as elsewhere one notes the debt to Hemingway. But O'Hara had ways of refining Hemingway's methods. "I can make it easier for the reader," the letter continued, "by filling up the block of type with nouns—rifles, machine guns, tanks, motorcycles, ambulances, other non-think words—but the reader is still being slowed down. He picks up the pace, is forced to, when I go back to dialogue."

O'Hara's dialogue is as rapid and natural as any that has been written in this century. In his big blocks of narrative, the style is plain, accurate, glassy-clear, and almost without metaphors, which O'Hara avoided on principle. It is the style of a man who wants to remain invisible while at the same time "mesmerizing the reader." The phrase is his own, and he is justified in using it, as one reader can testify. His books are easy not to pick up, but they have a compulsive quality that makes them hard to lay down; this is one of the effects he hoped to produce when writing in his study late at night. His headstone in Princeton Cemetery bears an inscription in his own words. One might well question the first phrase, but the rest of it is an accurate summation of his career: "Better than anyone else, he told the truth about his time, the first half of the twentieth century. He was a professional. He wrote honestly and well."

KEN KESEY AT STANFORD

K en Kesey was in my writing class at Stanford in the fall term of
1960. He wasn't there technically, in the sense that I passed in
his grade to the administration, but he was there in person and by virtue of what he was writing, which was a novel, then untitled, about
the psychiatric ward of a veterans' hospital. Kesey had spent the academic year 1958–59 as a graduate student at Stanford with a creative-
writing fellowship. As a matter of courtesy, fellows were invited to attend the class in later years without being formally enrolled. Kesey
and Tillie Olsen were two of the earlier fellows whom this instructor
was always glad to see.

It was a pretty brilliant class that year, including as it did some
professional writers already launched on their careers. Larry Mc-
Murtry, for instance, was working on what I think was his second
novel, *Leaving Cheyenne*. He was a light, sallow, bespectacled cowboy
who wore Texas boots and spoke in a pinched variety of the West Texas
drawl. Gradually I learned that he had read almost everything in English literature, besides a great deal in French, and that he had written
a dissertation on the scabrous poetry of John Wilmot, Earl of Roch-
ester. Larry supplemented his Stanford fellowship by finding rare
books on the ten-cent tables of Salvation Army outlets and reselling
them to dealers; *Book Prices Current* was his bible.

Peter S. Beagle was only twenty-one, with plump cheeks and a solemn boyish smile, but The Viking Press had already published his
successful first novel, *A Fine and Private Place*. I took a special interest
in Peter, since I was a literary adviser for Viking and since I knew and
liked his two famous uncles, the painters Raphael and Moses Soyer,
but I wasn't able to help him with his new project. He was trying to
write an autobiographical novel about his year in Paris, and he was too
young for autobiography; his bent was for gentle fantasy and humor.
There were other gifted students in the class. I remember James Baker
Hall, Judith Rascoe, Arvin Brown (now Artistic Director of the Long

Wharf Theatre), Gurney Norman, and Joanna Ostrow, who was the most beautiful woman I encountered in twenty years of teaching. It is hard to understand how Frank O'Connor, who succeeded me in the winter quarter, could bear to drop her from the class. Joanna had talent as well as beauty, but I suppose that she didn't manifest enough literary devotion to satisfy O'Connor's tough standards.

The class of fifteen assembled in the Jones Room at a huge oval table. One student would read his work aloud and others would offer comments. My problem at the head of the table was how to get the class working together. I believed that young writers learn more from one another than they do from an older instructor. I knew that their comments on stories revealed two contradictory impulses: first, to assert their egos by putting down their rivals; second, to advance the cause of good writing in an unselfish fashion by making useful suggestions. Aggression and *agape*. My tactic was always to put down the putter-downers and always to encourage the suggestions. In a good class like the one at Stanford in 1960, *agape* won out, jealousies were submerged, and stories were sometimes vastly improved in their second and third drafts.

I don't remember any comments that Kesey made. I do remember that he looked stolid and self-assured as he sat near the other end of the table. He had the build of a plunging halfback, with big shoulders and a neck like the stump of a Douglas fir. Chapters of his novel were read aloud in class and they aroused a mixed but generally admiring response. The instructor was excited by having found something original. Later Kesey showed me the whole of the unfinished manuscript and we discussed it in private sessions. Did I contribute anything? "Not even a sentence" is the answer; the book is Kesey's from the first word to the last. Probably I pointed out passages that didn't "work," that failed to produce a desired effect on the reader. Certainly I asked questions, and some of these may have helped to clarify Kesey's notions of how to go about solving his narrative problems, but the solutions were always his own.

From the beginning he had his narrator in the person of Chief Broom, a schizophrenic Indian who pretends to be deaf and dumb. He had his own crazy visions—induced by eating peyote, as he later explained—and these could be attributed to Chief Broom. Thus, when the Indian looks at Big Nurse, "She's swelling up, swells till her back's splitting out the white uniform and she's let her arms section out long enough to wrap around the three of them five, six times . . . she blows up bigger and bigger, big as a tractor, so big I can smell the machinery inside the way you smell a motor pulling too big a load." That hallucinated but everyday style, smelling of motor oil, was something new in fiction. Kesey's narrative problem, the central one, was how to use Chief Broom-or-Bromden's visions as the medium for telling an essentially simple, dramatic, soundly constructed story.

His first drafts must have been written at top speed; they were full of typing errors, as if the words had come piling out of a Greyhound bus too fast to have their clothes brushed. Later Kesey would redo the manuscript and correct most of the misspellings. He had his visions, but he didn't have the fatal notion of some Beat writers, that the first hasty account of a vision was a sacred text not to be tampered with. He revised, he made deletions and additions; he was working with readers in mind. I continued to be excited by Kesey's work as the manuscript grew longer (though I couldn't share his faith in the Randle P. McMurphy system of psychotherapy). I remember sending enthusiastic reports to Viking. A year later I was delighted when the manuscript arrived in the Viking office, this time with a title: *One Flew Over the Cuckoo's Nest*.

After turning over the advanced writing course to O'Connor—in private life Michael O'Donovan—I had spent the winter quarter at Stanford with less challenging assignments. Michael was a dear man with an Irish temper who wouldn't stand for nonsense. He couldn't have felt much sympathy for Kesey's narrator or his style or his hero. I heard that Kesey had stopped attending classes in the Jones Room and was persuading others to stay away too, sometimes by inviting them to his house on Perry Lane and keeping them there with drinks and conversation until the class was over. He had become the man whom other young rebels tried to imitate, almost like Hemingway in Montparnasse during the 1920s.

I paid perhaps two visits to Perry Lane, which was the Left Bank of Stanford, but the visit I remember was on the night when Kesey and his wife were throwing a big party. Most of the advanced writing class was there, with other friends of the Keseys including Vic Lovell, a graduate student with bold notions about psychology and a ducktail haircut. On a table by the window was a huge bowl of green punch from which clouds of mist or steam kept rising. Kesey explained that the punch was brewed with Kool-Aid and dry ice: the mist was carbon dioxide. "It looks like the sort of punch that Satan would serve," I said while politely accepting half a cupful. Was it the famous punch that Kesey had spiked with LSD? I haven't the faintest notion because I never drained my cup. Instead I wandered out to the kitchen, where my wife was talking with Faye Kesey and admiring the baby. I fell into conversation with Ken's grandmother. "If you don't like punch," she said, "I brought along a bottle of bootleg whiskey from Arkansas." "That suits me just fine," I said, taking a pull at the bottle. By that time the crowd around the punch bowl was growing noisy. Arvin Brown, who drank several cupfuls of the green stuff, tells me that he didn't recover full consciousness for twenty-four hours.

"OLD DOC WILSON"

Five years after his death, Edmund Wilson holds firmly to his place as the foremost American critic of our time. There have been grumblings at many of his judgments; there has been angry talk about his limitations, chiefly in critical theory; but nobody else has laid claim to his seat at the head of the table. This collection of his *Letters on Literature and Politics*, capably edited by his widow, Elena Wilson—with advice from Daniel Aaron and Leon Edel—reaffirms his ghostly but substantial presence there.

More than that, it reveals some aspects of Wilson's character that had not been clearly apparent in other books. One of those aspects was lifelong devotion to his friends. In the beginning they were friends he made at the Hill School or at Princeton, and particularly those who wrote for *The Nassau Lit* during the brilliant year when he was editor-in-chief: Scott Fitzgerald, John Peale Bishop, Stanley Dell. Later, in New York, his circle also included young writers from Yale (Phelps Putnam), from Vanderbilt (Allen Tate), and even one from Harvard (John Dos Passos)—though Wilson had written after a first visit to Cambridge that "Harvard is a helova place, and I wouldn't go to college there for money." Still later there were women friends, notably the poet Louise Bogan and the novelist Dawn Powell. He was always slow to welcome either men or women into his intimate circle, but once they had been accepted by the part of him that served as an admissions committee, he was most often slower still to let them go. Almost all those whose names I mentioned kept receiving letters from him until they died. Each death was a blow to Wilson, but especially that of Scott Fitzgerald. "Men who start out writing together," he wrote to John Bishop a few days later, "write for one another more than they realize till somebody dies."

"Writing together" is a significant phrase. For Wilson the advancement of literature—something he regarded as the central aim of his life—was in great part a collaborative venture. His friends, if they had talent, were to be enlisted in a broad campaign against the Philistines. Continually he urged and bullied them into producing more words and better words, then getting the words published. Thus, as early as 1919, he wrote to Fitzgerald exhorting him to contribute a new sort of story to a collection that Wilson was planning to edit. "No *Saturday Evening Post* stuff, understand! clear your mind of cant! brace up your artistic conscience, which has always been the weakest part of your talent! . . . Concentrate in one short story a world of tragedy, comedy, irony, and beauty!!! I await your manuscript with impatience."

That was a youthful outburst, with a touch of self-ridicule, but Wilson continued his exhortations long after he had become a respected critic and editor. In 1929 he urged John Bishop to come back from Europe. "I believe now that the principal reason why you haven't gotten it [your work] into more satisfactory shape is that you haven't been over here to be encouraged and spurred on by association with your fellow writers and—what is perhaps most important of all—to market your own productions." In 1933 he told Fitzgerald, "Now is your time to creep up on Hemingway." In 1936 he wrote to Phelps Putnam, who had failed to complete a long poem, "What the hell's the matter with you, you old fraud?—why don't you produce some literature? Haven't you heard about that one talent which is death to hide?"

Not only did Wilson exhort his friends to write, but he also offered them subjects, read their manuscripts if requested (but only if they were very good friends), and submitted their work to editors as an unpaid literary agent. In his favorite role of Old Doc Wilson, he offered advice about their private lives. If the friends had nervous breakdowns, as happened too often in the 1930s, he tried to cheer them with books and visits and sympathetic letters. I was impressed by a 1931 letter to Louise Bogan, then in Bloomingdale's sanitarium, because it expressed Wilson's feeling of obligation not only to friends but to the world. The letter reads in part:

> Dear Louise: I'm terribly sorry you've been in a bad state—I sympathize profoundly, having been there myself. But it is an excellent thing to go to bed on these occasions. . . .
>
> These are times of pretty severe strain for anybody, to lapse into

a vein of editorial generalization. . . . Still, we have to carry on, and people like you with remarkable abilities, even though they're more highly organized nervously than other people, are under a peculiar obligation not to let this sick society down. . . . The only thing we can really make is our work. And deliberate work of the mind, imagination, and hand, done, as Nietzsche said, "notwith-standing," in the long run remakes the world.

I don't want to present Wilson as a paragon of kindness and duti-fulness, but those qualities were part of the picture. Some less appeal-ing sides of it were revealed two years ago in *The Twenties*, a book compiled from his notebooks and diaries. Much of the book was con-cerned with his sexual adventures, which he reported as unfeelingly as if he were an ethologist jotting down notes on the behavior of chim-panzees. There is not much sex in the *Letters on Literature and Politics*, and the collection rather gains by the omission. Sex he observed with a cold eye, but he revealed a warm heart to his friends.

Most of the friends—as long as the older ones survived—were men and women "of the twenties," like Wilson himself. He remembered the twenties as the good time "when people mixed art and literature with their liquor." "The twenties over here," he wrote to a younger Englishwoman, "were quite different from the crops that have come since—the Depression has made the difference, because it cut down money and freedom and inhibited people in various ways. I find that I can only talk comfortably with the writers of my own era—am always shocking others or seeming frivolous to them."

Talk was vastly important to Wilson; that is another aspect of his personality revealed in this book. He talked uncommonly well, often in periodic sentences that were effective, if unpolished, and that might have been printed without revision (though Wilson, a born revision-ist, would have insisted on correcting them). "You see it's this way" was a phrase he used before expounding a book or a theory. When there was nobody to listen, he wrote letters to his friends. Thus, he spent the summer of 1925 at the house presided over by his mother, who was deaf. "I hope you will forgive these rambling letters," he told Stanley Dell at the time, "—they are the product of the unpeopled sol-itude in which I live. Having, as a rule, nobody to talk to at the highball hour, I have formed the habit of pouring it all into correspondence to avoid the necessity of talking to myself." Except when dealing with business matters, as writers often have to deal, the letters in this volume have the quality of lively and opinionated conversation at the highball hour, sometimes continuing late into the night.

The letters also confirm one's feeling that Wilson started out with an unusual store of intellectual energy. He had opinions on everything. Especially in the early days, he kept inventing new subjects for himself or others to write about. Later he somewhat reduced the number of his inventions, but chose bigger projects for himself and showed exceptional persistence in carrying them through. *To the Finland Station* involved an immense amount of reading in four languages and took him eight years to write and revise. *Patriotic Gore*, his book about Civil War literature, required even more reading, if in a single language; he worked on it, with interruptions, from 1947 until it was published in 1962. It was to be the last of his immense undertakings, but, by then in his late sixties, he carried out some smaller ones, including a survey of recent Canadian literature that appeared as a book in 1965. Meanwhile he studied Hungarian (after having learned to read Latin, Greek, French, Italian, German, Russian, and Hebrew), and he adopted a program "of getting through, before I die, all the celebrated books that I haven't read." With his obstinate energy, he also went back to his own earlier work, "revising and republishing everything I think is worth saving."

He was, however, feeling the effects of age while fighting against them. In the spring of 1965 he wrote to a friend on Cape Cod, "We're coming up to Wellfleet for the weekend, May 7–9, when I'll be seventy years old: it depresses me. I alternately think that I've had it and might as well call it a day, and that I must go into training and make an effort to accomplish a good deal more." He made the effort, once again, and his letters make us feel that there was something heroic in the accomplishments, against physical odds, of his last few years.

In April 1970 he wrote to Dos Passos, "Actually, since I have left the hospital"—that was after his first coronary—"I have been having a most enjoyable life: bed moved downstairs to the study, so that I only have to crawl from the bed to the writing table." He was then working

of the stone house in Talcottville, New York,
stors had lived and where Wilson spent most
was finished that fall, but not until after Dos
nber. Now almost the last survivor of his lit-
for Thornton Wilder), Wilson was feeling
and isolated and inclined to be crusty with strangers. Nevertheless he went back to work on other projects, including a book on
Russian writers (almost all of whose work he had read in the original).

In February 1971 he reported from New York, "I had a slight stroke
around Christmas, which has somewhat affected my right hand, and
given me some trouble in writing." Work continued "notwithstand-
ing," as he had once quoted from Nietzsche. In April he was back in
Wellfleet and, with the help of a grammar, was puzzling out some
apocryphal books of the New Testament that exist only in Old Church
Slavonic. During the year he prepared two books for the press; one was
A *Window on Russia* and the other was a collection of miscellaneous essays. He also partly revised his memoirs of the 1920s, though he now
realized that someone else would have to complete the revision, as well
as edit his later diaries; the man he wisely chose was Leon Edel. In May
1972 he reported from Wellfleet, "I had a slight stroke the other day
and now can't talk distinctly." Still he was unwilling to surrender. At
the end of the month he insisted on going alone to his beloved house
"upstate," and he died there two weeks later.

CONRAD AIKEN:
A PRIEST OF
CONSCIOUSNESS

Conrad Aiken, born in 1889, was the oldest of four children all of whom adored their parents, but Conrad, apparently, even more than the others. The father, a brilliant young physician, had gone from Harvard to Savannah and established a practice there. The beautiful mother belonged to an old New Bedford family; she liked to give dinner parties and sometimes indulged in a mild flirtation. The father was insanely jealous. One morning when Conrad was a boy of eleven, he heard two pistol shots, fearfully opened the bedroom door, and found his parents lying dead.

He went round to the local police station, where he knew the officers on duty, then followed them back to the house of his lost childhood. From that morning he was faced with the double problem of justifying himself to the dead parents, "those two angelic people," and of giving a new shape to his life.

It was not to be an adventurous life except inwardly. Separated from the three younger children, Conrad was taken north to be raised by relatives in New Bedford and Cambridge, Massachusetts. He was sent to a good preparatory school, Middlesex, and entered Harvard with the class of 1911. There he became known as a brilliant but self-willed student and formed a lifelong friendship with T. S. Eliot, his senior by one year. During his last semester he was elected class poet, an event that put his new life to the test. "He had known, instantly," Aiken tells us in his autobiography, "that this kind of public appearance, and for such an occasion, was precisely what the flaw in his inheritance would not, in all likelihood, be strong enough to bear. This was the kind of 'public' trial . . . which he must learn to circumvent: otherwise, the penalty might be tragic." To save himself he resigned from Harvard and fled to Italy. "It was his decision," he says, always speaking in the third person, "that his life must be lived *off-stage*, behind the scenes, out of view, and that only thus could he excel."

Excel he could and did, in the course of the next sixty years, but always in his own fashion, by means of the written word; he never appeared on a platform. A poet by trade and one of the most gifted, he also wrote novels, short stories, a play, and a considerable body of criticism in which he spoke his mind at any cost to himself or others. His books—fifty in all, by a rough count—were admired with reservations; they were never in fashion. Neither in England, where he spent many of his middle years, nor in America, which remained his spiritual home, did he choose to enter the literary establishment, a territory he regarded as a jungle full of ravening egos. The dramatic events in his life were strictly private.

In 1952, at the age of sixty-three, he published an account of himself in a book called *Ushant*, a puzzling title explained in the narrative. Ushant is the English name for Ouessant, an island off the coast of Brittany that is the westernmost point of metropolitan France. The cliff-guarded island is surrounded by shoals on which, over the centuries, hundreds of vessels have been wrecked; hence the French proverb, "Whoever sees Ouessant sees his own blood." In Aiken's private mythology, Ushant stands for the ultimate discovery of self and also, by extension, for whatever is forbidden: *you shan't*. It was his effort in the book to reach the perilous island by revealing himself completely.

What resulted from the effort was a complicated work of art. The author-and-protagonist, here called "D.," is returning to England after World War II on a hastily converted troopship. Night after night he lies awake in a stateroom crowded with strangers while reviewing his life from the beginning. He is trying to find a pattern in the life and to become fully conscious of his own motives. All this produces a triple movement in the book: first in space, from Halifax to Liverpool, with the stages of the voyage marked by ship's bells; then in time, from D.'s earliest childhood to the present, in a sequence interrupted by hilarious or dramatic episodes; then finally an inward movement of self-exploration. This last is also a backward movement in time and space, since it carries D.—or Aiken—to the nursery of his parents' house in Savannah. There, as a very young boy, he is lying on the floor and reading the epigraph to the first chapter of *Tom Brown's Schooldays*:

> I'm the poet of White Horse Vale, Sir,
> With liberal notions under my cap.

The boy, enchanted by those lines, asks what a poet is and learns that the admired father has also written poetry. From that moment—so the man decides fifty years later in the course of his relentless self-examination—his future course had been set: he would be a poet, he would cherish liberal notions, and he would go to live in England somewhere near White Horse Vale. All his adventures, Aiken tells us, "which seemed to be leading him farther and farther afield, and in ever-widening circles, whether outer or inner; all this was really the quite incredible equivalent of one very simple little thing: it had been the stratagem by which he could remain forever on that floor in the room at Savannah, reading, for the first time, a passage of verse."

It is indeed a simple answer to find after Aiken's long search for a pattern in his life, but the reader notes that it is surrounded by further complications. Why, for instance, did he start on the quest and pursue it compulsively? Was he trying to recover from the shock of finding his parents dead and of having to admit "the flaw in his inheritance"? Did he feel that the only means of restoring his mental health was by laying bare his motives, no matter how trivial they might be, and by confessing his shabbiest sins? So it would seem from a passage in his impressive cycle of poems, *Time in the Rock*:

> Out of your sickness let your sickness speak—
> the bile must have his way—the blood his truth—
> poison will come to the tongue. Is hell your kingdom?
> you know its privies and its purlieus? keep
> sad record of its filth? Why this is health.

Whatever the impulse that launched him on his quest and whether he was searching only to cure himself or to benefit others as well, the quest in itself became a moral imperative. It was his duty, he strongly felt, to discover everything hidden in his nature and then to find words for it that might be of value to humanity: "the self becoming word, the word becoming world." At the same time he must learn to divide the narrating D. from the other self that is the subject of narration, and he must approach the latter "with relentless and unsleeping objectivity." There were times when he felt himself to be laid on a cosmic operating table under a cruel and insupportable light. He took refuge in heavy drinking to cushion his nerves, and once, on a drunken night, he nearly succeeded in committing suicide. Rescued by accident (he makes it a comic story), Aiken went back to his quest: "The thing, of course, was not to retreat, never to retreat; never to avoid the full weight of awareness." He came to regard himself as "a priest of consciousness." "The only religion that was any longer tenable or viable," he says, "was a poetic comprehension of man's position in the universe . . . through self-knowledge and love. The final phase of evolution of man's mind itself to ever more inclusive consciousness: in that, and that alone, would he find the solvent of all things."

Aiken's religion of consciousness, which I have presented all too briefly, is a feature of the book that is certain to arouse questions. True, it has served to unify his immensely varied work from the beginning. True, it might well be adopted by other poets as a guiding faith (though a difficult one to follow). But can it be extended to all humanity, as Aiken tries to do at the end of *Ushant?* There he says of his fellow passengers on the converted troopship, "Well, they were all heroes, every one of them; they were all soldiers; as now, and always, all mankind were soldiers; all of them engaged in the endless and desperate war on the unconscious." But would being soldiers in that war provide them with any guidance in their daily lives?—help to make them better citizens or spouses or parents (any more than it had helped Aiken himself to be sober and faithful)?

The opposite might well be true. When the quest for complete self-knowledge led Aiken to divide himself into two persons, narrator and subject, it was the very transgressions of "the subject D." that made him interesting for "the narrating D." to study. Perhaps the narrating part of Aiken encouraged the subject to commit still more transgressions in order to make good stories out of them. One notes that the cathedral of consciousness has many confessional booths, most of them

scattered in nooks and crannies. For instance, Aiken keeps paying tribute to his many profane loves—Marian, Amabel, and Irene; Sara the
housemaid and the girl he calls Agnes Fatuous—as well as to his great
exaltations. Those "fly-by-nights and fall-by-nights," he asks: hadn't
they all provided "not only the creative value for the work, but the
substance of it as well—not to say its veritable heartbeat?"

Another continuing theme in the book is Aiken's "long, curious,
intermittent, and wandering association with that most engaging and
volatile and unpredictable of geniuses," the novelist Malcolm Lowry.
(In the text Lowry is called Hambo, but a 1971 edition of *Ushant* sup-
plies us with a key to the characters.) When Lowry-Hambo was eighteen years old, he read Aiken's novel *Blue Voyage* and traveled from
Cambridge, England, to Cambridge, Massachusetts, in order to become his disciple. There were later long meetings in Sussex, in Spain,
and finally in Mexico, when Lowry was writing *Under the Volcano*; the
year was 1937. This last time Lowry "as in the years before, but now
with an almost insane obsessedness," insisted on casting Aiken in the
role of father and declared his intention, moreover, of destroying and
absorbing him. Here is part of their conversation on a drunken afternoon:

HAMBO: (having compared himself to a starfish and D. to an
oyster): I shall wholly absorb you. I *am* absorbing you now. And
it's your own wish, moreover—you said so. Am I not your son, in
whom you are destined to be well pleased? . . . It is your fate simply to become a better "you" in me. . . . I shall become a better
"you," and you will be dead.

D.: How wonderfully tempting it is. . . . Could I backtrack
now?

HAMBO: Too late now. Your virtue has already passed
over. . . . You are a nation invaded. And as I'm younger, and as
I'm stronger, in appetite, in will, in recklessness, in sense of direction, it will be no use your trying to compete with me, you will
only appear to be echoing me, imitating me, parodying me—you
will no longer have a personality of your own.

D.: If I ever had one. Here's to betrayal and death.

HAMBO: Betrayal and death.

Hambo-Lowry went back to work on his novel and completed a first draft, although publication was to be delayed until after ten years and many revisions. *Under the Volcano* is an extraordinary book that incorporates everything the author had absorbed from Aiken, and from others, while transforming it by means of his special genius. Part of his prophecy was to be fulfilled when an academic critic—I forget his name—accused Aiken of copying Lowry. Aiken himself retained his personality and continued his lifelong quest for self-awareness. Eventually he found the words for which he was seeking and, in *Ushant*, he arranged them into their permanent form. If one borrows a phrase that he used in another connection, one might say that the book is "the perfected artifact which . . . was the ultimate good, and the ultimate obligation, of the creative mind."

And the rest of the story? Aiken lived for more than twenty years after *Ushant* was published and wrote several of his best poems, including "Hallowe'en" and "A Letter from Li Po." During those years he received a number of impressive honors: the National Book Award (1953), the Bollingen Prize (1956), the Gold Medal for Poetry of the National Institute of Arts and Letters (1958), and the National Medal for Literature (1969). But his work never reached a wide audience, and he reported by letter that his *Collected Poems, Second Edition* (1970), a volume of more than a thousand pages that contains the work of a lifetime, had a sale for the first half year of only 430 copies. Partly this public neglect was the result of his decision while at Harvard "that his life must be lived *off-stage*, behind the scenes, out of view." From the beginning the life had an intricate consistency like that of *Ushant*. Having completed the last of his ever-widening circles, Aiken spent his last years in Savannah only two or three doors from the house of his childhood. He died at the age of eighty-four and is buried in old St. Bonaventure Cemetery not far from his father and mother. Almost his last words were "I have never compromised."

ALLEN TATE
IN THE REPUBLIC
OF LETTERS

W hen Allen Tate died in Nashville in February 1979, he left an empty place in the lives of his friends, as also in the broader republic of letters. I call it a republic, as Allen liked to do, but rather it is a loose federation composed of many dukedoms and principalities. Allen was one of the very few American writers who were able to pass freely from one to another of those smaller states. That is, he was a complete man of letters: a poet primarily and sometimes a great one, but also an essayist, a biographer, an astute critic, a fictionist—his one novel, *The Fathers*, has been republished many times during the last forty years—and the author of candid memoirs. I needn't speak of his being a professor, a gifted editor, a correspondent with everybody, and a visiting lecturer at 150 colleges and universities: Oxford, Harvard, Virginia, Florence—name them one by one you will find that Allen had been there.

As the citizen of a world republic, he had taken out his first papers, so to speak, when he was 22 years old and a student at Vanderbilt. It was then he attended an early meeting of what was afterward known as the Fugitive Group, which had assembled to discuss philosophy and read the new poems of its members. Others of the group were John Crowe Ransom, Donald Davidson, and Robert Penn Warren; later they published a famous little magazine, *The Fugitive*. Still later the group, with additional members, became the Southern Agrarians and helped to shape the Southern renaissance of the 1930s and 1940s. Some of its members were active in the New Criticism, which was a force in the literary world of the 1950s.

Allen played a prominent part in all those movements, as initiator and theorist and also, thanks to his many friends abroad, as a sort of roving diplomat. One friend was St. John Perse, who had occupied a position that might be called permanent undersecretary of state in the French foreign service. It might be said that Allen had a corresponding place in the world republic of letters.

When he made his first trip to New York in June 1924, there was nothing cosmopolitan in his appearance except possibly the cane he carried. Hart Crane, with whom he had corresponded, introduced him to a Greenwich Village party, and it was there I met him. He was a slight young man with delicate features and an enormous forehead. Later I heard that when Allen was a boy, he was thought to have water on the brain. His mother once said, "Son, put that book down and go out and play with Henry. You are straining your mind and you know your mind isn't very strong." Was it as a delayed rejoinder that he wore a Phi Beta Kappa key conspicuously on his vest? I liked him at first glance, but I said severely, "*We* don't wear our Phi Beta Kappa keys any longer"; mine was in a pawnshop. Allen must have forgiven me for the remark because, two days later, we went together for a visit to Hart Crane on Brooklyn Heights. It was the beginning of a friendship that lasted—I have just been counting—for more than 54 years.

The friendship was often interrupted because both of us had to earn our livelihoods. That was an especially difficult problem for Allen during the early years. He believed deeply that one should achieve a unity between one's moral nature and one's economics. For him that meant earning a living by writing honestly and well. It was a hard thing to do in the 1920s, when honest writing was published, it is true, but not at the fees that were paid for writing pretentiously. A penny a word, or at most two cents, was what an honest writer earned. On this Allen was supporting a wife and a daughter, not well, but without making a moral compromise. The daughter, Nancy, was told not to touch the papers on his desk because they were Daddo's living. Once when she was four years old she disobeyed her parents and picked up the manuscript of a book review. "Is this your living, Daddo?" she asked. Allen grunted yes. Nancy felt a page of the manuscript between her thumb and her forefinger. "It's a mighty thin living," she said.

Later Allen would more or less solve the problem of earning a livelihood without compromising his standards. He spent two years in Paris on a Guggenheim fellowship, and afterward taught and lectured honestly as a wandering scholar. Those travels led to further interruptions in our friendship, not to mention that our political enthusiasms had carried us in different directions during the 1930s. I was a radical of sorts and Allen called himself a reactionary, but both of us put literature above politics and in literary matters we were likely to agree.

What a delight it was to meet him, sometimes to live beside him and his first wife, Caroline Gordon, in one city or country house after another! I set down the names as a litany: Robber Rocks, Caligari Cottage, Cloverlands, Princeton, Burlington, Vermont, Sherman, Connecticut, Minneapolis, Wellfleet (on Cape Cod), Sewanee, Tennessee, Nashville, and often at the American Academy, to which we were both inducted in 1964. An earlier meeting I remember was during the Prohibition years; it was in the big kitchen of a speakeasy, one of the very few that managed to exist in Clarksville, Tennessee. Allen and Caroline and I, with two or three friends, are sitting at a round oak table. What we are drinking out of kitchen glasses, with branchwater but no ice, is Between the Rivers, recommended by our host as the best bootleg liquor in the Middle South. We drink, we laugh, we tell stories about literary friends, we sing sailor ballads, and suddenly it seems to me that the Tates have abolished geography. The round oak table and all our laughter might have been transported on the instant to Greenwich Village or Soho or Montparnasse.

"You-all better make less noise," our host says. "Might be that the neighbors could turn us in." We scatter and drive to our separate beds over miles of dirt roads, through the wide stillness of tobacco fields.

All his life Allen revealed that mixture of cosmopolitanism and localism, his true home being anywhere in the republic of letters, but also definitely in the Middle South. One of his best poems, "The Mediterranean," is a brief recapitulation of The Aeneid, with a change of scene. In Tate's version Aeneas and his sailors escape from burning Troy, but their destination is the banks of the Cumberland, not those of the Tiber:

> Now, from the Gates of Hercules we flood
>
> Westward, westward till the barbarous brine
> Whelms us to the tired land where tasseling corn,

Fat beans, grapes sweeter than muscadine
Rot on the vine; in that land were we born.

The Middle Sea and the Middle South; Troy and Tate's Creek Pike: this was only one of the contradictions—Allen preferred to call them tensions—that gave depth to his poetry. He was classical in spirit but also wildly romantic, more so than any of his friends. He had an innate distinction of mind that everyone soon recognized, and he also had a touch of impishness and a roving eye. He was a proud man—the Romans would have called him *superbus*—who insisted on revealing his defaults and *défaillances*. He was determined to be loyal to friends with some of whom he had irrevocably quarreled. He was severe in his judgments, yet went out of his way to be kind. Lately I reread a dozen of his letters and found that in each of them he had strongly urged me to do something for somebody, usually for a younger writer of talent whose work was not being appreciated.

Allen wasn't happy during his last years, especially after the death in infancy of a favorite son. He suffered from more than his share of infirmities, with emphysema as the most crippling. His last expedition, in March 1974, was to the Library of Congress, where he read a magisterial paper on Robert Frost; the trip was nearly fatal. A year later his friends assembled in Sewanee, Tennessee, to celebrate his 75th birthday. They were a distinguished company and Allen appeared at the dinner to give a brief reading, but immediately he went back to his bed. Although he had received all sorts of honors and awards, including the National Medal for Literature, he nourished a feeling that often afflicts the old, a sense of being somehow pushed aside and also, in his case, of seeing poetry evolve in a different direction from the one he had bravely pioneered.

I saw him last in Nashville, where he had moved with his family to be close to a good hospital. By that time—it was July 1978—Allen was scarcely more than a skeleton with that immense forehead looming over it. He spent his days in a little room without books, since his vision had so deteriorated that he couldn't read; and neither could he leave the room except with a plastic tube dangling after him, the other end of it attached to an oxygen tank. As always he talked brilliantly about the world of letters and he laughed, too; both of us laughed until that little room without books—like the round oak table in Clarksville—might have been anywhere on two continents that good books were being written. I thought as we embraced and said good-bye that those deep lines on either side of his mouth were lines of laughter before they became lines of pain.

ZELDA FITZGERALD'S
PART IN THE STORY

This book consists of letters from and to Scott Fitzgerald that did not appear in three earlier collections. The letters here, with some exceptions, are not the most eloquent or the most revealing; Andrew Turnbull had the pick of these when compiling *The Letters of F. Scott Fitzgerald* (1963). A selection of correspondence with Maxwell Perkins and with Scott's literary agent, Harold Ober, went into *Dear Scott/Dear Max* (1971) and *As Ever, Scott Fitz* (1972). The new book does include, however, some important items that had been printed in studies of Fitzgerald and his contemporaries: for example, in Nancy Milford's moving biography of his wife, *Zelda* (1970), or in Bruccoli's *Scott and Ernest* (1978); here they are brought together in chronological order.

Some items in *The Correspondence of F. Scott Fitzgerald* are extremely useful to anyone who is trying to disentangle the Fitzgerald story. This is especially true of those bearing on Scott's relations with his wife and her psychiatrists. The best of the new items is Zelda's anguished recapitulation of their life together, a 42-page (in manuscript) letter written from her Swiss sanitarium; here as elsewhere, Bruccoli's footnotes identify the many persons mentioned. There are other letters that have only recently become available; most of them deal with business matters, or are simply pleas for money, but some of them cast new light on affairs of the heart. Letters to Scott from his friends, including many from John Peale Bishop, Ring Lardner, and the two candid but warmhearted Murphys, help to explain what he was talking about. A principal value of the collection is to set Scott and Zelda firmly in their world, with its people, its interiors, and its daily preoccupations.

But one can't help asking, "Why another book and a big one, compiled from Fitzgerald's posthumous papers?" My shelves are bending with such books already. Matthew J. Bruccoli, who also edits the *Fitzgerald/Hemingway Annual*, has himself produced more than a dozen of them. It is true that, as Bruccoli says, "The writer who died 'forgotten' in 1940 is the most fully documented American author of this century. . . . He made everyone else's work possible by preserving the evidence." But what is the charm that keeps Bruccoli and others going back to that evidence—and keeps people reading the volumes that are published year after year?

I suppose the answer is that Fitzgerald and his wife have become an American legend, of the sort that in earlier ages would have been embellished by scops and bards. Always there would have been music in the air. Youths and maidens, while they listened, would have imagined themselves as the hero or the heroine: the boy who became famous at 24 and "the girl of his dreams." One keeps falling into clichés—but isn't this a mark of legends, that their archetypes always harden into stereotypes?

What happened then in this particular romance? Boy lived with girl in an enchanted world; they spent without reckoning because their needs were supplied by what Scott called "great filling stations full of money"; and gradually the enchantment wore away. Girl went off to a series of sanitariums; boy worked desperately to pay the accumulated bills; but he was now an alcoholic, and the filling stations were closed for the decade. They lived on for a time (Scott for 10 years, Zelda longer) in an effort to recapture the magical past, without suspecting that their lives would some day be haloed with retrospective glory. Or did they suspect it? Scott frequently and Zelda at moments acted as if they regarded themselves as figures in a ritual drama, one that would mirror an age in which "success" and "failure" were mystical values for Americans.

This unwritten drama is more compelling than any of the plots that Fitzgerald laboriously found for his novels (though he had approached it in *Tender Is the Night*). For all his genius in evoking moods and atmospheres, he always had trouble with the story line. Often he tried to solve the problem by overcomplication, and one notes that many of his magazine stories have plot enough, in each case, for a medium-length novel. During the Hollywood years his trouble with plots was a mark against him—and this apart from his drinking, which would have been easier for the studio to forgive if his scenarios had worked. But meanwhile, more than a little consciously, he was living out the plot of a novel in which one scene followed another by inevitable steps and every detail rang true. Mightn't that be the essential charm of the Fitzgerald papers for biographers, critics, and scholars, those modern scops and bards? Isn't each of them trying to present, in each new book, some undiscovered aspect of the ritual drama and American tragedy that was Fitzgerald's life?

The aspect most sharply revealed in this new volume is by no means an undiscovered one, but it has often been underemphasized. Briefly it is the extent to which the Fitzgerald story—whether lived or turned by him into fiction—was a collaboration between Scott and Zelda. It is her part in the fiction that is widely neglected. Not only was she the Fitzgerald heroine—and he found it difficult to create another after her breakdown in 1930—not only did she enrich their common stock of material, but also she contributed to his style by her use of hallucinated language based on her intense perceptions. "Rewrite from mood" is an injunction to himself penciled in the margin of several manuscripts now in the Princeton library. Long after reading the injunction I decided what it really meant: that the passage was to be rewritten in the metaphorical terms into which Zelda fell naturally, but which Scott could achieve only by making an effort.

Here is an example, not from *The Correspondence*, but from the beginning of "A Millionaire's Girl," a story that Zelda wrote unaided from their joint stock of situations. Scott made revisions in proof and signed the story, so that it would bring a higher price from the *Saturday Evening Post*:

> Twilights were wonderful just after the war. They hung above New York like indigo wash, forming themselves from asphalt dust and sooty shadows under the cornices and limp gusts of air exhaled from closing windows, to hang above the streets with all the mystery of white fog rising from a swamp. . . . Through the gloom people went to tea. On all the corners round the Plaza Hotel, girls in short squirrel coats and hats like babies' velvet bathtubs waited for the changing traffic to be suctioned up by the revolving doors of the fashionable grill.

A few lines below one reads the mysterious statement: "It was always tea-time or late at night." Why? After hearing tales from their friends,

I guessed the reason: it was because Scott and Zelda got stoned at tea-time and didn't come back to the world until late at night. They were living too fast to keep up with themselves. Nevertheless Scott worked hard at his writing in the mornings and sometimes for days on end. Zelda hadn't that discipline, or any other, but in one way she pre-served a moral superiority over Scott. That was because she had less self-consciousness; most of the time she simply acted where Scott saw himself acting; she did not think of consequences. It was Scott, the spoiled priest, who believed in rewards and punishments.

There were more punishments than rewards during his last years in Hollywood. Money, money was the subject of his letters, to an extent that one wouldn't have realized from reading previous collections, which omitted his more abject pleas. If only he had money to pay the psychiatrists, to put Scottie through school and Vassar, to buy time for writing another novel. . . . Zelda the spendthrift spoke less of money in her letters from sanitariums; she was learning to do without it. Heartbreakingly she kept evoking the past. "O my darling," she wrote from North Carolina in the winter of 1937—

> That's what we said on the softness of that expansive Alabama night a long time ago when you invited me to dine and I had never dined before but had always just 'had supper.' The General was away. The night was soft and gray and the trees were feathery in the lamplight and the dim recesses of the pine forest were fragrant with the past, and you said you would come back from no matter where you are. So I said and I will be here waiting. I didn't quite believe it then, but now I do.

Scott did come back from the coast on several occasions. If Zelda had earned a reprieve from the sanitarium, they would go on a trip to-gether, but each of these was disastrous. Scott would drink suicidally and Zelda, back in her refuge, would sometimes lapse into catatonia. In April 1938 Scott wrote to her psychiatrist:

> . . . each time that I see her something happens to me that makes me the worst person for her rather than the best, but a part of me will always pity her with a sort of deep ache that is never absent

from my mind for more than a few hours: an ache for the beautiful child that I loved and with whom I was happy as I shall never be again.

It is hardly a wonder that scholars, no less romantic than the rest of us, keep going back to the Fitzgerald papers.

NELSON ALGREN'S
CHICAGO

W hen Nelson Algren was three years old, in 1912, his family
moved from Detroit to Chicago. The father was a skilled me-
chanic who could make machines behave but couldn't give orders to
people; he never became a foreman. Nelson spent his boyhood in two
working-class neighborhoods, south and northwest of the Loop. Chicago was to be the city that he hated and loved, abused and celebrated,
all through his life. He died at 72 in Sag Harbor, Long Island, where
he had lately established himself after some years in New Jersey, but
he would always be a Chicago author, by no means least and not the
last in a famous line.

Dreiser and Sandburg were two of his literary ancestors; Farrell was
a sort of cousin, but one he found it painful to admire. Those vastly
dissimilar writers had in common a Chicago spirit of bluffness and
down-to-earthiness that sets them apart from New Yorkers. Algren
had the spirit too, but expressed it in a different way. His Chicago was
"a Jekyll-and-Hyde sort of Burg," as he called it, a city whose various
aspects were organized into hostile pairs. It was a day city and a night
city (he preferred the night). It was a city of wide boulevards and lit-
tered alleyways. It was a city of mansions torn down to build towering
Bauhauses on the lakefront, and behind them mile after mile of dreary
streets. It was a city of prosperous, right-thinking citizens, and also—
passing over with hardly a mention the sober working class into which
Algren was born—another city of hustlers, pushers, junkies, hookers,
pimps, jackrollers, stewbums, crooked gamblers, and petty thieves,
all living at the mercy of the corruptible police.

This last was the Chicago that Algren memorialized in the best of
his novels and stories. He lived near these people for years, usually in
a two-room flat with books on the floor and a broken bed. He listened

to their talk, in which he found a savage type of poetry, and never betrayed their secrets to the police. In a sense he became their poet in residence.

Here are two passages from his long prose poem, *Chicago: City on the Make* (1951), that reveal his divided feeling about the city. The first expresses his contempt for prosperous people who live on the Gold Coast or in the northern suburbs:

> So if you are entirely square yourself, bypass the forest of furnished rooms behind The Loop and stay on the Outer Drive till you swing through Lincoln Park. Then move, with the lake still on your square right hand, into those suburbs where the lawns are always wide, the sky is always smokeless, the trees are forever leafy, the churches are always tidy, gardens are always landscaped, streets are freshly swept, homes are pictures out of *Town and Country*. And the people are stuffed with kapok.

Then a second passage, written from the heart and full of love for the dispossessed:

> . . . The nameless, useless nobodies who sleep behind the taverns, who sleep beneath the El. Who sleep in burnt-out busses with the windows freshly curtained; in winterized chicken coops or patched-up truck bodies. The useless, helpless nobodies nobody knows; that go as the snow goes, where the wind blows, there and there and there, down any old cat-and-ashcan alley at all. There, unloved and lost forever, lost and unloved for keeps and a day . . . there where they sleep the all-night movies through and wait for rain or peace or snow: there, there beats Chicago's heart.

I don't know why Algren adopted those nameless nobodies as the social class to which he owed allegiance. He seems to have started out with middle-class aspirations. After working his way through the University of Illinois, he had graduated in 1931 with a degree in journalism and with vague dreams, so he tells us, of becoming a sports writer like Ring Lardner or a foreign correspondent. Newspapers weren't hiring young men in that second year of the Depression. Big-city editors advised him to look for work in small towns, where the editors directed him back to cities. After trying his luck in Chicago and Minneapolis, he hitchhiked south through the Great Valley till he found himself in New Orleans, where he joined a crew selling coffee from door to door. Later he became one of the homeless young men— there were more than a million of them in 1932—who traveled in empty boxcars bound for they didn't know where. Unlike the others, Algren wanted to write and be published. The desire became so strong in him that he walked into a classroom in a Texas cow college and walked out again with a typewriter under his arm. For that misdemeanor he spent four months in jail while waiting for the circuit judge to appear and try his case. It may have been during those months that he lost his middle-class dreams and began to think of himself as a private in the mutinous army of the dispossessed.

After bumming his way back to Chicago, Algren wrote a story about his adventures—I don't know on whose typewriter—and it was printed in *Story* magazine. A publisher was impressed by it and offered him an advance of $100 against the putative royalties of a novel on which he had started working. The novel—he called it *Somebody in Boots*—was finished with that modest assistance and appeared in 1935. It was a book that spoke not only for the author but for other homeless and hopeless young men; it was a muttering from the depths. Not many people would read it at the time, but those who did would remember it. Later, during the years when Algren was on the Federal Writers' Project, his associates called him "the Dostoevsky of West Madison Street," which by then was Chicago's Skid Row.

He remained stubbornly loyal to the class for which he had chosen to be a spokesman. His second novel, *Never Come Morning*, dealt with low life in the Division Street neighborhood, then a Polish community, where he had lived for several years. The book had been started when he was on the Writers' Project, but Algren was always a slow worker and it wasn't finished until 1942. By that time—so he told Ernest Hemingway—he was working as a boilermaker's assistant in East St. Louis. Hemingway and others warmly praised the novel, but Algren didn't try to exploit their praise; instead he disappeared into the army. He served for three years, mostly in Europe, as a private in the Medical Corps and never rose in rank to private first class.

Once more in Chicago, he went back to Division Street and lived alone in a cheap two-room flat while trying to write another novel. His method was immensely wasteful of time. He started without a plot and with hardly more than a vague feeling of where he might go. "I've always figured," he said, "the only way I could finish a book and get a plot was just to keep making it longer and longer until something happens—you know, till it finds its own plot." *The Man with a Golden Arm*, his third novel, not published till 1949, started as the story of a returned soldier. Algren had typed hundreds of pages before it became a different story, that of a poker dealer with a monkey on his back. It was to be his only book that appeared on best-seller lists. The movie rights were sold, if for the miserly fee of $15,000; then Algren was offered a high salary to advise on the script. His advice wasn't taken. He appeared at the studio on a Monday, he says, and was fired on Wednesday for recalcitrance. Soon afterward he left Hollywood with a lasting hatred for the place and a reputation among producers of being impossible to deal with.

It wasn't the only time that a door to affluence opened in front of him, but he always slammed it shut. Later he formed one connection after another with magazines that paid high prices for his stories, but each connection was broken. Partly that was because he never learned to meet deadlines, but chiefly because he couldn't write anything to order unless it was something he truly felt. The standards he set for himself were those of what he called "the stomach"—others would call it the heart—and not of the head. He had a sort of visceral probity that made it impossible for him to become a hack. If he didn't feel that his writing was "from the stomach," he suffered from writer's block.

He was hard-working but unprofessional. "I don't know many writers," he used to say. He condemned critics as a group and sometimes reviled them individually. Always he resented what he took to be the literary establishment. I think he feared that some of its members might seize him and drive him blindfold in a Cadillac to one of those hated North Shore suburbs, where they would not only hold him in prosperous captivity but would stuff him with kapok and make him wear a necktie. Still, in his daily life he did make a sort of compromise with respectability. After the success of *The Man with a Golden Arm* he moved away from the Division Street neighborhood, but only to take possession of a hideous little green bungalow on a working-class street outside of Gary, Indiana. On weekends he went to Chicago and sat in on an all-night game of poker.

That was Nelson Algren as I knew him best in 1954. I didn't follow his career after he left Chicago twenty years later. Indirectly I heard that he was having trouble with a novel based on the life of Hurricane Carter, a Negro boxer convicted of a triple murder. Carter, who claimed to be innocent, brought bad luck to every writer—there were many—who became interested in his case. Algren wrote a long article about him, but it wasn't printed by the magazine that had ordered it. Then he expanded the article into a novel that he called *The Devil's Stocking*. After he had worked on it for years, this was rejected by American publishers and had to be issued in Germany after his death.

I haven't read it. During the months since Algren died, however, I have been reading earlier books that I missed when they first appeared. Once more I have been impressed by his talent, his probity, and his command of a tough language that he transforms into a raw and bleeding poetry. All his books are authentic, if unshaven, but I still like him best when he chants about Chicago, as in this singing paragraph:

> City that walks with her shoulder bag banging her hip, you gave me your gutters and I gave you back gold. City I never pretended to love for something you were not, I never told you you smelled of anything but cheap cologne. I never told you you were anything but a loud old bag. Yet you're still the doll of the world and I'm proud to have slept in your tireless arms.

ROBERT PENN WARREN, AET. 75

R ed Warren tells me that we first met in 1927, "when I was a student," he says, "and you were a big man." A big man? I was twenty-nine and was determined to keep my independence by not becoming a well-known author; precariously I supported myself by writing book reviews and an occasional poem for *The Dial*. Red was twenty-two and had just earned his M.A. at Berkeley; it was before his postgraduate year at Yale and his Rhodes scholarship. Already—if I remember correctly—he had published two poems in *The New Republic*, one of which was "Kentucky Mountain Farm." I admired the poems and had heard about Red as the youngest member of what was already known as the Fugitive group. Here he was at last, in person: tall, long-necked, angular, with a lot of curly dark-red hair. He made abrupt gestures and seemed self-conscious except when telling a story in his low Kentucky voice.

That's all I remember of our meeting, which must have been in Allen Tate's basement flat in the Village. More clearly I remember an evening in the summer of 1930, when Red was back from Oxford. We got drunk on Wall Street cocktails at the Dizzy Club—"One drink and we give you a seat on the Curb"—and talked poetry for hours among all those gangsters. Later I would recognize some impressions of that evening in Red's second novel, *At Heaven's Gate* (1943).

"That was the decade," he said in a recent letter, "when from poverty I was mostly South-bound, & knew little of the N.Y. complications of life," especially the political complications; Red has always been a deliberate innocent in politics. "Your book," he continued, referring to *The Dream of the Golden Mountains*, "is an eye-opener in many ways. I don't mean to say that I think N.Y. is the center of the U.S.A. (it may now be dying—and for whose woe or weal I don't know), but then (1930–40) I knew the South, West & Middle West very well & the East was a foreign country—wise and ignorant." Writers in the East were then preoccupied with political struggles as reflected in literature. Red took no part in the struggles, even after he went to Huey Long's university in 1934 and founded (with Cleanth Brooks) a distinguished quarterly, *The Southern Review*. The quarterly adopted no political position, though its contributors were permitted to adopt a variety of these, so long as they expressed their notions clearly. It was only when Red went to the University of Iowa as a visiting lecturer, in 1941, that he was exposed unwillingly to the New York City type of political arguments.

He has a story about them, as about everything else; most of his world is reduced to stories. "At Univ. of Iowa," he says, "there was a stalwart graduate student (female) from N.Y.C. who used to lecture me on American agriculture & how to save it. And driving in the country, we passed a flock of sheep. 'What,' she demanded in profound puzzlement, 'are those things?' 'Sheep,' says I, 'and I don't want to hear another word from you about Stalin unless he's got wool like that.' Long silence (for her a real feat) followed."

Red came through the political wars of the 1930s and 1940s without being wounded or inflicting wounds. He was never a politician, as I said, but rather a moralist, and this during a period when morality was going out of fashion. For him the confrontations at the heart of a drama are not between opposing doctrines, or social classes; they are between the individual and his own conscience, or consciousness. In his most famous book, *All the King's Men* (1946), he achieved the feat of writing a novel about Huey Long that is profoundly nonpolitical; nobody could use it in a campaign for votes. The one public issue on which he has taken a stand—in this case liberal—is race relations, and there he could do so because he approached the issue as essentially moral.

Although I have known Red Warren for more than fifty years, I never learned much about him directly. Largely that is the result of faulty communication: I have grown increasingly deaf and Red speaks rapidly, in a low voice, so that I have missed the point of his most illuminating stories. Once he took me into the store that his father was managing in Guthrie, Kentucky, after his little bank failed. It was in 1933 and Guthrie was then a singularly drab and impoverished railroad town. The post office displayed the names of everyone in the county who had paid a federal income tax for 1932; there were only two names. Red himself was a miserably paid instructor at Vanderbilt, out of favor with the administration because of his approach to literature. He told me that his father's boyhood ambition was to become a classical scholar, but that there hadn't been money enough for his education. His grandfather—but he didn't learn that until later—had been a major in Nathan Bedford Forrest's cavalry.

Little facts gleaned here and there. . . . One Sunday afternoon in that spring of 1933, the Fugitive group held a picnic on a houseboat moored in the Cumberland River upstream from Nashville. The river was in flood and the current swept past us at a rate to frighten timid swimmers. Red dived from the houseboat, swam arrow-straight across the river, and then swam back again as if the Cumberland in flood were a millpond. One of his friends told me that he liked to swim a mile before breakfast every morning. At twenty-eight he was already becoming a somewhat legendary character.

But what was he really like? The answer to that question was not to be found in conversation or in picnics on the river. The best place to look for it now is in his twelve published volumes of verse.

It occurred to me not long ago that, as a simple matter of statistics, Warren has published more lines of verse than any other major American poet of our century (exception being made for Conrad Aiken). He has produced a vast *oeuvre*, and that in itself is a considerable achievement, especially in an age marked until recently (fashions are changing) by the number of niggardly talents, men and women held back from writing by a dream of perfection and the fear of being caught out in errors of taste. Warren is generous, open, bold. He seems to be saying, "Why bother about possible errors of taste? The important matter is to get the thing said, accurately if possible, but at worst approximately, so long as the language shows a strict regard for truth."

The twelve volumes contain a great variety of subjects and moods and measures. Some of the verse is regular, rhymed in formal patterns, and some of it is so loosely hung together as to be almost invertebrate. One can't always be sure why a given line should end with a given word instead of rambling on through half a dozen others. But the poet knows—one gives him credit for that sure instinct—and the vast body of work is unified by being spoken in his unmistakable voice. Every poem is clearly by Robert Penn Warren; every line is distinctly signed.

This does not mean that every poem is of equal value. Some of them are rather too philosophical for my taste and not sufficiently relieved by Warren's matchless stories. Sometimes, having found what he thinks is the right pitch, he carries it too long—as if he didn't know how to break off except by making an inconsequential remark or by asking a vast question: "What is Love?" "What is History?" "What, ah, is Time?" That habit of asking questions tempts me to ask another in turn: whether it isn't the poet's task to answer those questions by giving examples, pictures, remembered moments that are truer than our philosophies? Warren does just that at his frequent best. He tells us what love is by picturing his wife naked on the seashore, his son raising both arms in the moonlight, his father speechless on his death-bed; those epiphanies are love in a poet's concrete terms. He tells us something about the nature of time by creating moments so absolute in themselves that time is momentarily abolished.

"What is it you cannot remember that is so true?" he asks at one point in his next-to-last book, *Now and Then* (1978). During recent years Warren has embarked, or has let himself be embarked, on a search for those half-forgotten truths. He is making what seems to me the most fruitful of all the efforts that are open to a poet in his eighth decade, namely, to remember and reconstitute his life, to reveal its essential form. The effort begins with his childhood in the Kentucky countryside and carries him through an extreme diversity of moods, landscapes, and—most important for him—persons; no other living poet has seen and felt so much of the world. His remembered life becomes a mixture of fact and fiction, "played against, or with," he says, "a shadowy narrative, a shadowy autobiography, if you will. . . . It may be said"—and he says it—"that our lives are our supreme fiction."

That is why the "real" Red Warren is to be found in his poetry, especially in his later books. What shall I say of him? He is a man who loves people but spends much of his time alone. He is extremely loyal to his friends, true to his lived background, but at the same time brutally realistic, with a fondness for depicting deeds of heartlessness or violence: murders, lynchings, suicides. He has bad dreams and remembers them. He is a countryman, a solitary walker, a swimmer (but not a hunter or a plowman), who seldom writes on urban themes;

the best of those exceptions is a poem that pictures the South Bronx covered with snow and transformed into an untouched wilderness. He prays, but he doesn't know for what. Kind as he is to others, he is ruthless in protecting his working hours (and I hear that the floor of his study is covered with unanswered letters).

After he sent me his last book (1980), I wrote a letter to Red that didn't have to be answered. Here is part of it:

> *Being Here*: I read the poems twice, and had the feeling that many of them were written especially for me. That effort to recover in age the memories of boyhood and to puzzle out their meaning. That country background, west of the mountains. Those questions about the dead who crowd around you asking only to be named ("Better Than Counting Sheep"). That undischarged debt to your mother. That burden of guilt (and why should you have it, you of all people?). Often you add to my own burden of guilt when I think, "I should have written that, I should have found the words." And to my sense of not having lived enough, felt enough, when I come across one of the scenes that you bring vividly to life—just as you bring the animals to life again: the six kittens beheaded with a corn knife, the other kitten with a broken leg saved from the garbage grinder, the deer in rut, the mountain lion, the drowned monkey on a Mediterranean beach. And yourself as a boy venturing deep into a cave and thinking, "This is me. . . . Who am I?" Or dreaming: how many dreams! till you think that yourself is only a dream of the moonlight. I read and envy you, being one who can seldom remember his dreams.

After mailing the letter I had some further reflections on one question it raised. Why did Red Warren—"of all people," I said once again—suffer often from a sense of guilt? Why should it afflict this upright man who has always worked hard and has never taken part in the vendettas of the literary life? Perhaps, I thought, there is one answer in a memory of childhood that he mentions several times: "How once I had lied to my mother and hid/In a closet and said, in darkness, aloud: 'I hate you.' " But his mother, long before she died, had absolved him of that sin. Perhaps it is a feeling of having neglected his duties to dead friends whose names he has forgotten. Perhaps it is connected with something vividly remembered: "how once, in total fascination, I watched a black boy/Take a corn knife and decapitate six kittens? Did I dream/That again last night? . . . Did I wake/With guilt? . . ./Sometime we must probe more deeply the issue of complicity." The issue remains, but we cannot live with the burden of being accomplices in all the sins of our culture. Perhaps the poet's real torment is the Protestant conscience that keeps urging him to be better than any human soul can be.

As a cure of conscience, I should recommend to Red Warren an exercise about him in which I indulged the other night. Only half dreaming I pictured the two pans of a balance that was weighing out his life. In the one pan were heaped all the gifts that he has received from the world: the three Pulitzer prizes (one for fiction, two for poetry), the National Book Award, the honorary degrees (fourteen by the last tally), the consultancy in poetry at the Library of Congress, the National Medal for Literature, the Presidential Medal of Freedom, the Bollingen Prize, the Commonwealth Award for Distinguished Service in Literature. . . . In the other pan were all the gifts he has bestowed on the world: the thirty-odd books (including, besides the poems, ten novels, a poetic drama in two versions, a prose drama, a collection of stories, a book of essays), the recreated boyhood in a Kentucky railroad town, the realization of his father's lost dream of scholarship, the years of devoted teaching, the inspiration of students—and of writers who have chosen his career as a model—all this and much more. It is a picture I recommend to Red Warren at seventy-five. "Heap up the gifts from the world," I said to myself (or to the court attendant who busied himself with medals and parchments). "There cannot be too many of them. They will never outweigh the gifts bestowed on the world that overflow the other pan."

JOHN CHEEVER:
THE NOVELIST'S LIFE
AS A DRAMA

L ate in the fall of 1930, John Cheever appeared in my office at *The New Republic*, where I was then a junior editor recently assigned to the book department. John was eighteen and looked younger.* He had a boyish smile, a low, Bay State voice, and a determined chin. We had just printed the first story he submitted to a magazine, a fictionized account of why and how he got himself expelled from Thayer Academy, in South Braintree. Promptly John had come to New York to make his fortune as a writer.

The story—we called it "Expelled"—had come to us marked for my attention. I had felt that I was hearing for the first time the voice of a new generation. There were some objections by the senior editors, who pointed out that we didn't often print fiction. "It's awfully long," Bruce Bliven said; he had the final voice on manuscripts. I undertook to cut it down to *New Republic* size and it went to the printer. When John appeared we talked about the story. I didn't tell him that it had caused a mild dispute in the office. Instead I invited him to an afternoon party, the first that the Cowleys had dared to give in their bare apartment a few doors down the street.

I had forgotten that party of Prohibition days, but John remembered it fifty years later when he went to Chicago and spoke at a dinner of the Newberry Library Associates. The Library had acquired my papers and wanted to hold a celebration, with John as the principal

---

*John always said "seventeen" in telling the story; he was inexact about his age, since he was born May 27, 1912. He also said that his manuscript was addressed to me because he had been reading my first book of poems, *Blue Juniata*, and thought I might sympathize.

speaker. "I was truly provincial," he said in evoking that long-ago afternoon. "Malcolm's first wife Peggy met me at the door and exclaimed, 'You must be John Cheever. Everyone else is here.' Things were never like this in Massachusetts. I was offered two kinds of drinks. One was greenish. The other was brown. They were both, I believe, made in a bathtub. I was told that one was a Manhattan and the other Pernod. My only intent was to appear terribly sophisticated and I ordered a Manhattan. Malcolm very kindly introduced me to his guests. I went on drinking Manhattans lest anyone think I came from a small town like Quincy, Masschusetts. Presently, after four or five Manhattans I realized that I was going to vomit. I rushed to Mrs. Cowley, thanked her for the party, and reached the apartment-house hallway, where I vomited all over the wallpaper. Malcolm never mentioned the damages."

John must have walked or staggered back to what he called "the squalid slum room on Hudson Street" that he had rented for $3 a week. At the time his only dependable income was a weekly allowance of $10 from his older brother Fred, who had kept his job during the Depression and believed in John's talent. His only capital was a typewriter for which he couldn't often buy a new ribbon. That first winter in New York he had lived—so he reported—mostly on stale bread and buttermilk. As time went on he found little assignments that augmented his diet; one of them was summarizing the plots of new novels for MGM, which was looking for books that would make popular movies. John was paid $5 for typing out his summary with I don't know how many carbons. *The New Republic* couldn't help him much except by giving him unreviewed books for sale; it was "a journal of opinion," mostly political, and John wasn't given to expressing opinions; by instinct he was a storyteller. He kept writing stories and they began to be printed, always in little magazines that didn't pay for contributions.

I told Elizabeth Ames about him. Elizabeth was the executive director and hostess of Yaddo, a working retreat for writers and artists in Saratoga Springs, and I had served on her admissions committee. She invited John for one summer, liked him immensely, and later renewed the invitation several times. John would never forget his indebtedness to Yaddo, which had fed and lodged him during some of his neediest periods.

In New York I sometimes gave him advice, not about his writing, which I had admired from the beginning, but about finding a market for it. Once I told him it was time for a novel that would speak for his new generation as Fitzgerald had spoken in *This Side of Paradise*. It turned out that John had already started a novel, and he showed me the first three or four chapters. They wouldn't do as the beginning of a book, I reported; each chapter was separate and came to a dead end. It might be that his present talent was for stories. . . . Then why wouldn't editors buy the stories? he asked me on another occasion. By that time I had been divorced from Peggy and had remarried, this time for good. It was a Friday evening and John had come for dinner in our new apartment. "Perhaps the stories have been too long," I said, "usually six or seven thousand words. Editors don't like to buy long stories from unknown writers." Then I had an inspiration. I suggested that he write four very short stories, each of not more than a thousand words, in the next four days. "Bring them to me at the office on Wednesday afternoon and," I said grandly, "we'll see whether I can't get you some money for them."

John carried out the assignment brilliantly. I doubt whether anyone else of his age—he was then twenty-two—could have invented four stories, each different from all the others, in only four days, but John already seemed to have an endless stock of characters and moods and situations. Although *The New Republic* seldom printed fiction, one of the four could be passed off as a "color piece" about a burlesque theater. "Yes. Short and lively," was Bruce Bliven's comment when I showed it to him. The other three ministories, plainly fictions, I sent along to Katharine White, then fiction editor of *The New Yorker*, and she accepted two of them. That event, which I have told about elsewhere, was the beginning of John's career as a professional writer. *The New Yorker* was his principal market for more than thirty years and it would end by printing 119 of his stories.

In the course of time John became impatient with the accurate reporting that was demanded of *New Yorker* writers, especially in the days when Harold Ross was editor. It set limitations on fiction, and

John always wanted to go farther and deeper into life. "This table seems real," he later said in an interview, "the fruit basket belonged to my grandmother, but a madwoman could come in the door any moment." In the stories he wrote after World War II, the madwoman appeared more often. Once she was a vampire; that was in "Torch Song." Once she assumed the shape of an enormous radio that picked up conversations from anywhere in a big apartment building. That story, his first with a touch of the impossible, was also his first to be widely anthologized.

Some future critic should trace John's development as a writer by reading his work from the beginning in its exact chronological order. The work changes from year to year and from story to story. "Fiction is experimentation," he was later to say; "when it ceases to be that it ceases to be fiction. One never puts down a sentence without the feeling that it has never been put down before in exactly the same way, and that perhaps the substance of the sentence has never been felt. Every sentence is an innovation." That is too seldom true of fiction, but it is true of John's best work, in which the sentences, apparently simple, are always alive and unexpected. Reading them makes me think of a boyhood experience, that of groping beneath roots at the edge of a stream and finding a trout in my fingers.

There were times of crisis when his purposes changed rapidly. One of these must have been during his work on *The Wapshot Chronicle*, his first novel and still his most engaging book. Perhaps it isn't a novel so much as a series of episodes connected with the imaginary town of St. Botolphs, on the south or less fashionable shore of Massachusetts Bay, and with the fortunes of the Wapshot family; John was right to call it a chronicle. The characters are presented with a free-ranging candor that must have embarrassed the Cheevers, to whom the Wapshots bore a family resemblance, but also with an affection not often revealed in his New York or Westchester stories. John felt that he couldn't publish the book until after his mother died. It appeared in 1957 while the Cheevers were spending a year in Italy. John was happy about the *Chronicle*, and this without seeing the reviews, most of which were enthusiastic. Writing it seems to have given him a new sense of scope and freedom.

Nevertheless he was having trouble with his second novel, *The Wap-*

shot Scandal, which was to be seven years in the writing. While work on it progressed slowly, or not at all, he published two more collections of stories (there would finally be six of these in all). One of the new collections bore a title that suggested another change in direction: *Some People, Places, & Things That Will Not Appear in My Next Novel*. In the title story he was performing what almost seems a rite of exorcism: he was presenting in brief, and then dismissing with contempt, a number of episodes that, in his former days, he might have developed at length. Not one of them, he now believed, would help him "to celebrate a world that lies spread out around us like a bewildering and stupendous dream."

He tried to present that dream in *The Wapshot Scandal*, but in writing the book he found little to celebrate. He had to record how the Wapshots, with their traditional standards, faced the new world of aimlessness, supermarkets, and fusion bombs. They died or went to pieces—all of them except Coverly Wapshot, more solid and unattractive than the others, who found himself working in a secret missile base and lost his security clearance. The book is almost as episodic as the *Chronicle*, but with the episodes more tightly woven together. Each of them starts with a scene that is accurately observed—it might correspond to Cheever's real table and his grandmother's fruit basket—but then everything becomes grotesque, as if his madwoman had come in the door. On one occasion she is followed by a screaming crowd of madwomen in nightgowns with curlers in their hair. The book has an unflagging power of invention and was praised by critics when it finally appeared; also it had a fairly impressive sale. John himself "never much liked the book," as he was to say when he was interviewed much later for *The Paris Review*, "and when it was done I was in a bad way. I'd wake up in the night and I would hear Hemingway's voice—I've never actually heard Hemingway's voice, but it was conspicuously his—saying, 'This is the small agony. The great agony comes later.' "

But first would come another agony that was not the greatest, but was not a small one either. After thirty years of intimate relations, *The New Yorker* rejected one of his longer and more treasured stories, "The Jewels of the Cabots." John sold the story to *Playboy* for twice what *The New Yorker* would have paid, but still his pride had been hurt. There were other rejections, one or two of them inexcusable, and John stopped publishing in *The New Yorker*. If one were plotting his life as a theater piece, one might say the curtain had fallen on a second act.

A few years later John published a third novel, *Bullet Park* (1969), that was more tightly plotted than the second. It pleased him more than the *Scandal*. "The manuscript was received enthusiastically everywhere," he reported, "but when Benjamin DeMott dumped on it in the *Times*, everybody picked up their marbles and went home. I ruined my left leg in a skiing accident and ended up so broke that I took out working papers for my youngest son." John was exaggerating, as he liked to do with gullible reporters. The son, then twelve years old, never thought about working papers; in due time he went off to Andover and Stanford. But John, horrified at going into debt, wasn't making progress with his writing, and he confessed to himself that he had become an alcoholic. He had a heart attack, nearly fatal, in 1972. Having recovered, he accepted teaching assignments, first at the Iowa School of Writing and then at Boston University, where, so he said, "I behaved badly."

For the black years that might be called a third act in his life, I'm not sure about the sequence of events, and I have to depend on his later accounts. I was seeing less of John. In 1967 our only son, Robert, had been married to John's daughter Susan in a high-church ceremony at St. Mark's in the Bouwerie. The elder Cowleys played no part in the preparations for an expensive wedding. At the reception, under an outsize tent in the churchyard, the Cheever connection drank their champagne on one side of the tent, while the smaller Cowley contingent sat grouped on the other. That marked a growing difference in styles of life between the two families. For ten years after *The Wapshot Chronicle* and before *Bullet Park*, John had earned a substantial income: there were Hollywood contracts and what seemed to me huge advances from publishers. The Cheevers had bought and remodeled a big stone house in Westchester County, to the disapproval of some *New Yorker* editors, who felt that authors should defend their economic freedom by living on a modest scale. The Cowleys did live modestly, farther out in the country, and spent rather less than they took in. I came to suspect that the Cheevers, who traveled widely, always in first class, now regarded us as tourist-class country cousins. Then Rob and Susan were divorced, after eight years of marriage. It was an amicable divorce, with no children to argue about (only two golden retrievers) and with no hard feelings. Still it was the end of casual family visitings.

I was always overjoyed to see John, but was a little tongue-tied even when we met at Yaddo, where we were both on the board of directors, or at various committee meetings of the American Academy; there was never much time for confidences. Later John would tell the public about his misadventures. After Boston University he went home to the big stone house, where he fell into utter depression. He used to wash down several Valium tablets with a quart of whiskey. He was trying to abolish himself—but why? Clearly it was less a matter of his finances or his physical state than of his concern with the art of fiction; he felt that his life as a writer was at an end. He was also a sincerely religious man, though he wouldn't talk much about the subject, and he must have felt that he had fallen from grace forever. His family, deeply concerned, told him that alcohol would kill him, as it had already killed his loved and resented older brother. "So what?" he said, taking another drink. In 1975 he finally listened to the family and committed himself to Smithers, a rehabilitation center. He was to speak darkly, in later years, of going mad when deprived of liquor and of being wrapped in a straitjacket.* The treatment was prolonged, whatever it was, and it worked; after being released from Smithers, John never again took a drink. He experienced a new sense of redemption, elation, and release from bondage. Almost immediately he set to work on a novel, which he finished in less than a year.

The novel, of course, was *Falconer*, published in 1977; John was to call it "a very dark book that displayed radiance." It was the story of Ezekiel Farragut, a moderately distinguished professor who becomes a drug addict, who kills his brother with a poker, and who is sentenced to ten years in Falconer Prison. There he is redeemed, partly through a homosexual love affair, and loses his craving for Methadone. The book reads swiftly and displays John's gift for economical prose with not a misplaced word, beside his amazing and unflagging talent for

---

*The treatment at Smithers did not include a straitjacket, but John had been confined briefly in another institution.

invention. Some of the episodes have a touch of the miraculous. A cardinal descends from the skies in a helicopter and carries off Zeke's lover to freedom. A young priest appears in the cellblock and administers last rites to the hero. "Now who the hell was that?" Zeke shouts to the guard. "I didn't ask for a priest. He didn't do his thing for anybody else." Symbolically Zeke is about to die, be entombed, and rise again. In life his cellmate dies instead. Attendants come to put the corpse into a body bag. Farragut zips open the bag, removes the corpse, and takes its place; then he is carried out of the prison. Walking in the street a free man, his head high, his back straight, "Rejoice," he thought, "rejoice."

Those are the last words of Cheever's longest continuous fiction. Judged purely as a novel, *Falcoln* has obvious faults. There are loose strings never tied up and events left unexplained. The reader is forced to wonder how Zeke Farragut will survive in his new life, considering that he has no money, no identity, and is still dressed in his prison clothes. Then one reflects that the faults don't matter much; that *Falconer* is not a novel bent on achieving verisimilitude, but rather a moving parable with biblical overtones of sin and redemption; it is Magdalen redeemed by divine grace and Lazarus raised from the dead. That is how it must have been read by thousands, and the book had an astoundingly wide sale, enough to pay off its author's debts for the first time in years.

And the fourth act in the drama?

The success of *Falconer* led to another change in John's character, as well as in his public image. He had always managed to keep from being a celebrity. When he was twelve years old his parents had given him their permission to earn his future living as a writer—if he could earn it—but only after he promised them that he had no idea of becoming famous or wealthy. In later years he had kept the promise, though with some latitude in the matter of income, since he liked to support the family on a generous scale. He had refused several offers that promised to make him rich, though he had always been shrewd in a Yankee fashion (and his agent was known for striking hard bargains). In the matter of fame, he had obdurately defended his privacy. Medals and honors he accepted when they came, if grudgingly, but he had done his best to avoid being interviewed—often by the simple device of getting drunk, or getting the interviewer drunk. But *Falconer* had made him a national figure as if by accident, and he found himself enjoying his new status.

For the first time in his life he gave interviews willingly—and brilliantly too, since he said without hesitation whatever was on his mind. Always the interviewers would mention his boyishness. I suppose the word was suggested by his lack of self-importance, his deprecatory smile, and his candor in speaking about intimate misadventures. In simple fact he was now an old man, wearied by the physical demands he had made on himself, so that he was older in body and spirit than his sixty-five years. He now had nothing to lose by telling the truth, so long as it made a good story. He was finding pleasure in addressing a new audience—as he explained more than once—but also he wanted to set things straight with himself and the world while there was still time.

His next book after *Falconer* would be a retrospective undertaking, *The Stories of John Cheever* (1978), collected at last in one big volume. He had chosen sixty-one stories for the book, after omitting all those printed before his army service in World War II (though some of that early work is worth preserving) as well as two or three stories written during his breakdown. Almost all the others he arranged in roughly chronological order. For the first time a wider public could note the changing spirit of his work over the years, not to mention its essential unity. John also had given the book a brief, illuminating Preface that has been widely quoted. "These stories," it says at one point, "seem at times to be stories of a long-lost world when the city of New York was still filled with a river light, when you heard the Benny Goodman quartets from a radio in the corner stationery store, and when almost everybody wore a hat. . . . The constants that I looked for in this sometimes dated paraphernalia are a love of light and a determination to trace some moral chain of being. Calvin played no part in my religious education, but his presence seemed to abide in the barns of my childhood and to have left me with some undue bitterness."

That moral element is always present, if concealed, in a Cheever story. At first the bad people, whose commonest sin is heartlessness, seem hard to distinguish from the good people, but they end by indicting themselves, and Cheever was an inexorable judge (especially when faced by women bent on expressing themselves at everybody's cost). He was not a tender judge of his own work, and there are only two sentences of the Preface that I think are in error as applied to himself. He says, "The parturition of a writer, I think, unlike that of a painter, does not display any interesting alliances to his masters. In the growth of a writer one finds nothing like the early Jackson Pollock copies of the Sistine Chapel paintings with their interesting cross-references to Thomas Hart Benton." That seems to me far from the truth. Among the important writers of this later time, Cheever reveals more alliances than others to three masters of the World War I generation.

Hemingway was his first master, as was evident in John's early and now forgotten stories. These copied many features of Hemingway's style, as notably the short sentences, the simple words, the paring away of adjectives, adverbs, conjunctions, and the effort to evoke feelings without directly expressing them, simply by presenting actions in sequence and objects seen accurately as if for the first time. I can testify that the novel John tried to write when he was twenty-one— and abandoned after three or four chapters—had as its obvious starting point a story by Hemingway, "Cross-Country Snow." It would have been the equivalent, in his case, of Jackson Pollock's attempts to copy the Sistine Chapel. Very soon Cheever developed a style of his own that became more effective than Hemingway's later style; he never parodied himself. Still, he retained what he had learned from that early master, including an enthusiasm for fishing and skiing. Hemingway as a father figure appeared in his dreams.

The resemblance to Fitzgerald was more often noted, especially during John's middle years. His characters, like Fitzgerald's, were mostly from the upper layers of American society (though Cheever didn't invest them with the glamour of great wealth). Like Fitzgerald he had the gift of double vision; he was both a participant in the revels and, at the same moment, a fresh and honest-eyed observer from a different social world. Both men were at heart romantics, even if they had different dreams. Cheever's was not the dream of early love and financial success; he was more obsessed with the middle-aged nightmare of moral or financial collapse. Sometimes, however, he wrote sentences that might grace a Fitzgerald story, as, for example, "The light was like a blow, and the air smelled as if many wonderful girls had just wandered across the lawn." Both men were time-conscious and tried to recapture the feeling, the smell, the essential truth of a moment in history. One can often guess the year when a Cheever story was written by internal evidence, without looking for the date of publication. It is the same with Fitzgerald, of whom Cheever was to say admiringly, "One always knows reading Fitzgerald what time it is, precisely where you are, the kind of country. No writer has ever been so true in placing the scene. I feel that this isn't pseudohistory, but the sense of being alive. All great men are scrupulously true to their times." It was one of the things that Cheever tried to be. His stories also imply moral constants that make them relatively timeless—but then Fitzgerald, too, was a moralist, "a spoiled priest."

And Faulkner? Here it is not at all a question of early influence or the relation between explorer and settler. I'm not sure that Cheever even read Faulkner during the 1930s, although he was an enormous reader. It is rather a question of natural resemblances in writing and in character as well. The two didn't look alike, but they were both short, handsome men attractive to women and blessed from childhood with enormous confidence in their genius. (The influence of mere stature on writers' careers is a subject that calls for more study. Often the Napoleons of literature—and the Balzacs—are short men determined not to be looked at from above.) Both Cheever and Faulkner were high-school dropouts and self-educated. Like Faulkner from the beginning, Cheever was a storyteller by instinct and kept turning description into narration. Note for examples the panoramic views of Bullet Park, at the beginning of the novel, and of St. Botolphs, in the first chapter of *The Wapshot Chronicle*. First we see the houses one by one, but each house recalls a family and each family suggests a story. That was how Faulkner proceeded too.

Like Faulkner again, Cheever depended at every moment on the force and richness of his imagination. Faulkner was preeminent in that gift, but Cheever had more of it than other writers of his own time, and he too created his "little postage stamp of native soil"; Westchester and St. Botolphs are in some respects his Yoknapatawpha. *Falconer*, the novel he liked best among his own works, was named for an imagined prison in Westchester County, but he usually pronounced the name in an English fashion: "Faulkner." Mightn't that be a form of tribute to the older novelist?

The two men had other points of resemblance, besides their common fondness for hard liquor. One trait of a different sort was their frequent use of symbols from the Bible, as if they were the last two Christians in a godless world. But I wanted to make the more general point about Cheever that he was carrying on a tradition. His age group or cohort has included many gifted novelists: Bellow, Welty, Updike, Malamud, to name only a few. I will never try to assign a rank to each of them like a schoolmaster noting down grades. Cheever may or may not be the best of them, but he is clearly the one who stands closest in spirit to the giants of the preceding era.

Most of the American authors admired in our time did their best work before they were forty-five. Many of them died before reaching that age. Most survived into their sixties, but their truly productive careers had been cut short by emotional exhaustion, alcoholism, or by mere repetition and drudgery. It was Scott Fitzgerald who said, "There are no second acts in American lives." We produced no Thomas Hardys or Thomas Manns (exception being made for Robert Frost) and no one who made a brilliant rebeginning after a crisis in middle life. More recently there have been other exceptions and Cheever is one of them. His career in literature not merely started over but had a last act as brilliant in a different way as the acts that preceded it.

After he published *The Stories of John Cheever*, honors came pouring down on him like an autumn shower. Among them was a doctorate from Harvard (1978), a Pulitzer prize for the stories, which also received the award for fiction of the Book Critics' Circle, both in 1979, the Edward MacDowell Medal in that same year, and finally, in 1982, the National Medal for Literature. He accepted the honors gladly, not with the indifference he had displayed toward the few that had been granted him in earlier years. Once he had acted like Faulkner, as if on the assumption that readers didn't exist; now he was delighted by their response. He gave public readings of his stories, most often of two favorites, "The Swimmer" and "The Death of Justina." His face and his Bay State voice became admiredly familiar on television. He was photographed on horseback, like Faulkner in his last years. Meanwhile he had started a new novel for which he had signed, so we heard, a magnificent contract. To interviewers he said merely that it would be "another bulky book." There wasn't much time to work on it in the midst of distractions. After he had spent so many years in the shadows, even his New England conscience would have absolved him for basking a little in a transcontinental light.

There is often an essential change in writers as they grow older, something beyond a mere ripening of earlier qualities. (I am thinking here mostly of men and not of women, who are likely to follow a different pattern.) The writer, if he has something of his own to say, begins under the sign of the mother, which is also the sign and banner of rebellion—against tradition, against the existing order, against authority as represented by the father. The change comes after a middle-aged crisis, or even before it in many cases. The writer becomes reconciled with his father, indeed with all the Fathers who suffer from having wayward sons. (Here again women are different; they are likely to sign a truce with their mothers.) Cheever said more than once that the Wapshot books were "a posthumous attempt to make peace with my father's ghosts."

Whether men or women, writers find themselves going back in spirit to the regions where they spent their childhoods. For more than forty years Cheever had been a Yorker, not a Yankee; he had been mistakenly called a typical writer for *The New Yorker*. Now he rebecame a New Englander. One can be more specific: he became a Bay Stater, a native son of the Massachusetts seaboard, which has a different voice and different traditions from those of the Connecticut Valley. If Bay Staters are of Puritan descent, they trace their ancestral histories back to the founder of the family. In John's case the founder was Ezekiel Cheever, a minister highly respected by Cotton Mather, who preached his funeral sermon. John quotes Mather as saying, "The welfare of the Commonwealth was always upon the conscience of Ezekiel Cheever . . . and he abominated periwigs." The commonwealth of letters was always on John's conscience and he abominated all sorts of pretension, almost as much as he abominated pollution and superhighways.

While writing *Falconer* he had still smoked furiously; "I need to have *some* vice," he explained. Now, after a struggle, he gave up smoking as well as drinking. In default of vices he practiced virtues, especially those native to the Bay State. That breed of Yankees are distinguished, and tormented as well, by having scruples; they keep asking themselves, "Was that the right thing for me to do?" John must have asked that question often in his prayers. Another Yankee precept is not to speak ill of people even if they are rivals. John, if he had grudges, now managed not to express them (except for a mild grudge against the fiction editor who had rejected "The Jewels of the Cabots"). He had become conservative in the Bay State fashion, that is, in manners though not always in politics, this last being a field that he continued to avoid. There was, however, one Yankee precept, "Be reticent about yourself!" that he now flagrantly violated. I suspect this was because he had come to regard himself as a fictional person, the leading character of a novel that he was composing not in written words, but in terms of remembered joys and tribulations.

The true Bay Stater discharges his obligations, and he sets high store by loyalty to his family, to a few old friends, and to chosen institutions. John became a devoted churchgoer, though he didn't often stay for the sermon. He worked for the institutions that had befriended him, as notably Yaddo and the American Academy, where he served for three years as chairman of the Awards Committee for Literature. In that post he had to read some two hundred novels a year; it was another of his unrecompensed services to the commonwealth of letters. He paid off his moral debts to friends; one example was his making a trip to Chicago in order to speak at a dinner held in my honor. He was like a man who puts his affairs in order before setting out on a journey.

The journey started, as always, sooner than was expected. In July 1981 John had an operation for the removal of a cancerous kidney. The operation appeared to be successful, but a few weeks later John was barely able to walk. The cancer had metastasized to the bones of his legs; then it appeared as a burning spot on his rib cage. There was no hope left except in chemotherapy and radiotherapy at Memorial Hospital. Once again John spoke of himself dispassionately, as if he were a character in fiction. He told an interviewer for *The Saturday Review*, "Suddenly to find yourself with thousands and thousands seeking some cure for this deadly thing is an extraordinary thing. It's not depressing, really, or exhilarating. It's quite plainly a critical part of living, or the aspiration to live."

Those were arduous months for John; I think one might call them heroic. Doggedly he prepared a manuscript for his publisher, though it was not the bulky novel he had planned. *Oh, What a Paradise It Seemed* was no more than a novella, but, like all the best of his work, it was accurate, beautifully written, and full of surprises. It appeared in the early spring of 1982. A few weeks later he wrote me, "I fully intend to recover both from the cancer, the treatment and the bills."

I last saw him in Carnegie Hall less than two months before his death. The occasion was the ceremony at which, among the recipients of lesser awards, he was presented with the National Medal for Literature. His face was gaunt after radiotherapy and almost all his hair had fallen out. I said that I admired him for having made the trip from Ossining and he answered, "When they give you fifteen thousand dollars you owe them an appearance." He hobbled out to the rostrum leaning on a cane—or was it two canes? From my folding chair in the wings I couldn't hear his little speech, but I heard the great rumble of applause; John had nothing but friends.

A few minutes later we met and embraced in an empty corridor; I remember feeling that the treatment at Memorial had altered his body. It was more than fifty years since John had first appeared in my office at *The New Republic*. We were two men who had grown old in the service of literature, but our roles had been transposed: John was now older than I and was leading the way.

Index

Acknowledgment is made to the following publications, in which some of the essays in this book originally appeared, some in different form:

American Heritage: "The Hawthornes in Paradise"; *The Georgia Review:* "Allen Tate in the Republic of Letters" (under the title "Remembering Allen Tate") and "Robert Penn Warren, *Aet.* 75"; *Interim:* "Gammon for Dinner"; *Mercure de France:* "Shakespeare and Company" (under the title "When a Young American . . ."); *The Nation:* "Nelson Algren's Chicago"; *The New Republic:* "The Red and the Black," "The Dispossessed," "Koestler: The Disenchanted," "Mr. Cholerton's Beard," "American Literature in Wartime," "Town Report: 1942," "The Streets of Palermo," "The Assassinated Poet," "The Battle Over Ezra Pound," "Some Dangers to American Writing," "Hemingway at Midnight," "In Defense of the 1920s," "Aidgarpo," "His World" (under the title "James Thurber's Dream Book"), "Dramatism" (under the title "Prolegomena to Kenneth Burke"), "His First Law of Aesthetics" (under the title "A Critic's First Principle"), "The Limits of the Novel," "We Had Such Good Times," "The Grammar of Facts," "Mencken and Mark Twain," "James T. Farrell: Time Obliterated" (under the title "Farrell's Time Obliterated"), and "Zelda Fitzgerald's Part in the Story"; *The New Yorker:* "Max Perkins" (under the titles "Unshaken Friend: I" and "Unshaken Friend: II"); *Northwest Review:* "Ken Kesey at Stanford"; *PM* magazine section: "Auden Edits Auden" (under the title "Auden's a Better Poet Than Editor in Collecting His Own Works"); *Reporter:* "His Words" (under the title "Lions and Lemmings, Toads and Tigers") and "Sociological Habit Patterns in Linguistic Transmogrification"; *Saturday Review:* "Old Doc Wilson" and "Walt Whitman's Buried Masterpiece"; *Quest '78:* "Conrad Aiken: A Priest of Consciousness"; *Sewanee Review:* "John Cheever: The Novelist's Life as a Drama."

"Aragon Victorious" appeared originally as the Introduction to *Aragon: Poet of the French Resistance,* edited by Hannah Josephson and Malcolm Cowley. Copyright 1945 by Duell, Sloan and Pearce, Inc. Copyright renewed 1972 by Malcolm Cowley.

"Communism and Christianism" appeared originally as "Faith and the Future" in *Whose Revolution?,* edited by Irving Dewitt Talmadge.